Civilian-Driven Violence and the Genocide of Indigenous Peoples in Settler Societies

Existing studies of settler colonial genocides explicitly consider the roles of metropolitan and colonial states, and their military forces in the perpetration of exterminatory violence in settler colonial situations, yet rarely pay specific attention to the dynamics around civilian-driven mass violence against indigenous peoples. In many cases, however, civilians were major, if not the main, perpetrators of such violence. The focus of this book is thus on the role of civilians as perpetrators of exterminatory violence and on those elements within settler colonial situations that promoted mass violence on their part.

Mohamed Adhikari is Emeritus Associate Professor in the Department of Historical Studies at the University of Cape Town, South Africa. His books include *Not White Enough, Not Black Enough: Racial Identity in South Africa's Coloured Community* (2005) and *Burdened by Race: Coloured Identities in Southern Africa* (2009).

Civilian-Driven Violence and the Genocide of Indigenous Peoples in Settler Societies

Edited by Mohamed Adhikari

LONDON AND NEW YORK

First published 2021
by Routledge
2 Park Square, Milton Park, Abingdon, Oxon OX14 4RN

and by Routledge
605 Third Avenue, New York, NY 10158

Routledge is an imprint of the Taylor & Francis Group, an informa business

© 2019, the Authors

This version of *Civilian-Driven Violence and the Genocide of Indigenous Peoples in Settler Societies* is published by arrangement with UCT Press.

Not for sale in Southern Africa (defined as South Africa, Namibia, Botswana, Zimbabwe, Zambia, Eswatini, Lesotho, Malawi, Uganda, Kenya)

The right of Mohamed Adhikari to be identified as the author of the editorial material, and of the authors for their individual chapters, has been asserted in accordance with sections 77 and 78 of the Copyright, Designs and Patents Act 1988.

All rights reserved. No part of this book may be reprinted or reproduced or utilised in any form or by any electronic, mechanical, or other means, now known or hereafter invented, including photocopying and recording, or in any information storage or retrieval system, without permission in writing from the publishers.

Trademark notice: Product or corporate names may be trademarks or registered trademarks, and are used only for identification and explanation without intent to infringe.

British Library Cataloguing-in-Publication Data
A catalogue record for this book is available from the British Library

Library of Congress Cataloging-in-Publication Data
A catalog record for this book has been requested

ISBN: 978-0-367-85891-9 (hbk)
ISBN: 978-1-032-04813-0 (pbk)
ISBN: 978-1-003-01555-0 (ebk)

Typeset in Minion Pro
by Apex CoVantage, LLC

For Rafiq and Zaheer

and

in loving memory of Helen Kies and Maureen Adriaan

CONTENTS

Acknowledgements ix

About the Contributors xi

1. 'No Savage Shall Inherit the Land': Civilian-driven Violence in the Making of Settler Genocides   *Mohamed Adhikari* 1

2. Raiders, Slavers, Conquistadors, Settlers: Civilian-driven Violencein the Extermination of Aboriginal Canary Islanders   *Mohamed Adhikari* 31

3. 'Shooting a Black Duck': Genocidal Settler Violence against Indigenous Peoples and the Creation of Canada   *Sidney L. Harring* 61

4. 'An Unbroken Line of Crimes and Blood': Settler Militia and the Extermination and Enslavement of San in the Graaff-Reinet District of the Cape Colony, c. 1776–1825   *Lance van Sittert and Thierry Rousset* 86

5. Establishing a Code of Silence: Civilian and State Complicity in Genocidal Massacres on the New South Wales Frontier, 1788–1859   *Lyndall Ryan* 114

6. 'Pale Death … Around our Footprints Springs': Assessing Violent Mortality on the Queensland Frontier from State and Private Exterminatory Practices   *Raymond Evans & Robert Ørsted-Jensen* 139

7. 'There Cannot be Civilisation and Barbarism on the Island': Civilian-driven Violence and the Genocide of the Selk'nam People of Tierra del Fuego   *Alberto Harambour* 165

8. Missionaries, Agents, Principals and Teachers: Civilian Complicity in the Perpetration of Genocide in Indigenous Boarding Schools in New Mexico and Manitoba, 1879–1975   *Andrew Woolford* 188

9. 'Little Kings': Farmers' 'Erasive' Practices in German South West Africa   *Robert Gordon* 218

10. Settler Genocide in Rwanda? Colonial Legacies of Everyday Violence   *Susan Thomson* 241

11. Colonialism, Frontiers, Genocide: Civilian-Driven Violence in Settler Colonial Situations   *Lorenzo Veracini* 266

Bibliography 285

Index 313

vii

ACKNOWLEDGEMENTS

The seed for this book was planted about a decade and a half ago when I first became interested in genocide studies. Having read about the iconic twentieth-century mass killings, where the role of the state as perpetrator looms large, I was intrigued by Tony Barta's idea that with the colonisation of Australia, 'relations of genocide' were embedded in the very encounter between coloniser and indigene and that government policy was of secondary importance.[1] Later, when my interest turned specifically to settler genocides, I realised that although Tony's insight was intrinsic to genocide in settler colonial situations, scholars in neither genocide studies nor settler colonial studies had applied his insights in meaningful ways. In analyses of settler genocides the emphasis has almost automatically and largely been on the doings of colonial and metropolitan states and their representatives. While some scholars did point to the insurgent character of frontier settler communities, there was little sustained analysis or reflection on the specific dynamic behind civilian-driven violence in settler genocides, on how such violence articulated with state-driven initiatives and imperatives, and on how civilians organised themselves to attack or destroy Indigenous societies. Because the issue is of fundamental importance to the broader scholarly project of mapping and understanding settler genocides, I thought that an edited volume on the subject would be useful. So, a huge thank-you to Tony Barta, whose seminal chapter provided the spark that lit this fire. It is a great pity that I was unable to twist his arm into contributing a chapter to this volume!

I would like to thank all the contributors for responding positively to my call for chapters. It was a great pleasure working with such a co-operative and collegial group. I am particularly appreciative of their prompt responses to my requests for reworking, added detail and 'fixing' of problems. The chatty exchanges that sometimes ensued brightened my day. I also wish to express my appreciation to those contributors who participated in the colloquium around the theme of the book that was held at the University of Cape Town in October 2018, as well as to Bodhisattva Kar of the History Access Programme at the University of Cape Town and Susan Thomson of Colgate University for their collaboration in putting together the associated

---

1 Barta T. 2000. 'Relations of genocide: Land and lives in the colonisation of Australia', in *Genocide and the Modern Age: Etiology and Case Studies of Mass Death*, eds. I. Walliman & M. Dobkowski. Syracuse: Syracuse University Press, 237–251.

three-day set of events. I am enormously appreciative of Lorenzo Veracini's support of the project from the start, and for his advice, help and intellectual companionship. My heartfelt thanks to the anonymous reviewers whose reports helped us improve the manuscript. I am extremely grateful to Colleen Petersen for her advice on and assistance with a range of administrative tasks relating to this project, and to Nabowayah Kafaar for helping me compile the bibliography. It is with gratitude that I acknowledge funding from the National Research Foundation and from the University of Cape Town's University Research Committee, without which the production of this book would not have been possible.

It has been a great pleasure working with the UCT Press team. I was very pleased once again to be collaborating with Sandy Shepherd, publisher of UCT Press. Her matchless proficiency, personal warmth and wonderful sense of humour made it an absolute delight to work with her. Alfred LeMaitre did a superb job of editing the manuscript, as did Deoni Conradie, project manager, of keeping the publishing process on track.

I dedicate this book to two of my beloved high school teachers, Helen Kies (1926–2017) and Maureen Adriaan (1939–2016), who had an important impact on my life and the lives of thousands of other students who passed through their hands. I was extremely lucky to have attended Harold Cressy High School in the latter half of the 1960s, where a dedicated core of teachers, through their unwavering commitment to fighting injustice and promoting egalitarian values, were determined to defy apartheid intentions of schooling black students for subservience and cheap labour. Not only did these teachers provide us with an excellent academic education under extremely challenging conditions, but they also imparted to us a critical mindset that encompassed a sense of social responsibility and resistance to oppression, among other things. Both Helen and Maureen worked tirelessly as teachers and activists, their lives exemplifying both the motto of the Teachers' League of South Africa — 'Let us live for our children' — and that of Harold Cressy High School — '*Volenti nihil difficile*' (To those who are willing nothing is difficult). I was hardly a model student, but their efforts did rub off on me, and continued to do so long after I left school. I will be forever grateful.

As always, the volume is also dedicated to my loving sons, Rafiq and Zaheer. And I am happy to be able to report that throughout the making of this book, Skipper did his skipping and Max his maxing, giving me endless pleasure. Alas, poor Kitty is no more.

ABOUT THE CONTRIBUTORS

Mohamed Adhikari is Emeritus Associate Professor in the Department of Historical Studies at the University of Cape Town, teaches courses on genocide studies in Stanford University's Bing Overseas Study Programme in Cape Town, and has served as vice-president of the International Network of Genocide Scholars since 2015. He has published widely on coloured identity and politics in South Africa. His books on the subject include *Not White Enough, Not Black Enough: Racial Identity in South Africa's Coloured Community* (2005), *Burdened By Race: Coloured Identities in Southern Africa* (2009) and *Against the Current: A Biography of Harold Cressy, 1889–1916* (2012). He now works primarily in the field of settler colonial genocide and published *The Anatomy of a South African Genocide: The Extermination of the Cape San Peoples* (2010) and the edited volume, *Genocide on Settler Frontiers: When Hunter-gatherers and Commercial Stock Farmers Clash* (2014).

Raymond Evans is Adjunct Professor in History at Griffith University and Senior Research Scholar at the Centre for Cultural Studies at the University of Queensland. He has been researching Australian race relations since the mid-1960s and has published widely on frontier history, gender and labour relations, reserves and missions, convicts, popular history, the History Wars and genocide in Australia. His most recent book is *A History of Queensland*.

Robert Gordon, formerly Senior Professor at the University of the Free State and Emeritus Professor at the University of Vermont, is a fellow at the Stellenbosch Institute for Advanced Study. He has authored several books, including *Law and Order in the New Guinea Highlands, The Bushman Myth and the Making of a Namibian Underclass* and, most recently, *The Enigma of Max Gluckman: The Ethnographic Life of a 'Luckyman' in Africa*. He is currently completing a project entitled *The Grand Delusion: How Ethnologists Fashioned Namibia*.

Alberto Harambour is Associate Professor at the Universidad Austral de Chile, researcher at Fondap's IDEAL Center, and principal investigator of the Fondecyt project, 'State and Market at the Frontiers of Civilization: Transnational Histories of Postcolonial Colonialism in South America, 1870's–1940's'. His most recent publications include *Soberanías Fronterizas. Estados y Capital en la Colonización de Patagonia: Argentina y Chile, 1830–1922* (2019) and the article, with José Barrena, 'Barbarie o justicia en la Patagonia occidental: las violencias coloniales en el ocaso del pueblo kawésqar, finales del siglo XIX e inicios del siglo XX', *Historia Crítica*, 71 (2019).

Sidney Harring is Professor Emeritus at the City University of New York. He holds both JD and PhD degrees from the University of Wisconsin and has worked in the area of indigenous law and history for more than forty years. He is the author of *White Man's Law: Native People in Nineteenth Century Canadian Jurisprudence* (1998) and *Crow Dog's Case: American Indian Sovereignty, Tribal Law, and United States Law in the Nineteenth Century* (1994). He has held three National Endowment for the Humanities Fellowships and three Fulbright Fellowships, teaching law in Malaysia, Namibia and Sweden.

Robert Ørsted-Jensen received an undergraduate degree in Social Science from Roskilde University and has a PhD from the School of Political Science and International Studies at the University of Queensland. His main research interest is frontier race relations in colonial Australia. In 2011 he published *Frontier History Revisited: Colonial Queensland and the 'History War'*.

Thierry Rousset completed his PhD in the Department of Historical Studies at UCT where he currently lectures. His work focuses on metropolitan representations of settler colonialism on Tristan da Cunha and other Atlantic islands, maritime histories of the Cape Colony and the use of 'destitute children' as a source of labour in the Cape Colony.

Lyndall Ryan is Conjoint Research Professor in the Centre for the History of Violence at the University of Newcastle, Australia. Her most recent books include *Tasmanian Aborigines: A History since 1803* (2012), and a coedited collection with Philip G. Dwyer, *Theatres of Violence: Massacre, Mass Killing and Atrocity throughout History* (2012). In July 2017 she launched stage one of an online map of Colonial Frontier Massacres in Eastern Australia 1788–1872 and expects to complete the second and third stages of the map to 1960 by the end of 2020.

Susan Thomson is Associate Professor of Peace and Conflict Studies at Colgate University. Her research is dedicated to understanding how systems of power structure the lives of individuals in so-called times of peace. She also studies the ethical challenges of doing field-based research in post-conflict settings. Thomson has authored *Whispering Truth to Power: Everyday Resistance to Reconciliation in Post-genocide Rwanda* (2013), coedited *Emotional and Ethical Challenges for Field Research in Africa: The*

Story Behind the Findings (2013), and is editor of the *Research in Difficult Settings* website. Her latest book is *Rwanda: From Genocide to Precarious Peace* (2018).

Lance van Sittert is an Associate Professor in the Department of Historical Studies at the University of Cape Town. He has written on the child labour market in the nineteenth-century Cape Colony and its links to the concomitant genocide of Indigenous hunter-gatherer peoples.

Lorenzo Veracini is Associate Professor of History at Swinburne University of Technology, Melbourne. His research focuses on the comparative history of colonial systems and settler colonialism as a mode of domination. He has authored *Israel and Settler Society* (2006), *Settler Colonialism: A Theoretical Overview* (2010) and *The Settler Colonial Present* (2015). He coedited *The Routledge Handbook of the History of Settler Colonialism* (2016), manages the settler colonial studies blog, and is founding editor of the journal, *Settler Colonial Studies*.

Andrew Woolford is Professor of Sociology at the University of Manitoba and former president of the International Association of Genocide Scholars. He is author of *'This Benevolent Experiment': Indigenous Boarding Schools, Genocide and Redress in the United States and Canada* (2015), *The Politics of Restorative Justice* (2009) and *Between Justice and Certainty: Treaty-making in British Columbia* (2005), and is co-author of *Informal Reckonings: Conflict Resolution in Mediation, Restorative Justice, and Reparations* (2005). He is coeditor of *Canada and Colonial Genocide* (2017), *The Idea of a Human Rights Museum* (2015) and *Colonial Genocide in Indigenous North America* (2014).

CHAPTER ONE

'No Savage Shall Inherit the Land': Civilian-driven Violence in the Making of Settler Genocides

Mohamed Adhikari

It is the fashion usually, to speak of these poor people as 'aborigines': the idea meant to be conveyed that they are a relic, so to speak, of the past, intruders in the path of the white man, and to be improved from the face of the earth accordingly. The argument seems to be, that God never intended them to live long in the land in which He placed them. Therefore, says the white man, in his superiority of strength and knowledge, away with them, disperse them, shoot and poison them, until there is none remaining; we will utterly destroy them, their wives and their little ones, and all that they have, and we will go in and possess the land.

This is no rhapsody or overstatement, but represents, in words, the actual policy which has been pursued towards the natives of the Australian colonies, and which is being acted upon vigorously in Queensland today.

George Carrington, 1871[1]

In the minutiae of quotidian life, in the presuppositions of service providers, in the structures of State actions and inactions, in the continuing struggles over land use, in a whole trajectory of policies and plans, the work of the conquest is being completed here and now.

Peter Kulchyski, 2005[2]

Major General Edward Braddock, commander-in-chief of British forces in North America at the start of the French and Indian War (1754–1763), emphatically asserted that 'no savage shall inherit the land'. With these

---

1 Carrington G. 1871. *Colonial Adventures and Experiences*. London: Bell & Daldy, 143–144.
2 Kulchyski P. 2005. *Like the Sound of a Drum: Aboriginal Cultural Politics in Denendeh and Nunavut*. Winnipeg: University of Manitoba Press, 3.

1

words Braddock flatly rejected a proposed alliance against the French by Delaware chief Shingas, in return for being allowed to retain their land in the upper Ohio Valley. The general paid heavily for his arrogance because the Delawares and several other Native American peoples in the area instead sided with the French. This allied force, consisting overwhelmingly of Indians, routed Braddock's army and killed him early on in the war.[3]

Although uttered by a likely sojourner rather than a settler,[4] Braddock's rebuff goes to the very heart of all settler colonial projects, particularly those that were part of Western global expansion since the fifteenth century. 'No savage shall inherit the land!' would have served as the perfect rallying cry for settlers around the world, especially those prepared to commit violence against Indigenous peoples to secure personal control of acreage, or more expansively, the territory they claimed as their new homeland. Braddock's pronouncement emphasises not only the centrality of exclusive control of land and homeland in perpetuity to settler projects, but also the racialised contempt in which Indigenous peoples were held. Proclaimed in a time of war by the supreme military commander, the underlying threat of violence was clear, as was the colonial state's backing of settler claims. More than a century later, and on the other side of the world, George Carrington, an Oxford graduate who travelled through, and worked in many parts of Queensland for four years during the mid-1860s, confirmed the centrality of these values to that settler society and elaborated on some of the justifications behind the murderous behaviour of sections of the civilian population toward indigenes. Similar sentiments, which echoed across virtually all settler frontiers through six centuries of Western expansion and conquest, were foundational to the violence visited upon Indigenous peoples.

Settler colonial projects do not primarily seek the domination, exploitation or conversion of Indigenous peoples, but rather the reproduction of their home societies or the creation of new ones through

---

3   Barr D. 2006. "'The land is ours and not yours": The Western Delawares and the Seven Years War in the Upper Ohio Valley, 1755–1758', in *The Boundaries Between Us: Natives and Newcomers along the Frontiers of the Old Northwest Territory, 1750–1850*, ed. D. Barr. Kent, OH: Kent State University Press, 29; Hixson W. 2013. *American Settler Colonialism: A History*. New York: Palgrave Macmillan, 49, 52; Anderson G. 2014. *Ethnic Cleansing and the Indian: The Crime that Should Haunt America*. Norman: University of Oklahoma Press, 74–75.

4   Settlers come to stay in the colony and make it their new home while sojourners intend returning to the metropole. Sojourners were integral to the making of settler colonies, could be every bit as destructive of Indigenous societies as settlers, and many subsequently became settlers.

CHAPTER 1: 'No Savage Shall Inherit the Land'

migration — more accurately, through invasion of other peoples' land in the sense that migrants can only settle vacant land, but of necessity invade occupied land. Settler regimes typically pursue total control of the newly claimed homeland, purged of any Indigenous claims to sovereignty, real or symbolic. In some instances, such as Australia, California, British Columbia and the Cape Colony, prior ownership of the land by Indigenous peoples was not even recognised in law.[5] In these and other cases, the legal fiction that Indigenous people did not own their land — retrospectively referred to as *terra nullius* (no one's land)[6] — was used to justify colonisation and to stake claims against competing powers.

Because settler colonialism is predicated on the invasion and expropriation of foreign land by largely civilian populations, civilian-driven violence against Indigenous peoples has always been congenital to frontier relations, and intrinsic to settler society after the closing of the frontier.[7] Given the prominent role of settler colonialism in European maritime expansion, civilian-driven violence was clearly integral to the making of Western global dominance. Civilian-driven violence on any significant scale was also specific to settler colonialism, for in other forms of colonialism the violence was of necessity largely perpetrated by metropolitan and colonial states and their military structures. Settler colonialism was

---

5   For discussion of *terra nullius* throughout the Pacific, especially Australia, California and British Columbia, see Banner S. 2007. *Possessing the Pacific: Land, Settlers and Indigenous People from Australia to Alaska*. Cambridge: Harvard University Press. For the Cape Colony, see Ülgen Ö. 2002. 'Developing the doctrine of aboriginal title in South Africa: Source and content'. *Journal of African Law*, 46, no. 2, 131–154; and for the formation of property rights during the first century of Dutch rule, see Dye A. & La Croix, S. 2018. 'Institutions for the taking: Property rights and the settlement of the Cape Colony, 1652–1750'. *Economic History Review*, 8 November 2018.

6   For a discussion of the lineage of the term *terra nullius* and its currency from the late nineteenth century onwards, see Fitzmaurice A. 2007. 'The genealogy of *terra nullius*'. *Australian Historical Studies*, 38, no. 129, 1–15; and Borch M. 2001. 'Rethinking the origins of *terra nullius*'. *Australian Historical Studies*, 32, no. 117, 222–239. Although the term itself did not come into use until the late nineteenth century, the juridical tactic of the blanket denial of Indigenous sovereignty over entire territories, subcontinents and even continents was deployed by invading settler regimes.

7   There is a sense in which only uninhabited land can be settled, and what are today generally referred to as 'settlers' are actually invaders; see Johnson A. & Lawson A. 2005. 'Settler colonies', in *A Companion to Postcolonial Studies*, eds. S. Ray and H. Schwarz. Malden: Blackwell, 364. That such invaders have managed to appropriate the term 'settler', and given it wide enough currency for almost universal use, is a measure of the degree to which these 'victors' have been able to determine the terms on which their histories have been written and the degree to which voices of the vanquished have been silenced. It also means that the full extent of the violence that has gone into the making of settler societies is seldom recognised — 'colonial amnesia' being a term that comes to mind.

3

particularly damaging to Indigenous communities as it sought not only to dispossess indigenes, but also usually to displace them completely from their habitations, except perhaps as rightless, cheap labour corralled into reserves to be exploited for the benefit of the colonial economy.[8] In many settler colonies, the destruction of Indigenous societies was clearly genocidal and the violence perpetrated by civilians, especially settlers, a primary contributor to Indigenous social erasure. In most settler colonies, especially where frontier conflict radicalised into genocide — in places as far apart as Queensland, the Cape Colony, California and Tierra del Fuego — the historical record is littered with calls from civilian sectors of the population for the extermination of indigenes. Although not proof of genocide, such demands are an indication of a genocidal mindset and a gauge of colonists' willingness to condone or perpetrate exterminatory violence against Indigenous peoples. Subsequently such violence has been routinely denied, minimised or misrepresented in ways that favour settler claims and self-perceptions.[9]

Whereas most studies of settler colonial genocide explicitly consider the roles of metropolitan and colonial states and their military forces in the destruction of Indigenous societies, specific attention to the nature of civilian-driven exterminatory violence has not featured in any significant way in the field of genocide studies, nor in investigations of settler colonial conquest. Occasionally, analyses have mentioned the phenomenon incidentally, or examined its significance in localised contexts. For example, Alison Palmer's *Colonial Genocide* cursorily describes the near extermination of Queensland's Aboriginal peoples as a 'societally-led' genocide.[10] Richard Price refers in passing to the '"unofficial" violence … of settlers against indigenous peoples … [as] baked into the everyday experience of empire'.[11] And Brendan Lindsay's *Murder State* restricts his analysis of how democratic

---

8 I am mindful of Veracini & Cavanagh's observation that settler colonialism 'is as much a thing of the past as a thing of the present', but use the past tense here as I am referring specifically to frontier violence and its role in the making of settler societies. See their definition of settler colonialism at https://settlercolonialstudies.blog/about-this-blog/ accessed 25 February 2019.

9 For a discussion of settler colonial narratives in this regard, see Veracini L. 2015. *The Settler Colonial Present*. Basingstoke: Palgrave Macmillan; see also Veracini L. 2010. *Settler Colonialism: A Theoretical Overview*. Basingstoke: London Macmillan, ch. 4.

10 Palmer A. 2002. *Colonial Genocide*. Adelaide: Crawford House Publishing, 3, 199.

11 Price R. 2018. 'The psychology of colonial violence', in *Violence, Colonialism and Empire in the Modern World*, eds. P. Dwyer and A. Nettelbeck. Basingstoke: Palgrave Macmillan, 25. Price also describes such violence as 'casual', 'quotidian' and 'everyday'. See Price, 'Psychology of colonial violence', 25, 27, 39, while the editors of the volume write of the 'private violence committed by colonial settlers'. See Dwyer P. and Nettelbeck A. 2018.

CHAPTER 1: 'No Savage Shall Inherit the Land'

structures were used to propel civilian-driven genocidal violence to parts of northern California.[12] In a seminal piece written in the 1980s, Tony Barta, however, recognised the significance of civilian-driven violence by arguing that in large parts of Australia it was a 'relationship of genocide ... structured into the very nature of the encounter' rather than government 'policy' or 'intention' that drove the destruction of Indigenous societies.[13] This important insight and its implications have, however, largely been overlooked within the discipline.

This collection thus seeks to shed light on a neglected area by exploring the dynamic behind civilian-driven violence in settler colonial situations globally, and to focus on those elements within civilian society that promoted genocidal attitudes, behaviour and outcomes in the making of Western global dominance.[14] This project is also fundamentally interested in how civilian, military and non-military state structures overlapped, collaborated and supported each other in the perpetration of genocidal violence against Indigenous peoples. The underlying question of why 'ordinary' people are so easily capable of perpetrating unspeakable atrocities, often with equanimity, is of course an extremely broad, highly complex and multidimensional subject that one cannot hope to address in any comprehensive way in a volume of this kind. The intention rather is to put the issue on the radar for scholars working on settler colonial genocide.

Civilians as perpetrators of genocidal violence

The term 'civilian' as used here needs some explanation as it has not in any systematic or categorical way been applied to perpetrators in the context of genocide or settler colonial studies, and its usage elsewhere is subject to a fair degree of controversy. In genocide studies, where the category of 'civilian' has entered the discussion, it has been as victims. Even as such, Martin Shaw correctly points out, their role has been sorely neglected.[15] In general usage, 'civilian' refers to non-combatants and anyone outside

---

"'Savage wars of peace": Violence, colonialism and empire in the modern world', in *Violence, Colonialism and Empire*, 9.

12 Lindsay B. 2012. *Murder State: California's Native American Genocide, 1846–1873*. Lincoln: University of Nebraska Press, ch. 5.

13 Barta T. 2000. 'Relations of genocide: Land and lives in the colonisation of Australia', in *Genocide and the Modern Age: Etiology and Case Studies of Mass Death*, eds. I. Walliman & M. Dobkowski. Syracuse, NY: Syracuse University Press, 237–239.

14 Martin Shaw places great emphasis on the importance of civilians to the concept of genocide — but as victims, not as perpetrators. See Shaw M. 2015. *What is Genocide?* Cambridge: Polity Press, 162–166.

15 Ibid., 162–166.

of a military chain of command, whether of formally constituted fighting forces under state control, or informal offensive units such as rebel armies or terrorist groupings.[16] Despite attempts to define the concept as clearly as possible in human rights legislation and formal documentation such as treaties and conventions, there is inevitably a considerable measure of ambiguity around the term, as military and civilian roles and activities are not dichotomous, and armed forces cannot operate entirely separately from the rest of society.[17]

'Civilian' covers very large and diverse categories of people, and being defined in negative terms — as those who are *not* part of the military — hardly helps. Most conflict situations are in any case sufficiently complex for neat distinctions between combatant and civilian to be confounded because a wide range of non-combatant individuals, organisations and sectors of society are complicit in myriad ways in military operations and in support of armed forces. Civilians are often anything but neutral, their situations ranging from passive hostility toward perceived enemies, through being indispensable to the war effort on the home front, to open resistance toward adversaries, which might include joining volunteer defence groups and bearing arms as irregular combatants. A further complication is that combatants sometimes disguise themselves as civilians, as is often the case with guerrilla wars and terror attacks. What is more, civilians can become combatants, and combatants civilians, with individuals possibly crossing this threshold multiple times.[18] Civilians can, of course, also be perpetrators of interpersonal and mass violence against purported enemies, ethnic minorities or subordinate populations, and it is in this capacity that they

---

16 'Non-combatant' is only applicable in situations of armed conflict. See Bellamy A. 2012. 'Massacres and morality: Mass killing in an age of immunity', *Human Rights Quarterly*, 34, no. 4, 927.

17 The original meaning of 'civilian', that of a practitioner of civil law, has been part of the English lexicon from at least the late fourteenth century. Although used to denote non-combatants as early as the seventeenth century, the term only came into common usage after the First World War as a result of growing international concern to protect the general public in times of conflict. The idea that non-combatants should enjoy protection during war long precedes the use of the term 'civilian' with descriptors such as 'the people', 'occupied populations' and 'unarmed inhabitants' used to refer to them. See Slim H. 2016. 'Civilians, distinction and the compassionate view of war', in *Protection of Civilians*, eds. H. Willmot, R. Mamiya, S. Sheeran & M. Weller. Oxford: Oxford University Press, 11–28; Slim H. 2007. *Killing Civilians: Method, Madness and Morality in War*. London: Hurst, 19. Leo Kuper's comment on the term 'genocide', 'The word is new, the concept is ancient', applies here as well; see Jones A. 2011. *Genocide: A Comprehensive Introduction*. Abingdon: Routledge, 3.

18 Coady C. 2007. 'Collateral immunity in war and terrorism', in *Civilian Immunity in War*, ed. I. Primoratz. Oxford: Oxford University Press, 138–139.

CHAPTER 1: 'No Savage Shall Inherit the Land'

are of greatest interest to this project. In situations of conflict and within perpetrating communities, as in the case of settler invasions, the lines between combatant and non-combatant are therefore blurred, sometimes to the extent that there are fairly broad spheres of uncertainty and overlap between the two.

An important question in distinguishing between combatant and civilian is: at what point should perpetrators who are not part of a formal military structure, but who commit violence, be seen to surrender their civilian status and be regarded as combatants? The standard view is that the transition occurs when such people take up arms or participate directly in military activity.[19] This approach emanates mainly from contemporary practical and legal concerns with civilians falling victim to violence and abuse, and being in need of protection in conflict situations. The conventional stance is not helpful for an enquiry of this sort, which is focused on developing a historical understanding of a particular social phenomenon, namely the perpetration of genocidal violence against Indigenous peoples by non-military personnel — 'ordinary' people as it were — in settler colonial situations. Is it, for example, appropriate to regard squads of settler farmers who for a few days, or a week or two, went on periodic killing sprees against Indigenous peoples, or on raids to acquire forced labour, as having yielded their civilian status? It makes far better sense, in my view, to regard such perpetrators as civilian, at least until they abandoned their civilian pursuits and became dependent on military activity for a living.

For the purposes of this project I have thus regarded as civilian anyone who is not part of a formal military or paramilitary force. And for those armed groups operating outside of state structures, such as insurrectionary forces or private militia, anyone whose main occupation is of a non-military description is regarded as civilian. Armed units of a temporary nature consisting variously of farmers, miners, loggers, fishermen, slave raiders, buccaneers, their dependants and employees, and other non-military personnel, as were regularly found on settler frontiers, are therefore considered to be civilian. While most members of such units were volunteers and part of the colonial establishment, they often also contained conscripts such as slaves, captives, convicts, indentured labourers or Indigenous servants recruited with varying degrees of force. This was, for example, the case with Canarian captives and chattels enlisted in Spanish slaving or

---

19 See Walzer M. 2006. *Just and Unjust Wars: A Moral Argument with Historical Illustrations.* New York: Basic Books, 135; Downes A. 2008. *Targeting Civilians in War.* Ithaca: Cornell University Press, 14; Slim, 'Compassionate view of war'.

conquering sorties in the Canary Islands and beyond; substantial numbers of Khoikhoi servants inducted into Boer commandos on the Cape colonial frontier; and Indigenous conscripts and collaborators used in various capacities by armed posses on several other settler frontiers.[20] These bands may well have been state-sanctioned, received some form of government assistance, organised military training for themselves, or may indirectly or retrospectively have received payment from the state as, for example, with bounty hunters or Indian hunting parties in the nineteenth-century United States. Those perpetrators not primarily dependent on military activity for a living are therefore regarded as civilian. On the other hand, a paramilitary unit such as the Queensland Native Mounted Police was clearly not civilian as it was officially constituted, financed and administered by the state and manned by full-time, salaried staff.[21]

Of course, it often happened that civilian and military structures collaborated closely, or that armed personnel from both sectors temporarily combined into a single fighting force as, for example, occurred from time to time on the Tasmanian, Queensland, Californian and other frontiers. Or, as with the conquest of the Canary Islands, that state agents were also expected to act in their private capacities, and as such wreaked genocidal violence on Indigenous communities. At the other end of the temporal scale, the hard-line Hutu government that came to power in Rwanda in the wake of Juvenal Habyarimana's assassination on 6 April 1994 was able to use its bureaucratic and military structures very effectively to mobilise over 150 000 civilians to kill Tutsis. After the closing of frontiers and in post-conflict situations, civilians in the form of employers, teachers, medical staff, clergymen, state officials, hired assassins, even neighbours and in various other capacities, inflicted violence or socially destructive behaviour on indigenes or victimised groups.

---

20 Adhikari, M. 2017. 'Europe's first settler colonial incursion into Africa: The genocide of aboriginal Canary Islanders'. *African Historical Review*, 49, no. 1, 1–26; Newton-King S. 1999. *Masters and Servants on the Cape Eastern Frontier*. Cambridge: Cambridge University Press, ch. 7; Penn N. 2005. *The Forgotten Frontier: Colonist and Khoisan on the Cape's Northern Frontier in the 18th Century*. Cape Town: Double Storey, ch. 4; Adhikari M. 2010a. *The Anatomy of a South African Genocide: The Extermination of the Cape San Peoples*. Cape Town: UCT Press, 39–43.
21 Skinner L.E. 1975. *Police of the Pastoral Frontier: Native Police 1849–59*. Brisbane: University of Queensland Press; Richards J. 2008b. *The Secret War: A True History of Queensland's Native Police*. Brisbane: University of Queensland Press; Richards J. 2008a. 'The Native Police of Queensland'. *History Compass*, 6, no. 4.

CHAPTER 1: 'No Savage Shall Inherit the Land'

While this project of necessity focuses largely on the 'sin of the settler', to use Elizabeth Elbourne's phrase,[22] it draws on the broader concept of 'civilian' because the non-military perpetrators of violence against indigenes in settler colonial situations extended beyond the settler category per se. Although settlers were usually the dominant grouping among civilian perpetrators of violence in settler colonies, culprits included sojourners, as well as a variety of other migrants including forced migrants such as slaves, transported convicts or indentured workers. Indigenous people, whether captive, coerced, allied or voluntary collaborators, were at times important agents as well. Perpetrators could include state actors, as many public employees were civilian. Thus, staff at state-run residential schools for Indigenous children, medical personnel at clinics conducting forced sterilisation of Indigenous peoples, reservation officials diverting food meant for starving inmates, or any other members of the civil administration enforcing socially deleterious policies could be civilian perpetrators of genocidal violence.

'Hordes of English Tartars': Settler insurgence and mass violence

That civilian-driven mass violence against indigenes was evident from the earliest days of European overseas settler expansion is confirmed by its central role in the fifteenth-century conquest of the Canary Islands analysed in the first case study presented in this volume. While an important part of European settler expansion from its inception, civilian-driven violence became especially prevalent through the long nineteenth century. During this period, industrialisation and the consequent growth of a much larger and more integrated global market accelerated the number of settlers flooding into, and extending the frontiers of, temperate-latitude colonies in the Americas, southern Africa and Australasia. A series of technological advances and successive economic booms, together with a much more positive attitude toward the opportunities offered by long-range migration among Europeans, resulted in what James Belich refers to as the 'settler revolution' and its adjunct, 'explosive colonisation', from the late eighteenth century onwards. Though a global phenomenon, the settler revolution was especially marked in the anglophone world and contributed greatly to Anglo global dominance.[23] Economic opportunities created on these expanding

---

22 Elbourne E. 2003. 'The sin of the settler: The 1835–36 Select Committee on Aborigines and debates over virtue and conquest in the early nineteenth-century British white settler empire'. *Journal of Colonialism and Colonial History*, 25, no. 3.

23 For authoritative overviews of this epochal shift, see Weaver J. 2003. *The Great Land Rush and the Making of the Modern World, 1650–1900*. Montreal: McGill-Queen's University

frontiers, especially commodity production feeding industrialising centres, provided the main impetus behind settler land invasions globally — what John Weaver calls the 'great land rush' and Timothy Bottoms, in the context of Queensland, more pointedly refers to as the 'great land theft'. This stoked conflict with, displacement of, and in several instances, the genocidal destruction of Indigenous communities.[24]

As Patrick Wolfe has emphasised, settler colonialism in the final analysis is a winner-takes-all proposition. More than a story of the total dispossession of Indigenous peoples within the claimed homeland, it also sought what he calls the 'elimination of the native', which is not equivalent to physical annihilation as it could include strategies such as expulsion, segregation or assimilation.[25] Settler violence toward Indigenous peoples, taken as a whole, has thus tended to be indiscriminate, aimed at the entire community, and generally not mitigated by any sense of proportionality. Unrestrained violence and collective punishment were among its hallmarks. While I do not regard settler colonialism as inherently genocidal, as has been suggested by some,[26] I would regard what is today known as 'ethnic cleansing' as intrinsic to it, because the inner drive of settler colonialism has always been to purge the new homeland of Indigenous claims to sovereignty, and to remove indigenes physically from that locale, except perhaps as segregated cheap labour. Ethnic cleansing can of course easily radicalise into genocide, as has often occurred in settler colonial situations.

In many settler colonies civilians were the main agents of destruction. This was of course in addition to, and usually in collusion with, a great deal of violence emanating from the colonial state and its military apparatus. The

---

Press; and Belich J. 2009. *Replenishing the Earth: The Settler Revolution and the Rise of the Anglo-World, 1783–1939*. Oxford: Oxford University Press.

24 Bottoms T. 2013. *Conspiracy of Silence: Queensland's Frontier Killing Times*. Sydney: Allen & Unwin, 45. While Bottoms refers specifically to Queensland, the comment is applicable to settler colonies generally.

25 See, for example, Wolfe P. 2016. *Traces of History: Elementary Structures of Race*. London: Verso, 36.

26 See, for example, Finzsch N. 2008. "'The Aborigines ... were never annihilated, and still they are becoming extinct": Settler imperialism and genocide in nineteenth-century America and Australia', in *Empire, Colony, Genocide: Conquest, Occupation and Subaltern Resistance in World History*, ed. A.D. Moses. New York: Berghahn Books, 253. See also Docker, J. 2008. 'Are settler colonies inherently genocidal? Rereading Lemkin', in Moses, *Empire, Colony, Genocide*, 97; Moses A.D. 2004. 'Genocide and settler society in Australian history', in *Genocide and Settler Society: Frontier Violence and Stolen Indigenous Children in Australian History*, ed. A.D. Moses. New York: Berghahn Books, for discussion of the issue and Lemkin R. 1944. *Axis Rule in Occupied Europe: Laws of Occupation, Analysis of Government, Proposals for Redress*. New York: Columbia University Press, xi, 79–80, for Lemkin's tendency to view it as such.

CHAPTER 1: 'No Savage Shall Inherit the Land'

more remote the frontier, the more influential the role of settlers tended to be. What is of particular interest to this book project is how civilian, military and non-military state actors within settler establishment collaborated to act against Indigenous societies, and how within this triad civilians organised themselves to initiate violence against indigenes or to participate effectively in state-sponsored violence.[27] Not surprisingly, all case studies in this collection to some degree focus on these partnerships in the making of the respective settler genocides they analyse. While civilian- and state-driven onslaughts on Indigenous peoples in settler colonial situations are almost inevitably interlinked, often integrally — and with shared codes of violence and silence — an analytical distinction nonetheless needs to be made between the two. While Patrick Wolfe is correct to point out that '[r]ather than something separate from or running counter to the colonial state, the murderous activities of the frontier rabble constitute its principle means of expansion', it would be counterproductive to conflate the two.[28] John Weaver, for example, points to 'a tension remarkable and fateful, between defiant private initiatives and the ordered, state-backed certainties of property rights' as being foundational to Western settler expansion.[29] Civilian-driven mass violence in settler colonial situations often had an impetus and motivation distinct to that emanating from their respective colonial or metropolitan states and their military structures, even though the two may have been closely intertwined, as demonstrated by the case studies in this volume.

It would be no exaggeration to claim that from the very outset of colonial projects, settler and metropolitan interests were rarely aligned, and settlers seldom compliant with metropolitan expectations and demands. Settlers tended to display an independence and an insurgent disregard for metropolitan sovereignty, policies and restraints from the start, despite usually being highly dependent on colonial and metropolitan states in various ways and regularly appealing for their help. Settlers often operated beyond colonial jurisdictions with the colonial state belatedly extending boundaries in a game of ongoing catch-up. And the more viable settler societies and

---

27 There are, of course, examples of genocides in settler colonial situations, such as those committed in German South West Africa and during the Nazi thrust eastwards, where frontiers were determined by warring armies, exterminatory campaigns were almost wholly driven by the state, and civilian-driven violence was inconsequential.

28 Wolfe P. 'Settler colonialism and the elimination of the native'. *Journal of Genocide Research*, 8, no. 4, 392; Wolfe P. 2008. 'Structure and event: Settler colonialism, time and the question of genocide', in Moses, *Empire, Colony, Genocide*, 108.

29 Weaver, *Great Land Rush*, 4.

economies became, the more their interests tended to diverge from those of the metropole. This resulted in growing demands for political autonomy, and in extreme cases rebellion, warfare and revolutionary breaks with the metropole. It can be taken as almost axiomatic that the greater control settlers gained over the colonial state, the more rapid land alienation, and the more intense violence against Indigenous societies tended to become. This trend is particularly noticeable when crown control gave way to settler self-government.

This fractiousness was recognised by Edmund Burke, political theorist and British parliamentarian, on the eve of the American Revolution as Native American resistance to settler advances on the western frontier started to crumble and a smallpox epidemic was about to devastate their numbers. In an oft-quoted parliamentary speech delivered in 1775, he characterised the tidal surge of settlers about to spill over onto the Great Plains as a refractory mass largely immune to government control:

> Already they have topped the Appalachian Mountains. From thence they behold before them an immense plain, one vast, rich, level meadow: a square of five hundred miles. Over this they would wander without a possibility of restraint; they would change their manners with their habits of life; would soon forget a government by which they were disowned; would become hordes of English Tartars; and, pouring down upon your unfortified frontiers a fierce and irresistible cavalry, become masters of your governors and your counsellors, your collectors and comptrollers, and of all the slaves that adhered to them.[30]

His observations about this spirit of insubordination and independence were as true of European and Anglo-American settlers in North America as they were of Australia, and of Iberians moving through Latin America, Russians advancing into the steppes, or Dutch-speaking farmers trekking into the southern African interior.

Focused primarily on land expropriation, settler incursions attacked the very foundations of Indigenous societies and undermined their communal existence in both calculated and unintended ways. Violence committed by civilians against Indigenous peoples in settler colonial situations covered a broad and multilayered spectrum of lethal and harmful activity

---

30 Barta, T. 2015. "'A fierce and irresistible cavalry": Pastoralists, homesteaders and hunters on the American plains frontier', in *Genocide on Settler Frontiers: When Hunter-Gatherers and Commercial Stock Farmers Clash*, ed. M. Adhikari. New York: Berghahn Books, 233, most recently drew my attention to this quote. For the smallpox epidemic, see Fenn E. 2001. *Pox Americana: The Great Smallpox Epidemic of 1775–82*. New York: Hill & Wang, especially 16–23.

CHAPTER 1: 'No Savage Shall Inherit the Land'

ranging from the arbitrary and opportunistic to the highly organised and meticulously planned; from the passionately intimate to the cold-heartedly detached; from the ferociously murderous to the calmly bureaucratic; from spectacular mass atrocities targeting entire Indigenous collectives to corrosive structural violence embedded in relationships of daily life.

Collectively, the contributions to this volume cover a very wide range of the violence used to destroy Indigenous societies. As one would expect, much of the analysis focuses on murder and massacre — the immediate physical destruction of Indigenous peoples and their societies. Genocide, of course, involves much more than just mass murder.[31] Besides killing, usually to clear land of its original inhabitants or in retaliation for Indigenous resistance to invasion, non-lethal means of social destruction such as taking captives, child confiscation, excessive forced labour, sexual violence, cultural suppression, confinement to reserves and destruction of the natural environment took their toll. Though usually foreseeable, but not necessarily premeditated, consequences of dispossession and expulsion from settler homelands included death by starvation, dehydration, exposure, disease and increased violence between Indigenous groups. Displacement, usually to marginal land, spelt disaster or even death for entire communities as they lost access to vital resources and were often pushed into conflict with neighbouring peoples. Where Indigenous peoples gained access to global markets, it usually served to foment competition and internecine conflict between them.[32] Broken treaties, fraudulent land deals and the peddling of tobacco, alcohol and narcotics also played a part. The debilitating personal and social impacts of psychological trauma that inevitably accompanied the shattering of their worlds is underestimated in the existing literature. One such consequence, lowered fertility rates, often severely undermined the ability of Indigenous communities to reproduce themselves.

---

31 The definition of genocide used in this chapter and the next is that it is the intentional physical destruction of a social group in its entirety, or the intentional annihilation of such a significant part of the group that it is no longer able to reproduce itself biologically or culturally. See Adhikari M. '"We are determined to exterminate them": The genocidal impulse behind commercial stock farmer invasions of hunter-gatherer territories', in Adhikari, *Genocide on Settler Frontiers*, 2. In the case of settler genocides, after the closing of the frontier with its overtly murderous impetus, survivors are usually reduced to forced labour or utter destitution, sometimes to the point of starvation. These remnant populations are subject to ongoing violence and social harm, cultural suppression, forced assimilation and purposeful marginalisation with a view to the elimination of an Indigenous presence in the new settler homeland.

32 For an interesting example of this, see Cavanagh E. 2014. '"We exterminated them, and Dr. Philip gave the country": The Griqua people and the elimination of San from South Africa's Transorangia region', in Adhikari, *Genocide on Settler Frontiers*, 88–107.

A great deal of scholarly attention, especially within genocide studies, has focused on the frontier and the bloodshed associated with dispossession — and with good reason, as so much of the carnage that obliterated Indigenous societies occurred during this earlier lethal phase in the making of settler societies. Here, by the very nature of the frontier, the state did not have a monopoly of power, and sometimes was effectively, or even completely, absent. On frontiers settlers thus did have a good deal of opportunity and strong motives for taking the law into their own hands in what was essentially a lawless situation — or, to borrow Julie Evans' phrase, 'where lawlessness is law'.[33] And much of this violence was perpetrated with little restraint.

An idea present in Western thinking from ancient times, even though often disdained by practitioners of warfare and perpetrators of mass violence, is that certain categories of people — the unarmed, the old, the young, women — in short, civilians — should be spared the wrath of rampaging armies and the cataclysm of combat. However, the resulting ideas of 'just war' or 'limited warfare' based on principles of restraint and proportionality often did not apply when settlers went to war with Indigenous peoples. The basic reason for this is that settlers, especially in the post-Enlightenment era, have regarded Indigenous peoples in a profoundly racist sense to be other, not fully human, and that 'civilised' rules, including those relating to warfare, did not apply to 'savages'. Dehumanisation of the 'savage' in effect brought into being, in the eyes of many perpetrators in settler colonial situations, an exceptional moral context in which the killing and maltreatment of Indigenous people required little more justification than settler need. With the rise of Social Darwinist thought in the latter half of the nineteenth century, this exceptional morality was elevated to a new level in that the supposed inevitable dying out of the unfit was attributed to the iron laws of nature, thus further exonerating perpetrators. For some, hastening the process through exterminatory violence, where the opportunity presented itself, was seen as salutary and perfectly justified, as for example Lothar von Trotha did in his exterminatory wars against the Indigenous peoples of Namibia between 1904 and 1908.

After the closing of the frontier, violence against indigenes did not cease, however. Survivors continued to suffer a great deal of violence and social harm at the hands of state and civilian actors to an extent that justifies

---

33 See Evans J. 2009. 'Where lawlessness is law: The settler-colonial frontier as a legal space of violence'. *Australian Feminist Law Journal*, 30, no. 1, 3–22.

CHAPTER 1: 'No Savage Shall Inherit the Land'

accusations of 'continuing genocide'.[34] After the homicidal phase of settler dispossession, the 'work of conquest' continued to be 'completed here and now' as Kulchyski puts it.[35] In settler societies the 'work of conquest' continues for as long as there are Indigenous survivors, and even when there are no longer any survivors left. One suspects that for as long as a settler consciousness exists there will always be a need for discursive and symbolic 'elimination of the native', indigenisation of the settler and reinforcement of settler claims to the land.

The post-frontier phase witnessed occasional mass atrocities, as well as interpersonal violence encompassing murder, corporal punishment, sexual exploitation and forced labour. Assaults on Indigenous survivors included child confiscation, incarceration, economic exclusion, cultural suppression, deliberate deprivation of basic needs — sometimes to the point of starvation — and death from easily preventable causes, among other abuses.[36] Inaction was at times a deliberately lethal strategy for dealing with surviving Indigenous communities. If, in addition, Indigenous labour was seen as unsuitable or not needed in the settler economy, the intensity of persecution increased.[37] Suppression of Indigenous cultures, including forced assimilation, and ubiquitous assertions of settler dominance became the norm. Violence, and, importantly, constant threats of violence, against Indigenous survivors became institutionalised in post-frontier settler society. Civilian protagonists played important roles in maintaining this state of ongoing genocidal persecution. Violence against indigenes was often seen as salutary, and was routinely used for didactic, coercive and disciplinary purposes by both state and civilian sectors of society, as many of the contributors to this volume demonstrate. Though post-frontier violence may have been less overt and on a smaller scale compared to the murderous frontier phase, the cumulative impact on the shattered remnants of Indigenous societies was devastating to their chances of demographic recovery and cultural rejuvenation. For such people, to survive was indeed to suffer.

---

34 For two case studies of ongoing genocide after the closing of the frontier see Short D. 2010. 'Australia: A continuing genocide?'. *Journal of Genocide Research*, 12, nos. 1–2, 45–68; Harring S. 2015. 'Dispossession, ecocide, genocide: Cattle ranching and agriculture in the destruction of hunting cultures on the Canadian prairies', in Adhikari, *Genocide on Settler Frontiers*, 273–285.

35 Kulchyski, *Like the Sound of a Drum*, 3.

36 See Harring, 'Dispossession, ecocide, genocide', 277–283.

37 Wolfe, *Traces of History*, 25–26; Curthoys A. 2014. 'Indigenous dispossession and pastoral employment in Western Australia during the nineteenth century: Implications for understanding colonial forms of genocide', in Adhikari, *Genocide on Settler Frontiers*.

15

This is of course not to suggest that frontier relations were a simple drama of relentless violence and unmitigated settler aggression, and that settler and Indigenous societies were not able to adapt to one another, negotiate modes of accommodation, form alliances, acculturate, or display tolerance or empathy toward those from the opposite camp. Nor is it to deny that Indigenous peoples had agency or that there was a degree of cooperation, peaceful exchange and mediation of differences. Such symbiotic, commensal and ambivalent relations were, however, temporary and generally lasted only for as long as settlers lacked the power to dominate and take possession of the land, or where settler projects failed. 'Middle grounds' or 'third spaces', where they existed, almost inevitably degenerated into land grabs, race wars and ethnic cleansing offensives, or, in a number of cases, escalated into exterminatory campaigns. The only times this did not occur was when settler communities were not sufficiently numerous or powerful to assert full control over the land they claimed. The inner drive of settler colonialism for exclusive control of the newly claimed homeland made lasting peaceful coexistence with Indigenous communities all but impossible. Bolstered by a range of cultural chauvinisms and racial assumptions with lethal implications,[38] the settler establishment demanded total security from any Indigenous challenge. The rise of the global industrial economy and its adjunct, the settler revolution, all but put paid to middle grounds. In Western imperial expansion, especially from the early nineteenth century onwards, settler claims were backed by unparalleled levels of resourcing, including a capacity for demographic swamping of Indigenous societies, as well as vastly superior technologies of warfare.

Civilian-driven genocidal violence in settler colonial situations: Case studies

Arranged in rough chronological order, the case studies in this book allow for an assessment of the dynamic behind civilian-driven violence in the making of settler genocides globally, and for a rough gauging historically of the pace and character of settler invasion and Indigenous dispossession — as well as a sense of their role in the making of Western global dominance. The concluding chapter by Lorenzo Veracini picks up on these themes, elaborating specifically on the relationship between mass violence, on the one hand, and colonialism and settler colonialism as distinct modes of domination, on the other.

---

38 Wolfe, *Traces of History*, 'Introduction', 1–30.

The first case study (Chapter Two) examines the Western world's earliest overseas settler colonial conquest, which resulted in the extinction of the Indigenous population of the Canary Islands, situated off the coast of southern Morocco. The obliteration of autochthonous Canarian societies on this archipelago of seven islands was initiated by marauding freebooters and slavers from the 1340s onwards after European mariners rediscovered the existence of the island cluster, and was propelled to completion by Iberian conquistadors and settlers toward the end of the fifteenth century. This extermination was to a large extent driven by civilians, if for no other reasons than the scant interest of the late medieval European state in acquiring overseas empire, and the limited capacity of its monarchs to exercise power across more than a thousand kilometres of ocean. The initial conquest of three of the seven islands between 1402 and 1405 was the product of private enterprise, being organised by two minor European noblemen and thus almost entirely a civilian-driven affair. Even after the Spanish crown took formal charge of operations in 1478, conquistadors and other state agents deployed in the Canaries acted as much in their personal capacities and private interests as in those of the sovereigns they represented.

Ongoing mass violence, land confiscation, scorched-earth tactics, enslavement, mass deportation, sexual abuse, child confiscation and cultural suppression ensured the utter annihilation of aboriginal Canarian societies by the end of the fifteenth century. It was in particular the enslavement and deportation of entire surviving island communities that made the liquidation of these societies genocidal. And it was especially the development of sugar plantations in Madeira and the Canaries themselves that drove the demand for slave labour. Besides arguing that the extermination of Indigenous Canarian peoples constitutes genocide — more accurately, a set of seven genocides — this chapter explores the role of civilian-driven mass violence in this process and establishes its centrality to the making of settler colonialism and Western global dominance from the start. The Canaries case is also significant as a proving ground for subsequent Spanish imperial ventures, especially the colonisation of the Caribbean.

In Chapter Three, Sidney Harring provides a sweeping survey of civilian-driven violence in the making of Canada, from seventeenth-century British claims to Newfoundland to present-day penetration of the Arctic north; and across the breadth of North America from the Maritime Provinces to British Columbia. Starting with settler extermination of the Beothuk people of Newfoundland by settlers by the late 1820s, Harring documents the role of civilian-driven violence in the destruction of Indigenous societies, and the way it meshed with state initiatives to dispossess Native

Americans as settlement and conquest spread westward, and later resource exploitation expanded northward. While Harring is clear that not all of the social devastation inflicted on Indigenous societies was genocidal, he is equally explicit that much of it was, and that the outcome was the same across Canada: Indigenous peoples were dispossessed, impoverished and marginalised, and their societies annihilated.

Harring elucidates this reality of ethnic cleansing and genocide with a view to demonstrating the hollowness of the Canadian national myth that the society came into being through peaceful and carefully controlled frontier settlement regulated by the rule of law. This narrative of Canadian exceptionalism is held up particularly in comparison to the United States — but also other British Dominions — where it is argued that a combination of unregulated settlement, a culture of rugged individualism and weak central government led to disorder and conflict with Indigenous peoples. Importantly, Harring's chapter helps provide a corrective to Canadian historiography, which places enormous emphasis on the genocidal consequences of residential schooling but too little on the earlier transgressions of colonisation itself. This is not to deny the genocidal impact of residential schooling but to place it in proper perspective — a genocidal measure of forced assimilation imposed upon communities that had survived prior processes of ethnic cleansing and genocide during colonisation. The power of Canada's national myth is such that few people — least of all, it would appear, Canadians — are accustomed to thinking about the settlement of Canada in terms of genocide. Those who engage with Sid Harring's chapter will be forced to do so.

The next four chapters reveal a variety of approaches by settler colonial establishments for taking control of the land and quelling Indigenous resistance, and civilian-driven strategies for perpetrating violence in pursuit of their objectives. For example, in the eighteenth-century Cape Colony, the weak and impecunious Dutch East India Company (VOC) government enabled mass violence by farmers against San communities through sanctioning both officially constituted as well as informal militias as a means of reinforcing its tenuous hold on frontier society and devolving most of the costs of frontier defence onto farmers. Settlers on the frontier accepted this burden in return for effectively being allowed to take the law into their own hands when dealing with Indigenous people, using the militia to clear new land for expansion, as well as to acquire captive labour. Not only did their destructive farming practices and demographic growth necessitate continuous expansion, but labour was also perennially in short supply. When the British administration tried to curb frontier

CHAPTER 1: 'No Savage Shall Inherit the Land'

conflict in the nineteenth century, this violence went underground in the form of clandestine militia activity that could be every bit as lethal as its official counterpart. In New South Wales a combination of covert civilian-driven assaults, together with state-sponsored violence to promote colonial expansion, cleared much of the land of Aboriginal people as settlement spread inland. A more direct and methodical approach was adopted by its northern neighbour and offshoot, Queensland, where the state maintained a paramilitary force for the express purpose of supporting lethal policies for Indigenous removal from the land. In the remote and sparsely inhabited Tierra del Fuego we observe the opposite. Here, commercial sheep farming companies, with the tacit approval of two essentially absent states, hired mercenaries to help clear the land of its Indigenous peoples.

In Chapter Four, Lance van Sittert and Thierry Rousset examine the role of state-sanctioned militia, especially the impact of their slaving activities, on the destruction of San societies along the Cape Colony's northeastern frontier district of Graaff-Reinet during the five decades straddling the turn of the nineteenth century. In the Cape Colony, mounted militia units consisting of farmers and their dependants, and known as commandos, were the main apparatus of both settler- and state-driven mass violence against Indigenous peoples. Official commandos were larger planned offensives, led by local officials, themselves farmers, that received instructions and ammunition from the VOC government. Importantly, the Cape government also allowed settlers to take the law into their own hands and to set up unofficial or informal commandos that could be formed on an ad hoc basis and only needed to report their activities after the fact. Though smaller, sometimes consisting of only a few farmers chasing after cattle raiders, unofficial commandos took to the field much more frequently than official ones, which tended to be annual affairs. There were, however, several large unofficial commandos that were as well-equipped and probably more murderous than their official counterparts, especially during the nineteenth century when the British administration curbed official commando activity. In their overall impact, unofficial commandos were every bit as destructive of San society as official commandos. Much of the activity of unofficial commandos went unreported, as many intentionally circumvented government scrutiny.[39]

---

39 Van der Merwe P.J. 1937. *Die Noordwaartse Beweging van die Boere voor die Groot Trek, 1770–1842.* The Hague: W.P. van Stockum & Zoon, 65; Adhikari, *Anatomy of a South African Genocide*, 40–41; Penn, *Forgotten Frontier*, 35.

Van Sittert and Rousset demonstrate how the officer corps of the militia, acting nominally for the state, used the commando system to further the interests of frontier farmers by securing a regular supply of forced Indigenous labour, suppressing Indigenous resistance, and opening up new land for occupation by enslaving and exterminating hunter-gatherer peoples on the frontier. They argue that, given a pervasive labour scarcity and because the Indigenous slave workforce was unable to reproduce itself biologically, it needed regular infusions of new captives — and the commando system was the only viable means of generating a sufficient supply. In a situation of growing social inequality, the militia leadership, having also to address the needs of rank-and-file members for labour, were nonetheless successfully able to pursue their own class interest of securing a larger share of the captive labour supply, and hence increased pastoral production and higher socio-economic status for themselves. The state, itself unable to police or maintain social order on the frontier, relied on frontier farmers conducting irregular militia offensives to do so, and paid the price of having its agenda subverted. On the Graaff-Reinet frontier, as on other Cape borderlands where settlers came into conflict with foragers over nearly two centuries, the violence was almost entirely civilian-driven, with much of it state-sanctioned. In the Cape Colony, two centuries of settler conflict with San, as the frontier moved inland, nearly always had the same outcome — the complete shattering of these aboriginal societies.

Lyndall Ryan (Chapter Five) analyses the dynamic behind frontier massacres in New South Wales during the first seven decades of the colony's existence, drawing on data produced by a long-range project to identify, describe and map frontier massacres that took place in central and eastern Australia between the start of colonisation in 1788 and 1930.[40] She traces changing patterns of civilian- as well as state-led massacres over this period, focusing on such aspects as techniques and motives, as well as collusion between civilian, military and government agents in the perpetration of violence against indigenes. Of the 71 massacres of Indigenous peoples she identifies, 45 were committed by civilians, 17 by the military, and 9 were joint operations. A very conservative estimate of casualties puts the average death toll at about 30 per incident of mass murder. Civilians were thus responsible for nearly two-thirds, and were involved in over three-quarters, of the massacres. The one mass slaying that stands out within Ryan's

---

40 'Colonial frontier massacres in central and eastern Australia 1788–1930'. Digital map. The Centre for 21st Century Humanities, University of Newcastle. Available at https://c21ch.newcastle.edu.au/colonialmassacres/map.php, accessed 26 October 2019.

compilation, because it led to the successful prosecution and execution of seven perpetrators — the Myall Creek massacre of June 1838 — clearly did not serve as a deterrent, as 21 civilian-led massacres were carried out within the following decade. This was by far the highest in any ten-year period she examines. This excessively high incidence indicates a certain confidence among offenders in the code of silence that had developed around frontier bloodletting. It is also apparent that economic interest trumped the danger of prosecution, as most of this conflict was generated by a land rush into the prime pastoral areas of what is today southern Queensland, especially the Darling Downs region. Using statistics and insights drawn from this survey of massacres, Ryan comes to the conclusion that the destruction of Aboriginal society in New South Wales was indeed genocide and was largely perpetrated by civilians.

In Chapter Six, Raymond Evans and Robert Ørsted-Jensen investigate the murderous confluence of civilian- and state-driven processes of Aboriginal dispossession in Queensland. They point out that Queensland serves as the primary example of genocide on the Australian continent, as it had the largest Aboriginal population, the most extensive land suitable for agriculture, and generated the most intense violence over the longest period of time. Here the state, for over half a century, administered and financed the Queensland Native Police, consisting of squads of Aboriginal troopers overseen by white officers, to protect settlers along its moving frontier. Native Police contingents assisted settlers with the displacement of Aboriginal peoples from their land, and often colluded with settler vigilante groups in perpetrating mass violence. It was especially when Indigenous resistance flared up and colonists were killed that the Queensland Native Police went on the rampage, indiscriminately slaughtering large numbers of Aborigines in paroxysms of collective punishment. The vigour with which the state defended settler interests, and its deliberate neglect of its duty to protect the rights of Aboriginal peoples, was a measure of the extent to which the Queensland government served squatter interests.

Noting the hopelessly inadequate approaches that have hitherto been used to estimate casualties in Queensland's frontier conflict and the acute underestimations that have resulted, Evans and Ørsted-Jensen develop a new methodology for assessing this loss of life more accurately. They do so by carefully mining information available from scattered and sketchy source material to project casualty rates for the entire period of frontier conflict. Starting with the number of Native Police camps that exist in the historical record, it is possible to calculate the aggregate number of years the camps were in operation. From this can be estimated the number of monthly patrols, the average number of times they were involved in assaults, and the average number of casualties per collision. Using a studiedly minimalist reckoning for each, they arrive at a figure in excess of 41 000 Aboriginal deaths from Native Police attacks alone. Using a similar methodology, they estimate just over 20 000 Aboriginal casualties at the hands of settlers on the Queensland frontier. This represents a radical upward revision of casualties resulting from Queensland's frontier violence, and has implications for assessments of casualties on other Australian frontiers as well. Their findings are bound to be controversial given that there is a strong denialist streak within Australian society about the lethality of violence in the dispossession of Aboriginal peoples and a long-standing tendency to understate frontier casualties in Australian historical writing. Whatever challenges critics may raise, what is clear is that all estimates of casualties on the Queensland frontier hitherto proffered are far too low. It bears repeating that what Evans and Ørsted-Jensen have produced is a minimalist estimate that was deliberately understated at every level of computation. Interestingly, this ratio of two-thirds of the casualties attributed to Native Police and one-third to settlers is an inversion of a tentative estimate that Evans made one and a half decades ago.[41] Clearly the Native Police was significantly more murderous than previously thought. No wonder that such care was taken to destroy its records.

This is followed by a case study (Chapter Seven) that elucidates a contrary strategy for destroying Indigenous society, and indicates that by the late nineteenth century the settler revolution had spread to the remotest habitable regions of the earth. In Tierra del Fuego both Argentina and Chile allowed an extreme form of laissez-faire capitalism by giving commercial companies a free hand in dealing with the challenges they faced, including Indigenous resistance. Alberto Harambour analyses the extermination of the Selk'nam people of Tierra del Fuego from the 1880s onward through the actions of a range of civilian agents, including gold prospectors, missionaries, sheep-farming companies and mercenaries, the last-mentioned employed to kill off the guanaco that competed with sheep for pasturage, as well as the Indigenous peoples who resisted settler encroachment. After the resolution of their border disputes through the Boundary Treaty of 1881, both Chile and Argentina privatised the productive land on the island both as a way of cementing their sovereignty in the face of their effective absence on the ground and of stimulating the economic potential of the region. While the

---

41 See Evans, R. 2004. "'Plenty shoot 'em": The destruction of Aboriginal societies along the Queensland frontier', in Moses, *Genocide and Settler Society*, 166.

CHAPTER 1: 'No Savage Shall Inherit the Land'

gold prospectors were brutal in their treatment of indigenes, their numbers were small and their impact both localised and episodic. It was sheep farming operations that had genocidal repercussions given their systematic occupation of the land, wilful destruction of the natural environment and ruthless response to Indigenous resistance. Hiring mercenaries mainly from English-speaking settler colonies, sheep farming companies embarked on a deliberate campaign of liquidating Selk'nam society through a combination of assassination, massacre and removal to remote mission stations of those taken captive. Missionaries, falsely lauded in settler mythology as saviours and civilisers of one of humanity's most primitive cultures, presided over the final stages of this extinction. Crowded together in unsanitary and extremely deleterious conditions at mission stations, Selk'nam who survived the violence unleashed by the sheep farming companies died off rapidly from communicable diseases, especially tuberculosis, until there was but a handful left and the stations became redundant.

Although it does not appear as a case study in this book, it is worth noting the example of the destruction of Californian Indian societies precipitated by the gold rush of 1848 as yet another way in which civilian-driven violence was integral to the perpetration of genocide in the making of Western global domination. In addition to a large number of indiscriminate murders and massacres, democratic institutions were also used by settlers to legitimate sprees of organised and sustained mass violence against indigenes. Farming communities, often with the backing of larger landholders, became adept at using democratic institutions and procedures to organise local, volunteer militia units to seize resources and extinguish Indigenous resistance. It was through these paid militia units used to hunt Native Americans, and which usually operated as mobile death squads, that much of the displacement and killing of Indians were perpetrated. The Californian state operated as a particularly vicious tyranny of the majority between the late 1840s and the mid-1870s, during which time the Native American population of the state was reduced by over 80 per cent.[42]

While vigilante parties operated irregularly and sporadically throughout the state, many voluntary militia units were formally constituted by means of petitions signed by male voters and endorsed by locally elected officials such as sheriffs and mayors. These petitions were addressed to the governor, with citizens claiming the need to protect themselves and

---

42 For a summary of estimated population declines, see Madley B. 2016. *An American Genocide: The United States and the California Indian Catastrophe, 1846–1873*. New Haven: Yale University Press, 346–347.

their property against marauding Indians. Governors, being sympathetic to settler claims and mindful of the need to retain the support of voters, endorsed the formation of paid militia units and sometimes used state resources to help them. After clearing a particular area of its Indigenous inhabitants, which might take several months, volunteer companies pressed claims for payment from the state government, which in turn passed on these claims to the federal government, which usually obliged. In this way, the killing of Indians in California — and many other parts of the American West — was largely a civilian-driven enterprise sponsored by state authorities, and partly financed by the federal government. Brendan Lindsay summarises the thrust of this genocide as one in which 'rather than a government orchestrating a population to bring about the genocide of a group, the population orchestrated a government to destroy a group'.[43]

Chapters Eight (Andrew Woolford), Nine (Robert Gordon) and Ten (Susan Thomson) deal with the mindsets of civilian perpetrators in setter colonial situations. An obvious question to ask of such perpetrating groups is what shared frames of reference, ideas and values motivated their communally held animosities toward indigenes? Or, more conventionally, what the were common ideological foundations of civilian-driven violence against indigenes in settler colonial situations, for it might be said that ideology was the glue that held imperial ventures together and that helped solidify settler societies. Ideology is of fundamental importance for its influence on how individuals, leaders, communities and state structures frame goals, perceive threats, devise solutions to problems, and deploy violence, and through which final solutions become imaginable. Ideologies play a central role in genocide as perpetrators do not kill or seek mindlessly to harm targeted social groups. They kill for a reason or a set of reasons, and at the very least with intentions they justify to themselves, and which point to victims as deserving of violence, suffering or death. Perpetrators of exterminatory violence generally act in groups and usually with the sanction of their broader societies, or sections of it. As such, they share ideas about their motives and the necessity for resorting to mass violence as a solution to a perceived social or political problem. Ideologies, moreover, are important enablers of mass violence to the extent that they help perpetrators overcome inhibitions and taboos against taking human life and mobilise sympathisers to their cause.

---

43 See Lindsay, *Murder State*, 22, for the quotation, and ch. 5 for the operation of these 'democratic death squads'; and Madley, *American Genocide*, especially chs. 6 and 7 for what he refers to as the 'killing machine'.

CHAPTER 1: 'No Savage Shall Inherit the Land'

All three contributors, however, push beyond the notion of ideology as commonly understood, namely, as a coherent system of ideas, values, beliefs, assumptions and other attitudinal and normative components shared by a social group, which influences their understanding of the world.[44] They seek more nuanced and deeper understandings of perpetrator perceptions of victims, as well as of the relationships between civilian- and state-led violence. While they agree that shared ideas and frameworks of meaning among perpetrators are critical in first making genocide thinkable, and then actionable, conventional understandings of ideology are too restrictive. Of these contributors, Andrew Woolford is the most explicit about the limitations of the usual academic conceptualisations of ideology, and deploys a more flexible theoretical framework to get to grips with questions of civilian participation in genocidal violence.

After the closing of their frontiers in the late nineteenth century, the governments of both the United States and Canada adopted Indigenous residential schooling as a key strategy for 'solving the Indian problem', as contemporaries often put it, or 'eliminating the native', as Patrick Wolfe would have it. Woolford examines processes of social destruction by civilian actors in four Indian residential schools — two each in New Mexico and Manitoba — from the 1870s to the 1970s, using the concept of collective action frames popularised by sociologist Erving Goffman. Woolford defines a collective action frame as 'a "schemata of interpretation" that allows actors to find common meaning in a complex world ... and the challenges they face therein'. Collective action frames are sufficiently flexible to accommodate individual negotiation of, adaptation to, and motivations within this shared understanding of social reality. They are far less circumscribed than what we understand as ideologies, in that they consist essentially of 'a set of assumptions that help co-ordinate interpretations' and responses to social situations. The idea, for example, that there was an 'Indian problem' and that the assimilation of Native Americans into settler society, especially of their children through Western schooling, represented an effective solution, constitutes a collective action frame.

Woolford explains that collective action frames can accommodate 'diverse motivations, intents, practices, and engagements to coalesce across varied temporal and spatial scales ... in fostering and occasionally

---

44 See, for example, Maynard J.L. 2014. 'Rethinking the role of ideology in mass atrocities'. *Terrorism and Political Violence*, 26, no. 5, 821–841; Freeden M. 2003. *Ideology: A Very Short Introduction*. Oxford: Oxford University Press, 72–77; Hamilton M. 1987. 'The elements of the concept of ideology'. *Political Studies*, 35, no. 1, 18–38.

disrupting group destruction' by civilian actors such as missionaries, teachers, principals and Indian agents. Given this flexibility, the notion of the collective action frame allows one to explain how actors with varying dispositions, having potentially very disparate points of view, not working in concert, not necessarily espousing the same values, and using very different strategies, can nevertheless participate in, or be compliant with, a common programme of social destruction with genocidal consequences. It helps explain how large numbers of 'ordinary people' who do not necessarily subscribe to the genocidal ideology of an elite or state can be recruited as 'foot soldiers', participants or sympathisers in a socially destructive project, and how individuals can play widely varying roles in these processes at different times. Woolford amply demonstrates the utility of the concept of the collective action frame for understanding motive, intent and complicity of participants in genocidal violence; as well as how civilian-driven violence and state-driven strategies intertwined in complex ways to drive forward processes of social destruction in the operation of these four schools over the better part of a century.

Robert Gordon's chapter also seeks to transcend conventional notions of ideology by exploring the roles of fantasy, imagination and particular kinds of ritualised and emotionally intense social interaction that promoted participation in acts of genocidal violence among settler farmers in German South West Africa. He does so by seeking to unravel two connected conundrums in German farmers' behaviour toward the San. The first is why settler farmers who had vehemently opposed General von Trotha's exterminatory campaigns during the 1904–1908 wars, for fear that their labour supply was being destroyed, indulged with some gusto in 'erasive' violence toward the San a few years later. The second is why, at a time of a labour shortage so severe that their very existence as farmers was being threatened, farmers nonetheless participated with enthusiasm in the unfolding genocide of the Namibian San.

Given the weakness of the colonial state in the Namibian countryside — it consisted of a 'veritable ragrug of islands of colonial power' — Gordon suggests that the situation on these farms was one of quasi-feudalism. With the weak state devolving a great deal of authority onto farmers to manage Indigenous people as they saw fit, farmers effectively ruled over petty fiefdoms and regarded themselves as feudal lords, or 'little kings'. Despite forming a small minority of the population and contributing very little to the economy or the fiscus, farmers nevertheless saw themselves as 'the backbone of the country'. Isolated and feeling threatened, and with their anxieties excited by the lurid dramas depicted in adventure novels

CHAPTER 1: 'No Savage Shall Inherit the Land'

popular at the time, German farmers allowed their 'imaginations to run wild' and engaged in 'a rich fantasy world' regarding threats emanating from San resistance to settler encroachment on their territory. Their fantasies exaggerated the San threat out of all proportion, prompting a frenzied settler overreaction of eradicatory violence toward the San. Gordon argues that it was not so much any particular ideology as recurring, ritualised and emotionally intense social interaction among farmers — especially around bouts of heavy drinking — that reinforced a macho culture of bravado in the face of danger and an over-hasty resort to violence when dealing with Indigenous people. He points to the much more composed reactions of Afrikaner farmers who settled in Namibia after the South African invasion in 1915 to prove his point that the reason for the near hysteria of German farmers on the frontier lay not in the actual situation but rather in their perceptions of it. Afrikaners faced the same conditions and had similar racist attitudes toward Bushmen, but did not resort to genocidal violence toward the San.

I have for more than a decade been intrigued by the Rwandan genocide, which provides interesting twists to the usual pattern of genocides in settler colonial situations. Although I cannot recall the term 'settler' being applied to the internal Tutsi population in the literature, their characterisation by Hutu nationalists as alien invaders of Caucasoid descent who had stolen Hutu land very clearly casts them as such. Hutu nationalists had from the 1950s already taken up the Hamitic hypothesis of their European rulers.[45] The internal Tutsi can thus be seen as having been annihilated as settlers and former oppressors. Also, after the Rwandan Patriotic Front invasion of 1990, the fear that external Tutsi would return to confiscate Hutu land and rule over them again clearly also construes them as potential settlers. One twist to the usual settler genocide pattern is that the internal Tutsi, purported settlers, were victims and not perpetrators of genocide. A second is that the perpetrators of genocide saw themselves as Indigenous, as formerly oppressed by alien invaders, and feared being overrun again by what in their eyes effectively was a new wave of Tutsi settlers. There is thus a sense in which the Rwandan cataclysm was a subaltern genocide — one in which the tables are turned, and the victims of oppression rise up against and destroy

---

45 Eltringham N. 2006. '"Invaders who have stolen the country": The Hamitic hypothesis, race and the Rwandan genocide'. *Social Identities*, 12, no. 4, 425–446; Mamdani M. 2002. *When Victims Become Killers: Colonialism, Nativism and the Genocide in Rwanda*. Princeton: Princeton University Press, 46–47, 79–87. See also Sanders E. 1969. 'The Hamitic hypothesis: Its origin and functions in time perspective'. *Journal of African History*, 10, no. 4, 521–532.

the dominating group. This is 'when the rabbit's got the gun', as Adam Jones puts it.[46] Thus, with the Rwandan genocide, one had former victims, who saw themselves as Indigenous, exterminating ostensibly former settler oppressors, under dire threat of an invading force of potential Tutsi settlers. What makes the Rwandan genocide of particular interest to this project is the exceptional level of popular participation, that is, of civilian violence.

Susan Thomson uses the concept of everyday violence to explore the historical legacies that made possible the Rwandan genocide, especially its high levels of popular participation. Thomson traces structural continuities in the social, political and cultural meanings and practices of intergroup violence in Rwanda from precolonial times onwards, as well as the ways in which they became embedded in the institutional, social and moral lives of the society. Demonstrating the potency of this legacy of everyday violence in modern Rwandan society, she shows how the postcolonial Hutu elite was able, in a time of acute crisis, to draw on historically conditioned and shared frames of reference about the existential threat the Hutu nation faced, to call successfully on Hutu civilians across the country to kill all Tutsi within reach, including neighbours, friends and even family members. She uses life history interviews with male Hutu perpetrators to demonstrate how at a personal level this mindset helped galvanise civilians into action when the Hutu extremist call for exterminatory violence was made.

The Rwandan genocide was state-driven, but the state did not have the capacity to execute its genocidal programme. It needed extensive civilian participation and large numbers of Hutu civilians responded to its call because of the acute and extended existential crisis they faced — of economic collapse, escalating social chaos, widespread political violence, looming defeat in war and the ultimate threat of the return of Tutsi — or, should one say, settler domination. Though the genocide was clearly state-orchestrated, on the ground most of the violence was committed by civilians.

In Chapter Eleven, Lorenzo Veracini concludes by theorising colonialism and settler colonialism as distinct modes of domination through their respective use of, and relationship to, violence. He argues, on the one hand, that colonialism tends to be centripetal in nature and systematically seeks to store up violence both as threat and for controlled future use in order to reproduce colonial relations of domination. Settler colonialism, on the other hand, tends to be centrifugal in nature and dissipates or expends

---

46 Jones, A. 2009. '"When the rabbit's got the gun": Subaltern genocide and the genocidal continuum' in *Genocides by the Oppressed: Subaltern Genocide in Theory and Practice*, eds. N. Robins & A. Jones. Bloomington: Indiana University Press.

CHAPTER 1: 'No Savage Shall Inherit the Land'

violence to prevent future settler–Indigenous relationships by destroying Indigenous society. On the basis of these insights, he engages with the contributions in this volume with a view to exploring the role of civilians in 'the shifting relationship between violence that is inflicted for the purpose of its storage and future use, and violence that is inflicted and dissipated at once for the purpose of pre-empting the possibility of its repetition'. He concludes that on remote frontiers 'settlers are hegemonic ... and if the settler is unleashing violence without the intention of reproducing it ... chances are that one is facing a civilian-driven genocide.'

Conclusion: Righteous violence and with 'justice on their side'

A generalisation I feel one can make with some degree of confidence about the mindset of death-dealing colonists in settler colonial situations is that they have, by and large, felt that their actions were morally sanctioned. Writing about violence in general, Alan Fiske and Tage Rai, in their book *Virtuous Violence*, present a persuasive argument that a great deal, if not most, violence is morally motivated *from the perspective of perpetrators*, rather than the product of psychological or social pathology, or genetic defect, as often assumed. They explain: 'Morality is about regulating social relationships and violence is one way to regulate relationships.'[47] Violence and threats of violence were the most important ways in which relationships between colonists and Indigenous peoples were regulated in settler colonial situations, even where ambivalent relations or middle grounds may have existed for substantial periods. Civilian-driven brutality toward indigenes in settler colonial situations was therefore largely the product of what I think of as righteous violence, where perpetrators believed themselves to have had some moral or principled justification for using force.[48]

Whether killing for God, country, culture, honour, revenge, land, liberty, some utopian future, to make a fortune or simply to make a living, righteous violence is particularly pernicious, as perpetrators feel little, if any, remorse and are motivated by what they regard to be honourable goals. This is amply reflected in the mythologies and manifest destinies that settler societies have constructed to justify their existence, their acquisition of the land and their treatment of Indigenous peoples. Theodore Roosevelt, a vocal advocate of settler entitlement at the expense of Indigenous peoples,

---

47 See Fisk A. & Rai T. 2015. *Virtuous Violence: Hurting and Killing to Create, Sustain, End, and Honor Social Relationships*. Cambridge: Cambridge University Press, xxii, 15–16, 136.

48 By 'moral' in this context I mean a set of subjective and culturally based evaluations of human behaviour, beliefs, attitudes and intentions.

provided the basic reasoning behind such thinking: 'The settler and pioneer have at bottom had justice on their side; this great continent could not have been kept as nothing but a game preserve for squalid savages.'[49] Walter Hixson provides the unspoken corollary to Roosevelt's premise with his observation that when indigenes 'resisted giving up colonial space "justice" was on the side of military aggression and ethnic cleansing'.[50] I would add 'genocide' and 'extermination' to his list and note that a great deal of this violence was committed by civilians.

---

49 Roosevelt T. 1889. *The Winning of the West: From the Alleghenies to the Mississippi, 1769–1776*. New York: G.P. Putnam's Sons, 90. Roosevelt came close to expressing the settler establishment's desire for the elimination of the native in its purest form when, in an 1886 speech in New York, he proclaimed: 'I don't go so far as to think that the only good Indians are the dead Indians, but I believe nine out of every ten are, and I shouldn't like to inquire too closely into the case of the tenth.' See also Hagedorn H. 1921. *Roosevelt in the Bad Lands*. Boston: Houghton Mifflin, 355; and Stannard D. 1992. *American Holocaust: The Conquest of the New World*. Oxford: Oxford University Press, 245.
50 Hixson, *American Settler Colonialism*, 70.

CHAPTER TWO

Raiders, Slavers, Conquistadors, Settlers: Civilian-driven Violence in the Extermination of Aboriginal Canary Islanders

Mohamed Adhikari

Modern Europe's earliest overseas settler colonial conquest resulted in the complete destruction of the Indigenous societies of the Canary Islands, situated off the southern coast of Morocco. The annihilation was initiated by marauding freebooters and slavers in the first half of the fourteenth century, after European mariners rediscovered the existence of the archipelago, and was propelled to completion mainly by Iberian conquistadors and settlers through the fifteenth century. The process was largely driven by civilians, if for no other reasons than the scant interest of the late medieval state in acquiring overseas empire and the limited capacity of its monarchs to exert their will across over a thousand kilometres of ocean. Even the state-appointed conquistadors who took charge of operations during the latter stages of the conquest acted as much in their personal capacities and private interests as those of the sovereigns they represented.

By the time Christopher Columbus set sail on his celebrated first voyage across the Atlantic Ocean in 1492, aboriginal Canarian societies had already been driven to the brink of oblivion by European invaders, with the last independent Canarians to resist Spanish colonisers surrendering in September 1496. Little more than 1 000 native Canarians, nearly all of whom were enslaved, were alive by the end of the fifteenth century. After a century-long process of conquest, which included ongoing mass violence, land confiscation, scorched-earth tactics, enslavement, mass deportation and child removal, it would not be long before continued bloodshed, sexual abuse and cultural suppression sealed the obliteration of Indigenous Canarian societies.

The reconnaissance and colonisation of three island clusters southwest of the Iberian Peninsula — the Azores, Madeira and Canary Islands — by the Spanish and Portuguese during the two centuries before Columbus' voyages were in part products of advances in ship design and navigation, as well as the extension out into the Atlantic of a long-standing European tradition of empire-building in the Mediterranean.[1] Since the Canaries were the only east Atlantic archipelago to be inhabited, it was the only one that needed to be conquered, in the process serving, via the experience of the *Reconquista*, as an apprenticeship for Castilian ultramarine empire.[2] These east Atlantic islands served as strategic bases for further European exploration and as testing grounds for Iberian colonialism in the New World. Not only were ideas, institutions and methods developed in the Canaries applied in the Americas,[3] especially the Caribbean, but the plunder of natural resources, development of plantation economies, widespread use of slave labour, unrestrained violence towards Indigenous populations and the devastating impact of disease also foreshadowed the holocaust that was to engulf the New World. The eradication of the archipelago's aboriginal societies is one of the least acknowledged of modern Europe's overseas settler colonial genocides.

The Canary Islands and their Indigenous peoples

The Canary archipelago, which is today part of Spain, consists of seven volcanic islands — Tenerife, Fuerteventura, Gran Canaria, Lanzarote, La Palma, La Gomera and El Hierro — strung out in a 450-kilometre latitudinal chain, at its closest point about one hundred kilometres off southern Morocco. Although much of the archipelago consists of rugged, mountainous terrain of jagged ridges with alternating ravines, and although there are many rocky outcrops and rock-strewn lava fields, there are also

---

1   Fernández-Armesto F. 1987. *Before Columbus: Exploration and Colonization from the Mediterranean to the Atlantic, 1229–1492*. London: Macmillan, 2, 12–13.

2   Fernández-Armesto F. 1982. *The Canary Islands After the Conquest: The Making of a Colonial Society in the Early Sixteenth Century*. Oxford: Oxford University Press, 1–2; Merediz E. 2004. *Refracted Images: The Canary Islands Through a New World Lens*. Tempe: Arizona Center for Medieval and Renaissance Studies, 2–3, 7–8; Stevens-Arroyo A. 1993. 'The inter-Atlantic paradigm: The failure of Spanish medieval colonization of the Canary and Caribbean islands', *Comparative Studies in Society and History*, 35, no. 3, 517; Carew J. 1992. 'The end of Moorish enlightenment and the beginning of the Columbian era', *Race and Class*, 33, no. 3, 4; Fradera J. 2004. 'Spanish colonial historiography: Everyone in their place', *Social History*, 29, no. 3, 368; Baily G., Phillips C. and Voigt L. 2009. 'Spain and Spanish America in the early modern Atlantic world: Current trends in scholarship', *Renaissance Quarterly*, 62, 44–45.

3   Elliott J.H. 1963. *Imperial Spain, 1469–1716*. London: Arnold, 58; Fernández-Armesto F. 2009. *1492: The Year the World Began*. New York: Harper Collins, 274–275; Crosby, A. 2013. 'An ecohistory of the Canary Islands: a precursor of European colonisation in the New World and Australasia', in *Spain, Portugal and the Atlantic Frontier of Medieval Europe*, ed. J. Lopez-Portillo. Farnham: Ashgate Variorum, 193; O'Flanagan P. 2017. 'Mediterranean and Atlantic settler colonialism from the late fourteenth to the early seventeenth centuries', in *The Routledge Handbook of the History of Settler Colonialism*, eds. E. Cavanagh and L. Veracini. Abingdon: Routledge, 38–40.

CHAPTER 2: Raiders, Slavers, Conquistadors, Settlers

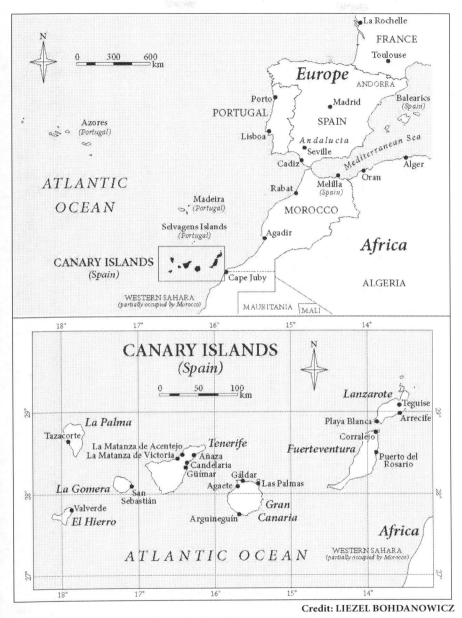

Credit: LIEZEL BOHDANOWICZ

Figure 2.1: The Canary Islands in the fifteenth century

extensive, verdant coastal lowlands. The steep gradient of their topographies means that a wide range of climatic conditions and natural vegetation occurs within relatively confined areas.[4] This made possible an Indigenous economy based on daily and seasonal movement between croplands and pastures, and made available a diversity of wild foods. Forests provided an abundant supply of wood, but the lack of metallic ores precluded the development of metalworking.[5]

Indigenous Canarians were derived from the Berber societies of northwest Africa. This is confirmed by close links between Berber and native Canarian languages, material cultures, blood types, physical appearance and cosmology. Despite cultural diversity across the islands, Canarian communities nevertheless shared a cultural genre indicative of common origins. Cultural variation arose because island communities developed in isolation from one another over long periods, and immigrants did not spread evenly across the archipelago.[6] Archaeological evidence and folklore indicate that migrants from the African mainland arrived in several waves between the second millennium BCE and the early centuries CE.[7] With prevailing winds and sea currents, it would have been relatively easy for simple vessels to have travelled from the Moroccan coast to the Canaries

---

4   Mercer J. 1980. *The Canary Islanders: Their Prehistory, Conquest and Survival*. London: Rex Collings, 117; Vallejo E. 1994. 'The conquests of the Canary Islands', in *Implicit Understandings: Observing, Reporting and Reflecting on the Encounters Between Europeans and Other Peoples in the Early Modern Era*, ed. S. Schwartz. Cambridge: Cambridge University Press, 134; Herrera S. 1978. *The Canary Islands Through History*. Madrid: Editorial Drosbe, 26, 58–59; Thornton J. 2012. *A Cultural History of the Atlantic World, 1250–1820*. Cambridge: Cambridge University Press, 7.

5   Major R. 1970. 'Introduction' to de Bethencourt J. 1970. *The Canarian, or Book of the Conquest and Conversion of the Canarians in the Year 1402*, trans. R. Major. New York: Burt Franklin (first published London: Hakluyt Society 1872).

6   Farrujia de la Rosa A. 2005. *Imperialist Archaeology in the Canary Islands: French and German Studies on Prehistoric Colonization at the End of the 19th Century*. Oxford: John & Erica Hedges; Flores C. et al. 2003. 'A predominant European ancestry of paternal lineages from Canary Islands', *Annals of Human Genetics*, 67, 138; Maca-Meyer N. et al. 2004. 'Ancient mtDNA analysis and the origin of the Guanches', *European Journal of Human Genetics*, 12, 160; Maca-Meyer N. et al. 2004. 'A tale of aborigines, conquerors and slaves: Alu insertion polymorphisms and the peopling of Canary Islands', *Annals of Human Genetics*, 68, 603–604; Schwidetzky, I. 1976. 'The pre-Hispanic population of the Canary Islands', in *Biogeography and Ecology in the Canary Islands*, ed. G. Kunkel. The Hague: Dr W. Junk Publishers, 16–19, 24–25, 34.

7   Fernández-Armesto, *After Conquest*, 5; Schwidetzky, 'Pre-Hispanic population', 34; Gil J. & Martin F. 1993. *History of the Canary Islands*. Santa Cruz: Centro de la Cultura Popular Canaria, 22; Pérez M. 2011. 'Role of interpreters in the conquest and acculturation of the Canary archipelago', *Interpreting*, 13, no. 2, 157; de Espinosa A. 1907 [1594]. *The Guanches of Tenerife: The Holy Image of Our Lady of Candelaria and the Spanish Conquest and Settlement*, trans. C. Markham. London: Hakluyt Society, 26–27.

but near-impossible for them to have made the return journey.[8] It is also clear that early migrants had the intention of settling there, as they came with domesticated animals and seeds, and as families. They lived in isolation from the adjacent continent as well as from other islands.[9]

Canarians were agro-pastoralists. They cultivated crops of barley and in some areas wheat, while also gathering fern roots, which were roasted and ground into flour. A variety of fruits and vegetables were grown in small-scale horticultural initiatives, while wild foods, including berries, seeds, honey and yams, were foraged. On all the islands, shepherds tended substantial herds of goats, which provided them with meat, milk, tallow and hides, as well as bones and tendons for tools. Sheep and pigs were also present on some islands. Shellfish and fish formed an important part of the Canarian diet. Birds, small rodents and several varieties of lizard were also available.[10] The pre-contact Canarian economy most likely supported a population of somewhere between 50 000 and 80 000, with some estimates as high as 100 000.[11]

Canarian society consisted mostly of dispersed settlements, often no larger than the extended family. Gran Canaria, socially and economically the most developed of the island societies, had a few larger settlements. Islanders often lived in caves and constructed simple stone dwellings with thatched roofs. Canarian societies had hierarchical social structures of hereditary ruling families, a small nobility and commoners. Caste-like social divisions were reinforced by founding myths, social customs, status markers in dress and grooming styles, and by the exercise of force where necessary. At the upper end, a small order of high priests had considerable influence, while at the lowest butchers were a despised, segregated group.[12] Canarian society

---

8   Thornton J. 1998. *Africa and Africans in the Making of the Atlantic World, 1400–1800*. Cambridge: Cambridge University Press, 15; Crosby A. 2007 *Ecological Imperialism: The Biological Expansion of Europe, 900–1900*. Cambridge: Cambridge University Press, 112. Rodger N. 2011. 'Atlantic seafaring', in *The Oxford Handbook of the Atlantic World, 1450–1850*, eds. N. Canny and P. Morgan. Oxford: Oxford University Press, 75–76.

9   Mercer, *Canary Islanders*, 17–18; Farrujia de la Rosa A. 2014. *An Archaeology of the Margins: Colonialism, Amazighity and Heritage Management in the Canary Islands*. New York: Springer, 10–11.

10 Farrujia de la Rosa, *Archaeology of the Margins*, 5–6; Mercer, *Canary Islanders*, 117–123; Cook A. 1900. 'The Aborigines of the Canary Islands'. *American Anthropologist*, New Series, 2, no. 3, 463–468; Benjamin T. 2009. *The Atlantic World: Europeans, Africans, Indians and Their Shared History, 1400–1900*. Cambridge: Cambridge University Press, 107.

11 Crosby, *Ecological Imperialism*, 82, 92; Stevens-Arroyo, 'Inter-Atlantic paradigm', 527; Herrera, *Canary Islands*, 167; Benjamin, *The Atlantic World*, 24.

12 Abulafia, D. 2008. *Discovery of Mankind: Atlantic Encounters in the Age of Columbus*. New Haven: Yale University Press, 56, 63; Mercer, *Canary Islanders*, 101–111.

was politically organised into rudimentary, hereditary chiefdoms with a fair degree of fluidity in power relations.[13] On the more populous islands, chiefs were capable of marshalling substantial fighting forces efficiently in the face of outside threats, as several European expeditions found to their cost.[14]

Although they were limited to weapons of wood and stone, Canarians proved to be formidable adversaries in combat. Island warriors were legendary for the force and accuracy with which they hurled rocks and stones at opponents, often breaking the shields of European soldiers and sometimes the arms holding them. Combatants also used a variety of fire-hardened wooden lances reinforced with horn tips. Acclimatised to local conditions, Canarians moved swiftly over the rocky, rugged terrain, in contrast to clumsy European soldiers usually hampered by heavy, inappropriate armour and gear. Many Canarians used wooden staves to vault nimbly down inclines or across rough ground. The craggy, precipitous uplands and deep, narrow gullies, especially when forested, provided many natural fortresses, as well as opportunities for escape or surprise attack, which favoured the island defenders. Given the rudimentary military and maritime technologies available to Europeans, they were usually outnumbered and ill-equipped for the unconventional methods of the Canarians. These advantages, together with adept use of guerrilla tactics, meant that many of the islanders' military successes came through ambushes in rough terrain.[15]

Reconnaissance, raiding and slaving

The Canaries came to the attention of European mariners for the first time since the fall of the Roman Empire when the Genoese navigator Lancelotto Malocello landed on the easternmost isle, Lanzarote, in 1336.[16] The archipelago became the object of Portuguese, Genoese, Majorcan, Aragonese, Catalan, Norman and Castilian voyages of exploration, raiding and ultimately conquest by Castile. Trading and proselytisation occurred

---

13 At the time of colonisation Tenerife, for example, was divided into nine polities, Fuerteventura into two, Palma into twelve and Gran Canaria into two. Two generations earlier, Gran Canaria had as many as nine or ten chiefdoms, which were consolidated into a single state under a charismatic ruling couple, that was then split between two heirs.

14 Mercer, *Canary Islanders*, 80, 90–91, 96–98; Fernández-Armesto, *After Conquest*, 8–9; Stevens-Arroyo, 'Inter-Atlantic paradigm', 526.

15 Merediz, *Refracted Images*, 68; Thornton, *Cultural History*, 25–26, 161–162.

16 Crosby, *Ecological Imperialism*, 71; Abulafia, *Discovery of Mankind*, 34; Diffie B. and Winius G. 1977. *Foundations of the Portuguese Empire, 1415–1580*. Minneapolis: University of Minnesota Press, 25; Merediz, *Refracted Images*, 22.

CHAPTER 2: Raiders, Slavers, Conquistadors, Settlers

but were completely overshadowed by violent encounters.[17] Between Malocello's landing and the onset of conquest in 1402, European interlopers came to the Canary Islands mainly with the intention to loot and raid for slaves. Plundering expeditions to the Canaries were organised by pirates as well as merchants, aristocrats and monarchs of various southern European polities. One of the earliest and best documented accounts is that of the 1341 venture sponsored by Alfonso IV of Portugal and led by Genoese navigator Nicoloso da Recco.[18] Expeditions were disappointed at not finding the urban settlements, precious minerals, spices, fine fabrics or other spoils coveted by late medieval brigands. The Canaries did, however, offer a commodity that made raids worthwhile, namely, slaves. Persistent hopes of finding gold nonetheless motivated adventurers and freebooters to visit the islands.[19]

In addition to hides and tallow, the Canaries provided Europeans with sealskins from the two easternmost islands; orchil, a lichen used in the making of a rare purple dye much in demand in Europe; and dragon's blood, the bright red resin tapped from the dragon tree (*dracaena draco*) and used in dyes, medicines and varnish for musical instruments. The most valuable commodity obtained from the Canaries, however, was the inhabitants themselves. The presence of Canarian slaves was reported in Majorca already in the early 1340s, and they were subsequently sold in Iberian, Italian and North African slave markets. Canarian slaves were also sought after on other east Atlantic islands, and with the onset of conquest were used to build the colonial economies of the Canaries themselves.[20]

From very early on, European aristocrats laid private claim to feudal overlordship of the Canaries or parts thereof. The first claim was by the Infanta Luis de la Cerda, the disinherited and exiled claimant to the

---

17 Vallejo, 'Conquests', 134, 139–142; Fernández-Armesto, *Before Columbus*, 158; O'Callaghan J. 1975. *A History of Medieval Spain*. Ithaca: Cornell University Press, 484, 538, 557; Abulafia, *Discovery of Mankind*, 65–67, 70–75.

18 This expedition is generally regarded as the start of Portuguese maritime expansion. See Disney A. 2009. *A History of Portugal and the Portuguese Empire, Vol II*. Cambridge: Cambridge University Press, 99–100; Vicens Vives J. 1969. *An Economic History of Spain*. Princeton: Princeton University Press, 210–211

19 Abulafia, *Discovery of Mankind*, 39; Smith S. 2010. 'The mid-Atlantic islands: A theatre of early modern ecocide?', *International Review of Social History*, 55, supplement 18, 55; Kicza J. 1992. 'Patterns in early Spanish overseas expansion'. *William and Mary Quarterly*, 49, no. 2, 231, 233.

20 Abulafia, *Discovery of Mankind*, 66; Crosby, *Ecological Imperialism*, 79–80; Fernández-Armesto, *Before Columbus*, 226. A few Canarians were also brought to Europe as a result of trading and missionary activities. See Vallejo, 'Conquest', 139, 140; Campos C. 2013. 'The Atlantic islands and the development of southern Castile at the turn of the fifteenth century' in *Spain, Portugal*, ed. Lopez-Portillo, 153.

37

Castilian throne, who tried to have his fictitious title legitimated through a grant by Pope Clement VI of Avignon in 1344. Over the next one and a half centuries, until Spain finally wrested full control of the archipelago, various southern European states and aristocratic families competed for a stake in the Canaries.[21]

There were numerous slave raids on the Canaries during the latter half of the fourteenth century that continued throughout the period of conquest. In many instances, redoubtable Canarian warriors staved off attacks, and on other occasions slavers, who usually surprised their victims with sneak attacks at night, carried off boatloads of captives. The French conquerors of Lanzarote noted that slave raids had so depleted that island's population that there were little more than 300 inhabitants left by the time they invaded in 1402. Three such raids on Lanzarote, in 1385, 1393 and 1399 resulted in as many as 500 slaves, including the island's ruler and his wife, being captured and sold in Spain.[22] Hierro also suffered continuous raiding, which thinned the population markedly. The larger, more populous islands of Tenerife and Gran Canaria, better able to defend themselves, were generally avoided by slavers but nevertheless experienced periodic raids.[23]

The Portuguese settlement of Madeira from the 1420s, and of the Azores from the late 1430s onwards, created increased demand for Canarian slaves. The temperate Azores, with an economy based on wheat, stock farming and timber, had limited demand for slaves, although Canarians were prized for their animal husbandry skills. Madeira, however, had a greater demand for forced labour. Its tropical climate and the availability of water meant that it was suitable for sugar cultivation, a highly profitable but labour-intensive undertaking. Insatiable demand for sugar in Europe ensured explosive growth of the sugar industry from the mid-15th century onwards.[24] Canarians were among the first slaves to be used on Madeira, which lay

---

21 O'Callaghan J. 2013. 'Castile, Portugal and the Canary Islands: Claims and counterclaims, 1344–1479, in *Spain, Portugal,* ed. Portillo-Lopez, 171–173; Merediz, *Refracted Images,* 11–12; Herrera, *Canary Islands,* 97–98; Glas G. 2006. *The History of the Discovery and Conquest of the Canary Islands.* London: Adamantine Media Corporation (first published London: R. & J. Dodsley, 1764. Translation of Abreu de Galindo J. 1632. *Historia de las siete Islas de Canarias*); Fernández-Armesto, *Before Columbus,* 171–172.

22 Mercer, *Canary Islanders,* 151–159, 163; Fernández-Armesto, *Before Columbus,* 175; Abulafia, *Discovery of Mankind,* 66.

23 Papal bulls in 1434 and 1476 prohibiting attacks on, and the enslavement of, Canarians were ignored. Vallejo, 'Conquests', 142; Fernández-Armesto, *Before Columbus,* 238; Abulafia, *Discovery of Mankind,* 74; Glas, *Conquest of Canary Islands,* 80–82.

24 Vieira A. 2004. 'The sugar economy of Madeira and the Canaries, 1450–1650', in *Tropical Babylons: Sugar and the Making of the Atlantic World, 1450–1680,* ed. S. Schwartz. Chapel Hill: University of North Carolina Press, 42–84; Smith, 'The mid-Atlantic islands', 66;

CHAPTER 2: Raiders, Slavers, Conquistadors, Settlers

conveniently on the route from the Canaries to Portugal. Canarians were particularly sought after to cut *levadas*, the intricate system of watercourses that carried precipitation from the mountains to the coastal plains where sugar cane was grown, because of their legendary agility over rocky terrain. Their skills as drovers also meant that they were used to look after settlers' flocks in the highlands.[25] By the 1480s an even larger sugar industry was being established in the Canaries, fuelling intensified demand for slaves.[26]

The invasion of Lanzarote, Fuerteventura and Hierro

From pillaging and slave raiding in the fourteenth century, the emphasis of European activity in the archipelago swung towards conquest in the fifteenth. The subjugation of the Canaries was a slow, fitful process that took the better part of a century. The two main islands of Gran Canaria and Tenerife, with their large, doggedly defiant populations and difficult terrain, took a long time and great effort to vanquish. In the first phase of conquest, Lanzarote, Fuerteventura and Hierro were subjugated between 1402 and 1405. Their flatter, more open and drier terrains made Lanzarote and Fuerteventura easier targets. Hierro, given its small size and a population considerably thinned by slave raids, was particularly vulnerable.

The expedition to subjugate these islands started as a private Norman enterprise that placed its conquests under Castilian sovereignty.[27] It set sail from La Rochelle on 1 May 1402 with 280 men, and was led by Gadifer de la Salle and Jean de Bethencourt, two aristocratic Norman adventurers. The imaginations and cupidity of the two crusading knights were captivated by tales of the riches the Canaries had to offer. Bethencourt financed the undertaking by raising a loan against his estate and intended using his political connections to find a royal patron, while La Salle, a warrior of some renown and a veteran of many campaigns, provided the ship and military leadership.[28] Whatever chivalrous, crusading and missionary ideals they espoused, it was clear that their main aims were mercenary — the plunder

---

Verlinden C. 1970. *The Beginnings of Modern Colonization*. Ithaca: Cornell University Press, 21.

25 Crosby, *Ecological Imperialism*, 78–79, 82; Vieira, 'Sugar economy', 57–58; Fernández-Armesto, *Before Columbus*, 197–198.

26 Vieira, 'Sugar economy', 74. Verlinden, *Modern Colonization*, 151, 153, 156.

27 Goodman J. 1998. *Chivalry and Exploration, 1298–1630*. Woodbridge: Boydell Press, 113; Keen M. 1986. 'Gadifer de La Salle: a late medieval knight errant', in *The Ideals and Practice of Medieval Knighthood: Papers From the First and Second Strawberry Hill Conferences*, eds. C. Harper-Bill and R. Harvey. Dover: Boydell Press, 80.

28 Mercer, *Canary Islanders*, 161; Goodman, *Chivalry and Exploration*, 105–106

of any valuable commodities they might find and the establishment of personal fiefdoms.[29]

Things got off to an inauspicious start when the crew mutinied upon reaching Cadiz, and most deserted. The remaining 63 men pressed on and reached Lanzarote in July 1402, where they made exceedingly heavy weather of seizing the island from its severely diminished population. Pretending to come in friendship and being well received by the islanders, the Normans gained permission from Lanzarote's ruler to construct a fort in the far south of the island in return for protecting the population against European raiders. In that same month, another mutiny broke out among the invaders. Bethencourt sailed back to Europe with the mutineers who had commandeered the ship, leaving La Salle with about two dozen men, scant supplies and a promise that he would soon return with reinforcements and fresh provisions.[30] La Salle and his depleted force nevertheless persevered in their efforts to conquer Lanzarote.

La Salle's express aim in subduing Lanzarote, as recorded by his biographers and chaplains, Pierre Boutier and Jean le Verrier, who accompanied him on the expedition, was to kill all the men of fighting age, and to capture, baptise and enslave the rest of the island population. This represents as clear an indication of genocidal intent as any, especially as this was subsequently largely accomplished, and enslavement entailed deportation from the island. It is also an accurate description of the intentions of subsequent conquerors and would-be conquerors in the Canaries, who counted on the sale of slaves to cover part of their costs.[31]

The first tactic used by La Salle was that of divide and rule. He befriended Afche, a Lanzarotean leader who challenged the chief's authority. La Salle recruited Afche as an accomplice on the promise that he would be made ruler. La Salle's plan started off well, with the capture of the island chief in a surprise attack on his stronghold, but ended badly, with the chief's escape and execution of Afche. Open hostilities between the invaders and the islanders ensued. Given the small size of their force, the privations they suffered and the difficult terrain, subsequent fighting consisted of a series of small skirmishes in which the French used the security of the fort and their superior weaponry to capture islanders individually and in small groups, some of whom were exchanged for supplies with passing ships. Those who evaded capture or supported the king in his guerrilla campaign were unable

---

29 Keen, 'Gadifer de La Salle', 80; Fernández-Armesto, *Before Columbus*, 31–32, 181.
30 Bethencourt, *Canarian*, 11–16.
31 Goodman, *Chivalry and Exploration*, 122; Mercer, *Canary Islanders*, 160–161, 168.

CHAPTER 2: Raiders, Slavers, Conquistadors, Settlers

to tend their fields or flocks, and most of their food and seed stores were confiscated by the interlopers. Some died of starvation while others gave themselves up to be taken prisoner, baptised and enslaved. The high death rate reported among prisoners was probably as much due to malnutrition and disease as brutal treatment by their vanquishers.

It was only in July 1403 that La Salle and his party received supplies from a Castilian ship sent by Bethencourt, allowing him over the next six months to capture most of the islanders still at large. In January 1404, the island chief and about twenty of his followers were among the last of the Lanzaroteans to be captured. With the surviving population enslaved and most shipped off for sale in Europe, Lanzarotean society was destroyed.[32] Motivated by chivalric considerations, Bethencourt subsequently allowed the chief to live on the island, allotting him a small parcel of land.[33]

Back in Europe, Bethencourt meanwhile solicited royal backing for the venture, which needed the legitimacy and protection of a sovereign. The erratic French monarch, Charles VI, given to bouts of insanity, was hardly suitable, but Henry III of Castile proved to be receptive to Bethencourt's lobbying. He was willing to sponsor the enterprise to pre-empt Portuguese claims to the islands. Bethencourt also managed to persuade Henry III to recognise him as 'Lord of the Islands', and his conquests in the Canaries as his fiefdom under the sovereignty of the Castilian crown, in the process betraying La Salle. Bethencourt's gambit set the stage for the eventual Castilian conquest of the archipelago.

When Bethencourt finally returned to the Canaries with reinforcements and fresh supplies in April 1404, the marauders turned their attention to Fuerteventura. There was great tension between the two leaders and their followers. Besides having left La Salle to fend for himself while he furthered his own interests in Castile, Bethencourt on his return asserted himself as 'Lord of the Isles'. What is more, Bethencourt kept most of his supplies for his own fresh, well-fed party, while the ragged, worn-out group loyal to La Salle remained deprived. The two factions, Bethencourt's by far the larger and better provisioned, built separate forts on Fuerteventura and competed for control of the island. Soon after an unsuccessful foray to Gran Canaria in mid-1404, in which he was forced to retreat under a hail of stones, La Salle returned to Europe for good.[34]

---

32 Bethencourt, *Canarian*, 63–75; Mercer, *Canary Islanders*, 160–168; Goodman, *Chivalry and Exploration*, 125.
33 Bethencourt, *Canarian*, 191.
34 Ramsey J. 1973. *Spain: The Rise of the First World Power*. Birmingham: University of Alabama Press, 245; Mercer, *Canary Islanders*, 175–176; Abulafia, *Discovery of Mankind*, 79.

Bethencourt, by then styling himself 'King of the Canaries', headed the offensive to conquer Fuerteventura. Throughout 1404 there were numerous skirmishes, at times daily, between the French and Fuerteventurans. Outnumbered and occasionally outmanoeuvred, the French armed some Lanzarotean slaves who fought and died for their cause. The security of their fort and superior arms nonetheless gave the French major advantages. Islanders taken captive were ferried back to Lanzarote. Worn down by this war of attrition and unable to engage in subsistence activities, the two Fuerteventuran chiefs and their subjects surrendered together in January 1405, marking the fall of the island. The two chiefs were baptised, and in a show of chivalry, were given small land grants and allowed to live on the island. Their subjects, however, were baptised and enslaved, some shipped off for sale in Europe, the rest to Lanzarote. Bethencourt immediately set off for Normandy where he recruited nearly 200 settlers to repopulate the island. Since most were single men, many took Canarian women as wives or concubines.[35]

Looking to extend his control of the islands Bethencourt in October 1405 went on an ill-advised sortie to Gran Canaria in which over 20 of his men were killed. Chastened, he then waged war on La Palma for six weeks, claiming to have killed over a hundred of its inhabitants before turning his attention to tiny Hierro. Here, a ruse against the trusting Canarians proved successful. Bethencourt persuaded Augeron, brother of the island leader, to propose a mass meeting to seal a peace agreement between the two groups. The French used this gathering of indigenes to round up and enslave them. A reported 112 islanders were taken prisoner. Only a small number of Hierroans remained free in the mountains, as the island had already been substantially depopulated by slave raids, with perhaps as many as 400 people taken in 1402 alone.[36] Bethencourt immediately settled some 120 families on the island. After a fruitless reconnaissance of Gomera, Bethencourt left the Canaries for good in December 1405, appointing his nephew Maciot de Bethencourt as governor of the conquered isles.[37]

Portuguese intervention

Between the end of 1405 and serious incursions into Gran Canaria in the late 1470s, very little headway was made in the conquest of independent islands. The situation was complicated by the entry of the Portuguese as serious contenders for control of the Canaries from the mid-1420s onwards.

---

35 Bethencourt, *Canarian*, 162.
36 Pérez, 'Role of interpreters', 161; Mercer, *Canary Islanders*, 172.
37 Bethencourt, *Canarian*, 183–185; Herrera, *Canary Islands*, 117.

CHAPTER 2: Raiders, Slavers, Conquistadors, Settlers

The Portuguese challenge to Castilian control was based partly on the assertion that because Malocello had been a vassal of the Portuguese king, who had also sponsored de Recco's expedition, Portugal had prior claim to the archipelago.[38]

Portuguese military intervention was facilitated by none other than Maciot de Bethencourt. The younger Bethencourt had become increasingly tyrannical, eliciting a chorus of complaints from settlers, especially for extorting tax payments. In response, the Castilian crown in 1414 ordered Count Guzman of Niebla to unseat him. Guzman dispatched three warships under the command of Pedro Barba, forcing Maciot to cede title to the conquered islands.[39] Both Barba and Guzman now claimed title to the islands, including Gomera, subsequently selling them to other members of the Andalusian aristocracy. Multiple cessions, sales, bequests and inheritances gave rise to a bewildering array of private claims to the Canaries, the most significant of which was that of the Peraza family. Unlike other claimants, they were doggedly determined to give effect to their claims by residing there, trying to subdue and govern the indigenes, and attracting settlers from mainland Europe.[40]

After being deposed, Maciot agreed to 'sell' the four islands to Prince Henry the Navigator of Portugal although his uncle Jean, the 'King of the Canaries', was still alive. Maciot's ploy, aided by protracted civil strife in Castile following Henry III's death in 1406,[41] suited Prince Henry, who coveted control of all the eastern Atlantic islands for the immediate profit they would yield, their potential as colonies and as strategic bases from which to realise his ambitions along the west African coast. This farcical transaction triggered nearly six decades of competition between Portugal and Castile for control of the archipelago.[42]

---

38 Verlinden, *Modern Colonization*, 13; O'Callaghan, 'Castile, Portugal and the Canary Islands' 169–191.

39 Glas, *Conquest of Canary Islands*, 34–35

40 Herrera, *Canary Islands*, 123–125; Diffie and Winius, *Foundations of the Portuguese Empire*, 58, 64, 94; Glass, *Conquest of Canary Islands*, 2, 10, 35, 40; Major R. 1967. *The Life of Prince Henry of Portugal, Surnamed the Navigator, and its Results; from Authentic Contemporary Documents*. London: Cass (first published London, A. Ascher & Co. 1868), 214.

41 Russell P. 2000. *Prince Henry the Navigator: A Life*. New Haven: Yale University Press, 278–279; Livermore H. 1968. *A History of Spain*. New York: Minerva, 169.

42 Verlinden C. 2013. 'Feudal and demesnial forms of Portuguese colonisation in the Atlantic zone in the fourteenth and fifteenth centuries, especially under Prince Henry the Navigator', in Lopez-Portillo, *Spain, Portugal*, 317; Disney, *History of Portugal*, 101; Fernández-Armesto F. 2006. *Pathfinders: A Global History of Exploration*. Oxford: Oxford University Press, 133–134; O'Callaghan, 'Castile, Portugal and the Canary Islands',

CIVILIAN-DRIVEN VIOLENCE AND THE GENOCIDE OF INDIGENOUS PEOPLES

The Portuguese launched several fruitless military expeditions to the Canaries to give substance to their claims. There were four major assaults. The 1424 offensive under Fernando de Castro, which deployed 2500 foot soldiers and 120 horsemen, was the first and most ambitious. A concerted campaign in 1446, which resulted in a two-year occupation of Lanzarote and Hierro, came to nought, as did another in 1468 focused on Gran Canaria. The last of the major campaigns came in 1477, lasted for two years, and formed part of a larger Portuguese-Castilian war of succession between 1474 and 1479.[43] On each occasion a combination of high cost, diplomatic protest by Castile and resistance from islanders, both native and settler, thwarted Portuguese ambitions in the Canaries. In addition to military action, contestation between the two powers for control of the island cluster was pursued through lawsuits, as well as through an ongoing diplomatic chess game. It was finally resolved in 1479 by the Treaty of Alcaçovas in terms of which the Portuguese abandoned their claims to both the Castilian throne and the Canaries in return for having their claims to the Azores, Madeira and the northwest African coast recognised. Ironically, Castilian conquistadors subsequently brought in large numbers of Portuguese settlers, many from Madeira, to help establish the sugar industry.[44]

The subjugation of Gran Canaria

Gran Canaria withstood attempts at European invasion for much of the fifteenth century even though its substantial, fertile lowlands and population of perhaps 25000 made it an attractive prize. The fierce, well-organized fighting forces its leaders were able to summon with remarkable rapidity kept intruders at bay. Invading parties, such as those of Bethencourt in 1405 and the Portuguese expedition under Fernando de Castro in 1424, were sent packing under a hail of missiles. For a period of 16 years after 1461, Diego de Herrera, who claimed title to the conquered islands through marriage into the Peraza family,[45] led expeditions to Gran Canaria at great cost but without success. He and other private claimants were sidelined in 1477 by Ferdinand and Isabella, whose marriage in 1469 unified the crowns of Aragon and

---

176; Miller R.J. 2010. 'The doctrine of discovery', in *Discovering Indigenous Lands: The Doctrine of Discovery in the English Colonies*, eds. R.J. Miller, J. Ruru, L. Behrendt & T. Lindberg. Oxford: Oxford University Press, 10–11.

43 Russell, *Prince Henry*, 265; Fernández-Armesto, *Before Columbus*, 203.

44 Russell, *Prince Henry*, 290; Benjamin, *Atlantic World*, 107–108; Kamen H. 1983. *Spain, 1469–1714*. London: Longman, 5; O'Callaghan, *History of Medieval Spain*, 557.

45 Herrera married Inez Peraza in 1445 and in 1454 inherited the title to the Canaries upon the death of her father, Fernan, whose only son, Guillen, was killed in a raid on Palma in 1447.

CHAPTER 2: Raiders, Slavers, Conquistadors, Settlers

Castile. They decided that the Spanish crown should take responsibility for conquering the Canaries, paid Herrera and wife Inez Peraza compensation for the loss of their right to the unconquered islands, and recognised their entitlement to the three conquered islands as well as Gomera. Ferdinand and Isabella then organised their own military expedition to conquer Gran Canaria, under the command of General Juan Rejon.[46] The timing of this intervention was determined by Portugal's launching a renewed military effort in the archipelago during its war of succession with Castile. Moreover, the monarchs feared that Herrera might defect to Portugal. Taking control of the Canaries was also part of their broader strategy of centralising monarchical power and undermining the feudal nobility, evident also in their approach to the reconquest of Granada.[47]

Ferdinand and Isabella's intercession marks a new phase in the conquest of the Canaries. Henceforth, the main difference between seigneurial and royal islands was that in the former the lord and titleholder provided access to land in return for rent and taxes, whereas in the latter the crown distributed land to those who had financed and participated in the conquest.[48] Despite the considerably greater resources of the Castilian crown, little was available for the Canarian venture as the primary commitment was to the conquest of Granada. Conquistadors were thus expected to raise most of their own finance from merchants and noblemen, who were promised a share in the immediate spoils of conquest, such as slaves, orchil harvests and land grants, as well as privileged access to the colonial economy, of which sugar production was the most attractive prospect.[49]

In mid-1478 Rejon set sail with a force of 600 soldiers, 30 horsemen and a number of mercenaries hungry for loot and land. He set about establishing a garrison at the present-day site of Las Palmas. Before the fort could be completed, the invaders were engaged by a force of 2 000 Canarian fighters. The Europeans narrowly won this battle through effective use of cavalry and cannon, and through the protection provided by the partially completed fort. In flat, open spaces, mounted warriors gained considerable advantage from the height, speed and manoeuvrability of their horses.[50]

---

46 O'Callaghan, 'Castile, Portugal and the Canary Islands', 189.
47 Stevens-Arroyo, 'Inter-Atlantic paradigm', 520, 522; Fernández-Armesto, *1492*, 278–279.
48 This dual system of seigneurial control of Lanzarote, Fuerteventura, Hierro and Gomera, and royal control of Gran Canaria, La Palma and Tenerife remained in place until it was abolished under the Napoleonic occupation of Spain in the early nineteenth century.
49 Fernández-Armesto, *Before Columbus*, 203–207; Herrera, *Canary Islands*, 104, 129; Vallejo, 'Conquests', 135–136; Verlinden, *Modern Colonization*, 124, 149, 155.
50 De Espinosa, *Guanches of Tenerife*, 106–107.

45

Once the fort was complete, the Spanish launched raids throughout the fertile northeastern part of the island, destroying crops, confiscating flocks, and taking captives. Gran Canarians were forced to retreat to the mountains. The Spanish did not have it all their own way, though. On a sortie into the southern part of the island, at Arguineguin, the Spaniards were ambushed by Canarian forces while passing through a gorge and completely routed, resulting in over 20 dead, 80 taken prisoner and over 100 wounded. Rejon also had to fight off a Portuguese seaborne attack, and a subsequent naval blockade hampered the delivery of supplies to his garrison. Rejon's inability to pursue the Canarians into their mountain fastnesses led to a stalemate. These and other difficulties resulted in morale-sapping intrigues and conflict within the Castilian camp, culminating in Rejon's rash execution of the governor appointed by the Spanish crown. Ferdinand and Isabella dismissed Rejon and in August 1480 replaced him with Pedro de Vera, whose reputation for ruthlessness made him an ideal candidate for rescuing their foundering Gran Canarian enterprise.[51]

De Vera's military strategy was to build a second fort on the northwestern coast of the island and to launch a two-pronged campaign against the mountain strongholds of the Gran Canarians while implementing an even more comprehensive scorched-earth policy than that of Rejon. This plan paid dividends from 1482 onwards as Gran Canarians were prevented from engaging in subsistence activities. Most of the fortified mountain refuges in the northern part of the island were taken one by one, often with the help of Gomeran and Lanzarotean fighters. There is also evidence that contagious diseases introduced by Europeans weakened Canarian resistance.[52]

An intriguing feature of the Spanish campaign on Gran Canaria is the strategic use made of collaborators, most notably of one of its two chiefs, Tenesor Semidan. In February 1482 Semidan, who 14 years earlier had allowed a large force of besieged invaders to go free,[53] was taken prisoner at his residence in Galdar. He was immediately sent to Spain and put on public display in his traditional goat-skin dress as an example of the Canarian savage. Later, attired in the finest European clothes, he was baptised Fernando Guanarteme and paraded around the realm. This treatment, and the promise that he would be allocated a tract of land on Gran Canaria and allowed to live there with his family and entourage, won Semidan's unwavering loyalty. Presumably overawed by the wealth, power

---

51 Fernández-Armesto, *1492*, 278–279.
52 Mercer, *Canary Islanders*, 191–192; Crosby, *Ecological Imperialism*, 92–94.
53 For an account of this bizarre incident, see Glas, *Conquest of Canary Islands*, 46–48.

CHAPTER 2: Raiders, Slavers, Conquistadors, Settlers

and technological advancement of the Europeans, he henceforth cooperated fully with the Spaniards, even in the most devious and damaging of their strategies, and played an important role in the final phase of the conquest of Gran Canaria. He later also assisted in the occupation of La Palma and the invasion of Tenerife.[54] On his return to the island, Semidan was sent by de Vera to try and persuade Canarian defenders to surrender. Though unsuccessful he nevertheless provided valuable information about Canarian fortifications and strategies, which de Vera used to great advantage. In the closing stages of the war, Semidan was allowed to lead an attacking force of 500 baptised islanders.

With their backs to the wall, most defenders fought to the bitter end. Some preferred ritual suicide by leaping from cliffs to being taken prisoner. At least one leader, Aytami, a high priest, defected and accepted baptism. The Gran Canarians were not without their successes in the latter stages of the conquest, though: a force of 200 Spaniards suffered near-annihilation in a reckless attack on the coastal fortress of Ajodar.[55] The closing encounter in the conquest of Gran Canaria came in April 1483 with the siege of the mountain fortress of Ansite, where approximately 600 men, 1 500 women and a large number of children were forced to surrender. The Spaniards once again sent Semidan to make empty promises of immunity in return for their surrender. This time the defenders opted to submit. Their leader, Ben Tegui, a high priest, together with one of his officers, however, flung themselves from the fortress summit, reportedly shouting 'Atis Tirma!' (for my land!). De Vera saw to it that the Bishop of Lanzarote was on hand to oversee the performance of a *Te Deum* and the baptism of prisoners, which marked their descent into slavery.[56]

It was decreed that all Canarians be deported from the island for fear of subsequent uprisings. The majority were exiled on conquered islands, where they served as slave labourers. A contingent of several hundred, including many of the island's elite, was shipped off to Castile. Gran Canarian children were distributed among settlers on the pretext that they were to be raised as Christians but were used as slaves. Only 40 Canarians, who formed part of the household and retinue of Semidan, were allowed to stay on a stretch of

---

54 Glas, *Conquest of Canary Islands*, 114–117; Fernández-Armesto, *1492*, 281.
55 Herrera, *Canary Islands*, 144–145.
56 See 'Atis Tirma', sculpture by Manuel Bethencourt, 1981. http://vanderkrogt.net/statues/object.php?webpage=ST&record=esca159, accessed 28 October 2019; Mercer, *Canary Islanders*, 193.

CIVILIAN-DRIVEN VIOLENCE AND THE GENOCIDE OF INDIGENOUS PEOPLES

poor pasturage along the northwestern coast promised to Semidan by King Ferdinand.[57]

The occupation of Gomera

From the mid-fourteenth century Gomera had endured slave raids and some attention from missionaries. Despite Gomera being one of the smaller islands in the Canaries, its people were well capable of defending themselves, as demonstrated by a European slaving expedition to the island in 1384, which met an ignominious end when its members were trapped on a rocky outcrop by an Indigenous fighting force. The raiders had little option but to surrender but were allowed to go free. Gomera became a significant site of struggle between Castile and Portugal for supremacy in the archipelago for two decades from the mid-1420s onwards because it was the easiest of the remaining isles to subdue. There was an ongoing tussle between the Portuguese and the Castilians for influence on Gomera, with each allied to factions within the Gomeran population, which was split into four chiefdoms. Though divided, and enduring the presence of both the Portuguese and the Spanish, the island chiefdoms remained independent, as they could muster significant fighting forces and had ready access to highland refuges.[58]

When the Portuguese withdrew from the island in 1448, a permanent Castilian presence remained in the form of the precariously fortified Peraza residence. Although the Peraza family claimed title to the island from 1446 onwards, they had little control over it. When Fernan Peraza died in 1452, title to the Canaries passed to his son-in-law, Diego de Herrera, as his only son, Guellen, had been killed in a raid on Palma in 1447. The next four decades witnessed ongoing skirmishes with islanders, alliances being formed with one or other Gomeran faction against others, and a good deal of intrigue all round. The Castilians meanwhile shipped off whatever orchil and captives they could take. The stalemate continued until Pedro de Vera made a concerted effort to subdue the island in the late 1480s after consolidating control of Gran Canaria.

In 1486 De Vera quelled a localised Gomeran uprising, after which 200 of its inhabitants were deported into slavery on Gran Canaria, which he governed. Two years later, the Gomeran titleholder and self-proclaimed

---

57 Vallejo, 'Conquests', 148–149; Fernández-Armesto, *After Conquest*, 129; Merediz, *Refracted Images*, 20; Mercer, *Canary Islanders*, 194.

58 Azurara, G. 1971. *The Chronicle of the Discovery and Conquest of Guinea*, trans. C. Beazley and E. Prestage. New York: Franklin, 242.

CHAPTER 2: Raiders, Slavers, Conquistadors, Settlers

governor, Hernan Peraza, was killed when he was surprised in the cave of his Gomeran lover by a small group of insurgents.[59] De Vera's tactic for suppressing this incipient insurrection and subduing the island permanently was to order all Gomerans to attend the funeral of the slain 'governor', and to take prisoner all of those who complied. De Vera then used these hostages, together with false promises of amnesty, to procure the surrender of a substantial number of fugitives who had taken to the mountains. All prisoners over the age of fifteen who hailed from the rebellious regions of Agana and Orone were sentenced to death and were hanged, drowned, impaled or torn apart by horses. Children were distributed among the colonists as slaves. The rest were baptised, enslaved and deported to Lanzarote, with a good number thrown overboard along the way. De Vera learned that some Gomerans he had deported to Gran Canaria in 1486 had encouraged this later insurrection. His response was to hang all the males in this group. A further hundred Gomerans were sold into slavery in Spain. Being by then in principle against slavery, especially of people who professed Christianity, Ferdinand and Isabella manumitted this contingent and sent them back to the Canaries. In contravention of the crown's intentions, de Vera saw to it that they were detained on Gran Canaria to replace the labourers he had executed the year before.[60] Denuded of indigenes and occupied by an influx of European settlers, Gomera subsequently developed a productive sugar industry.

The vanquishing of La Palma

La Palma was subject to slave raids but retained its independence until the early 1490s because its terrain was particularly rugged, and its population had a well-earned reputation for ferocity. Among the better-known forays it repulsed were those by Maciot de Bethencourt in the mid-1420s and a Portuguese slave raid aided by native Gomeran allies in 1443. The most notable slaving sortie to this island came in 1447 when the Palmans successfully defended themselves against a Castilian invasion by 200 European soldiers and 300 hundred Canarian subalterns. Ambushed in rugged terrain in the interior, the invaders had little defence against the rocks hurled at them with pinpoint accuracy, and were soon put to flight.[61] From mid-century slave raids were mounted by settlers from neighbouring

---

59 Glas, *Conquest of Canary Islands*, 129–130.
60 Ruiz, T. 2001. *Spanish Society, 1400–1600*. Harlow: Pearson Education, 113; Herrera, *Canary Islands*, 148.
61 Herrera, *Canary Islands*, 125–127; Fernández-Armesto, *Before Columbus*, 184; Azurara, *Conquest of Guinea*, 206–211.

CIVILIAN-DRIVEN VIOLENCE AND THE GENOCIDE OF INDIGENOUS PEOPLES

Hierro and Gomera. Hostilities were punctuated by ephemeral peace pacts, trade agreements and attempts at evangelisation. Missionaries had some success, resulting in several Palman leaders being baptised in 1488. They and their followers were now *bandos de pazes*, or people of peace, who could not be enslaved, while heathens, or *bandos de guerra*, remained fair game for slavers.[62]

Alonso de Lugo, who had played an active role in the subjugation of Gran Canaria under both Rejon and de Vera, emerged as the foremost conquistador of the Canaries in the 1490s after de Vera had been deployed to the siege of Granada. With a mandate from the Spanish crown to conquer the two remaining Canary Islands and with the financial backing of mainly Italian merchants, in 1491–1492 de Lugo mustered a force of nearly a thousand men for an attack on La Palma. Many were Gran Canarians, and among them was Semidan.

Landing on the central west coast of La Palma at the end of September 1492, de Lugo set about building a fort at Tazacorte. With this defensive measure in place, he presented an ultimatum to the island leaders, representing 12 chiefdoms. Those who accepted Spanish rule and conversion to Christianity were offered peace and freedom as *bandos de pazes*, while those who resisted would be attacked and enslaved. Those amenable to the offer were further lulled into a false sense of security by assurances of fair treatment by Francisca Palmesa, an enslaved Gran Canarian woman who was used as intermediary by the Spaniards. Half the chiefs, particularly in the vulnerable southern part of the island, accepted the offer. Those who refused were not able to resist for long, and were captured and enslaved. The last of the resisters, chief Tanausu and his followers, holed up in the mountain fortress of Ecero and were tricked into submission. Tanausu refused to consider a peace treaty until de Lugo left his territory. De Lugo withdrew, his departure visible from high ground, but left a force of men hidden near the fortress. Lured from his sanctuary, Tanausu was easily overcome. This event, on 3 May 1493, symbolised the fall of Palma.[63]

Once in full control of the island, de Lugo immediately shipped off into slavery those he could classify as *bandos de guerra*, including Tanausu's party. Tanausu refused to speak or eat and soon died en route to Spain.[64] It did not take long before de Lugo also started transporting *bandos de pazes* into slavery. The predictable rebellion by Palmans gave de Lugo the excuse

---

62 Mercer, *Canary Islanders*, 195.
63 Herrera, *Canary Islands*, 152–154.
64 Gil and Martin, *Canary Islands*, 139.

CHAPTER 2: Raiders, Slavers, Conquistadors, Settlers

he needed to declare all Palmans *bandos de guerra*. He then rounded up the entire surviving population of about 1 200 people, appropriated perhaps 20 000 head of stock, executed the leaders, and sold the rest into slavery. European settlers soon repopulated the island, with sugar becoming the staple crop.[65]

The conquest of Tenerife

Tenerife, the last of the Canary Islands to be subjected, had a pre-conquest population that might have been as much as 30 000. Populous, relatively prosperous, and politically well organised, this island was the one most capable of defending itself against intruders. Tenerife was thus generally avoided by plunderers, who sought easier pickings elsewhere. Among those who tried were Fernan Peraza, who organized a minor raid on Tenerife in the mid-fifteenth century, which netted a few captives. Diego de Herrera landed 400 men there in 1464 but hastily retreated at the menacing sight of Guanches, as Indigenous Tenerifans were called,[66] massing to confront them. Herrera's son Sancho subsequently gained permission from the chief of Anaga to build a fort to garrison 80 men on the northeast coast. It was not long before the Spaniards' offensive behaviour led to a Guanche attack on the fort, in which many of its occupants were killed and the rest put to flight. The next major incursion came nearly two and a half decades later, in 1490, when Francisco Maldonado, governor of Gran Canaria, led a quixotic attempt to conquer the island. A hare-brained attack on a Guanche force reputedly many times the size of his own soon turned into a rout, with over a hundred killed.[67]

Meanwhile, in the decades prior to Maldonado's attack, an Indigenous religious cult had emerged in Guimar, along the east coast of the island. It centred around a wooden image of the Virgin Mary carrying the infant Christ that had washed ashore during the 1390s. Believed to have supernatural powers, the image was housed in the Guimar chief's cave.[68] One of the captives taken during Fernan Peraza's mid-fifteenth-century raid had been a seven-year-old boy who was taken back to Lanzarote, christened

---

65 Vallejo, 'Conquests', 150.
66 The Indigenous name Guanche is a corruption of *Guan Chenerche* meaning 'man of Tenerife'. See C. Markham, 'Introduction', de Espinosa, *Guanches of Tenerife*, v. For the names of Indigenous peoples of individual islands, see Abulafia, *Discovery of Mankind*, 54.
67 Mercer, *Canary Islanders*, 199–200; de Espinosa, *Guanches of Tenerife*, 87.
68 Markham, 'Introduction', de Espinosa, *Guanches of Tenerife*, x–xi; Merediz E. 2001. 'Travelling icons: The Virgin of Candelaria's transatlantic journeys'. *Arizona Journal of Hispanic Cultural Studies*, 5, 128; Abulafia, *Discovery of Mankind*, 44–48.

Anton Guanche, and instructed in Christianity. In his teens, Anton Guanche escaped from a ship stopping off at Tenerife on its way to Gomera. Anton used his knowledge of Christianity to establish himself as priest of the cult centred on the wooden engraving, which came to be known as 'Our Lady of Candelaria'. Converted to Christianity through the influence of this sect, the leaders and people of Guimar became the foremost collaborators of the Spanish.

Until the mid-1490s, the logistical problems of mounting an effective campaign on Tenerife, its challenging terrain and the military prowess of its defenders deterred invaders. In the early 1490s, the prospects for conquest by Spain, by now the only contender for control of the Canaries, improved considerably. The capture of Granada in January 1492 freed resources that could be deployed in the Spanish colonial enterprise, and Columbus' reconnoitring of the Caribbean later that year provided a considerable boost to Spanish colonial ambitions. By this time, firearms, though still relatively primitive, were coming into wider circulation and helped swing the balance of power in favour of Europeans.[69] Barely a year after concluding his campaign on La Palma, Alonso de Lugo was commissioned by the Spanish crown to conquer Tenerife. De Lugo's quest began in April 1494, was concluded in little less than two and a half years, and consisted of two campaigns. The first ended in disaster for the Spaniards, the second in victory — not only because of their superior weaponry and resources but also because they gained considerable advantage from invisible helpers, in the form of disease-causing microbes.

De Lugo landed at Anaza on 30 April 1494 with a force of 1 000 infantry and 120 horsemen, funded partly by the sale of his personal assets.[70] Fearing an attack before they could set up fortifications, De Lugo sent Semidan to the chief of Anaga to request that the landing party be left in peace, a mission he accomplished. A few days later, when he was ready to venture forth from his Santa Cruz fortress, De Lugo was confronted by a Guanche force under Ben Como, the chief of Taoro, located in the north-west. Como emerged as the pre-eminent leader on Tenerife, and Taoro as the epicentre of resistance to Spanish rule. De Lugo made Como an offer of freedom and peace in return for his adoption of Christianity and acceptance of Spanish rule. Como declined, asked De Lugo to leave, and, in a gesture of goodwill, offered him some supplies. A battle was averted, both sides retreating to consider their strategies.

---

69 Mercer, *Canary Islanders*, 199–200.
70 De Espinosa, *Guanches of Tenerife*, 98.

CHAPTER 2: Raiders, Slavers, Conquistadors, Settlers

Guanche leaders called a joint council a few days later to plan a course of action. Only eight chiefs attended, Guimar having thrown in its lot with the Spanish. Besides the influence of the cult of Candelaria, the Guimar chief, Acaymo, was involved in an ongoing feud with Ben Como. With Anton Guanche acting as interpreter, Acaymo, together with 600 soldiers, visited de Lugo's camp, accepted Spanish authority, cemented a formal alliance with the invaders, and was baptised Anaterve el Bueno (Anaterve the Good). Mercer suggests that Acaymo had ambitions of acting as surrogate ruler for the Spanish after the conquest.[71] The four westerly chiefdoms of Icod, Daute, Adeje and Abona rejected Como's proposal of united action under his military leadership because of internal rivalries, while the chiefs under immediate threat, those of Anaga, Tegueste and Tacoronte, allied themselves under Como's chieftainship.

Deciding to wait out the winter, which lasts into March, de Lugo resumed his campaign in the spring of 1495. His plan was to confront Como in his own territory. De Lugo marched with 800 men from his base camp at Anaza towards Taoro. He became suspicious at not encountering any Guanches and decided to call off the attack. Returning through the Acentejo ravine, the Spanish invaders were ambushed by a contingent of 300 Guanches under Tinguaro, Como's brother. The Spaniards were caught completely off-guard and had little defence against the rocks hurled at them, and the boulders and tree trunks that came crashing down. Trapped in the gorge, and in disarray, the Spanish suffered major casualties and came off second best in the hand-to-hand combat that followed. Two hours into the battle, Como arrived with a large force, ensuring the utter defeat of the Europeans. Over 600 Spanish soldiers were killed, with scattered bands of survivors fleeing to the Santa Cruz fort.[72] The massacre was by far the Spaniards' worst defeat in the Canaries.

Acaymo sent his ally 300 men and supplies to help shore up their depleted garrison. De Lugo, ever in need of funds, reciprocated with a remarkable act of treachery and myopia. He placed the islanders in chains and shipped them to Spain to be sold as slaves. An annoyed Spanish crown, which placed higher value on their Guimar confederates, freed the men and sent them back to Tenerife in the hope of saving the alliance. Worn down by harassing attacks on his demoralised garrison, de Lugo packed up camp and returned to Gran Canaria in early June 1495.

---

71 Mercer, *Canary Islanders*, 201.
72 de Espinosa, *Guanches of Tenerife*, 91–95.

Despite this setback, de Lugo managed to gain the backing of Italian and Castilian merchants and a few Spanish noblemen to sponsor a second campaign in return for a share in the spoils of conquest. De Lugo almost immediately went about reassembling a force of 1 100 men and 70 cavalry for a second invasion of Tenerife. By early November 1495 he had once again landed at Anaza and rebuilt the fort. This force was better equipped than the last, with more soldiers carrying firearms.[73]

Shortly after landing, the Spanish were fortunate to capture a Guanche spying on their camp. From him they extracted information about Ben Como's whereabouts and tactics. De Lugo outmanoeuvred Como by marching on his encampment through the night. Taken by surprise, the Guanche army was comprehensively defeated, suffering 1 700 deaths. In the wake of this display of military superiority, Acaymo, who had remained on the sidelines, once again declared his support for the Spaniards and contributed men and supplies to their war effort.

As in the previous year, de Lugo suspended his campaign and dug in for the winter. Although relatively mild, the Canary winter can be wet and uncomfortable with snowfalls in higher-lying areas. Forced to abandon the lowlands, the Taoro confederacy clearly had the worst of the weather, which was unusually wet and cold. The Guanches also had to cope with the loss of their croplands and disruption to other subsistence activities. Hunger was widespread and despair at the imminent destruction of their way of life must have taken a toll. Among the Guanches, the outbreak of an unknown epidemic decimated the population, with several thousand succumbing. Though there can be little doubt that the plague stemmed from micro-organisms introduced by the invaders, while malnutrition, psychological distress, the large number of rotting corpses strewn across the land and the Guanche practice of embalming the bodies of deceased nobles contributed to the severity of the outbreak. Spanish foraging parties reported large numbers of corpses littering the landscape, settlements deserted, and flocks left untended. They nevertheless came under periodic attack from enfeebled Guanche forces.[74]

De Lugo had to contend with a different set of problems during the winter break. Insufficient funding from his backers in Europe meant a serious shortfall in provisions. Captured Guanche flocks and food supplied by Acaymo were not sufficient to tide his troops over the winter. By the

---

73 Campos, 'The Atlantic islands', 149–501; Glas, *Conquest of Canary Islands*, 159; de Espinosa, *Guanches of Tenerife*, 98–100.
74 de Espinosa, *Guanches of Tenerife*, 104–105, 108; Crosby, *Ecological Imperialism*, 82–103.

CHAPTER 2: Raiders, Slavers, Conquistadors, Settlers

end of November 1495, the situation had deteriorated to the point where soldiers were forced to forage for wild foods to supplement their daily rations. An outbreak of disease and growing ill-discipline among the rank and file resulted. The situation was saved by one of de Lugo's lieutenants volunteering to sell two Gran Canarian sugar estates, as well as houses, slaves and stock, to buy provisions. The supplies bought from this fire sale arrived none too soon, at the beginning of December 1495.[75]

Revitalised, de Lugo decided to go on the offensive and before the end of that month marched on the Taoro league. A substantial force of Guanches under Ben Como engaged the invaders a few kilometres from the site of their victory the previous year. Once again learning of their battle plan from a captured Guache, de Lugo was able to counter the attack successfully. As many as 2000 Guanche warriors were killed while Spanish casualties amounted to 64 dead. Preferring not to press home his advantage, de Lugo returned to his Santa Cruz fortress to await the arrival of further provisions. These came at the end of May, and by early July he was ready to confront the Taoro alliance head-on and marched into the heart of their territory. Como, observing the strength of the opposing force, and how his own army was weakened by disease and hunger, decided to sue for peace. De Lugo required that the Guanches accept Spanish sovereignty, convert to Christianity, and help him subdue the rest of the island. Como agreed, and the two sides joined together in revelry to celebrate their pact and the Guanches' new status as Spanish subjects.

During August and September, de Lugo moved against the four remaining polities. Realising they had no chance against the forces ranged against them, their chiefs formally submitted to de Lugo on 29 September 1496. Tenerife had finally been conquered. The obligatory religious ceremony to thank God for this victory followed. Surrendered Guanches were baptised, which for nearly all marked their descent into slavery. In the immediate aftermath of conquest, all Guanches were treated as enslaveable, notwithstanding previous assurances to the contrary. Substantial numbers were immediately shipped off to Spain, or to other islands, some not even baptised. The rest were taken up as slaves on Tenerife itself. A handful of collaborating nobles were displaced to marginal lands. Women, both slave and free, were sexually exploited in a variety of ways. Some were taken as concubines and domestic drudges, while sexual violence seems to have been common and perpetrated with impunity. A small number of islanders who refused to submit to Spanish rule, together with escaped slaves, lived

---

75 Mercer, *Canary Islanders*, 206–207.

CIVILIAN-DRIVEN VIOLENCE AND THE GENOCIDE OF INDIGENOUS PEOPLES

in the mountains, foraging and preying off settler flocks. From 1499 de Lugo formed squads of settlers to hunt down and kill refugees. There were fugitives in the mountains till at least the mid-1530s.[76]

A case of genocide?

Individually and collectively, all seven Canarian cases represent clear examples of genocide. Not only were all Indigenous Canarian societies utterly destroyed and their populations removed, but this was also accomplished with a great deal of violence directed at entire communities. The Castilian conquerors practised near-total confiscation of the land and near-total enslavement and deportation of survivors from their home islands, not simply for immediate profit but also for the explicit purpose of repopulating the islands with European settlers and establishing completely new economies and ways of life. The realisation that highly lucrative sugar-cane crops could be cultivated in much of the archipelago spurred on this process.

More so than the slaughter of Canarians, mass enslavement, together with mass deportation of captives — mostly within the archipelago, but also beyond, notably to Europe and Madeira — were the main forms of social destruction. Enslavement and deportation went hand in hand and were in effect as destructive as killing because the victims, generally the most fertile and productive members of their communities, were permanently lost to their societies. The twinned assaults of enslavement and deportation of entire surviving island communities formed the lynchpin of the genocidal process not only because it accounted for more victims than any other means of social erasure but also because it represented intentional and irreparably damaging acts of social destruction. Individual raids purely for the sake of acquiring slaves, though highly detrimental to Canarian society, were not genocidal in themselves. However, in the cases of Lanzarote, Fuerteventura and Hierro the cumulative impact of slave raiding depleted the population so severely that it would be no exaggeration to describe it as being of genocidal proportion. Much more damaging, and unquestionably genocidal, were the slaving activities of conquerors, for whom captives formed the most lucrative part of the virgin bonus offered by the Canaries. For conquistadors, the taking of chattels was counted on to help cover the costs of conquest, and as immediate reward for those who both funded and fought on these ventures.[77] Deportation was used to realise higher prices

---

76 Mercer, *Canary Islanders*, 228–229; Fernández-Armesto, *After Conquest*, 11.
77 Stevens-Arroyo, 'Inter-Atlantic paradigm', 523, 530.

56

CHAPTER 2: Raiders, Slavers, Conquistadors, Settlers

for slaves, to channel labour where it was needed most, and as a security measure to subvert resistance.[78] From the 1480s onwards, increasing numbers of slaves were imported from the African mainland to replace the declining Indigenous labour pool and to meet burgeoning demand from the settler economy.[79]

There were other forms of social destruction as well. Scorched-earth tactics severely undermined the subsistence and communal lives of Canarian societies, resulting in malnutrition, starvation, disease, psychological distress and social dislocation. Child removal, usually into slavery or some form of forced labour, was common. After conquest, cultural suppression was the norm, most consistently and insistently through the imposition of Christian beliefs, values and customs by settlers, as well as through state and church structures.[80] Cultural suppression also came indirectly in that Canarians needed to abide by Western standards and modes of behaviour to survive under the new order.[81] Both during and after conquest, Canarian men were commonly recruited as fighters, and often deliberately used as cannon fodder. While this provided some opportunity for preferment and allowed Canarian genes to be spread into Latin America, Africa and beyond, it was extremely dangerous work that contributed to the post-conquest extinction of Indigenous Canarian cultures.[82] Communicable diseases introduced by Europeans and poor health due to depressed living conditions continued to take a heavy toll on the vestigial Canarian population.[83] The Italian adventurer Girolamo Benzoni, who visited the islands in 1541, attested to hardly any indigenes being alive by then, and Alonso de Espinosa, a Dominican priest who lived on Tenerife and published an influential history of the Canaries in the mid-1590s, claimed that none bar a few of 'mixed' descent had survived.[84]

Two aspects of the Canarian saga are sometimes cited by romanticisers and apologists to parry accusations of extermination and to argue for the continued survival of a substantive but hidden Indigenous Canarian

---

78 Fernández-Armesto, *After Conquest*, 40, 128.
79 Mercer, *Canary Islanders*, 234–237; Fernández-Armesto, *After Conquest*, 36–38, 40, 160–161, 174.
80 Abulafia, *Discovery of Mankind*, 59; de Espinosa, *Guanches of Tenerife*, 41.
81 Fernández-Armesto, *After Conquest*, 5; Pérez, 'Role of interpreters', 158.
82 Crosby, *Ecological Imperialism*, 98; Mercer, *Canary Islanders*, 213.
83 Fernández-Armesto, *After Conquest*, 11.
84 Benzoni G. 1858. *A History of the New World*, trans. W. Smyth. London: Hakluyt Society, 260; Crosby, 'Ecohistory of the Canary Islands', 207; de Espinosa, *Guanches of Tenerife*, 120.

presence on the islands.[85] The first points to marriages between Canarian women and settler men, and the second to land grants made to indigenes as means for their assimilation into colonial society. Both were supposedly aided by the benevolence of church and monarchy.

Regarding intermarriage, there is a tendency to celebrate a handful of unions involving the very elite of Canarian society, the most prominent of which were the marriages between Maciot de Bethencourt and Teguise, the Lanzarotean chief's daughter; and between the Guanche princess Dacil and the conquistador Gonzalo del Castillo. These marriages are seen as symbolic of a cultural blending in which a covert autochthonous Canarian presence survived, even thrived, under the aegis of the new imperial order. In reality, sexual relations between settlers and Indigenous women were generally exploitative and often violent. Even where more permanent unions occurred, as when several of the Norman settlers recruited by Bethencourt took Canarian women as concubines, these women were the spoils of genocidal war and were utterly powerless. While such unions may have aided in the survival of Canarian genes, they were also a by-product of genocide, and did little to mitigate its destructive impact. DNA studies indicate a significant presence of Indigenous Canarian genes in the archipelago's contemporary gene pool. This distribution is largely skewed in favour of female survivors, which is consistent with a much higher death rate among Canarian males due to their higher exposure to violence, and with the sexual exploitation of Canarian women by settlers.[86]

As regards land grants, while a few allotments were made to Indigenous Canarians, these allocations were small, of poor-quality land, and were given to a handful of the aboriginal elite as reward for their collaboration in the destruction of their societies, and did not remain in Canarian hands for long.[87] Indeed, the Hispanicisation of the remnants of their ruling classes helped kill off Indigenous Canarian cultures. Both church and monarchy were ineffective in curbing violence toward, and extreme exploitation of, Canarians, as settlers and conquerors easily evaded or ignored their injunctions. The romanticised view represents little more than a denial of the

---

85 Herrera, *Canary Islands*; Gil and Martin, *Canary Islands*; Vallejo, 'Conquests'; and Pérez 'Role of interpreters' are good examples.

86 Fregel R. et al. 2009. 'Demographic history of Canary Islands male gene-pool: replacement of native lineages by European'. *BMC Evolutionary Biology*, 9, 181–194; Bortolini M. et al. 2004. 'Ribeiro's typology, genomes, and Spanish colonialism, as viewed from Gran Canaria and Colombia'. *Genetics and Molecular Biology*, 27, no. 1, 1–8; Maca-Meyer et al., 'Origin of the Guanches', 160–161; Maca-Meyer et al., 'Aborigines, conquerors and slaves', 604; Flores et al., 'A predominant European ancestry', 145–148.

87 Fernández-Armesto, *After Conquest*, 38–39, 54–64, 66.

CHAPTER 2: Raiders, Slavers, Conquistadors, Settlers

true extent of colonial violence and a legitimisation of settler conquest.[88] An alternative, eco-historical interpretation is provided by Alfred Crosby. His analysis, however, downplays the significance of mass violence, exaggerates the impact of disease, and is unduly focused on Tenerife.[89]

This conflict was, moreover, informed by a quasi-racist ideology in that European conquerors unequivocally saw Canarians as culturally and spiritually inferior, despite Canarians, being of Berber origin, to a large degree resembling them physically. This was especially true of settlers from southern Europe, who tended to be swarthier than their northern counterparts. Spain, with its doctrine of *limpieza de sangre* (purity of blood), which emerged during the fifteenth century and was used to ascribe an inherited and intrinsic inferiority to Jews and Moors, had developed the most advanced racist ideology in Europe at the time. Canarians were, however, regarded as 'wild men' who were taken to inhabit areas beyond the world known to Europeans. They were clearly not one of the 'monstrous races', the other trope medieval Europe used to speculate about strange peoples living in unexplored lands. European conquerors thus felt that they had the right to enslave, dispossess and if necessary kill Canarians.[90] That Canarians were pagans rather than infidels, and thus more deserving of forbearance, evoked a more benevolent attitude from the church and the Castilian monarchy. It, however, did little to mitigate the aggression of conquerors and settlers blinded by material interests and whose intolerance of the racial other had been conditioned by centuries of conflict against infidels on the Iberian Peninsula itself.[91]

Civilian-driven nature

Brigandage and private commercial interests always played an important role in European colonial expansion. This was even more the case during

---

88 This romanticised denialism dates back to at least the early seventeenth century when epic poet Antonio de Viana sought to counter indictments of Spanish colonial occupation of the Canaries implicit in de Espinosa's history. Merediz's *Refracted Images* and 'Travelling icons' deals with this in some detail. See also Mercer J. 1979. 'The Canary Islanders in Western Mediterranean politics', *African Affairs*, 78, no. 3,

89 Crosby, *Ecological Imperialism*, 79–103.

90 Frederickson G. 2002. *Racism: A Short History*. Princeton: Princeton University Press, 30–47; Hannaford I. 1996. *Race: The History of an Idea in the West*. Baltimore: Johns Hopkins University Press, ch. 5; Jahoda, G. 1999. *Images of Savages: Ancient Roots of Modern Prejudice in Western Culture*. New York: Routledge, 11, 15.

91 Cohen Y. 2012. *The Spanish: Shadows of Embarrassment*. Brighton: Sussex Academic Press, 92; Merediz, *Refracted Images*, 35, 57; Stone P. 2014. *The Canary Islands: A Cultural History*. Oxford: Signal Books, 3. Two papal bulls forbidding the enslavement of Canarians were ignored, as were similar injunctions by the Castilian monarchy.

its pre-Columbian phase when states were relatively weak and uninterested in overseas expansion but entrepreneurs were prepared to risk capital, and adventurers their lives, to make their fortunes.[92] As would later happen with the conquest of Spanish America, the subjugation of the Canaries was largely funded not by the Spanish crown but rather through private means raised by conquistadors themselves.[93] Conquistadors were as much entrepreneurs as they were military leaders, risking ruination by selling personal assets and taking on crippling debt. In the Canaries, campaigns were chiefly financed by venture capital provided by merchants and aristocrats, who were recompensed through the spoils of conquest — plunder, slaves, land grants and privileged access to the colonial economy. It was for the most part Italian, especially Genoese, but also Flemish and Iberian, merchants who came to form the commercial elite in post-conquest Canarian society.[94] Even after the seigneurial phase of conquest ended in 1477 and the Castilian state took charge, conquistadors were nonetheless highly dependent on venture capital, which they were expected to raise themselves, effectively conducting private campaigns for personal gain, licensed by the Spanish crown. According to Campos, the 'crown's main contribution ... was the umbrella of a just, legal and sanctified war [which] opened coffers and convinced the undecided'.[95]

The Western world's first overseas settler colonial conquest thus very much consisted of a set of civilian-driven genocides. They demonstrate that civilian-driven mass violence was integral to settler projects from the start of Western overseas expansion, even though later settler invasions may have taken very different forms.

---

92 Harari Y. 2014. *A Brief History of Humankind*. London: Harvill Secker, 304, 315.
93 Restall M. 2003. *Seven Myths of the Spanish Conquest*. Oxford: Oxford University Press, 65–67; Elliott, *Imperial Spain*, 63–65.
94 Fernández-Armesto, *Before Columbus*, 199.
95 Campos, 'Atlantic islands', 149; Benjamin, *Atlantic World*, 108, 150–154, 157.

CHAPTER THREE

'Shooting a Black Duck': Genocidal Settler Violence against Indigenous Peoples and the Creation of Canada

Sidney L. Harring

Canada has a foundational myth of a peaceful frontier, settled according to the rule of law. In this view Native people were protected by the Crown and the legal system and were peacefully incorporated into a now-thriving, multicultural society. This is in contrast to the many violent Indian wars of the neighbouring United States. On a broader scale, this is also held in contrast to the violence suffered by Indigenous peoples in other British colonial societies — Australia, South Africa and New Zealand. The end result in all these countries was, however, the same: Native people were forced from their land to live in poverty, their cultures destroyed, while white settlers became rich developing all this now-empty land.[1]

Canada lacks a narrative of how settler-driven violence shaped both Native policy and the resulting status of Indigenous peoples. Indeed, the myth of the peaceful — and in the west 'policed' — frontier is inconsistent with this reality of civilian-driven violence. This is in contrast to the United States' experience, in which settlers drove a policy of 'Indian hating and empire building,'[2] which is abhorrent to Canadians. Indeed, much of what is seen to define Canadian history is that it was unlike that of the United States: it had national policies that avoided the rampant racism, violence and imperialism of its southern neighbour. This is still seen as a defining difference between the histories of the two nations.

Not only is there now, to varying degrees, historical amnesia, and denial of the shape and violence that underlay the disposession of Indigenous peoples, but Native people themselves are also blamed for the result. Most white Canadians still claim that dispossession was 'inevitable' and that

---

1 Harring S.L. 1998. *White Man's Law: Native People in Nineteenth Century Canadian Jurisprudence*. Toronto: University of Toronto Press, 16–34. Until Confederation in 1867, Canadian Indian policy was British Indian policy, with some deference to local politics.
2 See for example, Drinnon R. 1997. *Facing West: The Metaphysics of Indian-Hating and Empire Building*. Norman: University of Oklahoma Press.

Native people now living on the margins of Canadian society are somehow responsible for their own fate. Most Canadians are unaware of the role of settler-driven violence in this process. Even worse, the resulting white racism focuses on Native people as lazy and somehow enjoying their lives on 'welfare'.[3] Yet settler invasion devastated Indigenous Canada, leaving the whites rich and the First Nations not only poor, but also sick and dead.

The word 'genocide' is objectionable to most Canadians when applied to their settlement of the country. Stephen Harper, Prime Minister of Canada from 2006 till 2015, went so far as to deny that the word 'colonialism' had any place in Canadian history.[4] This is a wrong-headed and dishonest position to be taken in a former colony.[5] At the same time, recent developments relating to Indian residential schools in Canada have, for the first time, opened up a discourse on genocide in Canadian history.[6] There can be no question that residential schools had the clear policy goal of destroying Native culture, thus meeting one of the definitions of genocide under the UN convention, which Canada has ratified.[7] Now that it is clear that Canada did, in fact, commit genocide through its residential schooling system, it is time to move beyond this narrow framework and inquire further into the historical

---

3   Shrubb R. 2014. '"Canada Has No History of Colonialism." Historical Amnesia: The Erasure of Indigenous Peoples from Canadian History'. MA dissertation, University of Victoria. Any number of articles and editorials in the *National Post*, a conservative newspaper with nationwide circulation, also take this view.

4   Stephen Harper, in a speech at the G20 meetings in Pittsburgh in September 2009, said: 'We are one of the most stable regimes in history. We are unique in that regard. We also have no history of colonialism. So we have all of the things that many people admire about the great powers but none of the things that threaten or bother them'. Quoted in Dearing S. 2009. 'Harper in Pittsburgh: Canada has no history of colonialism'. *Digital Journal*, 3 October 2009. Available at digitaljournal.com/article/280003, accessed on 29 October 2019.

5   This statement is so bizarre that it might be useful to imagine what Harper was thinking. My reading of it is that Harper, being of British heritage, has a race-based understanding of the term 'colony', and simply didn't understand British domination of Canada to be 'colonial', a word that he believes refers to white European countries taking non-white 'colonies' in the undeveloped world. This is speculation, but it is important to note that Harper has never clarified what he meant. He apparently denies that white Canada has a colonial relationship with Indigenous Canada.

6   *Indian Residential Schools, Truth and Reconciliation Commission Report: Truth, Healing, Reconciliation*, 18 August 2008; Palmater P. 2016. 'The ongoing legacies of Canadian genocide'. *Canadian Dimension*, 50, no. 1; Woolford A. & Benvenuto J. 2015. 'Canada and colonial genocide'. *Journal of Genocide Research*, 17, no. 4, 373–390.

7   United Nations Convention on the Prevention and Punishment of Genocide, General Assembly Resolution 260, 9 December 1948. Beverley McLachlin, former Chief Justice of Canada, has said that Canada 'attempted' to commit 'cultural genocide', so this issue has reached the heart of Canadian national discourse. See *Independent*, 30 May 2015.

CHAPTER 3: 'Shooting a Black Duck'

amnesia involving genocide in other aspects of Canadian history.[8] There are a number of paths an analysis of this sort might take. One possibility is re-examining the relationship between settlers and Native people from the very beginnings of Canadian colonial history.

What is today Canada consisted of distinct colonies, including Newfoundland, Nova Scotia, Prince Edward Island, New Brunswick, Upper and Lower Canada (precursors to Ontario and Quebec, respectively) and British Columbia, with their own governments, until Confederation in 1867. Four colonies became the original provinces of Canada in 1867, with other provinces being added later. British control of these colonies varied over time, was often weak, and largely ended in 1867. Through most of the nineteenth century there were few colonial institutions aimed at controlling settler activities, especially on the frontier. This was, however, the result of a series of, first British, and later Canadian, political choices not to protect Indian rights, leaving Indians exposed to settler violence. This runs counter to official versions of Canadian history, but can be demonstrated in all historical contexts throughout the making of Canadian society and the displacement of Native people from their land. Much of this violence is clearly genocidal, while other settler activity complemented the destruction of Indigenous societies.

The extermination of the Beothuk of Newfoundland

There are a handful of now-classic stories of the genocide of Native peoples. One of these is the extermination of the Beothuk, the original inhabitants of Newfoundland,[9] which rivals the annihilation of the Tasmanian Aborigines.[10] This extinction was accomplished through civilian killings, as

---

8   There is some discussion within Canada about the issue of genocide, largely following the residential schools debate, but there is no agreement that it occurred. Not surprisingly, this follows political lines, with the Conservative Party and its members strongly in denial. There is a substantial literature on this. For discussion of this issue in the context of the UN Convention, see MacDonald D. & Hudson G. 2012. 'The genocide question and Indian residential schools in Canada', *Canadian Journal of Political Science*, 45, no. 2, 427–449; and Palmater, 'The ongoing legacies of Canadian genocide', 3.

9   Budgel R. 1992. 'The Beothuks and the Newfoundland mind', *Newfoundland Studies*, 8, 15–33; Pastore R. 1993. 'Archaeology, history and the Beothuks', *Newfoundland Studies*, 9, no. 2, 260–278; Pastore R. 1987. 'Fishermen, furriers, and Beothuks: The economy of extinction', *Man in the Northeast*, 33, 47–62.

10 The killing of the Tasmanians has been a foundational story in Australian history for generations. As with all genocides, this account has been denied. See Windschuttle K. 2004. *The Fabrication of Aboriginal History, vol. 1, Van Diemen's Land, 1803–1847*. Sydney: Macleay Press. This account was repudiated in Manne R. 2004. *Whitewash*. Melbourne: Black Inc.

CIVILIAN-DRIVEN VIOLENCE AND THE GENOCIDE OF INDIGENOUS PEOPLES

well as by settlers forcing the Beothuk from their coastal communities into the much more hostile climate of the interior. This occurred in an isolated and sparsely populated colony with weak adminstration, but certainly with the knowledge and tacit approval of the Crown. Every white person in the colony knew what was happening, its occurrence widely accepted as necessary.

There is a voluminous literature on this extermination, with some difference in detail because the events were poorly documented, but the basic outline is clear. There were two related causes.[11] First, the Beothuk, facing increased competition for land and resources from white settlers and itinerant fisherman, moved their villages away from the coastal sites that they had traditionally occupied. Their traditional economy was based on the exploitation of coastal resources, a rich ecological system providing much food and a relatively mild climate. Moving to the interior put them in a different ecosystem, requiring hunting, trapping and gathering in a harsh north-woods environment, far colder and less productive than their former fishing and gathering economy on the coast.

Second, and inextricably interconnected with this demographic shift, is that the Beothuk faced great violence on the coast. Settlers, especially fisherman, shot them because they were in competition for scarce coastal resources or to occupy their village sites. The literature is replete with references to the Beothuk as stealing from white settlers. This was exaggerated, because much white settler occupation was seasonal. Seasonal settlements were left vacant much of the year, and the Beothuk, often finding these settlements at the same location as their former settlements, freely used the resources, helping themselves to metal utensils, tools, stores and whatever else they could use. This, in turn, escalated the cycle of violence as settlers and fishermen came to view the Beothuk as a threat. Increasing violence against the Beothuk forced them from the coast into the harsh interior. There are dozens of stories of settler hunting parties killing Beothuk men, women and children.

One example was reported by Lieutenant Pulling of the Royal Navy in 1792, describing civilian expeditions to retaliate against the Beothuk for killing settlers and stealing:

---

11 Upton L. 1977. 'The extermination of the Beothuks of Newfoundland', *Canadian Historical Review*, 58, no. 2, 133–153; reprinted in Miller J.R., ed. 1991. *Sweet Promises: A Reader on Indian–White Relations in Canada*. Toronto: University of Toronto Press, 68–89; Marshall I. 2001. *The Beothuk*. St John's: Newfoundland Historical Society; Rowe E. 1977. *Extinction: The Beothuks of Newfoundland*. Toronto: McGraw-Hill Ryerson.

CHAPTER 3: 'Shooting a Black Duck'

> Eight whites revenged the death of Rousell, travelling eighty miles before finding an encampment. According to their account, they let the Indians run away, all except two women ... Several veterans of that expedition went looking for stolen nets in the following year. They found an empty punt and assumed its crew had been killed. Discovering a wigwam, they let two women run away, but shot a man who emerged carrying a child. Both were left to die ... That same summer one of the principal employers of the area, John Peyton, led a group whose members were most reluctant to talk about what happened. Three days' travel up Main Brook brought them to their quarry, they fired into the midst of the Beothucks — Peyton had thirty-six pistol balls in his gun — but did not report their kill. They found a wounded Indian lying in a wigwam, the man tried to defend himself and Peyton beat his brains out with a stolen trap.[12]

At the time, much of this went unrecorded because settlers did not want the extent of the killing to be known. British colonial administrators were aware of the bloodshed, and may even have helped to suppress it. In addition, the geography of Newfoundland made any kind of government intervention difficult. The island has a very rugged coastline, settled with dozens of small fishing villages accessible only by boat, and then only during part of the year. As long as settlers in these villages kept quiet about the killings, the authorities would not know. At the same time, the British authorities were focused on the colonies as sources of profit, and Newfoundland contributed mainly as a lucrative fishery. As long as the fishing was good, there was little reason to intervene to protect Native people.

It became worse when the French and British fought wars over their North American lands and enlisted other tribes, particularly the Mi'kmaq, to fight for them in Newfoundland. The extent to which the Mi'kmaq also killed Beothuk is not clear, and is denied in Mi'kmaq lore. In any event, the Mi'kmaq were drawn into Newfoundland by Europeans.

By 1829 the 'last' Beothuk, a woman named Shawandithit, was reported dead at age 28. Like other reported 'extinctions' of Native people, this was not the end of the Beothuk because remnant populations moved inland and merged with other tribes, particularly the Mi'kmaq, some of whom had settled in Newfoundland. Shawandithit had, in fact, been found starving in 1823 with four other women, and reported that there were no more than 15 people left in her band. Four years earlier, in 1819, Demasduwit was also captured by a colonial force composed of both soldiers and settlers, organised by the colonial government. Her husband, Nonobawsut, was

---

12 Upton, 'Extermination of the Beothuks' in Miller, *Sweet Promises*, 74.

65

CIVILIAN-DRIVEN VIOLENCE AND THE GENOCIDE OF INDIGENOUS PEOPLES

bayoneted in the process, and she later died of tuberculosis. By this time there may only have been a handful of Beothuk left living in the interior.[13]

By the late 1700s and early 1800s, the colonial government made some effort to protect the Beothuk, but by then it was too late to reverse the damage that had been done to these people.[14] Governor Hugh Palliser in 1766 informed the secretary of state that 'the barbarous system of killing prevails amongst our people towards the Native Indians — whom our People always kill, when they can meet them.'[15]

Newfoundland to this day stands as one of the classic examples of the destruction of people by settlers. This destruction was intentional. It was meant to remove the Beothuk threat to settler property and their fishing economy. Whether this was done by actual killing, or by forced removal from their former villages on the coast, or by disease brought on by their weakened condition, the result was extinction. The term 'genocide' applies in this case because of the intentional nature of the violence committed. While no person intended to kill every last Beothuk, settlers intended to kill many of them, and intended to force all of them from their villages on the coast to the interior, where they succumbed to starvation and disease.

Settler violence against the Native peoples of Nova Scotia and New Brunswick

Nova Scotia, from which New Brunswick was separated in 1784, had a diverse economy, based mainly on agriculture. Settlement occurred with little or no legal regulation, allowing settlers on the frontier to confiscate land from Indians, mostly Mi'kmaq, through whatever means available, including threats of violence and murder. The Crown facilitated the process by refusing to protect Indian land from illegal settler occupation, referred to as 'squatting'. This failure of law made the settlement of rural Canada an inexpensive measure for the Crown. A similar process, with local variations, occurred in Ontario and as settlement moved westward.[16]

These developments followed on from the violence of the origins of the colony, when Lord Cornwallis in 1749 settled 2 500 colonists at the current site of Halifax. The Mi'kmaq resisted this settlement, launching several

---

13 Heritage Newfoundland and Labrador. 2013. 'Disappearance of the Beothuk', July. Available at http//:www heritage.nf.ca, accessed 29 October 2019; Pastore R. & Story G. 1987. 'Demasduwit', in *Dictionary of Canadian Biography*. Toronto: University of Toronto/University of Laval Press, 5.

14 Upton, 'Extermination of the Beothuks', in Miller, *Sweet Promises*, 74.

15 Ibid.

16 Harring, *White Man's Law*, 35–90.

CHAPTER 3: 'Shooting a Black Duck'

fatal attacks on colonists working outside the village. These events are now known as the Mi'kmaq War of 1749, but were in reality a continuation of the long-standing conflict between the French and English, both with Indian allies, that culminated in the French and Indian War of 1754–1763.[17] In reaction, Cornwallis issued a proclamation of a bounty for every Mi'kmaq scalp—men, women, and children.[18] Daniel Paul, a Mi'kmaq elder, has called this proclamation genocide, causing some controversy in Canada.[19] This, on the face of it, appears to be genocidal although some have attempted to contextualise it as 'normal' in the language of eighteenth-century colonisation.[20]

There clearly were killings of Native people by British soldiers and settlers thereafter in Nova Scotia. The record is very thin about the extent of colonial settler violence, but clearly Lord Cornwallis's proclamation sent a message that supported settlers and their violent measures to remove Indians.[21] Settlers directly benefited from these killings in that they gained access to Indian land. As in Newfoundland, the colonial authorities knew that the killing of Native people by settlers was occurring but did nothing to intervene. Justice Brenton Halliburton of the Nova Scotia Supreme Court wrote that 'whenever British soldiers or hunters shot an Indian they 'boast of killing a black duck'.[22] There are, accordingly, no records of these killings, but this was the process by which lands were cleared for settlement. Moses Perley, the New Brunswick Commissioner of Indian Affairs, wrote in an 1841 report that white squatters 'hunted the Indians off the reserve like wild beasts' and faced them 'in hostile array'.[23] Landry describes repeated attacks by squatters on Indians in mid-nineteenth-century New Brunswick: 'There was long and continuous conflict between loggers and Indigenous

---

17 Patterson S. 1993. 'Indian–White relations in Nova Scotia, 1749–61: A study in political interaction', *Acadiensis*, 23, no. 1, 23–59

18 Ibid., 31.

19 Paul D. 2011. 'The hidden history of the Americas: The destruction and depopulation of the Indigenous civilizations of the Americas by European invaders', *Settler Colonial Studies*, 1, no. 2, 167–181; Paul D. 2006. *We Are Not Savages*, 3rd ed. Winnipeg: Fernwood Publishing.

20 The *National Post*, a conservative newspaper with a wide readership, has characterised the proclamation as 'a necessary response' and Cornwallis as 'more a victim than a villian'. *National Post*, 2 February 2018.

21 Once a proclamation offers a reward for Indian scalps, the impact on colonial legal culture must last for at least several generations. The taking of Indian lands by settlers would seem to follow as a matter of course, all in the shadow of this violence.

22 Upton L. 1979. *Micmacs and Colonists: Indian–White Relations in the Maritime Provinces, 1713–1867*. Vancouver: University of British Columbia Press, 145.

23 Upton L. 1974. 'Indian affairs in colonial New Brunswick', *Acadiensis*, 3, no. 2, 3–26. Perley himself 'accidentally' shot and killed an Indian while a teenager.

CIVILIAN-DRIVEN VIOLENCE AND THE GENOCIDE OF INDIGENOUS PEOPLES

peoples, likely since logging began.'[24] Andrea Bear Nicholas reports an attack on women on the Kingsclear reserve in 1861, carried out by 'an army of woodsmen'.[25] In 1791 a complaint was filed by Barnaby Julia, an Indian, against white men, alleging that they had 'assaulted and abused' his wife, but a grand jury found there was insufficient evidence to proceed to trial.[26] What this demonstrates is that settlers were violently confronting Indians.

There are extensive records, however, on the theft of land by settlers in Nova Scotia and New Brunswick. Settlers moved on Indian land wherever they wanted, with no legal regulation. The literature is replete with references to white 'squatters' taking up Indian lands — including on Indian reserves, and forcing Indians to move elsewhere. Nova Scotia, however, was a settled colony, with a colonial administration dating from 1749. Indians could have been protected but were left to fend for themselves, beyond the protection of British colonial law. There were times, however, when settlers were held accountable. But this history is uneven, as British law was rarely applied. For example, two Loyalists in New Brunswick were arrested for killing an Indian whom they claimed was trying to steal their hogs. They were tried for murder and one of them was hanged. This episode, however, also shows that white settlers thought that they could engage in this behavior openly.[27] Its significance also needs to be read in the context of the efforts by the British authorities to tame the reckless conduct of many Loyalists, who had moved to Canada after the American Revolution, and to create a different legal culture in Canada. This becomes very clear in the history of white settlement of Upper Canada, now Ontario.

In the end, while it is clear that settler violence played some role in the settlement of Nova Scotia, and later New Brunswick, we cannot say how many Indians were killed, nor how prevalent these killings were. What we can say is that white settlers were able to move onto Indian land with

---

24 Landry M. 2010. 'Pokemouche Mi'kmaq and the Colonial Regimes'. MA dissertation, St Mary's University, Halifax, 64.

25 Ibid. This event needs to be understood in the context of the massive violence described in Nicholas A. 2011. 'Settler imperialism and the dispossession of the Maliseet, 1758–1765', in *Shaping an Agenda for Atlantic Canada*, eds. J. Reid & D. Savoie. Halifax; Fernwood Publishers, 21–57; Nichols A. 2015. 'The role of colonial artists in the dispossession and displacement of the Maliseet, 1790–1850s', *Journal of Canadian Studies/Revue d'études canadiennes*, 49, no. 2, 25–86. The latter article demonstrates how colonial artists changed their depiction of the Maliseet as settler efforts to dispossess them increased.

26 Grandy L. 2017. 'First nations and local courts of New Brunswick: Negotiated relationships, Atlantic Loyalist connections', The Loyalist Collection, University of New Brunswick. Available at https://loyalist.lib.unb.ca/atlantic-loyalist-connections/first-natins-and-local-courts-new-brunswick; accesssed 29 October 2019.

27 Upton, *Micmacs and Colonists*, 145.

CHAPTER 3: 'Shooting a Black Duck'

impunity and Indians were unable to resist, instead removing themselves under threat of violence to less desirable land. As one colonial observer wrote, 'You will scarcely meet an Indian, but who will tell you that he has cleared and cultivated land some time or other, but that the white men have taken it from him.'[28] Fishing streams were blocked by nets set by white settlers, preventing Indians from fishing. Game animals were hunted to extinction.[29] Their forced removal led to impoverishment and disease, and the deaths of most of the Indians of Nova Scota. Unlike the Beothuk, the Mi'kmaq survived as a people, and were able to reassert their Indigenous rights in the twentieth century. They still lost almost all of their lands, and occupy a few small reserves today. The removal of the Maliseet, a people who lived to the south of the Mi'kmaq in New Brunswick, Quebec and Maine, followed this now-familiar pattern. White settlers moved onto Maliseet land, depriving them of subsistence opportunities in the interior.[30] By the late 19th and early 20th centuries, the children of Indians left on these reserves were removed to residential schools where they were forbidden to speak their native languages and forced to renounce their traditional cultures.[31] The inherent violence behind settler-driven land dispossession is at the core of the forced assimilation that ended in residential schooling, which closed the circle of the genocidal process in Canada.

This completed a three-stage process of genocide: the killings and removals led to a loss of land and displacement; this resulted in impoverishment and death by disease, destroying communities, and ended with children being removed from their families and communities to residential schools where their culture was forcibly beaten and also 'educated' out of them.

Settler displacement of the Indigenous peoples of Ontario

Building on these developments on the Atlantic coast, Indian policy in Upper Canada (later Ontario) became the template for what is now known as 'Canadian' Indian policy, as Ontario came to dominate Canada after Confederation in 1867. Like New Brunswick, Upper Canada was settled by Loyalists with the ending of the American Revolution in 1783. Mindful of the

---

28 Reid J. 2009. 'Empire, the maritime colonies, and the supplanting of Mi'kma'ki/ Wulstukwik, 1780–1820', *Acadiensis*, 38, no. 2, 10.

29 Ibid., 5–6.

30 Nicholas, 'Settler imperialism', 21–29.

31 Peters M. 2016. 'A Respectable Solution to the Indian Problem: Canadian Genocidal Intent, Non-Physical Conceptions of Destruction and the Nova Scotia Mi'kmaq, 1867–1969'. BA Honours thesis, Acadia University.

American example, Britain was determined to have a strictly administered colony, with a more developed colonial government. Accordingly, a colonial administrative body, including a legal system, was created at Fort York, now Toronto.[32] At the same time, Britain's loss of the American colonies resulted in thousands of settlers moving just north of the United States border within a short span of time. These settlers were land-hungry and expected Britian to reward them for their loyalty to the Crown. There was thus a contradiction between the demand for land and the ideal of a more orderly settlement of Canada. As in Atlantic Canada, colonists, often squatters without any legal entitlement, drove land settlement, with the Crown unable to control the process.

Unlike in the Atlantic colonies, it was decided that Indian lands were not to be settled until they were first purchased by treaty, marking the beginning of the treaty system in Canada.[33] This determination was directly related to British thinking that the wild and uncontrolled United States frontier had been a cause of the American Revolution. Britain also believed that it had some responsibility to protect Indians from settlers, also based on their experience with the American colonies.[34] Among the Loyalists who moved to Upper Canada were Iroquois allies of the Crown. They were settled at Grand River, not on the reserves, as used in the rest of Canada, but on a land grant purchased by treaty from the previous Native occupants. By the 1850s, British authorities were negotiating treaties with all the other Indigenous inhabitants of Upper Canada. This treaty process was, however, undermined by the haste with which it was enacted and by the unequal power of the two parties.

For the British, the treaty system was honourable, in contrast to the wars and policy of Indian removal prevalent in the United States. At the same time, the British seemed unaware of the damage that the process was doing to Indian Nations. This policy became the foundation of Canadian Indian policy as the frontier moved west. While each treaty was unique, the level of damage done to Indian Nations varied according to the circumstances of each treaty. To the extent that this Crown-centred policy avoided Indian

---

32 Harring, *White Man's Law*, 16–90.

33 Surtees R. 1969. 'The development of an Indian reserve policy in Canada', *Ontario History*, 61, no. 2, 87–90; Surtees R. 1984. *Report: Indian Land Surrenders in Ontario, 1763–1867*. Canadian Department of Indian and Northern Affairs Treaty Research Centre; Blair P. 2008. *Lament for a First Nation: The Williams Treaties of Southern Ontario*. Vancouver: University of British Columbia Press, 14–37.

34 Tobias J. 1991. 'Protection, civilization, assimilation: An outline history of Canada's Indian policy', in Miller *Sweet Promises* 127–144.

CHAPTER 3: 'Shooting a Black Duck'

wars and established a peaceful frontier, it clearly cannot be called genocide. It was, however, a fragile system, leading to great injustice on several levels. Ultimately, it led to the impoverishment of Indigenous peoples and the cultural genocide of the residential school system.

First is the reality of American violence against Indians all along the Canadian frontier. This not only drove Indians to Canada but also sent a clear message to all Indians that they could be violently displaced from their lands. While the Revolutionary War ended in 1783, the frontier west of the Appalachian Mountains was the scene of considerable violence against Indians until after the War of 1812. While the border between the United States and Canada was legally determined after the revolution, these borderlands were not settled for another generation, with Indians and colonists freely moving back and forth across the border. American violence against Indians set the context for Canadian Indian policy.[35] The border between the United States and Canada was open through much of the nineteenth century, and thousands of Americans, both white and Indian, moved to Upper Canada. American Indians who fled American violence to Canada were then confronted with American squatters who had moved to Canada in search of cheap land.

Second, the simple reality is that the treaties were very unequal in both their conception and their execution. Small and weak tribes had little choice but to enter into these treaties, giving up most of their land in return for annuities and a guarantee by the Crown that they would be protected from further encroachment. Once the treaty was signed, these tribes had very little ability to get the Crown to protect them. Indians were resettled in small villages, often under the influence of some religious order, where they took up small farms, with varying degrees of success. Some Indians became successful farmers, while others were impoverished.[36] Many contemporary First Nations view their treaties as unfair and a denial of their rights. This is obvious from the continuing litigation over treaty and land rights in

---

35 Taylor A. 2006. *The Divided Ground: Indians, Settlers, and the Northern Borderland of the American Revolution*. New York: Random House; Taylor A. 2010. *American Citizens, British Subjects, Irish Rebels, and Indian Allies*. New York: Alfred Knopf; Skaggs D. & Nelson L. 2010. *The Sixty Years War for the Great Lakes, 1754–1814*. East Lansing: Michigan State University Press; White R. 1991. *The Middle Ground: Indians, Empires, and Republics in the Great Lakes Region, 1650–1815*. Cambridge: Cambridge University Press.

36 Harring, *White Man's Law*; Schmalz P.S. 1991. *The Ojibwa of Southern Ontario*. Toronto: University of Toronto Press, 121–179.

CIVILIAN-DRIVEN VIOLENCE AND THE GENOCIDE OF INDIGENOUS PEOPLES

Ontario, where there are currently more than a hundred legally contested land claims.[37]

Thirdly, there was great settler demand for land in Upper Canada, including Indian land. There was not enough land to meet this demand, nor did the colonial state have the capacity to survey and allocate Crown land. The result was wholesale illegal occupation of land by squatters. The Crown, in turn, did not respond to this crisis adequately both because of concerns about political instability and because it was not prepared to defend Indian treaty rights against the white settlers. Also, many of these squatters were Americans, moving west to get better and cheaper land, and the Crown was not eager to confront anti-authoritarian American rebels again.[38]

The result was that white settlers were allowed to force Indians off their land. Treaties were renegotiated, reducing the size of already-small reserves. Whites were allowed to move onto Indian land, take Indian property, and generally make life miserable for Indian farmers.[39] Chief Bauzh-Giezhig-Waeshikum of Walpole Island reported to Samuel Jarvis, Superintendent General of Indian Affairs, that squatters had killed a hundred of their pigs, stolen their horses, and shot their dogs 'at the very doors of our lodges'.[40] Sir Walter Bagot, in his 1845 Report on the Indians of Ontario, put the problem clearly: 'They hold large blocks of land ... which they can neither occupy nor protect against the encroachments of white squatters, with whom in the vain attempt to guard their lands, they are brought into a state of constant hostility and conflict.'[41] This replicates the process that had occurred in Nova Scotia almost a hundred years earlier.

Indian Department officials who were beholden to settlers, or engaged in land speculation themselves, colluded in this process. Land administration became chaotic as whites not only squatted on Indian land, but also illegally 'purchased' Indian land, or engaged in illicit land deals with poverty-stricken Indians. Jarvis, himself corrupt, took money from Indians and engaged in his own speculative land deals. There was no real

---

37 Coyle M. 2005. *Report: Addressing Aboriginal Land and Treaty Rights in Ontario: An Analysis of Past Policies and Options for the Future*. Attorney-General of Ontario. Available at https://www.attorneygeneral.jus.gov.on.ca/inquiries/ipperwash/policy_part/research/pdf/Coyle.pdf, accessed 29 October 2019. See also *Report of the Ippwerwash Inquiry*, 31 May 2007. Available at http://www.attorneygeneral.jus.gov.on.ca/inquiries/ipperwash/report/, accessed 29 October 2019.
38 Harring, *White Man's Law*, 35–61.
39 Blair, *Lament for a First Nation*, 38–61.
40 Schmalz, *Ojibwa*, 169.
41 Baton C. 'Report on the affairs of the Indians in Canada laid before the Legislative Assembly 20 March 1845', cited in Blair, *Lament for a First Nation*, 39.

CHAPTER 3: 'Shooting a Black Duck'

access to the Canadian legal system for these Indians, so there was nothing they could do about white squatters. This was a forced occupation of Indian land. While this process of land dispossession was aggressive, there was little direct interpersonal violence, both because Indians did not resist with force and because it was clear to whites that direct violence against Indians would not be tolerated by the authorities, a fundamental principle of Canadian Indian policy after this period.[42]

This is not genocide but a policy of forced assimilation and removal of Indians to small reserves where they were unable to earn a living, nor practise their traditional cultures. After their land had been confiscated, boarding schools became the central means for destroying Indian culture through forced assimilaton. Several denominations started proselytising in reserves and began a range of religious activities designed to 'help' Indians. This ultimately led to the establishment of residential boarding schools.[43] In Ontario, the process goes back at least to the 1820s when Sir Peregrine Maitland and his chief advisor, Anglican cleric John Strachan, first recommended aboriginal children's participation in immersive forms of colonial pedagogy.[44]

While the government of Upper Canada — and later the government of Canada — structured all of these actions, most of the actors were private individuals or religious institutions, acting in their own interests. Some of these interests were selfish, such as settler demands for more and more land. Others were altruistic, such as the desire of various missionaries to 'civilise' Indians by providing schools and religious education. The system of forced assimilation was predicated on the collapse of Indian reserves. The reserves were undermined at every turn by both white settlers and Canadian government policy. The removal of Indian children to boarding schools formed part of this process.

This paternalistic system reached its full development in the years after the settlement of the prairies and the ending of the fur trade in the north. In the east, Indians remained on small reserves, and the residential school system originated there.

---

42 The lack of direct violence against Indians in Canada is notable. The hanging of the American Loyalist in New Brunswick for shooting an Indian was a clear message from Canadian authorities. British colonial authorities in Canada were repulsed by the violence of the American Revolution and were determined that it not be repeated in Canada. There were a few other hangings of settlers for violence against Indians.

43 Hutchings K. 2016. 'Cultural genocide and the first nations of Upper Canada: Some romantic-era roots of Canada's residential school system', *European Romantic Review*, 27, no. 3.

44 Ibid., 1.

The removal of Indians and the settlement of the prairies

While the settlement of Ontario was not driven by clear policy, but rather succumbed to expediency, expansion into western Canada after Confederation in 1867 was driven by wilful implementation of policies highly destructive of Indian society by the new Canadian state. The plan was to clear the prairie provinces of Manitoba, Saskwatchewan and Alberta of Indians ahead of settlement, with the respective bands removed to enclaves modelled after the small reserves in Ontario. There, it was hoped, Indians would become small farmers or wage labourers and support themselves.[45]

Unlike Ontario where masses of uncontrolled squatters drove settlement, the west would be a policed frontier, with a new police force, the North-West Mounted Police (NWMP), created to manage settlement. This was an armed, paramilitary organisation, expressly created in 1873 to protect Canadian expansion from the depredations of Americans, who were operating freely north of the border. It also operated hand in glove with agricultural and business interests to settle the prairies and drive economic development.[46]

Americans were hunting buffalo, selling whisky, trading with Indians, grazing cattle, and essentially anything else they wanted to do there throughout the latter half of the nineteenth century, especially after the Sioux Wars of 1868. The Missouri River was a highway to the west, bringing thousands of Americans to what is now Montana and North Dakota, within easy access of the Canadian border. Further south, the railway crossed the United States in 1868, bringing an end to the buffalo hunt, and bringing many thousands more settlers west. Armed parties of Americans were operating north of the border, killing the last of the buffalo herds, and bringing about the ecological transformation of the prairie from vast grasslands to small farms.[47] This was a civilian-driven clearing of the plains, with American settlers forcing the Canadian government to clear the plains for settlement. As this occurred, increasing numbers of Canadians, including government workers, cast in their lot with the settlers, becoming businessmen and land

---

45 Daschuk J. 2013. *Clearing the Plains: Disease, Politics of Starvation, and the Loss of Aboriginal Life*. Regina: University of Regina Press, 79–126.
46 Macleod R. 1976. *The North-West Mounted Police and Law Enforcement, 1873–1905*. Toronto: University of Toronto Press.
47 Harring S. 2015. 'Dispossession, ecocide, genocide: Cattle ranching and agriculture in the destruction of hunting cultures on the Canadian Prairie', in *Genocide on Settler Frontiers: When Hunter-Gatherers and Commercial Stock Farmers Clash*, ed. M. Adhikari. Cape Town: UCT Press.

CHAPTER 3: 'Shooting a Black Duck'

speculators. As in Ontario, a large proportion of the settlers in Western Canada were Americans, driven by the promise of cheap land.

The NWMP was largely successful in structuring the settlement of the Canadian frontier, but it has to be remembered that it was equivalent to a small army, given the coercive power it needed by government to accomplish its mission. Its purpose was to control the settlement of the prairie provinces so as to unite the Dominion of Canada's western and eastern shores. Already there were plans for a trans-Canadian railroad and for the recruitment of farmers and ranchers to settle these lands. While Indians were removed to reserves by the Crown, acting through local authorities and backed by the NWMP, they were kept there by the fact that they had no place else to go, with farmers having settled all the land around their reserves. Many Indians were forced to accommodate themselves to this reality and either tried to farm, or went to work as labourers for local farmers.[48]

While in Ontario the fiction was that Indians could survive as small farmers, this was even less of a possibility on the prairies. The prairies were too dry to sustain small-scale farming. Agriculture there would be either pastoral, copying the vast ranching operations then dominating the American West, or, later, industrial dry-land farming, creating the vast fields of wheat that later gave way to canola, sunflower and mustard crops. Indeed, even wheat farming did not succeed on the prairies until new strains of wheat were developed based on Russian and Ukrainian varieties.[49]

Thus, while Ontario-style reserves were created all over the prairies, the Indians were never able to support themselves there, and everyone knew it. Canadian Indian policy thus became punitive, deliberately based on forced assimilation and reserves effectively operating as prisons. The result was famine, as Indians couldn't farm well enough to support themselves. Mass death by starvation and disease followed. Finally, children were removed to boarding schools. This, in brief, characterises the genocidal destruction of the Plains Indians. The documentation supporting this is extensive and convincing, although still denied by many Canadians.[50]

Following the impoverishment and starvation of the early years of the reserve system, Canada experienced its worst Indian uprising, the North-West Rebellion of 1885, where some Indians, particularly from the

---

48 Macleod, *The North-West Mounted Police*; Carter S. 1990. *Lost Harvests: Prairie Indian Reserve Farmers and Government Policy*. Montreal: McGill-Queen's University Press, 159–258.

49 Buckley H. 1992. *From Wooden Ploughs to Welfare: Why Indian Policy Failed in the Prairie Provinces*. Montreal: McGill-Queen's University Press.

50 Daschuk, *Clearing the Plains*, is exhaustive in making this argument.

CIVILIAN-DRIVEN VIOLENCE AND THE GENOCIDE OF INDIGENOUS PEOPLES

Battleford area (of Saskatchewan), joined Métis in a last-ditch effort to save their way of life.[51] This war, which did not last very long, was a watershed in Canadian history as it served as a pretext for a harsher policy toward the prairie Indians.[52] Punitive measures toward Indians continued for years afterwards. Dozens of Indians were tried for treason, even though, as their lawyers pointed out, there was no evidence that they owed any allegiance to the British Crown. When Big Bear, a Cree chief, was read the charges in open court, translated as 'stabbing the Queen from behind and knocking off her bonnet', he angrily responded that the charge was a lie, because he had never met the Queen and had no reason to knock off her hat. The injustice of this kind of trial is transparent.[53] Although Métis had led the uprising, many more Indians were tried for treason.[54] Dozens of Indians were hanged, dozens more sentenced to long prison terms, and others kept in chains for months after the uprising was over. The impact of this violence still endures. Stony Mountain Prison, northwest of Winnipeg, was built in part by Native forced labor. After its construction, subsequent generations of Indians have seen their fathers and sons locked up there. Many returned to their reserves impoverished and suffering from tuberculosis.[55]

Disease and death were hallmarks of prairie reserves and most Indians sent there were dead within a few years. The Native population of the prairies dropped precipitously, with death rates exceeding 10 per cent a year on many reserves.[56] Cole Harris argues that while there was considerable local variation, probably about 90 per cent of Indigenous people in Canada died of contagious diseases such as smallpox, tuberculosis, influenza, typhoid fever and measles in the first hundred years of colonisation.[57] It was thus debilitated Indigenous societies that faced the full force of settler colonialism. Disease was a deliberate instrument of colonial

---

51 Waiser B. and Stonechild B. 1997. *Loyal Till Death: Indians and the North West Rebellion.* Calgary: Fifth House, 155–170.
52 It is not clear to what extent this ever was an Indian war. In *Loyal Till Death,* Waiser and Stonechild suggest that most of the killings attributed to Indians were directed at individual whites who had abused them. In any case, most Indians did not take part.
53 Harring, *White Man's Law,* 239–272.
54 Daschuk, *Clearing the Plains,* 159. Eighty-one Indians were charged with crimes, with 44 being convicted and imprisoned; 46 Métis were charged, with 7 incarcerated.
55 Ibid., 160–161. So many chiefs died during imprisonment that it destroyed the leadership of the tribes.
56 Ibid., 159–180. The death rate of Crees at Thunder Child Reserve reached 233.5 per 1 000 in the two years after 1885, and the rate at Sweet Grass Reserve was 185 per 1 000.
57 Harris C. 1997/1998. 'Social power and cultural change in pre-colonial British Columbia', *BC Studies,* no. 115/116, 45–82, 55.

CHAPTER 3: 'Shooting a Black Duck'

domination, intended by the Crown to weaken and remove Native people from their lands.[58]

This demographic disaster was not only the product of Western diseases that swept Indigenous societies across America. Much of the death was caused by malnutrition and starvation, which weakened Indigenous peoples on most of the reserves. The starvation, it is now clear, was a deliberate plan on the part of the Crown, implemented by John A. Macdonald, Prime Minister of Canada and former Minister of Indian Affairs. He wanted to force reserve Indians to work, so calculatingly decided to provide just enough food to keep them above starvation level, a cruel policy applied to men, women and children. He is on record admitting that: 'We cannot allow them to die for want of food ... We are doing all we can by refusing food until the Indians are on the verge of starvation, to reduce the expense.'[59] This has led some to accuse Macdonald of genocide.[60] On the face of it, what Macdonald intended, if not genocide, was just as vicious. He intended to keep Indians alive, but on the edge of starvation, so that they, as a people, would be forced to submit to Canadian authority in this weakened state. Now we know that most of these Indians died under these conditions.

Although not legally required, Indians were forced to stay on these impoverished, disease-ridden reserves, requiring a pass to leave.[61] This, in effect, made the reserves not much more than prison camps and enforced racial segregation on the prairies. The NWMP imposed this illegal regime, keeping starving Indians from leaving their reserves.[62] Indians were taught Canadian farming techniques by resident farming instructors, although no farming culture had ever existed among the Plains Indians, unlike the Indians of Ontario.[63]

This is the context in which residential schooling was imposed on Plains Indians. By the second generation of the reserve system, it was obvious that the children confined to these reserves were not losing their

---

58 Lux M. 2001. *Medicine that Walks: Disease, Medicine and Canadian Native People, 1880–1940.* Toronto: University of Toronto Press.

59 Quoted in Daschuk, *Clearing the Plains*, 123.

60 Stanley T. 2015. 'John A. Macdonald's Aryan Canada: Aboriginal genocide and Chinese exclusion'. *Active History*, 7 January. Available at http://activehistory.ca/2015/01/john-a-macdonalds-aryan-canada-aboriginal-genocide-and-chinese-exclusion/, accessed 29 October 2019.

61 Tang E. 2003. 'Agriculture: The relationship between aboriginal farmers and non-aboriginal farmers'. Research paper, Western Development Museum/Saskatchewan Indian Cultural Centre Partnership Project, 24 April.

62 Gavigan S. 2012. *Hunger, Horses, and Government Men: Criminal Law on the Aboriginal Plains, 1870–1905.* Vancouver: University of British Columbia Press.

63 Carter, *Lost Harvests.*

CIVILIAN-DRIVEN VIOLENCE AND THE GENOCIDE OF INDIGENOUS PEOPLES

cultures, and not assimilating into white Canadian society. The limited residential school system in the east was then expanded. It removed Indian children from reserves and taught them dominant white values, as well as the skills they might need to fit into Canadian society. Their families and their communities, weakened by Macdonald's policies, were unable to intervene to protect their children.

There is a clear link between the collapse of the reserve system and the beginning of the residential school system. While residential schools dated back to early Roman Catholic schools in French Canada in the late seventeenth century, and were used in Ontario after the 1830s, the reliance on residential schools to enforce mass assimiliaton began in the 1880s when policy-makers realised that the reserve system was not working to assimilate prairie Indians. The removal of their children to church-run residential schools was an obvious solution.[64]

By the early twentieth century the plains had been 'cleared' of Indians, while white settlers flocked to take up 'empty' farmlands on formerly Indian land. While this policy was initiated by the Crown, and not by settlers, it was initiated by a Crown mindful of the experience of land-hungry squatters in Ontario who had broken the law and pushed onto Indian lands, destabilising the frontier.[65] Determined not to have a repeat of this process, the Crown took the initiative to 'clear the plains' of Indians to create an orderly settled frontier.

Again, this occurred in the context of American Indian policy. Just as the violence of Indian removal and related wars east of the Mississippi had structured Ontario's Indian policy, the spectre of Indian wars and a lawless frontier had structured the settlement of the Canadian prairies. Just as many settlers in early Ontario were Americans, who tried to reproduce their own ideas of democracy and land ownership in Canada, many of the prairie settlers were also American. They were after cheap land on the Canadian side of the border but had no respect for Canadian traditions, nor for Canadian law.

Settlers and Indian land in British Columbia

The settlement of British Columbia was managed independently of the settlement of the eastern parts of Canada and the prairies. British Columbia,

---

64 Milloy J. 1999. *A National Crime: The Canadian Government and the Residential School System*. Winnipeg: University of Manitoba Press.

65 Daschuk J. 2013. 'When Canada used hunger to clear the west', *Globe and Mail*, 19 July 2013.

CHAPTER 3: 'Shooting a Black Duck'

unlike Ontario and the plains, was settled without treaties, much as occurred in the Maritime provinces. Originally penetrated by the Hudson's Bay Company, whose traders came over the Rocky Mountains even before Lewis and Clark claimed the American Northwest, the colony was then settled from the Pacific, in competition with the Americans for its rich resources. Settlement began about 1770 but was slow to expand until the latter part of the nineteenth century. A proprietary colony was not established on Vancouver Island until 1849, and a Crown colony was not proclaimed on the mainland until 1858. By 1870 two cities, Victoria and Vancouver, had been established, along with a large number of smaller settlements based on resource extraction, mainly along the rugged coast.[66] Without treaties, the settlement of British Columbia was settler-driven, with settlers moving as they chose, to maximise their access to resources. Indians were displaced and left to fend for themselves as best they could.[67]

One account of settlement on Vancouver Island well illustrates this process, which was repeated over and over again, site by site:

In August 1860, a young English businessman, Gilbert Malcolm Sproat, and some fifty hired men sailed up a long, steep sided fjord on the west coast of Vancouver Island with the intention of establishing a logging camp and sawmill. Sproat had purchased land from the Crown at the head of the fjord ... but enocuntered a summer settlement there of a people whom he called the Aht (Nuu-chah-nulth). When the chief of the Aht said that the land Sproat intended for his camp and mill belonged to him and his people, Sproat purchased it again, in goods worth some twenty pounds, on condition that the Aht move the next day. However they did not move, and their behaviour soon convinced Sproat that they intended to fight. Only, he said, when he brought up his ships armed with cannon, and the Aht 'saw that resistance would be inexpedient', did they begin to remove themselves. Three days later, they were re-established at another location nearby.

Sproat then visited the chief who, in Sproat's account, said that his people 'hear things that make our hearts grow faint. They say that more King-George-men will soon be here, and will take our land, our firewood,

---

66 Harris C. 2008. *The Reluctant Land: Society, Space, and Environment in Canada before Confederation.* Vancouver: University of British Columbia Press, 416.

67 Harring, *White Man's Law*, 186–216; Fisher R. 1977. *Contact and Conflict: Indian–European Relations in British Colombia, 1774–1890.* Vancouver: University of British Columbia Press.

> our fishing grounds; that we shall be placed on a little spot, and shall have
> to do everything according to the fancies of the King-George-men'.[68]

This epitomises the painful process through which British Columbia was settled. The use of gunboats was effective against Indigenous coastal villages, which were shelled by settler and, later, British ships. As in the rest of Canada, many of the settlers were Americans, used to taking direct action against Indians and to getting what they wanted. While the details differ, all the white settlements of British Columbia followed a similar pattern. While the above action occurred with the permission of the Crown, which had sold the land, it was completely driven by settlers. In other places, the settlers acted without even this pretence.[69]

For the Indigenous people, this occupation of their land occurred in a context of violence that had been established by the fur trade. The maritime fur trade had been characterised by violence as ship's captains kidnapped or flogged Indigenous people and held them hostage in exchange for furs, fired grapeshot at Native canoes, cannons at villages, and generally extorted wealth from Indigenous people.[70] In the interior, the Hudson's Bay Company and other trading companies relied on 'club law' to settle trade-related disputes, using guns or cutlasses ruthlessly.[71]

The settlement of British Columbia occurred relatively late, with Victoria, the first town, established in 1852. Setting a pattern, the settlement was founded on the site of an Indian village, with the Indians removed across the harbour to a small reserve.[72] Like Atlantic Canada, the colony was settled from the coast, which was already occupied by Indigenous villages that, by the nineteenth century, had long exposure to fur traders. Compared to Newfoundland and Nova Scotia, relatively few Indians were shot.

In the interior, the violence of the fur trade gave way in the late 1850s to the gold rush. The lure of gold in the Fraser Valley and elsewhere drew settlers who also came ahead of any governmental regulation, acting to maximise personal gain, and pushing Indigenous peoples out of their way. Most of the gold miners were also American. This was a different kind of

---

68 Harris C. 2002. *Making Native Space: Colonialism, Resistance, and Reserves in British Columbia*. Vancouver: University of British Columbia Press, xv.
69 Tennant P. 1990. *Aboriginal People and Politics: The Indian Land Question in British Columbia, 1849–1989*. Vancouver: University of British Columbia Press.
70 Gough B. 1984. *Gunboat Frontier: British Maritime Authority and Northwest Coast Indians, 1846–1890*. Vancouver: University of British Columbia Press; Harris, *Reluctant Land*, 421.
71 Loo T. 1994. *Making Law, Order, and Authority in British Columbia, 1821–1871*. Toronto: University of Toronto Press, 18–19.
72 Ibid., xviii.

CHAPTER 3: 'Shooting a Black Duck'

violence, but direct violence underlay the entire process.[73] More Indians were shot or beaten, while others avoided violence by moving away from these settlers.

Settlers and Indian land in Quebec and the North

The dominance of the fur trade in Canadian history is always cited as one of the major reasons why Canadian Indian policy differed from that of the United States. In this trade, the Indians were not only respected and necessary partners but also sharp businessmen, often making large profits from their trade in furs. Indians engaged in the fur trade were not in the way of the agricultural frontier, but were rather partners in a substantial economy. It was, however, a brutal economy as Indigenous peoples competed for furs, often driving rivals off traditional land. The trade was under settler control, with Indians acting as agents or middlemen. The fur traders were a law unto themselves, and their propensity for violence was restrained mostly by their need to return year after year to buy more furs.[74] Given that traders' livelihoods depended on cooperation with the same people year after year, killing them was counterproductive. There was nonetheless substantial violence, corruption and theft in the trade.

The fur trade, like the fisheries, had a long history in Canada, extending from the early 1600s until well into the twentieth century. Over time, it took many forms, some well organised, some rapacious. Indeed, the whole history of the French in Canada merges into the history of the fur trade. At the time of the British capture of French Canada in 1763, there were not more than 60 000 French settlers, with about half of them living in Montreal and Quebec. Some of the settlers were farmers, but these farms were largely confined to the St Lawrence River valley and did not expand across Quebec, leaving the Indians free to move away from the river and away from French settlement, and allowing them largely to be left alone. Most of the French economy in Canada stemmed from the fur trade. The trade took French and Indian fur traders across Canada by the early 1700s, and made many merchants in Montreal and Quebec exceedingly rich. The French colony, with its small population not dependent on an expanding agricultural economy, did not need to dispossess Indians as rapaciously as

---

73 Harris C. 2004. 'How did colonialism dispossess? Comments from the edge of empire', *Annals of the Association of American Geographers*, 94, no. 1, 165–182.

74 Loo, *Making Law*, 18–53.

CIVILIAN-DRIVEN VIOLENCE AND THE GENOCIDE OF INDIGENOUS PEOPLES

British settlers did. After 1763, the British took control of the fur trade in Canada.[75]

By 1900 the fur trade had collapsed in almost all of North America, although it had been diminishing for some time, and had also been moving west and north for two hundred years. As Indians moved beyond the frontier, they could protect their cultures from settler incursion. Once the fur trade ended, these people came upon hard times as traditional hunting, fishing and gathering could no longer feed their families. Northern communities became government-dependent slums, filled with alcoholism and despair. This was indirectly a product of settler colonialism as the fur trade had disrupted their traditional economies.[76]

Their remote location was not enough to protect these Indigenous peoples from further exploitation by settlers as mining, fishing, timber harvesting and other extractive activities moved settlers onto Indian land as well. In the Robinson-Huron Treaties of 1850, a large swathe of northern Ontario, the area north of Lakes Huron and Superior, was purchased by treaty from Indians who resisted the incursions of copper prospectors. Similarly, Treaty 3 (1873) purchased the Rainy River Country of northern Ontario for white settlers who were prospecting there.[77]

Because actual settlement was slow in the north, Indians were able to remain in traditional communities until well into the nineteenth century. But the hunting, trapping and fishing economies were either gone or moving into the hands of settlers. The Indians in this vast region were left to fend for themselves, until their resources failed. With the decline of hunting, trapping and fishing, these communities became impoverished, disease and starvation taking a toll. The Indians were allowed to live on their lands until these were needed for fishing, logging or mining, or for the extraction of whatever natural resources might exist there. These were the last Native peoples to be displaced from their lands, and the displacement occurred at the hands of both individual miners and the corporations that now dominate the north. The Canadian government, anxious to exploit the mineral wealth of the north, facilitated removals, working hand in glove

---

75 Ray A. 1974. *Indians in the Fur Trade: Their Role as Trappers, Hunters, and Middlemen in the Lands Southwest of Hudson Bay, 1660–1870.* Toronto: University of Toronto Press.

76 Tough F. 1996. *As Their Natural Resources Fail: Native Peoples and the Economic History of Northern Manitoba, 1870–1930.* Vancouver: UBC Press.

77 Harring, *White Man's Law*, 130–131. Ma-we-do-pe-nais, a Salteaux, made this point at the first treaty negotiation in 1872: 'We think where we are is our property. The sound of gold is under my feet where I stand; we have a rich country; it is the Great Spirit who gave us this; where we stand upon is the Indians property and belongs to them', 131.

CHAPTER 3: 'Shooting a Black Duck'

with mining interests. The Alberta tar sands are probably the best example of this destruction but by no means the only one. The tar sands, much of which lies on Indian land, is a vast oil-soaked wasteland that will take many generations to recover from mining operations. This has been characterised as yet another act of genocide.[78]

Similarly, uranium mining in northern Ontario in the 1950s and 1960s has been labelled genocide because it caused high levels of cancer and other diseases among aboriginal populations. These mines have long since been abandoned, but the radioactive waste was never cleaned up, leaving the land poisoned for generations to come, with little or no notice given to local bands.[79] Most of northern Canada is now open to industrial development. In fact, Canadian mining and other extractive industries depend on it. Mining and other companies move in, take the land they need, exploit it under licence from the government, then leave an ecologically shattered landscape. Canadian mining companies are among the richest in the world, and engage in the same kind of destruction of Indigenous communities in other parts of the world as well.

Conclusion

First, any attempt to use the concept of genocide must take into account the historical context, as well as the specific behaviour and motivations of perpetrators. The settlement of Canada occurred in diverse historical contexts over four centuries. Settler colonisation of the country, which started in Newfoundland in the 1600s, is still continuing in the Canadian north. Secondly, genocide is a process more than it is a definition. Each genocide is different, and each of its phases may look different. Thirdly, any genocide includes violent actions aimed at destroying the targeted social group. Starting with the killings of Indians in Newfoundland by settlers, and ending with the killing of Indians and in the north, it is clear that genocide occurred in Canada, especially over the last two centuries. The bloodshed was not isolated in time or space, but rather was pervasive. This was a general process that followed the logic of settler colonialism that sought to clear the land for white settlement. Although it took different forms, and

---

78 See especially Huseman J. & Short D. 2012. *Extreme Energy as Genocidal Method: Tar Sands and the Indigenous Peoples of Northern Alberta.* Extreme Energy Initiative Research Paper. Available at http://extrmeenergy.org/files/2013/07/EEI-Tar-Sands-RP. pdf, accessed 29 October 2019.

79 McNamara P. 2011. "'Nuclear genocide" at Serpent River First Nation, Elliot Lake, Ontario'. *Beyond Nuclear*, 26 November. Available at http://www.beyondnuclear.org/uranium-mining/2011/11/26/nuclear-genocide-at-serpent-river, accessed 29 October 2019.

while it might not have been genocidal at every point, the overall outcome can certainly be regarded as such.[80]

Also, it is best to discard the phrase 'cultural genocide' as used in the context of the residential schooling system. Forcibly removing more than 150 000 aboriginal children from their families and communities to beat their cultures out of them; killing perhaps 6000 in the process with many more succumbing to disease and depression; and jailing many of their parents and relatives in order to achieve this end — this is more than cultural genocide. The basic evidence in the report of Canada's Truth and Reconciliation Commission demands this conclusion.[81] While the concept of 'cultural genocide' has meaning and contributed to the genocide, it is also important not to lose sight of the actual violence and murder subsumed under this label. As early as 1907, the report of Dr Peter Bryce on the residential schooling system revealed that in many of the Indian residential schools, large percentages of the student population were dying. In individual schools, typically 25 per cent of students succumbed; in some, the figure was as high as 70 per cent.[82] The government suppressed the report and took no action, although it knew that in Indian residential schools large numbers of the children were dying.[83]

The work of the Truth and Reconciliation Commission is important because it has contributed greatly to introducing the concept of genocide into Canadian national discourse, and in informing people about the experience of Indigenous people. Also, it has enhanced basic understanding of the violence suffered by Indigenous people, especially children. The stories in its *Final Report* are horrific: employees of religious bodies, funded by the Crown, stuck needles through the tongues of aboriginal children who dared speak in their own language; starved children as punishment for dozens

---

80 Woolford A. 2009. 'Ontological destruction: Genocide and Canadian Aboriginal peoples'. *Genocide Studies and Prevention*, 4, no. 1, 81–97.

81 Truth and Reconciliation Commission of Canada. 2015. *The Final Report of the Truth and Reconciliation Commission of Canada. Vol. 6: Reconciliation: Canada's Residential Schools.* Montreal: McGill-Queen's University Press. There are, in all, six volumes in this final report. The massive and thorough nature of the report anticipated the controversy that it would provoke in Canada.

82 Bryce P. 1907. *Report on the Indian Schools of Manitoba and the Northwest Territories.* Ottawa: Government Printing Bureau, 18.

83 Wattam J. 2016. 'Dr Peter Henderson Bryce: A story of courage'. First Nations Child and Family Caring Society of Canada, July. Available at https://fncaringsociety.com/sites/default/files/dr._peter_henderson_bryce_information_sheet.pdf, accessed 29 October 2019.

CHAPTER 3: 'Shooting a Black Duck'

of offences; beat children, often very severely; and sexually abused them.[84] All of this to promote a government agenda of the forced assimilation of Indigenous peoples. Residential schools were promoted as the solution to the 'Indian problem'. The reasoning was that if Indian children could be forcibly assimilated, then there would eventually be no more Indians. Their parents would inevitably die off, and these children would assimilate into communities in Canada where they would be gainfully employed and intermarry.[85] This is not what happened.

What has happened is that Canada has remained divided between Native people living in poverty on isolated reserves across the country, and the rest of the population living in wealth in a handful of crowded urban areas — Canada being among the most urbanised countries in the world. Canada thus consists of two very different societies. Bringing these societies together requires policies sufficiently insightful and benevolent to surmount this genocidal past. Overcoming this past, at the very least, requires a deep understanding of the violence with which Indigenous peoples were dispossessed of their land, and respect for all of the Indigenous lives lost in this process. Here, the use of the term 'genocide' is not meant to be an accusation, but rather an explanation of how Canada got to where it is today. There can be no reconciliation in Canada until the majority comes to understand this and the historical processes behind it.

---

84 It is these stories, in fact, that form the core of the *Final Report*. The Commission viewed it as central to its responsibility to visit as many Indigenous communities as it could, and to hear as many stories as they could find. In the end, they heard over 6700 stories, from all across Canada. Many of these are published in *The Survivors Speak* (2015). See www. trc.ca/.

85 Defining who is an 'Indian' in Canada is left to the Crown, under the Indian Act. In the United States, the Indian nations, as an attribute of their sovereignty, determine their own membership. Thus, in Canada, the Crown has the ultimate power to end Indian status. This discussion is extremely complicated. See Lawrence B. 2003. 'Gender, race, and the regulation of native identity in Canada and the United States: An overview', *Hypatia*, 18, no. 2, 3–31. There are thousands of Indians in both the United States and Canada who have been detribalised, that is, who have lost their status as Indian; see Palmater P. 2014. 'Genocide, Indian policy, and legislated elimination of Indians in Canada', *Aboriginal Policy Studies*, 3, no. 3, 27–54.

CHAPTER FOUR

'An Unbroken Line of Crimes and Blood': Settler Militia and the Extermination and Enslavement of San in the Graaff-Reinet District of the Cape Colony, c. 1776–1825

Lance van Sittert and Thierry Rousset

The growing colony presents on its borders an unbroken line of crimes and blood. Such is the picture of almost every new settlement in an uncivilized country; and the result has almost uniformly been either the extirpation of the original inhabitants, or their degradation to the condition of slaves or of bondsmen.

John Philip, 1828[1]

The missionary John Philip was absolutely clear that the settler militia was the primary instrument of the crimes committed and blood spilt on the north-eastern border of the Cape Colony in the half-century after 1776, more specifically the extirpation and degradation to the condition of slaves or bondsmen of the San. English-speaking historians have been more equivocal for two main reasons.[2] First, there is a commitment to the

---

1 Philip J. 1828. *Researches in South Africa: Illustrating the Civil, Moral and Religious Condition of the Native Tribes*, vol. 1. London: James Duncan, 2.
2 Here we are thinking of, among others, Malherbe V.C. 1978. 'Diversification and Mobility of Khoikhoi Labour in the Eastern Districts of the Cape Colony Immediately Prior to the Labour Law of 1 November 1809'. MA dissertation, University of Cape Town; Newton-King S. & Malherbe V.C. 1981. *The Khoikhoi Rebellion in the Eastern Cape, 1799–1803*. Communication no. 5. Cape Town: Centre for African Studies, University of Cape Town; Szalay M. 1995. *The San and the Colonisation of the Cape, 1770–1879: Conflict, Incorporation, Acculturation*. Köln: Rüdiger Köppe; Malherbe V.C. 1997. 'The Cape Khoisan in the Eastern Districts of the Colony before and after Ordinance 50 of 1828'. PhD dissertation, University of Cape Town; Newton-King S. 1999. *Masters and Servants on the Cape Eastern Frontier*. Cambridge: Cambridge University Press; Penn N. 2005. *The Forgotten Frontier: Colonist and Khoisan on the Cape's Northern Frontier in the 18th Century*. Cape Town: Double Storey; Penn N. 2013. 'The British and the Bushmen: The massacre of the Cape San, 1795 to 1828'. *Journal of Genocide Research*, 15, no. 2, 183–200; McDonald J. 2015. 'Subjects of the Crown: Khoesan Identity and Assimilation in the Cape Colony, c. 1795–1858'. PhD dissertation, University of London.

CHAPTER 4: 'An Unbroken Line of Crimes and Blood'

idea that the changeover from Dutch to British control of the Cape Colony at the end of the eighteenth century marked a qualitative shift away from forced to free labour. San extermination and enslavement does not fit this narrative and, if admitted, exposes it, as Philip pointed out in the 1820s, as a fraud. Secondly, there is a commitment to San agency in making their own history. This outlook is most comfortable in celebrating resistance as the highest expression of individual or collective agency and no more able to accommodate the complete negation of agency by extermination and enslavement than is its companion Whig meta-narrative. The challenge posed by the twinned processes of settler extirpation and enslavement of the San to these respective ideological commitments is usually resolved by lumping the two together; agency is expressed through assimilation by conversion or contract to the new liberal order of the Pax Britannica. Yes, the San disappeared, but they did so by their own choice. Philip's claim of settler culpability thus ironically remains as much a heresy today as it was at the time it was written, and one which Mohamed Adhikari has recently reiterated to similar effect.[3]

A close reading of the Graaff-Reinet archive for the period c. 1776–1825 follows Philip's unbroken line in a specified, although vast and shifting, space over a fifty-year period, to trace the changing processes and practices of settler extermination and enslavement of the San. The administrative district of Graaff-Reinet was created in 1786 out of the eastern extremities of two older districts, Stellenbosch and Swellendam, administered from the south and south-west and with its undefined northern border shading into 'Bushman country'. Two major delimitations followed: the southern third of the district being excised in 1804; and the western and eastern thirds of the remainder in 1825 to form new administrative units, while the rump doubled its size to the north by ingesting part of the 'Bushmen country' and planting its border on the Orange River.[4]

---

3   See Adhikari M. 2010b. 'A total extinction confidently hoped for: The destruction of Cape San society under Dutch colonial rule, 1700–1795'. *Journal of Genocide Research*, 12, no. 1–2, 19–44; Adhikari M. 2011. *Anatomy of a South African Genocide: The Extermination of the Cape San Peoples*. Athens: Ohio University Press; and Adhikari M. ed. 2014. *Genocide on Settler Frontiers: When Hunter-Gatherers and Commercial Stock Farmers Clash*. Cape Town: UCT Press. See also McDonald J. 2016. '"We do not know who painted our pictures": Child transfers and cultural genocide in the destruction of Cape San societies along the Cape Colony's north-eastern frontier, c. 1770–1830'. *Journal of Genocide Research*, 18, no. 4, 519–538.
4   See Smith K.W. 1976. *From Frontier to Midlands: A History of the Graaff-Reinet District, 1786–1910*. Grahamstown: Institute of Social and Economic Research, 1–40.

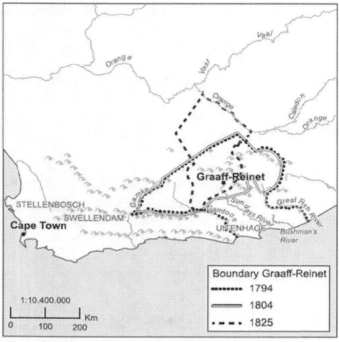

Figure 4.1: Graaff-Reinet District, 1786–1825[5]

In this study, the usual sources are supplemented by two as-yet-unexplored archives: Moodie's unpublished fourth volume of *The Record*, dealing with the crucial period c. 1785–1805, and the Graaff-Reinet tax censuses 1787–1828 (extracted by the Cape Panel project in the Department of Economics at Stellenbosch University and generously made available to us by its principal investigator, Johan Fourie).[6] The new source material provides a comprehensive record of militia expeditions against the San, as well as of San reprisals, which can then be read against the settler tax census data of the district. This confirms Philip's central contention that the militia was the key instrument of settler primitive accumulation through the extirpation and enslavement of the San as Khoisan ('Hottentot') slaves.

---

5   From Cilliers J. & Green E. 2018. 'The land-labour hypothesis in a settler economy: Wealth, labour and household composition on the South African frontier'. *International Review of Social History*, 63, no. 2, 247.

6   See Moodie D. 1838/1839. *The Record or Official Papers Relative to the Condition and Treatment of the Native Tribes of South Africa*. Cape Town: A.S. Robertson (for the published parts) and Cape Town Archives Repository (KAB), VC 871-897 (for drafts of unpublished parts II and IV); Fourie J. & Green E. 2018a. 'Building the Cape of Good Hope Panel'. *History of the Family*, 23, no. 3.

CHAPTER 4: 'An Unbroken Line of Crimes and Blood'

Neither the Khoisan nor the much smaller chattel slave population on settler farms were self-reproducing, requiring regular infusions of new captives to sustain pastoral production. The British demobilisation of the militia and extension of legal protections to the Khoisan through contracting, in response to the mass popular uprising of Khoisan in the east in 1799–1803, created a dual crisis for the militia system of indigenous slavery in Graaff-Reinet by limiting both the supply and exploitation of Khoisan labour. The settler militia was central to the resolution of this crisis, exploiting its remobilisation by the British in 1811 as irregular auxiliaries to the colonial garrison to resume the enslavement of San on the district's open northern border. At the same time, its officers, in their civilian guise, turned the system of contracting to settler advantage as a means of arresting the movement of Khoisan, securing access to their children, and legalising the child slaves generated by the militia's renewed war against the San. The militia officer corps was also instrumental in ending missionary and military recruitment of San and Khoisan labour and in advancing the district's northern border to the Orange River.

Enslaving the San, c. 1770–1798

In the 1770s the eastward movement of European settlers breached two environmental frontiers governing human occupation of the subcontinent; the 350 mm isohyet and the escarpment. In so doing, they were following a route pioneered by Indigenous pastoralists a millennium earlier and entered a world in which pastoralists occupied the forelands and foragers the escarpment, tracking the seasonal shifts in grazing and game.[7] The abundant water, pastures and game on the north-eastern frontier quickly drew settlers, who converted the region into the colony's livestock 'nursery'.[8] Settler pastoralists initially benefited from the practices of coexistence that had been developed to mediate relations between pastoralists and foragers over the *longue duree*, the San's diligent recovery and restoration of stray settler livestock constituting a stock settler narrative of first contact in the

---

7 See Hall S. 1986. 'Pastoral adaptations and forager reactions in the Eastern Cape'. *South African Archaeological Society, Goodwin Series*, 5, 42–49; Hart T. 1989. 'Haaskraal and Volstruisfontein: Late Stone Age Events at Two Rock Shelters in the Zeekoe Valley, Great Karoo, South Africa'. MA dissertation, University of Cape Town; Neville D. 1996. 'European Impacts on the Seacow River Valley and its Hunter-Gatherer Inhabitants, AD 1770–1900'. MA dissertation, University of Cape Town.

8 See Barrow J. 1806. *Travels Into the Interior of Southern Africa*. Vol. 1. London: T. Cadell & W. Davies, 189 & 204.

CIVILIAN-DRIVEN VIOLENCE AND THE GENOCIDE OF INDIGENOUS PEOPLES

region.[9] Such inviting circumstances led to a rush of poorer settlers into the northeast who, in addition to the wealth of other pastoral resources, also looked upon the resident San as a source of slave labour and the militia warband as its means of production. The settler militia or commando had successfully displaced the Khoi and San from the arid plains in the west by seizing scarce permanent water sources, but the mountainous terrain and abundance of permanent water in the north-east blunted this militia strategy, enabling the San to force the abandonment of the initial settler land seizures on the escarpment.[10] As the *landdrost* (magistrate), *heemraden* (councillors) and militia officers of the Stellenbosch District explained to the governor at the end of 1773, 'in consequence of the great extent of the mountains in the said countries, it is impossible to attack the said Hottentots at one and the same time, by the small number of men under the orders of the respective field corporals, without entirely denuding the country of its means of defence, and exposing it to the depredations, in other quarters, of another gang of Bosjesmans Hottentots'.[11]

The need to force the door on the escarpment against San resistance along the northern frontier led to the 'institutionalisation' of the settler militia by the Dutch East India Company government in 1774 to increase its size, as well as its spatial and temporal reach.[12] The small settler adult male population available for conscription was doubled by making settler-dependent 'Bastard' and Khoisan adult male servants also subject to commando requisition. More than just increasing the number of fighters, Bastards and Khoisan provided the reorganised militia with vital intelligence and skirmishing capacities it lacked in the new terrain, being employed as 'spies' and to assault fortified forager settlements in caves and on mountain tops. A new form of mass militia mobilisation, the 'general

---

9   See Bradlow E. & Bradlow F., eds. 1979. *William Somerville's Narrative of His Journeys to the Eastern Cape Frontier and to Lattakoe, 1799–1802.* Cape Town: Van Riebeeck Society, 26–27; Sparrman A. 1977. *A Voyage to the Cape of Good Hope: Towards the Antarctic Polar Circle, and Round the World but Chiefly into the Country of the Hottentots and Caffres, from the Year 1772 to 1776.* vol. 2. Cape Town: Van Riebeeck Society, 113 for this narrative.

10 See Guelke L. & Shell R. 1992. 'Landscape of conquest: Frontier water alienation and Khoikhoi strategies of survival 1652–1780'. *Journal of Southern African Studies*, 18, no. 4, 803–824.

11 Bergh M.A. 1838/1839 'Extract of records of a meeting of the combined boards of landdrost and heemraden, and landdrost and militia officers of Stellenbosch, 28 December 1773'. In Moodie, *Record*, part III, 19–20.

12 See Penn, *Forgotten Frontier*, 111 for the quote and Roux P.E. 1925. 'Die vedigingstelsel aan die Kaap onder die Hollandse-Oosindiese Kompanje, 1652–1795'. MA dissertation, University of Stellenbosch, for a history of the settler militia during the Dutch period.

CHAPTER 4: 'An Unbroken Line of Crimes and Blood'

commando', was also created, along with new ranks to command it, and a Company ammunition subsidy to keep it in the field for weeks rather than days.[13] Slave production was also written into the founding charter of the new model militia. The Company deemed war captives an unavoidable by-product of its operation, and instructed that some be divided 'among the poorest of the inhabitants ... in order to continue to serve them for a fixed and equitable term of years, in consideration of their receiving proper maintenance'.[14] In reality, the settler militia retained all its war captives, the great majority women and children, and divided them among members of the commando, many of whom had been conscripted from among the poorest of the inhabitants. For the latter, the militia was a vital collective form of frontier bootstrap capitalism, forging Indigenous slave labour from the San in the furnace of war.

By simultaneously reproducing and collapsing the racialised male hierarchy of the farm in the field, the new model militia also brought to the surface its barely sublimated tensions. Settlers worried about the levelling effects on their authority and social status of the Khoisan's right to bear arms that came with militia service. The threat from below was often imagined as a mass uprising and inversion of the settler social order in which the indigenes took over settler land and women.[15] Thus the initial settler request to the Company for material support included both 90 quality guns for the newly conscripted Khoisan, who had long been forbidden from owning firearms, and '3 chests, covered with painted canvas, and provided with locks, in order to keep the same locked up and secured at night from the accompanying Hottentots [Khoisan]'.[16] The hard manual labour of commando duty, like that of pastoral farming, depended on Khoisan, but settlers were also always deeply mistrustful of them in both these capacities. They constantly worried that Khoisan herders and 'skuts' (shooters) were conspiring with San stock thieves and bandits. As they told Barrow in 1797, the Khoisan servant 'takes the first opportunity that offers of escaping to his countrymen, and

---

13 Bergh, 'Extract of records, 28 December 1773', in Moodie, *Record*, part III, 19–20.
14 Ibid.
15 See, for example, Theal G.M. 1904. *Records of the Cape Colony*. Vol. 4. London: William Clowes & Sons Ltd, 'Provisional justification of Honoratus Christiaan David Maynier in his quality as commissary of the District of Graaff Reinet, concerning several accusations preferred against him, with the investigation of which a special commission appointed by the government is at present occupied in', 320–323; Theal, *Records*, vol. 7. 'Lieutenant Colonel Collins to the Earl of Caledon, 6 August 1809', 116.
16 Bergh, 'Copy of a letter from the combined boards of landdrost and heemraden, and landdrost and militia officers, Stellenbosch, to Governor van Plettenberg and Council, 19 April 1774'. In Moodie, *Record*, part III, 25–26.

contrives frequently to carry off a musquet, and powder and ball. With tales of cruelty he excites them to revenge; he assists them in their plans of attack; tells them the strength of the whole district, and of individuals; the number of their cattle, and of the advantages and the dangers that will occur in the attempt to carry them off; puts them in possession of the manner in which expeditions are conducted against them; and, in short, of everything he knows respecting the colonists.[17] The official 'Hottentot'/'Bushman' binary was blurred on the north-eastern frontier, where settlers used the terms interchangeably and in combination and set more store by what they called the 'faithfulness' of servants.[18] Thus Jacob Erasmus, after being relieved of 60 cattle and 300 sheep, lamented that 'the worst is that I am obliged to arm them [Indigenous slaves] with so much powder and lead that I would be in great danger if they prove unfaithful.'[19]

The 'faithfulness' of Indigenous slaves was a function of their owner's wealth, which determined the resources they had to dispense beyond their immediate kin. The first enumeration of Khoisan on settler farms in Graaff-Reinet in 1805 revealed that the top 11.8 per cent (hereafter rounded up to top 12 per cent) of settler household heads (or 132 out of 1 121) controlled one-third of all livestock and with it more than half the Khoisan employees in the district, namely, 54.5 per cent (see Table 4.1).

Table 4.1: Percentage distribution of settler labour and property in the Graaff-Reinet district by number of Khoisan employed, 1805[20]

	Number of Khoisan employed			
	(a) < 10	(b) 10–19	(c) ≥ 20	(b) + (c)
Settlers	88.1	8.9	2.9	11.8
Khoisan	45.5	33.5	21.0	54.5
Slaves	58.9	25.4	15.7	41.1
Horses	68.0	19.9	12.1	32.0
Cattle	65.7	21.9	12.4	34.3
Sheep	67.1	22.4	10.5	32.9
Goats	71.8	18.2	10.0	28.2

17 Barrow, *Travels*, vol. 1, 190.
18 Bergh, 'Record of meeting, 19 April 1774'. In Moodie, *Record*, part III, 22–23, 25–26.
19 See KAB, VC 886, Jacob Erasmus, Veldwagtmeester, Tarka, 7 February 1793.
20 Calculated from data contained in Graaff-Reinet Tax Censuses, 1787–1828.

CHAPTER 4: 'An Unbroken Line of Crimes and Blood'

The 88.2 per cent of settlers having just two-thirds of the collective pastoral wealth had on average only two Khoisan per household, half the district average and only one tenth the household average of the top 12 per cent. Lacking the means, these settlers depended on coercion to secure and retain labour against the centripetal pull of the top 12 per cent. Thus the 88.2 per cent of 'common men' owned three-fifths of the slaves in the district and employed a Khoisan population, two-thirds of whom were adult. The demographic skewing of the latter, despite having the same sex ratio as the Khoisan employed by the top 12 per cent, suggests its origins in militia slaving, the first two slave generations having graduated to adulthood by 1805, while the third was serving its youth apprenticeship.[21] If the 'faithfulness' of the Khoisan of the top 12 per cent was secured through their incorporation into the extended households of their patrons, that of the rest, more or less forcibly attached to settler households barely able to reproduce themselves, was always tenuous and in doubt. The Company initially assuaged this doubt by prohibiting Khoisan from owning guns and horses, but by the 1770s could no longer afford to indulge settler fears and ordered that they be armed.[22]

As the settlers' firearm monopoly broke down, not only in the field but also on the farm, where San attacks on their livestock made it increasingly necessary for them to arm herders, so too did their sense of safety and security. This was further eroded by the desertion of slaves and killing of herders, which, by the end of the 1780s, had also made firearms available to San. The experience of being fired on in the field with guns by Khoisan, first reported in 1789, signalled the final levelling of a colonial hierarchy marked and maintained as much by technological monopolies as by race.[23] The settlers' other legislated technological monopoly was horses, a weapon made redundant by the mountainous terrain of the north-east, where success in the field depended on stealth, not speed. The horse was also an expensive weapon, owing to its acute susceptibility to the endemic horse sickness, which required settlers to remount themselves annually, at an estimated cost of 50–100 rix-dollars for a well-trained animal.[24] They reportedly also would

---

21 A slave generation was 14 years, thus two full generations had passed by 1805 since the start of militia slaving in the north-east in c. 1770.

22 See Sparrman, Voyage, vol. 1, 227–228, for the 1755 ban on Khoisan owning guns.

23 See KAB, VC 886, P.E. Kruger, Veldwagtmeester Sneeuberg to the Landdrost Graaff-Reinet, 6 November 1789 and 26 December 1789, for the first reports of settlers being fired on with guns by San.

24 See KAB, VC 886, Extract from records of landdrost and heemraden of Graaff-Reinet, 5 January 1789; Combined meeting of heemraaden and military court Graaff-Reinet, 21 December 1791.

CIVILIAN-DRIVEN VIOLENCE AND THE GENOCIDE OF INDIGENOUS PEOPLES

need at least three remounts for up to six weeks in the field as required by the new general commandos.[25] This was an investment few settlers could afford. The greater majority, up to 80 per cent, could manage no more than one horse and about 10 per cent of settlers owned none at all.[26] The animal's role in the reorganised militia was largely symbolic rather than real, to differentiate settlers from the Khoisan, who were forbidden from owning horses and consequently served on foot. The overdetermination of the horse as a totem of settler identity was reflected in the use of the term 'murdered' for those horses killed by San, and in the acceptance by militia officers that not having a horse was a valid reason for settlers' refusing a call-up.[27] The intimate relation between settlers and their equines was not lost on the San either. They killed one settler horse on the farm for every one they stole, compared to just one in ten cattle and sheep.[28]

The general commando was distinguished from the traditional commando by its greater size and operating regionally rather than locally for periods of a month to six weeks at a time. Because of this scaling-up, the general commando also required its own commissariat over and above the roughly one week's subsistence that the individual militiaman was traditionally expected to provide and transport themselves. Wealthier farmers, easily able to insulate themselves and their sons from militia service through substitution by Khoisan retainers, were also expected to provision the militia and provide wagon transport for its commissariat, ammunition and booty in the field. Shut out from a direct share in war captives by their non-participation in commando, the wealthy nonetheless sought to claim a share of its slave booty by bluntly asserting the equivalence of their capital risk to the lives ordinary settlers staked to claim a share as co-adventurers. In 1792 the district administration duly informed settlers that, in future, 'Those who furnish oxen and wagons are to share in the allotment of Bushmen prisoners, equally with those who serve personally on the Commandoes ... When the men present on the Commando, and the owners of oxen and wagons employed on it, shall have received by lot each, one Bushman, and no more, the remaining prisoners shall be distributed among those who

---

25 See KAB, VC 886, Extract, 5 January 1789, for the need for at least three horses on general commando.
26 Calculated from data contained in Graaff-Reinet Tax Censuses, 1787–1828.
27 See Burchell W. 1824. *Travels in the Interior of Southern Africa.* Vol. 2. London: Longman, 83–84.
28 Calculated from data contained in KAB, VC 872–898.

94

CHAPTER 4: 'An Unbroken Line of Crimes and Blood'

have contributed to the expenses.'[29] The 'common men' were also sternly admonished to 'not leave the wagons behind, but take care of them that no one may be thus deterred from supplying wagons'.[30] All this pointed to growing class differentiation in settler society on the frontier, slackening kinship bonds, and the erosion of customary principles of co-adventuring.

The newly reorganised and subsidised militia took the field for the first time in 1774.[31] It depended on its Khoisan spies to locate San settlements for ambush. More than 1 000 San were killed and over 350 captured in the first decade in a rough 3:1 ratio that remained constant until the end of the eighteenth century.[32] This ratio suggests that militia slaving — killing three-quarters of the San it encountered and capturing only one in four — was economically inefficient. This inefficiency was structural and reflected social rather than economic utility. The militia was drawn from a settler population of less than 1 000 adult males bound together by ties of kinship and religion, which aided its organisation and discipline but also made it highly averse to taking casualties. Militia officers were thus sternly admonished to 'not pursue ... [the San] in an inconsiderate manner, and expose their men to needless danger' and to always attack 'in such a cautious manner ... that our own inhabitants may be as little as possible exposed to danger, and not rashly led to slaughter'.[33] They were also granted wide powers to make treaties, recognise chiefs and allocate them land on the Company's behalf in preference to violence. The militia officer's obedience to this injunction was reflected in the militia's preferred strategy of ambush and reliance on its Khoisan auxiliaries for all scouting and close-quarter skirmishing.[34] The settler militia thus always retreated or negotiated if outnumbered and attacked only when guaranteed the element of surprise. Its greatest leaders were celebrated for their trickster ability to conjure opportunities for ambush violence out of the rituals of retreat or negotiation. Such inbuilt

---

29 KAB, VC 886, Extract from the Records of the Military Court Graaff-Reinet, 7 February 1792.

30 KAB, VC 886, Extract, 7 February 1792.

31 Bergh, 'Copy of letter, 19 April 1774', 25–26.

32 Calculated from the data contained in Moodie, *Record*, and KAB, VC 872–888. To justify their 75 per cent kill rate and to pass off slaving as self-defence, the militia inflated the martial prowess of the San, portraying them as fearless warriors who would rather die than surrender.

33 See 'Instructions — according to which the newly-appointed field commandant Godlieb Rudolph Opperman shall have to regulate his conduct upon the expedition about to attack the Bosjesmans Hottentots, who still continue to commit murder and robbery, 19 April 1774', in Moodie, *Record*, vol. 3, 29.

34 See, for example, 'Provisional justification of Honoratus Christiaan David Maynier', 286, 306, 328, for the importance of Khoisan labour to the success of the settler militia.

risk aversion, coupled with the Company ammunition subsidy, predisposed the militia to overkill, yielding a killed-to-capture ratio that was socially, if not economically, efficient. Settler casualties from militia slaving were all but non-existent. Militia overkill was further structurally conditioned by the need of settlers to create sufficient levels of natal alienation in San war captives to enable their enslavement en masse and *in situ*.[35] The natal alienation of massacre served both to condition child captives to accept their enslavement and to lure their mothers after them to share in it, 'for it has been observed, that the mothers can seldom persuade themselves to flee from their tender offspring. The amiable tenderness of the mother ... is the very circumstance laid hold on by her persecutors, in order to rivet the chains of this wretched female so much the faster'.[36]

The establishment of the new administrative district and drostdy of Graaff-Reinet at the foot of the north-eastern escarpment in 1786 enabled the intensification of militia slaving by improving its discipline and resupply.[37] The new district administration purchased two wagons from the public purse for the militia, required every settler adult male to arm themselves with 'proper weapons' and Company-issue ammunition, and threatened heavy fines for officers and men who failed to muster when ordered, or who went to Cape Town without permission.[38] General commandos followed annually for the next decade, being closely integrated into the annual agricultural cycle. This saw the militia mobilised locally in summer in defence of the new season's crop of lambs and calves, and in a general commando during winter when severe cold forced San to light fires and so reveal the location of their settlements (see Figure 4.2).

Commando activity was seasonally suppressed by horse sickness in autumn (March–May) and the labour demands of cultivation and travel to Cape Town in spring (September–November). The proximity of a landdrost and company arsenal greatly improved the militia's output of war captives, enabling it to kill more than 3 500 San and capture over 1 000 in a decade and a half after 1786, in the same 3:1 ratio as during the 1770s.[39]

The militia's capture ratio, however, declined steadily as a consequence both of San flight and defensive reorganisation in response to slaving. The latter took the form of a shift from dispersed to concentrated settlements

---

35 Newton-King, *Masters and Servants*, 122–127.
36 Sparrman, *Voyage*, vol. 1, 200–201.
37 See Smith, *From Frontier to Midlands*, 1–40.
38 KAB, VC 886, Colonial Secretary to Landdrost Graaff-Reinet, 1 September 1786; Extract of Records of Military Court Graaff-Reinet, 14 November 1786 and 3 June 1788.
39 Compiled from data contained in KAB, VC 872–898.

CHAPTER 4: 'An Unbroken Line of Crimes and Blood'

located in raised defensible positions, such as caves or mountain tops, the acquisition of firearms and attacks on settler farms.[40] The need to feed and defend their new concentrated settlements led to a surge in San raiding settler herds and farms, the former for food and the latter for firearms and ammunition. More than 110 000 head of livestock, of which 84.1 per cent consisted of sheep, were killed or taken by San raiders in the decade and a half from 1786.[41] In addition, nearly 400 farm Khoisan and chattel slaves were killed by San raiders, mostly while herding livestock. More than 50 farms suffered arson attacks, and over 75 firearms were taken during this period. Khoisan and slaves deserting to the San further added to this arsenal, as did the illegal settler traffic in Company arms and ammunition across the frontier.[42] The settler militia's aversion to casualties greatly magnified the impact of San firearms.[43]

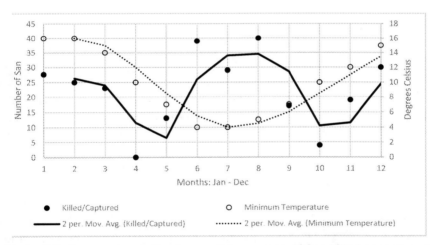

Figure 4.2: Seasonal variation in monthly average of San killed or captured in the Graaff-Reinet district, 1786–1799[44]

---

40 See Sparrman, *Voyage*, vol. 2, 110–111, for San population concentration.
41 Calculated from data contained in KAB, VC 872–898.
42 See 'Diefstal van buskruit', 21–22 July 1794, in Naude S.D. & Venter P.J. 1949. *Kaapse Plakkaatboek*. Part 4. Cape Town: *Cape Times*, 242, for the theft of Company gunpowder and 'Verbod op die verkoop en veruil van gewere, kruit en lood aan Basters en Hottentote', 13 July–1 October 1792 105, for the reissue, at the request of the Graaff-Reinet settlers, of the mid-eighteenth-century prohibition on the sale of arms and ammunition to indigenes.
43 See Storey W.K. 2008. *Guns, Race and Power in Colonial South Africa*. Cambridge: Cambridge University Press. Khoisan skill with firearms had sometime been acquired through prior settler and militia service.
44 Compiled from data contained in KAB, VC 872–898.

The San's defensive response to militia slaving, including the emergence of armed and mounted Khoisan commandos by the mid-1790s, greatly increased the production cost of slaves to individual settlers, not just in the increased investment of farm labour and assets in militia service for a diminished or even no return in slaves, but also from the San threat to their unprotected farms during their absence.[45] The latter's use of firearms and attack in numbers on multiple fronts against farms required several shooters to defend a farmhouse successfully, making settlers ever more reluctant to leave their own farms or immediate vicinity, especially for extended periods of slaving in other wards. As a result, a growing number of settlers refused militia conscription, offering a variety of excuses in which their poverty was the recurring refrain, leading in turn to a high turnover in militia officers. Growing non-compliance and resignations from its officer corps in turn eroded the militia's slave production capacity, in both its local and general incarnations, further steepening the decline in slave production.[46] Settlers flatly refused a Company proposal to establish a 35-strong armed and mounted Bastard militia to police the district, nor were they prepared to foot the estimated annual bill of 55 000 rix-dollars required to keep a 225-strong settler militia permanently in the field.[47]

Increasing land prices extruded poorer settlers to the district's northern and eastern borders where their rudimentary settlements formed straggling breastworks along the open San slaving frontier, protecting the lives and property of the top 12 per cent by absorbing the escalating costs of militia service and San raiding.[48] The ability of the poorest households to do so was severely constrained by their being mired in debt, including to the Company for land rent arrears. They were also subject to imminent ruination from a successful San raid. By the early 1790s these 'common men' were demanding land rent relief and an open frontier in the east as the price of their continued militia service. The Company refused and pushed

---

45 See, for example, KAB, VC886, Extract from the Records of Landdrost and Heemraaden, 10 May 1790 and 3 May 1792, for Graaff-Reinet Heemraaden meeting quarterly and resigning their positions because they were unwilling to be absent from their farms owing to the threat of San attacks.

46 See KAB, VC 886, Extracts from the Records of the Landdrost and Military Court Graaff-Reinet, 21 June 1791; 6 September 1791; 11 January 1794 and Landdrost Woeke to Veldwagtmeester Bester, 6 February 1792, for threats to prosecute militia officers for failing to order and lead commandos.

47 KAB, VC 886, Combined Meeting of Heemraaden and Military Court Graaff-Reinet, 21 December 1791. The proposed settler–Khoisan ratio of the latter was 2:1.

48 See Sampson C.G., Sampson B.E. & Neville D. 1994. 'An early Dutch settlement pattern on the north east frontier of the Cape Colony'. *South African Archaeological Bulletin*, 3, no. 2, 74–81.

CHAPTER 4: 'An Unbroken Line of Crimes and Blood'

instead for their greater incorporation into its tax net.[49] Denied relief, the Zuurveld militias went into rebellion in 1795, calling themselves 'the voice of the people' (*Die Volkstem*) and marching under the republican banner of co-adventuring.[50] They appointed their own *landdrost* and *heemraden* and proposed a revision to the customary division of militia spoils that would allow them to convert the captive labour of their San prisoners into slave capital.[51] In 1790 already, the 'common men' wanted the Company to pay a bounty of 20–30 rix-dollars per head on war captives sent to Cape Town as a means of encouraging their 'additional vigilance and exertion on Commando [and] to procure in this way some compensation for their losses'. Now they demanded the right to capitalise their war captives in their own names:

> The slowness of the inhabitants in the performance of commandoes being spoken of it was unanimously resolved humbly to request the Government that hence forth all such inhabitants of this District ordered on commandoes, as should produce to the landdrost or secretary, a certificate from the leader that they had been present in action against the plundering Bushmen nation should be graciously permitted after payment of 10 rds, or such other sum as should be thought fair, into the Company's chest, for each prisoner, to dispose of the same by legal transfer, even as a slave. It is thought that the departed military ardour would thus be at once restored. The enemy would be more eagerly beaten or slain and the inhabitants relieved from the payment to foreign nations of the enormous sums now paid for slaves.[52]

The Company agreed to the right to 25 years' indenture for captives registered with the *landdrost*, and the new British regime wrote off land rent arrears in a desperate bid to ensure that poor settlers did not 'desert their places, and leave an open entrance to the enemy' — all to no avail.[53]

---

49 See, for example, KAB, VC 886, Extract from Records of Landdrost and Heemraden of Graaff-Reinet, 5 January 1789; Extract from the Records of the Landdrost and Heemraaden Graaff-Reinet, 1 November 1790; Memorial of Adriaan van Jaarsveld submitted to the Board of Landdrost and Heemraaden and Military Court, Graaff-Reinet, 12 July 1791 and Combined Meeting of Heemraaden and Military Court Graaff-Reinet, 21 December 1791.

50 Marais J.S. 1944. *Maynier and the First Boer Republic*. Cape Town: Maskew Miller.

51 KAB, VC 886, Extract from the Records of the Landdrost and Heemraaden Graaff-Reinet, 16 March 1795, and Extract from the Records of the Military Court Graaff-Reinet, 2 June 1795.

52 See KAB, VC886, Combined Meeting of Heemraaden and Military Court Graaff-Reinet, 21 December 1791, for the first demand, and Extract from the Records of the Landdrost and Heemraaden Graaff-Reinet, 16 March 1795, for the second.

53 See KAB, VC 886, Extract from the Records of the Military Court GR, 7 February 1792, for the quote, and Extract from the Records of the Military Court Graaff-

Graaff-Reinet's frontier breastwork of poorer settlers were the areas of greatest settler labour hunger and coercion, and whose Khoisan population was largely derived from, and supplemented by, recently enslaved San. The latter took the opportunity of the republican rebellion to desert in growing numbers across the frontier, often taking firearms and horses with them. The settler militias, already starved of ammunition by the 1795 rebellion and collapse of Company rule, now faced San strengthened and resupplied by former Khoisan spies and skirmishers. Little wonder, then, that settler militia were repeatedly routed in the field by commandos of their erstwhile Indigenous slaves during a burgeoning Khoisan uprising in the east at the end of the eighteenth century. As a result, the colonial frontier was rolled back a third of the way to Cape Town and nearly 500 settler farms were destroyed.[54] The new British regime, alarmed at the defeat of settler militias and the collapse of settler farming in the east, and fearing a repeat of the Haitian revolution, hastily sued for peace with the Khoisan militias, offering the demobilisation of the settler militia, land and legal protection in exchange for their return to settler farms. [55]

The solitude of peace, 1799–1824

In the wake of the collapse of the defensive network provided by poorer settlers along the district's borders, the settler top 12 per cent extended a hand of patronage to the San, offering livestock in return for an end to raiding and residence on settler farms.[56] The first San refugees to accept the offer began to settle on Graaff-Reinet farms in the winter of 1798, leading to their owners' being denounced for their treachery and vilified by the 'common men'.[57] The new British rulers were quick to adopt this ad hoc

---

Reinet, 2 June 1795, for 25 years' indenture conditional upon registration.

54 See Newton-King & Malherbe, *The Khoikhoi Rebellion*; Malherbe V.C. 1980. 'David Stuurman: Last chief of the Hottentots'. *African Studies*, 39, no. 1, 47–64; Malherbe V.C. 1982. 'Hermanus and his sons: Khoi bandits and conspirators in the post-rebellion period, 1803–1818'. *African Studies*, 41, no. 2, 189–202.

55 See 'Provisional justification of Honoratus Christiaan David', 292, for the fear of a repeat of San Domingo.

56 See KAB, VC 888, T.P. van der Walt to the Landdrost Graaff-Reinet, 3 October 1798, and Landdrost Graaff-Reinet to T. van der Walt, 18 November 1798, for the first evidence of livestock gifting to the San in Graaff-Reinet; Sampson C.G. 1995. 'Acquisition of European livestock by the Seacow River Bushmen between AD 1770–1890'. *South African Field Archaeology*, 4, no. 1, 30–36; and McGranaghan M. 2015. 'Hunters-with-sheep: The /Xam Bushmen of South Africa between pastoralism and foraging'. *Africa*, 85, no. 3, 521–545, for the archaeological evidence and the practice in the west of the colony.

57 See, for example, 'Journal of a tour made by Lieutenant Colonel Richard Collins to the north-eastern boundary, the Orange River and the Storm Mountains', in Theal, *Records,*

CHAPTER 4: 'An Unbroken Line of Crimes and Blood'

local practice of the top 12 per cent as official policy, withdrawing the settler militia's ammunition subsidy and autonomy of action to force obedience on the 'common men' with the intention that:

> As soon as a quiet intercourse shall have been by these means established, the feldwachtmeesters ... shall endeavour to persuade the Bosjesmen to consider themselves as under the protection and authority of the English government, and to appoint chiefs or captains of their own nations over them, which are to be distinguished by metal-headed canes and brass gorgets, in the same manner as the chiefs and captains of the other Hottentot tribes, dependent on the government. A sufficient district beyond the Sack River, towards the Kareeberg or Mountains shall be traced and assigned to the Bosjesmen, to inhabit and be acknowledged and respected as such by both parties ... The Bosjesmen are then to be left in possession of their just rights and habitations and are not to be molested, nor their children taken from them, or made slaves or servants of, on any pretence whatsoever.[58]

Two years later, the Khoisan were also offered their own land on mission stations or the eastern front, and protection from settler rapaciousness on the farms. *Landdrosts* were instructed —

> [t]o see that a Register of the Hottentots, Men, Women and Children who are employed in the service of the different farmers is established and kept at the Drostdy by the Landrost in which is to be specified the names of the parties, Farmer and Hottentot, with the age condition and term of service of the latter, and the Landrost is likewise instructed not to suffer with impunity any acts of Violence or Cruelty as have been usual on the part of the Farmers towards the Hottentot.[59]

While hundreds of Khoisan chose to leave the district, the mission stations or the military, some 400 signed contracts to return to settler farms, with 70 per cent demanding remuneration in livestock.[60] That the San were willing to settle for the paltry comforts and tenuous security offered by the new policies of settler reconciliation and restraint is a stark indicator of the decimation of their societies by the decades of exterminatory violence and

---

vol. 7, 23, for the Van der Walts being driven out of Tarka. See 'Collins to Caledon', 117, 121, for gifting as conspiracy and sign of settler fear.

58 Proclamation of Lord Macartney, 24 July 1798, in Theal, *Records*, vol. 7, 116–117.

59 See 'Tour made by Lieutenant Colonel Richard Collins', 20–57, for the offer of land, and Major General Dundas to Sir George Yonge in Theal, *Records*, vol. 3, 51, for the quote. See also Major General Dundas, Answers to Questions proposed by Sir George Yonge relative to the District of Graaff-Reinet, 24 February 1800, in Theal, *Records*, vol. 3, 67.

60 See Newton-King, *Masters and Servants*, for an analysis of these more than 400 contracts.

slaving visited on them by bands of musket-wielding horsemen on both sides of the frontier.

Only the top 12 per cent had the livestock means to accommodate the new British labour regimes of San gifting and Khoisan contracting. The 'common men' had barely sufficient means to subsist and certainly no surplus with which to either attract the San or remunerate the Khoisan. They relied instead on coercion to secure their labour supply through the militia's capturing San children and their permanent detention on the farm into adulthood as Khoisan. As an official visitor reported in 1809, a decade after the introduction of labour contracting:

> [T]he measure which I conceive of the first importance to the protection of the Hottentot and the improvement of his situation, is a sacred observance of his annual engagement. A Hottentot can now seldom get away at the expiration of his term. If he should happen not to be in debt to his master, which he must have more caution than is characteristic of his race to prevent, he is not allowed to take his children, or he is detained under some frivolous pretence, such as that of cattle having died through his neglect, and he is not permitted to satisfy any demands of this nature otherwise than by personal service.[61]

Day-to-day docility on the farm was induced through narcotic addiction. Only the top 12 per cent produced alcohol, the 'common men' cultivating cannabis for this purpose. Thompson reported from the Agter Sneeuberg in 1823 that —

> [w]e found a large quantity of the herb called dacha, a species of hemp, hung up on the rafters [in settler houses]. The leaves of this plant are eagerly sought after by the slaves and Hottentots to smoke, either mixed with tobacco or alone. It possesses much more powerfully stimulating qualities than tobacco, and speedily intoxicates those who smoke it profusely, sometimes rendering them for a time quite mad. This inebriating effect is in fact the quality for which these poor creatures prize it. But the free use of it, just like opium, and all such powerful stimulants, is exceedingly pernicious, and gives the appearance of old age in a few years to its victims. It is, therefore, the more extraordinary, that the whites, who seldom use the dacha themselves, should cultivate it for their servants. But it is, I believe, as an inducement to retain the wild Bushmen in their service, whom they have made captives at an

---

61 'Collins to Caledon', 111.

CHAPTER 4: 'An Unbroken Line of Crimes and Blood'

early age in their commandoes—most of these people being extremely addicted to the smoking of dacha.[62]

With the demobilisation of the militia and the granting of legal protection, Khoisan labour gravitated inexorably to the settler top 12 per cent, whose share of the total rose from 54.5 per cent in 1805 to 61.1 per cent by 1825, creating an acute and worsening labour shortage among the majority of settlers with fewer than ten Khoisan. Their average labour per capita was half the district average and declined by 20 per cent between 1810 and 1815 (see Table 4.2b).

Table 4.2a: Percentage distribution of Khoisan labour in the Graaff-Reinet district by number of Khoisan employed, 1805–1825[63]

		1805	1810	1815	1820	1825
(a)	<10	45.5	43.3	48.0	37.4	38.9
(b)	10–19	33.5	31.7	33.0	39.4	38.9
(c)	≥20	21.0	25.0	19.0	23.2	22.2
(b) + (c)	Top 12%	54.5	57.7	52.0	62.6	61.1

Table 4.2b: Average Khoisan labour per settler by number of Khoisan employed, 1805–1825

	1805	1810	1815	1820	1825
<10	2.04	2.02	1.66	1.96	1.99
10–19	14.8	14.0	14.9	14.4	13.6
≥20	28.1	28.3	28.2	27.6	26.7
Average	3.9	4.1	3.1	4.4	4.3

This sudden sharp decline, not felt by the top 12 per cent at all, was the result of the mass exodus of Khoisan from the hardscrabble farms of the 'common men' to the mission stations established on the district's northern border in 1814–1815, and its recovery by 1820 from the abolition of these

---

62 Thompson G. 1967. *Travels and Adventures in Southern Africa*. Vol. 1. Cape Town: Van Riebeeck Society, 52. See also Sampson C.G. 1993. 'Zeer grote liefhebbers van tobak: Nicotine and cannabis dependency of the Seacow River Bushmen'. *The Digging Stick*, 10, no. 1, 2–6.
63 Calculated from data contained in Graaff-Reinet Tax Censuses, 1787–1828.

missions in 1818.[64] The reproductive capacity of this population was also impaired by its low operational sex ratio of sexually receptive males to sexually receptive females. In addition, the fragmentation of this population averaging just two per farm over the first quarter of the nineteenth century, its tightly constrained mobility, the heavy labour demands made on it and poor subsistence greatly restricted their ability to reproduce.

Table 4.3a: Operational sex ratios of male:female among Khoisan labourers in the Graaff-Reinet district by number of Khoisan employed, 1805–1825[65]

	1805	1810	1815	1820	1825
<10	1.28	1.17	1.00	1.05	0.98
10–19	1.33	1.27	1.13	1.08	1.10
≥20	1.30	1.21	1.26	1.21	1.15
Average	1.30	1.21	1.08	1.10	1.06

Table 4.3b: Percentage of children in Khoisan labouring population in the Graaff-Reinet district by number of Khoisan employed, 1805–1825

	1805	1810	1815	1820	1825
<10	28.7	34.6	34.7	38.7	39.1
10–19	45.4	41.7	41.3	46.0	46.6
≥20	48.5	46.7	48.6	47.1	49.4
Average	37.6	39.9	39.5	43.5	44.3

Rather than being self-reproducing, the Khoisan population of the 'common men' depended for its replenishment and growth on labour secured through participation in the annual slaving expeditions of the settler militia against the San. As the *landdrost* explained in 1807, 'the Hottentots ... [were] mostly generated from the Bosjesmans', or as his successor put it in the 1820s, the San were 'at length ... confounded with the Hottentots, [and] often bind themselves voluntarily by contract'.[66] The first official enumeration of San,

---

64 See Schoeman K. 1993. 'Die Londense Sendinggenootskap en die San: Die Stasies Toornberg en Hephzibah, 1814–1818'. *South African Historical Journal*, 28, no. 1, 221–234.
65 Calculated from data contained in Graaff-Reinet Tax Censuses, 1787–1828.
66 'Earl of Caledon to Viscount Castlereagh, 25 July 1807', in Theal, *Records*, vol. 6, 183, and British House of Parliament Papers (BHPP) 202, *Correspondence on Treatment of Slaves and Hottentots at Cape of Good Hope: Account of Expedition against Bonshmen; Census of Population, 1826–27*, 18.

ordered in 1822, specifically excluded '[s]uch of the Bosjesmens children who from long residence have mixed with the Hottentots, and have been considered as such, and who have as Hottentot children been apprenticed among the inhabitants' and 'those who, by a long residence in the colony, are considered as belonging to the Hottentots, and have as such entered into agreements with the inhabitants'.[67]

The 'common men' in Graaff-Reinet also depended on militia officers, in their civil guise, for the retention of their Khoisan labour. The Batavian regime (1803–1806) delegated authority for Khoisan contracting from *landdrosts* to the militia officer corps, and the returning British administration, despite its low opinion of these field cornets, tripled their number in Graaff-Reinet in the next two decades.[68] They also organised a mail system between the capital and the district drostdys. Communication between *landdrost* and field cornets, however, continued to be 'very negligently' conveyed unsecured 'from house to house', with the result that 'it often happens that these despatches miscarry, or that they are not received for two or three months after their date'.[69] The same was true of the colonial state's own mouthpiece to the settler countryside, the *Courant*, which was 'seldom regularly sent around for the perusal of the inhabitants'.[70] Thus, although standard printed contract forms were distributed to the drostdys, the first commission of circuit in 1812 reported that many of the contracts in Graaff-Reinet were handwritten by field cornets in which they 'either only make a general memorandum that such a Hottentot has hired himself to such or such a farmer, or they draw up a contract in their own manner, which is therefore frequently deficient in all the necessary requisites of such an instrument'.[71]

If the militia officer corps played a key role in preventing contracting from spreading into the countryside, they were no less important in maintaining the existing system of Indigenous slavery by turning a blind eye to the continued routine use of physical violence to manage social relations on the farm. Such violence was not excessive in the sense of being superfluous to the system, but rather was integral to providing the necessary regular reminder of the primal scene of capture and the absolute power

---

67 BHPP 584, *Reports of Royal Commission on the Condition of Hottentots and other Native Tribes of South Africa and their Relations with Cape Colony, 1830*, 9.

68 Calculated from data contained in the *African Court Calendar*, 1802–1825.

69 'Collins to Caledon', 147–148.

70 Ibid.

71 'Report of the Commission of Circuit for 1813', in Theal, *Records*, vol. 10, 86.

CIVILIAN-DRIVEN VIOLENCE AND THE GENOCIDE OF INDIGENOUS PEOPLES

of life and death that all settlers held over all Khoisan slaves. As the LMS missionary James Read declared:

> Indeed the complaints have become so numerous we can no longer pinch our consciences. There are of late several Hottentots missing, but we fear little will be done, as those who are accused as their murderers are not arrested. Some of the falsely called Christian Boers are accused of 8 or 9 murders. Many of our poor people have also lost their children, whom they keep as slaves, and will not restore. A poor old man has been travelling 9 or 10 times backwards and forwards to the Cape, and has now brought a Letter from the Fiscal, and an order from the Landdrost of Graaff-Reinet, after waiting several years, to the Boer to give him up his children, but is deterred from going thro' fear of being killed. He entreated an officer of Justice to be sent, but was refused. With such kind of complaints we could fill a volume ... [S]uch crimes still continue, upwards of 100 murders have been brought to our knowledge in this small part of the colony. If we take the whole into account, what a field of blood, of innocent blood crying to God for vengeance.[72]

The high level of endemic violence on settler farms was confirmed by the first commission of circuit in 1812. In Graaff-Reinet, 90 per cent of criminal cases involved settler assault or murder of servants, and two-thirds of civil cases were of settlers withholding children, livestock or wages from servants.[73] The violence of the militia internalised on the farm to manage the slave labour population made desertion a common form of escape, re-seeding the district's Cisgariep border with maroon communities of armed and mounted Khoisan who raided settler farms for livestock and ammunition.[74]

Neither of Graaff-Reinet's slave populations were self-reproducing, and both stagnated after 1805 owing to the British abolition of the import slave trade in 1807 and the demobilisation of the settler militia.[75] The British

---

72 'Extracts from the letters and journals of the missionary James Read, relating the murders of numbers of Hottentots, 9 January 1811', in Theal, *Records*, vol. 8, 126.
73 Calculated from data contained in 'Report of the Commission of Circuit for the Districts of Graaff-Reinet, Uitenhage and George for 1812', in Theal, *Records*, vol. 9, 54–128.
74 See, for example, 'A. Stockenstrom to Major Bird, June/July 1811', in Theal, *Records*, vol. 8, 109–110; Challis S. 2012. 'Creolisation on the nineteenth-century frontiers of Southern Africa: A case study of the AmaTola Bushmen in the Maloti-Drakensberg'. *Journal of Southern African Studies*, 38, no. 2, 265–280; King R. 2017. 'Cattle, raiding and disorder in southern African history'. *Africa*, 87, no. 3, 607–630 and King R. & Challis S. 2017. 'The interior world of the nineteenth-century Maloti-Drakensberg Moutains'. *Journal of African History*, 58, no. 2, 213–237, for San maroon communities along the Gariep.
75 See Fourie J. &. Green E. 2018b. 'Wage labour and slavery on the Cape frontier: The impact of the abolition of slave imports on labour relations in the Graaff-Reinet district'.

CHAPTER 4: 'An Unbroken Line of Crimes and Blood'

sought to alleviate the problem by coercing Khoisan into contract service. From 1809 all Khoisan were required to have a registered 'place of abode' and permission from the *landdrost* or settler to leave it for any purpose.[76] Settlers were instructed that, 'every one is to ask a pass from any Hottentot that happens to come to his place, and in case of his not being provided with it, to deliver him up to the field-cornet, landdrost or fiscal'.[77] This was the one aspect of contracting diligently administered by the field cornets to ensure Khoisan labour was detained within the ward if not on a specific farm. A subsequent enquiry thought it 'not unfair to presume that the veld cornets and landdrosts have been disposed generally to abridge the period as well as the distance to which their permissions have extended, with a view to the monopoly of labour in their respective districts'.[78] Khoisan pass-law offenders were arrested as 'vagrants' and recycled back onto the farms through the district gaol-keeper to masters who 'either advanced or became responsible for the expenses of detention'.[79] Three years later, in 1812, the colonial state forced the door of the Khoisan household by extending contracting to include Khoisan children born on farms and purportedly maintained by settlers. Finally, in 1819, *landdrosts* were empowered to act in *loco parentis* to contract with settlers on behalf of Khoisan and other Indigenous orphans.[80]

The intensifying labour shortage also focused renewed attention on one of the district's original sources of Khoisan labour, the San. Reconciliation and the settler provision of 'flesh and tobacco' had drawn increasing numbers of the latter onto settler farms after 1803, but they showed little desire to settle there permanently.[81] As Collins said in 1809: 'I fear it will be a considerable time before the plan of engaging the Bosjesmen to serve the inhabitants during registered periods can be conveniently adopted; until long accustomed to the way of living of the colonists, they leave them for some months every year to enjoy a ramble, and to eat locusts, wild roots,

---

In *Colonialism, Institutional Change and Shifts in Global Labour Relations*, eds. K. Hofmeester & P. de Zwart. Amsterdam: Amsterdam University Press.

76 See 'W.S. van Ryneveld, a plan for amending the interior police in the Colony of the Cape of Good Hope, 31 October 1801', in Theal, *Records*, vol. 4, 88–96, for the origin of the idea; and 'Proclamation by the Earl of Caledon, 1 November 1809' in Theal, *Records*, vol. 7, 212.

77 'Proclamation by the Earl of Caledon, 1 November 1809', 216.

78 'Report of J.T. Bigge, upon the Hottentot and Bushmen population of the Cape of Good Hope and of the Missionary Institutions', in Theal, *Records*, vol. 35, 317.

79 Ibid.

80 'Proclamation by Lord Charles Somerset, 9 July 1819', in Theal, *Records*, vol. 12, 249–250.

81 See Campbell, *Travels*, Vol. 1, 310, for the quote.

CIVILIAN-DRIVEN VIOLENCE AND THE GENOCIDE OF INDIGENOUS PEOPLES

and the larvae of ants.'[82] Rather, the British demobilisation of the settler militia enabled San refugees to reoccupy territories abandoned in the face of militia slaving and to attempt to resuscitate traditional seasonal foraging beats. Wild game initially remained plentiful, but settlers increasingly substituted it for livestock as the staple of the San gift economy, the local militia being mobilised in hunting parties for this purpose.[83] By the end of the 1810s the wild game was gone.[84] Although officials made much of any evidence of San livestock keeping, this too, like the migration onto settler farms, was an ad hoc innovation, not an abandonment of foraging. The great majority of settlers, though, were opposed to the reconciliation policy of the top 12 per cent and colonial state. As Colonel Collins shrewdly observed in 1809, the 'beneficial effects [of reconciliation] have probably been produced, not more by the friendly intercourse that the farmers have endeavoured to establish, than by the restrictions that have been attached to commandos.'[85] In particular the prohibition on taking captives 'greatly served to dampen the ardour for commandos, and has actuated the farmers as much as humanity in their tenderness to the Bosjesman, a feeling that their great want of servants has also tended to promote.'[86]

In 1811 the British mobilised the settler militia again for the first time in a decade to assist the colonial garrison in clearing the Xhosa from the Zuurveld. A third of Graaff-Reinet's military-age settler males remained in the field on rotation until 1813, patrolling the district's eastern border on the Fish River, making the British anxious to demobilise them for fear that prolonged military service might 'too much excite among farmers and the lower classes of the community, that spirit of warfare and enterprise, which cannot but keep alive an uncivilized and ferocious character, which it must be the peculiar wish of the Government in this part of the world to moderate and suppress.'[87] This fear was heightened by the rebellion of elements of the Zuurveld militia in 1815, but imperial austerity and the concomitant

---

82 'Collins to Caledon', 118.
83 See, for example, 'Report of the Commission of Circuit 1812', 82, and 'Report of the Commission of Circuit for 1813', 94–95.
84 See Plug I. & Sampson C.G. 1996. 'European and Bushmen impacts on Karoo fauna in the nineteenth century: An archaeological perspective'. *South African Archaeological Bulletin*, 51, no. 163, 26–31.
85 'Collins to Caledon', 111.
86 Ibid., 113.
87 'Memorandum of Sir John Cradock, 19 December 1813', and 'Sir John Cradock to Lord Bathurst, 5 February 1814', in Theal, *Records*, vol. 9, 285–287 and 326, respectively; 'Lord Charles Somerset to Earl Bathurst, 25 September 1814', in Theal, *Records*, vol. 10, 191. See also Philip, *Researches*, vol. 2, 42–44.

CHAPTER 4: 'An Unbroken Line of Crimes and Blood'

reduction in the size of the colonial garrison made demobilising the settler militia impossible. A third of Graaff-Reinet's settler adult males were called up again in 1819 for another major campaign against the Zuurveld Xhosa. General militia service on the eastern frontier, together with regular local militia deployments in hunting parties and against San raiders on the northern border, did indeed reanimate the primary primitive accumulation apparatus of settler pastoralism, the commando, and excited its spirit of 'warfare and enterprise'. Graaff-Reinet's settler militia killed over 176 San and took as many as 466 captive in the decade after 1815, the latter being 'according to an old custom, ... distributed among the inhabitants, to try to bring them to peaceable habits ... so that most of them have returned to their kraals, and the remainder are living with the farmers in the same way as their Hottentot servants'.[88] The striking inversion of the historical 3:1 killed-to-captured ratio in the 1820s, however, gives the lie to claims of self-defence and points instead to the militia's primary function as a vehicle for San slaving on the district's Cisgariep frontier. It is no coincidence that its reappearance in the Graaff-Reinet countryside, after an absence of more than a decade, coincided with that of Indigenous child slaving.

Some form of reciprocity had always been implicit in settler gifting to the San. Whereas its promoters originally hoped for repayment in the gold standard of adult labour contracting, by the 1810s it was increasingly being extorted by settlers in the base metal of child slavery. This was done in the guise of custom, with settlers claiming that because San were 'unnatural parents' prone to routinely abandoning or trafficking their children, they had an 'ancient custom' of adopting such children into their households as servants on a temporary or permanent basis to save their lives.[89] When the British introduced slave registration in 1816, specifically to 'prevent the possibility of ... free persons, or their offspring, merging into a state of slavery, or being confounded with the domestic or other slaves, the property of individuals in this settlement', the *landdrost* of Graaff-Reinet, himself a

---

88 BHPP 202, *Correspondence on Treatment of Slaves and Hottentots at Cape of Good Hope; Account of Expedition against Bonshmen; Census of Population, 1826–27*, 27. Calculated from data contained in BHPP, 50, *Papers Relative to the Condition and Treatment of the Native Inhabitants of Southern Africa, within the Colony of the Cape of Good Hope, or beyond the Frontier of that Colony: Part I Hottentots and Bosjesmans; Caffres; Griquas, 1835.* See also BHPP 202, *Correspondence on Treatment of Slaves*, 27, for the quote, and Thompson, *Travels*, vol. 2, 37–58, for an eyewitness account.

89 'Landdrost of Graaff-Reinet to the Colonial Secretary, 5 May 1817', in Theal, *Records*, vol. 11, 325–327.

CIVILIAN-DRIVEN VIOLENCE AND THE GENOCIDE OF INDIGENOUS PEOPLES

wealthy farmer and comfortable member of the top 12 per cent, belatedly reported that custom was being 'seriously abused' in his district:[90]

> That these children got in the above manner are transferred from one hand to another, and that payment is secretly taken; that many by these means are gradually taken from the frontier, brought into the inner districts, and passed off as orphans; that itinerant merchants begin to be supplied with them through some channel or other; that parents even begin to be disputed their claim to such children; from all which enormities I should think may result, that men may be found base enough for the sake of some paltry gain, to give what the Bosjesmen may consider a great deal for such children, in order to supply other anxious to procure them—this would be a sufficient inducement for one kraal to make an attack upon another, to murder the old ones and dispose of the children, independent of other excesses, to which men used to and leading the unpolished life of some of our most remote colonists may be seduced by such easy profit ... Two little Bosjesmen girls ... [were] brought through the village a few days since, by a merchant from Cape Town, Jacob Theron, who could give me no other account but that he had got them at a Bosjesmen kraal, where he was told that they were orphans.[91]

The following year the *landdrost* reported that San children were also being slaved in Transorangia by Bastard (Griqua) militias for the Graaff-Reinet market.[92] Rather than suppressing the burgeoning trade in San child slaves, the *landdrost* wanted it legalised on the same logic as the contracting of Khoisan children, that settlers were entitled to recoup the cost of maintaining such children for the first eight years of their lives through an equivalent period of indentured labour service.[93] A later investigation revealed that while settlers showed 'no reluctance ... to avail themselves of the opportunities which these laws, especially the last, have afforded, of increasing the number of unpaid labourers on their estates', the *landdrost* evidenced 'great negligence'

---

90 'Proclamation by Lord Charles Somerset, 26 April 1816', and 'Lord Charles Somerset to Earl Bathurst, 18 May 1816', in Theal, *Records*, vol. 11, 102–105 and 108–109, respectively.
91 'Landdrost of Graaff-Reinet to the Colonial Secretary, 5 May 1817', in Theal, *Records*, vol. 11, 326.
92 'Landdrost of Graaff-Reinet to the Colonial Secretary, 18 August 1818', in Theal, *Records*, vol. 12, 34–36. The missionary reported 1 500 military-age males and more than 300 guns at Philippolis, with the latter growing rapidly.
93 'Landdrost of Graaff-Reinet to the Colonial Secretary, 5 May 1817', and 'Proclamation of Lord Charles Somerset, 8 August 1817', in Theal, *Records*, 11, 325–328 and 365–367, respectively.

CHAPTER 4: 'An Unbroken Line of Crimes and Blood'

in documenting this traffic, which was directed as 'patronage to the master instead of an instrument of benefit to the children'.[94]

By the mid-1820s there were reported to be at least 1 088 San child slaves on farms in Graaff-Reinet 'without contract or indenture', equivalent to one fifth of the district's total Khoisan population.[95] These were supplemented with Tswana and Korana 'orphans' imported from Transorangia. A remnant San adult population continued to be maintained on the farms through gifting and force, but on bare subsistence rations of offal and narcotics, to ensure on-site reproduction of the child slave labour supply.[96] Indeed, so numerous were San children on settler farms that they depressed Graaff-Reinet's adult wage rate to the lowest in the colony.[97] Any attempt by the slaves to redress the balance was severely punished as a warning to others: 'publicly flogged under the scaffold, branded with a hot iron, put in irons, and condemned to hard labour'.[98] As the missionary Philip saw it, 'the landdrasts [sic], and clerks, and farmers, have all the same views respecting the Hottentots and other Aborigines: they consider them as the absolute property of the colonists, and as much made for their use as their cattle and sheep'.[99] In this all-pervasive slave-owner *mentalité*, the idea that labour should be 'free' was a peculiar British affectation indulged in only by the tiny urban middle class huddled around the drostdy in Graaff-Reinet town for whom contracting was as much an indicator of their wealth and status as the number of Bushmen children they 'owned' was to a settler farmer in the surrounding countryside.

Conclusion: The strong hand

In the mid-1830s John Philip reported that '[a]ny traveller who may have visited the interior of this colony, little more than 20 years ago, may now stand ... in the midst of a district of 42 000 square miles on the north side of Graaff Reinet, and ask the question, "Where are the aboriginal inhabitants of this district which I saw here in my former visit to this country?" without any one being able to inform him where he is to look for them "to find them"'.[100] Nearly a decade after his initial 'researches' into the enslavement of the San

---

94 'Report of J.T. Bigge', 325–326.
95 Ibid., 326.
96 See Thompson, *Travels*, vol. 2, 1–11.
97 'Report of J.T. Bigge', 315.
98 Philip, *Researches*, vol. 2, 37.
99 Ibid., vol. 1, 15.
100 BHPP 538, *Report from the Select Committee on Aborigines (British Settlements) together with the Minutes of Evidence, Appendix and Index, 1836*, 692.

CIVILIAN-DRIVEN VIOLENCE AND THE GENOCIDE OF INDIGENOUS PEOPLES

in Graaff-Reinet, the missionary Philip returned to 'the country between the Snewbergen and the Orange River' on the district's vast northern shield, which, he estimated, had once held around 5 000 San in the mid-1810s:

> In 1832 I spent 17 days in that country, travelling over it in different directions. I then found the country occupied by the boors, and the Boschmen population had disappeared, with the exception of those that had been brought up from infancy in the service of the boors. In the whole of my journey, during the 17 days I was in the country, I met with two men and one woman only of the free inhabitants who had escaped the effects of the commando system, and they were travelling by night and concealing themselves by day, to escape being shot like wild beasts. Their tale was a lamentable one. Their children had been taken from them by the boors, and they were wandering about in this manner from place to place, in the hope of finding out where they were, and of getting a sight of them.[101]

As Philip indicated, the settler militia was the key mechanism in the 'disappearance' of the San in Graaff-Reinet, routinely exterminating adult males and incorporating the women and children into an Indigenous slave population of Khoisan ('Hottentots') assembled under its aegis. Despite the militia's enemy image of the San as animals, slaving was not restricted to them. Commandos moved on to gather Tswana, Korana, Mfengu and emancipated slave children into its resident Khoisan slave population once the local San population had disappeared.

The militia's reach extended far beyond the commando into the day-to-day management of its rank and file's social relations of production on the farm. Here the militia officer corps reappeared in civilian garb as agents of judicial authority, superintending the very limited ordinary movement allowed Khoisan slaves and disciplining them by enacting the occasional exemplary violence on the delinquent as a reminder to the rest of the primal violence of capture and the power of life and death that their owners held over them. While the militia notionally made war and managed peace in the name and on behalf of the state, in reality it did so in the collective interest of the local settler population who furnished its manpower, weaponry and resources. Their common interest lay in securing a regular inflow of Indigenous slave labourers to replenish their non-self-reproducing Khoisan slave population, and the militia was their preferred means for doing so. The Company and the colonial state could exercise some control over the militia by extending or retracting their consent and munitions for its actions,

---

101 BHPP, 538, *Report from the Select Committee on Aborigines*, 694.

but were discouraged from withholding ideological or material support by the militia's willingness to rebel and destabilise the whole of the colony's eastern front. Thus, for two generations, settlers in Graaff-Reinet enjoyed a free hand to exterminate and enslave Indigenous foragers along the open frontier. Their effectiveness at doing so was evidenced by the near-complete disappearance of San from the north-eastern frontier by the 1830s.

CHAPTER FIVE

Establishing a Code of Silence: Civilian and State Complicity in Genocidal Massacres on the New South Wales Frontier, 1788–1859

Lyndall Ryan

In November 1838 the citizens of Sydney, New South Wales, were in turmoil over the guilty verdict of the second trial of stockmen charged with the murder of 28 Aboriginal people camped at the Myall Creek cattle station on the far northern frontier of the colony.[1] The trials not only exposed the way stockmen were killing Aboriginal people on the frontier en masse and for no apparent reason, but also demonstrated that absentee owners of cattle stations were prepared to cross class lines to support stockmen by hiring the best barristers in the colony to defend them. This tactic was so successful that two trials were required before seven of the eleven stockmen were found guilty and hanged.[2]

Frontier massacres of Aboriginal people were not unknown in New South Wales, but it was the first time since the colony was founded, 50 years earlier, that perpetrators were brought to justice and hanged. Indeed, the trials only took place because of a set of extraordinary circumstances. First, station manager William Hobbs decided to report the massacre to the authorities in Sydney and his report arrived just as the British government's new policy, clarifying the rights of Indigenous peoples in the British Empire, was coming into effect. The policy was introduced by the Colonial Office in London in the wake of the House of Commons Select Committee Report on the status of Aboriginal people in British settler colonies and stressed that Aboriginal people were British subjects and that an inquest should be held into the suspicious death of any Aboriginal person.[3] Secondly, the colony's

---

1 Lydon J. & Ryan L., eds. 2018. *Remembering the Myall Creek Massacre*. Sydney: NewSouth Books.

2 For the most recent analysis of the trials, see Tedeschi M. 2016. *Murder at Myall Creek: The Trial that Defined a Nation*. Sydney: Simon & Schuster.

3 See *Report from the Select Committee on Aborigines (British Settlements)*, British Parliamentary Papers, 1837, vol. VII, no. 425. For the outline of the new policy, see *Historical Records of Australia*, Series I, vol. xix, Glenelg to Gipps, 31 January 1838, 252–255.

CHAPTER 5: Establishing a Code of Silence

Attorney-General, John Hubert Plunkett, was determined to bring the perpetrators to justice. It was he who despatched police magistrate Edward Denny Day to the Gwydir River to arrest the perpetrators and to take depositions from the key witnesses, including hutkeeper George Anderson.[4]

Anderson's evidence at the trials revealed the anarchy that prevailed on the colony's northern frontier in 1838. He told the court how settler John Henry Fleming led the posse of 12 armed horsemen that galloped into Myall Creek Station late in the afternoon of Sunday 10 June 1838, knowing that the manager, William Hobbs and two of the station's three stockmen were absent droving cattle. Those who remained, stockman Charles Kilmeister, hutkeeper Anderson and two 'naturalised' Aboriginal youths, Yintayintin and Kiumanga, were in no position to force the posse to leave. Anderson knew that the stockmen had come for the group of 40 Aboriginal people from the Wirrayaraay nation who were camped at the station, although the posse did not know that on this particular day, ten of the leading warriors were cutting bark at another station about 16 kilometres away. He also told the court that when the Wirrayaraay people heard the horses approaching, they fled into Anderson's hut for safety. But to no avail. He stood by helplessly as Fleming and his second-in-command, George Russell, dragged most of them out of the hut and tethered them by the wrists with a leather strap so they could not escape. At that point Kilmeister, clearly intimidated by the stockmen's threatening behaviour, saddled his horse and joined them in driving the Wirrayaraay up the muddy track out of sight of the station huts. Fearing that he would also be forced to join them, Anderson locked himself in the hut with Kuiminga and two Wirrayaraay women and their children who had escaped detection. He then heard two shots ring out, and later the sound of assassins galloping away into the falling darkness.[5]

Yintayintin remained outside and hid behind a tree to witness the proceedings. He saw Fleming fire two shots at the victims and then watched while the stockmen slaughtered the others with swords and cutlasses, cutting off many of their heads in the process. But they kept one woman, Impeta, for themselves and galloped away from the station. Yintayintin then returned to the hut and told Anderson all he had seen. Several hours later, the Wirrayaraay warriors arrived from the neighbouring station. After hearing what had happened to their people, they were determined to bury

---

4   Molony J. 1973. *An Architect of Freedom: John Hubert Plunkett in New South Wales 1832–1869*. Canberra: Australian National University Press, 140–150.

5   Ryan L. 2018. "'A very bad business": Henry Dangar and the Myall Creek massacre 1838', in *Remembering the Myall Creek Massacre*, 20–22.

their bodies. But Anderson knew the assassins would return and told them to take two women left in the hut and their children to another cattle station over the hills 40 kilometres to the east, where the overseer, Daniel Eaton, might offer them protection.[6]

Anderson was correct in his assessment. Late the following afternoon, the killers returned to Myall Creek Station, knowing that they had to dispose of the bodies. After sleeping overnight in Anderson's hut, the next morning Fleming, Russell and Kilmeister, holding lighted firesticks aloft, mounted their horses, and after ordering another to keep guard over Anderson so that he could not witness their work, Fleming led the others to the massacre site. But they had not reckoned on Yintayintin. Once again, he witnessed the proceedings from behind a tree. He saw the men drag great logs down to the site, and when the fire was well alight they all returned to the hut. After a while, Fleming ordered Kilmeister back to the fire to 'make sure that all was consumed' and he remained there for the rest of the day trying to burn the rotting flesh. After remaining another night in Anderson's hut, early the next morning, Tuesday 12 June, the killers took Kuimunga hostage and threatened to kill him unless he showed them a quick way over the ranges to Eaton's cattle station. Promising him two women for his efforts, they galloped off, leaving behind a broken sword.[7]

The Wirrayaraay men had arrived at Eaton's Station the day before and told him that 'soldiers' — the name they gave to any group of white men on horseback — had massacred their people. When they heard horsemen in the bush on Tuesday morning, Eaton, alone and powerless against so many, urged them to hide in the ranges. But the assassins went after them and shot a little boy and nearly all of the men. Two women were spared. On Thursday 13 June the assassins dispersed, well satisfied with the operation. They kept their word to Kuimunga and sent him back to Myall Creek with the two women.[8]

Despite the sheer terror of the massacre, or perhaps because of it, when Hobbs returned to Myall Creek two days later, he decided to report it to the authorities. It was an incredibly brave decision. Hobbs knew of at least three other frontier massacres along the Gwydir River, and by breaking the code of silence, he placed his own life at risk. His decision set in motion a tumultuous chain of events.

---

6   Ibid., 22–23.
7   Ibid., 23.
8   Ibid.; for another account of the events at Myall Creek, see Tedeschi, *Massacre at Myall Creek*, 100–108.

CHAPTER 5: Establishing a Code of Silence

Once it was known that Hobbs had reported the massacre, ringleader John Fleming vanished, leaving the 11 stockmen to take the rap. In their support, a group of settlers formed what became known as the Black Association, to raise funds to hire the colony's three leading barristers to defend the perpetrators. At the first trial the barristers were successful in persuading the jury to return a 'not guilty' verdict. The Attorney-General, however, was determined to overturn the verdict, and with new evidence available, secured a second trial in which seven of the eleven accused were found guilty and hanged. This was the only time a 'guilty' verdict for the massacre of Aboriginal people was achieved in nineteenth-century New South Wales.[9] Hobbs would also pay dearly for his decision to report the massacre. He was sacked by his employer and vilified in the press. He would never hold a similar position again.[10]

The significance of the Myall Creek massacre to Australian frontier history cannot be overstated. As lawyer Mark Tedeschi points out, the massacre has come to represent —

> the multitude of massacres that occurred all over Australia during a period of more than 120 years. This because we know more today about the murders at Myall Creek than any of the hundreds of other massacres of Indigenous people that occurred all around Australia. We know so much today about this one largely because of the investigation and the two trials of the perpetrators that were conducted in 1838.[11]

The trials failed to stop settlers' determination to annihilate Aboriginal people on the frontier. Indeed, the massacre, the disappearance of the ringleader, the furore surrounding the trials, and the hanging of the seven stockmen so deeply divided the colony that for the remainder of the nineteenth century the atrocity was not recorded in colonial histories.[12] It was as if the colonists could not accept that the practice of civilian massacre on the pastoral frontier was a crime. Rather, it would appear that they saw it as a necessary and socially sanctioned practice, for it is known to have continued long after the Australian colonies federated in 1901 and at least until the 1930s.

---

9   Tedeschi, *Massacre at Myall Creek,* 269–270.
10   Ryan, 'A very bad business', 36.
11   Tedeschi, *Massacre at Myall Creek,* 161.
12   Withycombe P. 2018. 'The twelfth man: John Henry Fleming and the Myall Creek massacre', in *Remembering the Myall Creek Massacre.*

Myall Creek and the historiography of frontier massacre

The atrocity was only brought back to public view in 1973, when John Molony published an account of the Myall Creek trials in his biography of prominent nineteenth-century New South Wales politician John Hubert Plunkett.[13] Molony was closely followed by Aboriginal history specialist R.H.W. (Bob) Reece, who placed the massacre and the trials within the context of other frontier massacres of the time, and was the first historian to list 'massacres' in the index.[14] As more information about the massacre and the trials surfaced in the 1980s, a raft of scholars analysed every aspect of the incident. A study of the assassins, for example, revealed that apart from Fleming, the rest were either former or serving male convicts from the industrial towns of England and Ireland, with one of them a former black slave from North America.[15] Although they worked as stockmen, the convicts under sentence were officially known as assigned servants, and most of the former convicts worked as managers or overseers on the pastoral stations of absentee owners. These men, it would appear, operated on the frontier without fear of restraint and behaved as civilian employees rather than as servants of the Crown.

Another study explored the details of the massacre operation, the decision by the Attorney-General in Sydney to issue warrants for the arrest of the perpetrators, the depositions that were taken by the magistrate in charge of the investigation, and detailed analyses of the trials that led to the conviction and hanging of seven of the twelve perpetrators.[16] Finally, the detailed account of the Gwydir River frontier in the 1830s by Roger Milliss revealed that the massacre was simply one of many in the region at the time.[17]

The extensive research on Myall Creek generated studies of other frontier massacres in other parts of New South Wales. They include Geoffrey Blomfield's pioneering study of the massacres of Aboriginal people of the Hastings, Manning and Macleay rivers region in the 1830s and 1840s, and Gordon Reid's masterful study of the Hornet Bank massacre in the Dawson

---

13 Molony, *Architect of Freedom*. See also Harrison B. 1978. 'The Myall Creek massacre', in *Records of Times Past: Ethnohistorical Essays on the Culture and Ecology of the New England Tribes*, ed. I. McBryde, Canberra: Australian Institute of Aboriginal Studies.
14 Reece R. 1974. *Aborigines and Colonists: Aborigines and Colonial Society in New South Wales in the 1830s and 1840s*. Sydney: Sydney University Press.
15 Anon. 1985. 'The evidence of murder'. *The Push from the Bush*, 20, 58–87.
16 Aveling M. & Ryan L. 1987. 'At the boundaries', in *Australians 1838*, eds. A. Atkinson & M. Aveling. Sydney: Fairfax, Syme & Weldon Associates, 54–60.
17 Milliss R. 1992. *Waterloo Creek: The Australia Day Massacre of 1838. George Gipps and the British Conquest of New South Wales*. Melbourne: McPhee Gribble.

CHAPTER 5: Establishing a Code of Silence

River district in 1857, in which eight white men and three white women were killed, leading to the wholesale slaughter of up to 300 Aboriginal people in the aftermath.[18] This was followed by Bruce Elder's Australia-wide study of frontier massacre, in which he noted that military massacres were a feature of the first decades of settlement in each of the six Australian colonies.[19] The findings were matched by the detailed study of the frontiers of New South Wales and Tasmania between 1788 and 1838 by military historian John Connor, in which he argued that British military forces brought Aboriginal people under control by deploying the tactic of massacre.[20] Ian Clark and Peter Gardner, in their respective studies of incidents of frontier massacre in the Port Phillip district, now the state of Victoria, argued that the usual preconditions were the Aboriginal killing of a settler or stockkeeper, or stock theft. In the aftermath, regardless of whether the massacre was carried out by civilians or the military, a code of silence prevailed, making detection difficult.[21] All of these studies indicated that because Myall Creek was not a reprisal massacre and was reported to the authorities, it was not suitable for comparison with other known incidents.

Nonetheless, Patrick Collins' study of the Mandanjanji land war in the Maranoa pastoral district in the 1840s did offer important insights for comparison. He pointed out that in the decade following Myall Creek, sheep and cattle farmers were largely left to their own devices in their search for new grazing lands. In their determination to bring Maranoa under their control, they carried out some brutal opportunity massacres of Aboriginal people that resonated with the incident at Myall Creek. By the end of the 1840s, however, settlers were prepared to pay a levy to enable a native police force to bring the region under their control.[22] Lesley Skinner's study of native police operations in the region between 1848 and 1859 leaves the reader in no doubt as to their effectiveness.[23]

---

18 Blomfield G. 1981. *Baal Belbora: The End of the Dreaming*. Sydney: Alternative Publishing Co-operative; Reid G. 1981. *A Nest of Hornets: The Massacre of the Fraser Family at Hornet Bank Station, Central Queensland 1857, and Related Events*. Melbourne: Oxford: University Press.
19 Elder B. 1988. *Blood on the Wattle: Massacres and Maltreatment of Australian Aborigines since 1788*. Sydney: Child & Associates.
20 Connor J. 2002. *The Australian Frontier Wars, 1788–1838*. Sydney: UNSW Press.
21 Clark I. 1995. *Scars in the Landscape: A Register of Massacre Sites in Western Victoria, 1803–1859*. Canberra: Australian Institute of Aboriginal and Torres Strait Islander Studies; Gardner P.D. 2000. *Gippsland Massacres*. Ensay: Ngarak Press.
22 Collins P. 2002. *Goodbye Bussamarai: The Mandandanji Land War, Southern Queensland 1842–1852*. Brisbane: University of Queensland Press.
23 Skinner L.E. 1975. *Police of the Pastoral Frontier: Native Police 1849–59*. St Lucia, Brisbane: University of Queensland Press.

CIVILIAN-DRIVEN VIOLENCE AND THE GENOCIDE OF INDIGENOUS PEOPLES

Placing these findings in the context of the Myall Creek massacre, new questions arise about the colonial frontier in New South Wales. Were civilian massacres the most common practice on the New South Wales frontier? How did they compare with frontier massacres in Tasmania and Victoria? Were civilians left to their own devices on the frontier in the decade following Myall Creek, leading to the practice of poisoning Aboriginal people? Finally, were the frontier massacres in New South Wales an expression of genocide?

The publication in 2018 of stage 2 of an interactive digital map of more than 250 frontier massacres in central and eastern Australia from 1794 to 1930 — hereafter referred to as the 'massacre map project' — could help resolve these questions.[24] The map is based on both the conceptual framework of massacre devised by historical sociologist Jacques Semelin from his international study of massacre and the characteristics of colonial frontier massacre identified by Ian Clark and Peter Gardner from their studies of colonial Victoria.[25] Semelin observes that new colonial settlements required extensive land for major economic enterprises, such as sheep and cattle farming, which often resulted in the massacre of Indigenous owners.[26] He points out that frontier massacres were typically not the product of rash and impulsive decision-making, but rather were carefully planned operations. In general, frontier massacres were either a response to a particular act of perceived aggression, such as the alleged killing of a settler or stockkeeper by Aboriginal people, even though the original aggression may have been by settlers themselves. To this end, a frontier massacre was intended either to intimidate the Aboriginal owners of the land into subjection or to eliminate them entirely. The act was usually carried out by settlers who lived in fear of the alleged aggressors and believed that by engaging in massacre, they would regain the upper hand. The act of massacre was thus usually an expression of weakness. For this reason, it was usually carried out in secret, making it difficult for the perpetrators to be identified in the immediate aftermath. However, witnesses and perpetrators sometimes spoke out long after the event, when fears of prosecution and reprisals by other perpetrators had passed.[27]

Both Clark and Gardner found that frontier massacres in the Port Phillip district between 1835 and 1859 were usually carried out in secret by

---

24 'Colonial Frontier Massacres in Central and Eastern Australia 1788–1930', digital map, The Centre for 21st Century Humanities, University of Newcastle. Available at https://c21ch.newcastle.edu.au/colonialmassacres/map.php, accessed 26 February 2019.

25 Semelin J. 2007. *Purify and Destroy: The Political Uses of Massacre and Genocide*, trans. C. Schoch. London: Hurst; Clark, *Scars in the Landscape*; Gardner, *Gippsland*.

26 Semelin, *Purify and Destroy*, 366–383.

27 Ibid.

CHAPTER 5: Establishing a Code of Silence

armed groups of settler men on horseback with the intention of eradicating or destroying Aboriginal victims. A code of silence surrounded the event, preserving the anonymity of the assassins and making detection extremely difficult. These factors were compounded by the colonial legal system, which prevented Aboriginal witnesses from presenting evidence in court, thus allowing assassins to escape conviction. They also found that many frontier massacres took place at campsites, or in creek beds, lagoons and waterholes — places where Aboriginal people were likely to be found in larger groups. Sometimes groups of Aboriginal people were trapped and killed in ravines.[28]

By combining Semelin's conceptual framework with the characteristics provided by Clark and Gardner, the massacre map project defines a colonial frontier massacre in Australia as the indiscriminate killing of six or more undefended Aboriginal people in a single operation.[29] Why six? The sudden loss of what would usually constitute about a third of an Aboriginal hearth group leaves the survivors vulnerable to further attack. They are left with a greatly diminished ability to hunt or gather food, to carry out ceremonial obligations, and to reproduce the next generation. They also become vulnerable to introduced diseases. All of these factors radically reduce their long-term chances of survival.

This framework was initially deployed to compare the impact of the raw wool industry on Aboriginal people in Van Diemen's Land (Tasmania) between 1817 and 1832, and the Port Phillip district between 1835 and 1851. In Tasmania, I found that despite sustained Aboriginal resistance, frontier massacres were the defining feature of their dramatic population decline and that most were carried out as joint operations between civilians and the military. In the Port Phillip district, however, most incidents of frontier massacre were carried out by civilians whose landholdings were located beyond the colonial government's jurisdiction.[30]

Applying Semelin's conceptual framework and the characteristics of frontier massacre more broadly, the massacre map project allows us for the first time to consider the scale and practice of frontier massacres in New South Wales from first settlement in 1788 to the formation of Queensland as a separate colony in 1859. As the first systematic study of the frontier

---

28   Clark, *Scars in the Landscape*, 5–7; Gardner, *Gippsland Massacres*, 60–70.
29   'Colonial Frontier Massacres in Central and Eastern Australia 1788–1930' 'Introduction'.
30   'Ryan L. 2014. "No right to the land": The role of the wool industry in the destruction of Aboriginal societies in Tasmania (1817–1832) and Victoria (1835–1851) compared', in *Genocide on Settler Frontiers: When Hunter-Gatherers and Commercial Stock Farmers Clash*, ed. M. Adhikari. Cape Town: UCT Press, 205–209.

massacres of Australia's oldest colony in the first 70 years of colonisation, this chapter produces new insights about civilian and state-sanctioned massacres in a critical period of the colony's history.

The colony of New South Wales and its Aboriginal peoples

New South Wales was named and claimed for Britain by Captain James Cook in 1770. He noted that the Aboriginal owners of the territory were 'a warlike, stout people' and never allowed the British to 'land without various attacks'.[31]

The Aboriginal people of New South Wales were in possession of the country for at least 40 000 years and possibly as long as 65 000 years. They lived in hearth groups of about 20 or so, as members of an extended family, comprising three or four warriors and their wives and children, and sometimes visitors from other clans. Hearth groups were part of a clan group of several hundred people, which in turn was part of a nation of several thousand people, defined by language and territory. Each hearth group usually camped near fresh water and each was part of an elaborate system of clan, kin and totem relationships that determined their spiritual relationships to country. Each clan was responsible for a clearly defined territory, which could range in area from as little as 16 square kilometres along the coastline to several hundred square kilometres in the dry interior. They managed the land through firestick farming to enable the planting and harvesting of root vegetables, such as yams, and seeds, and the hunting of animals, such as kangaroo and emu. They also gathered shellfish and fished in fresh- and saltwater creeks, rivers and lagoons. Their land management practices were derived from each clan's obligations to their territory or country, which were an integral part of the Dreaming, the set of ideas and beliefs that underpinned Aboriginal cultural, political and social practices. 'Singing' the country was an important way of caring for the country after the death of a traditional owner, or of restoring it to life in the aftermath of drought or flood, ensuring that particular trees and plants associated with their ancestors and totems had properly recovered.[32]

---

31 Cook J. 1955. *The Journals of Captain James Cook in his Voyage of Discovery, Vol. I: The Voyage of the Endeavour 1768–1777* ed. J.C. Beaglehole. Cambridge: Cambridge University Press, 653.

32 For dates of arrival, see Lourandos H. 1997. *Continent of Hunter-Gatherers: New Perspectives on Australian Prehistory.* Cambridge: Cambridge University Press, 80–85; for agriculture and firestick farming and 'singing the country', see Pascoe B. 2013. *Dark Emu, Black Seeds: Agriculture or Accident?* Broome: Magabala Books. For fishing practices, see Kohen J. & Lampert R. 1987. 'Hunters and fishers in the Sydney region', in *Australians 1788*, eds. D. Mulvaney & J.P. White. Sydney: Fairfax, Syme & Weldon Associates,

CHAPTER 5: Establishing a Code of Silence

Visiting rights to the country of neighbouring clans and nations were carefully managed on a seasonal basis through the presentation of gifts, such as ochre, an item of universal spiritual significance, or necklaces made of shell and kangaroo tail, or special foods, such as parts of large sea mammals such as whales, or the offer of particular weapons, such as spears and clubs, known as waddies. In abundant seasons, important ceremonial gatherings could attract up to 1 000 people, and in the early colonial period sightings of 600 or more were not uncommon.[33] Nevertheless, clans were often at war with one another or with nearby nations. Some conflicts were resolved through elaborately staged fights between groups of warriors that concluded with a ceremonial feast and dance known as a *corroboree*. Others were resolved in payback killings and the abduction of women for wives. As historian Stephen Gapps points out, men's hunting skills were precisely those required for guerrilla warfare.[34] But it was their land management practices that attracted the most attention from the British. As environmental historian Bill Gammage points out, it was the way Aboriginal people used firestick farming to manage their crops and turn their kangaroo hunting grounds into an English parkland that made their lands so attractive to sheep and cattle farmers, and in turn became the trigger for frontier violence.[35] The Aboriginal population of the original colony of New South Wales at the time of British colonisation in 1788 was possibly 400 000.[36]

Apart from the comments made by Cook and other members of his expeditions along the east coast of New South Wales in 1770 and 1777, little was known in Britain about Australia's Aboriginal people. Cook considered them to be less hostile than the Maori of New Zealand, and that the south-eastern part of the territory would be suitable for British settlement on the grounds that the Aboriginal people, despite clear evidence that they did not want intruders in their country, were simply too 'primitive' to be accorded respect as a sovereign people. There was thus no need for treaties or land purchases. Nevertheless, when the British did establish a settlement

---

342–369. See also Gammage B. 2011. *The Biggest Estate on Earth: How Aborigines Made Australia*. Sydney: Allen & Unwin. 'Singing' refers to a person talking and singing to the plants, rocks, creeks and physical features of a territory and recalling stories associated with the person who previously 'owned' the area.

33 For visiting rights and population estimates, see Karskens G. 2009. *The Colony*. Sydney: Allen & Unwin, 19–32.

34 Gapps S. 2018. *The Sydney Wars: Conflict in the Early Colony, 1788–1817*. Sydney: NewSouth Books, 269–270.

35 Gammage, *Biggest Estate on Earth*, 92–93.

36 The population estimate is based on White J.P. & Mulvaney D.J. 1987. 'How many?', in *Australians to 1788*, 114–119.

in Sydney Cove, at Port Jackson, on the south-eastern coast of New South Wales in 1788, the governor Captain Arthur Phillip estimated the size of the Aboriginal population in the immediate vicinity to be about 1 500. From the outset, the settlement was well prepared for Aboriginal attack.[37]

Between 1788 and 1859 the geographical boundaries of New South Wales changed several times. In 1788 the colony comprised the entire eastern part of the Australian continent, including Tasmania. The first boundary changes came in 1825 when Tasmania became a separate colony. Then in 1835 a section of the south-western part of New South Wales was detached to form part of the colony of South Australia. A year later in 1836 the Port Phillip district, located south of the Murray River, was placed under separate administration and became the colony of Victoria in 1850. A further change occurred in December 1859 when a large part of the Northern district was excised from New South Wales to form the colony of Queensland.

New South Wales was not only the first colony where civilians and the military were known to instigate frontier massacres, but was also the first to implement a range of policies to suppress Aboriginal resistance, as well as the first to arrest civilian perpetrators of frontier massacre and bring them before the courts. To make better sense of changes in both the policy and practice of frontier massacre over the first 70 years of the colony's existence, the rest of the chapter is divided into four chronological sections, each identifying key changes that occurred, and determining the parts played by civilians and agents of the state and military.

Frontier massacres, 1788–1827

New South Wales began its existence in 1788 as a penal outpost of the British Empire. The 736 transported British convicts, guarded by 550 officers and marines, were expected to transform themselves into subsistence farmers, even though families were difficult to establish because the men outnumbered the women by four to one.[38] The fledgling colony did not start to become self-sufficient in food production until the first grain crops were harvested in 1794 at the Hawkesbury River settlement 55 kilometres west of

---

37 Gapps, *Sydney Wars*, 19. For Philip's views and Aboriginal population estimate, see *Historical Records of New South Wales*, vol. 1, part 2, Phillip to Lord Sydney, 15 May 1788, 129.

38 Karskens G. 2013. 'The early colonial presence', in *The Cambridge History of Australia*, vol. 1, eds. A. Bashford & S. Macintyre. Melbourne: Cambridge University Press, 91.

CHAPTER 5: Establishing a Code of Silence

Sydney.[39] It was here, six years after the British arrived in New South Wales, that the first frontier massacres took place.

The Hawkesbury River area was central to the homeland of the 500-strong Bediagal clan of the Darug nation, and they had no intention of yielding it to the British. In September 1794 they made their intentions clear when they tried to prevent a settler from establishing a farm on their yam grounds. In reprisal, a group of farmers, most of whom were former soldiers and armed with muskets, attacked a Bediagal campsite at night and killed at least seven of them. The government responded by stationing a sergeant and ten soldiers of the garrison in the heartland of the new settlement, intending that their presence would serve as a warning to the Bediagal to keep away from British settlers and their crops.[40]

The Bediagal, however, considered the grain crops planted in their yam fields as belonging to them, and as harvest time approached in May 1795, the government deployed a further 66 soldiers and two officers of the garrison to Hawkesbury with orders to 'kill any [Bediagal] they found and hang their bodies from gibbets as a warning to the rest'.[41] After forcing a Bediagal boy to guide them to his people's forest encampment at night, the soldiers again killed seven or more of them and captured a man, five women and some children. When the soldiers returned to the camp the next morning to string up the bodies, they were missing. The Bediagal boy explained that his people would have carried them away for a proper burial. After one of the children died in custody and one of the women miscarried, the rest were released.[42]

The first state-sanctioned massacre may have been messy, but it made the British realise that they had to contend with a well-prepared enemy. Over the next two years a permanent garrison of 93 soldiers and 2 officers were deployed in three different locations along the river, and carried out several sorties against the Bediagal, though few details survive. We do know, however, that the garrison remained in the region until 1808, by which time the Hawkesbury area was considered 'safe'.[43]

As British settlement spread south-west along the Hawkesbury-Nepean

---

39 Ryan L. 2013. 'Untangling Aboriginal resistance and the settler punitive expedition: The Hawkesbury frontier in New South Wales, 1794–1810', *Journal of Genocide Research*, 15, no. 2, 224.

40 Ibid., 225–226.

41 Collins D. 1975. *An Account of the English Colony in New South Wales*, vol. 1, ed. B. Fletcher. Sydney: A.H. & A.W. Reed, in association with the Royal Australian Historical Society, 348.

42 Connor J. *Australian Frontier Wars*, 38.

43 Ibid., 46.

River system after 1810, more state-sanctioned massacres by soldiers took place. Among the best known is the night-time military attack on an Aboriginal campsite at Appin in April 1816, ending in the slaughter of 14 Dharawal people. Appin was then on the south-western frontier of settlement and the Dharawal people firmly resisted the expansion onto their hunting grounds.[44] The purpose of these frontier massacres was to protect farmers by instilling fear into the Dharawal and bringing about their surrender, or to eradicate them entirely.

The final cluster of military-led massacres in the period to 1827 took place on the Bathurst Plains across the Blue Mountains, more than 160 kilometres west of Sydney, and in the Hunter Valley, more than 240 kilometres north-west of Sydney. Bathurst was in the homeland of the Wiradjuri people and the Hunter Valley was in the homelands of the Worimi and Wonnarua peoples. Both regions were opened up by the colonial government in 1822 for broad-acre sheep and cattle farming. After two alleged Wiradjuri attacks on civilian stockkeepers in the Bathurst region, the latter retaliated with night-time attacks on Wiradjuri camps, in which it is estimated 12 Wiradjuri people lost their lives. Convinced that the Wiradjuri were engaged in a major uprising in defence of their homeland, the governor declared martial law and between August and December 1824 sent more than 70 British troops under the command of Major James Morisset to 'clear' the region of Wiradjuri 'insurgents'. In one particular operation, the troops massacred 45 undefended Wiradjuri, the largest number known to have been killed in one operation to that date.[45]

In summarising the period 1794–1827, it is clear that the colonial government deployed the garrison to protect the frontiers of settlement and used the strategy of massacre to force Aboriginal surrender of their land. The killing of colonists was usually the trigger for the despatch of military forces to a site of conflict. Overall, the massacre map project indicates that at least 200 Aboriginal people died in 13 recorded frontier massacres, while 3 civilian men lost their lives. Five of the massacres were carried out by the military in which 126 Aboriginal people were killed, 6 were carried out by the settlers with a tally of 58 killed, and 2 were joint operations in which 26 Aboriginal people were killed. The statistics, however, are incomplete. There is no record of the sorties carried out by the military along the Hawkesbury River between 1795 and 1808, nor of their deployment against Aboriginal people along the new road over the Blue Mountains in 1816,

---

44 Ibid., 49–52.
45 Ibid., 59–62.

CHAPTER 5: Establishing a Code of Silence

about which information is just beginning to emerge, nor of their mopping-up operations in the Bathurst region during the final weeks of martial law in 1824.[46] The statistics do show that although the settlers appear to have carried out more instances of recorded massacre, they appear to have killed fewer than half the number of Aboriginal people killed by the military. If we make allowances for limited information being available about the military engagements, the findings would suggest a revision of the conclusion by Elder and Connor that most of the frontier massacres in the foundation years of the Australian colonies were carried out by British soldiers and that civilian massacres of Aboriginal people were harder to detect. Rather, the findings of the massacre map project show that the military killed more Aboriginal people than the settlers.[47]

Frontier massacres, 1828–1838

The year 1828 presaged a major shift in the practice of frontier massacre because of the wider availability of horses. According to Connor, horses 'tilted the balance on the Australian frontier'.[48] They not only enabled stockmen to push cattle and sheep into new pastures well beyond the colony's 'limits of location', but they also led the colonial government to replace the infantry with more mobile mounted police units that were better suited to the task of patrolling the frontier. Comprised of troopers and army officers seconded from British regiments serving in New South Wales, the mounted police force's brief was to suppress Aboriginal resistance without imposing martial law.[49] The changes were part of the transformation of the economic and social fabric of the colony in the aftermath of the Napoleonic Wars. No longer just a penal outpost, New South Wales attracted settler capitalists from Britain seeking large tracts of land to graze sheep to produce raw wool for export to Britain and live cattle for export to India. Between 1828 and 1838 the British population of New South Wales more than doubled from 35 960 to more than 80 000. According to historian Angela Woollacott, the free settlers brought with them a set of ideas and beliefs about political rights and racial, gender and class superiority that led them to believe that they had an inherent right to occupy Aboriginal land. And they expected

---

46 For the emerging information about violence along the new road over the Blue Mountains, see Gapps, *Sydney Wars*, 248–251.
47 Elder, *Blood on the Wattle*, 24; Connor, *Australian Frontier Wars*, 21.
48 Connor, *Australian Frontier Wars*, 67.
49 Ibid., 62.

the colonial government to clear Aboriginal people, whom they considered to be savages, from the land.[50]

The new conditions were first played out in the fertile Hunter Valley in the homelands of the Wonnarua and Worimi nations. Following tit-for-tat killings by the Wonnarua and settlers in 1826, the settlers petitioned Governor Ralph Darling to declare martial law and to despatch detachments of infantry to the region to eradicate the Wonnarua. Darling, however, considered the measure 'too extravagant to put down a few naked savages' and instead sent a detachment of Mounted Police under the command of Lieutenant Nathanial Lowe to suppress the Wonnarua insurgents.[51] Although few details of Lowe's operations survive, we do know that over the succeeding two years many Wonnarua people lost their lives. He also facilitated the opening up of the track from the Upper Hunter Valley across the Liverpool Range to the grazing lands of the Gamilaraay and Wirrayaraay nations on the Liverpool Plains and beyond to the Namoi and Gwydir Rivers. The Gamilaraay were the largest and most powerful Aboriginal nation in the central west of New South Wales, with an estimated population of more than 4 000.[52]

Between 1828 and the end of 1838, ten frontier massacres were recorded in the Hunter Valley, the Liverpool Plains and the Namoi and Gwydir River Valley regions, with an estimated loss of more than 500 Gamilaraay and Wirrayaraay people and 20 settler lives. In this decade, all but two of the massacres were perpetrated by settlers and stockmen.

The civilian massacre that took place near Quirindi, just across the Liverpool Range, in late 1827 revealed the changes taking place in the conduct of frontier massacre. According to historian Roger Milliss, a posse of mounted stockmen at a cattle run near Quirindi slaughtered a large group of Gamilaraay people in broad daylight. So great were the casualties that it took three stockmen more than two days to bury the bodies. Milliss believes that the massacre was 'hushed up, the government not wishing to give the matter any publicity'.[53] The incident bore some resemblance to the massacre at Myall Creek ten years later. The assassins were armed, mounted stockmen

---

50 For population statistics see Caldwell J.C. 1987. 'Population', in *Australian Historical Statistics*, ed. W. Vamplew. Sydney: Fairfax, Syme & Weldon Associates, 26; Woollacott A. 2015. *Settler Society in the Australian Colonies*. Oxford: Oxford University Press, 152–178.

51 *Historical Records of Australia*, series I, vol. xii, Darling to Hunter Valley Landholders, 5 September 1826; Enclosure in Darling to Bathurst, 6 October 1826, 577, 609.

52 Gamilaraay population estimate taken from Belshaw J. 1978. 'Population distribution and the pattern of seasonal movement in northern New South Wales', in *Records of Times Past*, 74.

53 Milliss, *Waterloo Creek*, 78–82.

CHAPTER 5: Establishing a Code of Silence

who slaughtered innocent victims in broad daylight and encountered considerable difficulty in disposing of the bodies.[54]

The six frontier massacres of Gamilaraay people in the Namoi and Gwydir River valleys between 1836 and 1838 provide the best illustration of the close relationship that was developing between the Mounted Police and civilians. The first took place in the Namoi River valley in early 1836, when a posse of stockmen staking out pastoral leases, or 'runs', for their absentee employers corralled a large group of Gamilaraay people near the base of the Nandewar Range and slaughtered them.[55] After the Gamilaraay fought back by attacking a cattle station on the Gwydir River and killing a station worker and wounding a stockman, settlers called on the government in Sydney for assistance.

The government responded by sending a detachment of Mounted Police to the region under the command of Sergeant John Temple. Over several weeks between April and June 1836, he joined with settlers and stockmen in a search-and-destroy operation in the Barraba area. The Reverend Lancelot Threlkeld estimated that they slaughtered 'upwards of 80' Gamilaraay people.[56] The stockmen called the operation a 'bushwhack', and in the following winter of 1837 they led other stockmen in the region in another bushwhack to clear the Gamilaraay from another part of the Gwydir River. The operation included the corralling of about 200 Gamilaraay people in a gorge at Gravesend Mountain and over several days hacking them to death with a variety of weapons, including swords and hatchets.[57]

Despite the loss of more than 300 of their countrymen in less than 2 years, the Gamilaraay continued to resist the intrusion of stockmen. Once again, the government sent help. This time the detachment of Mounted Police consisted of 28 troopers under the command of Major James Nunn. Assisted by at least three civilians, over eight weeks from the beginning of December 1837 to the end of January 1838, they conducted a bushwhack culminating in the massacre at Waterloo Creek on 26 January 1838, where at least 40 Gamilaraay were killed.[58] There is no doubt that the tactics deployed by the Mounted Police in the war to exterminate the Gamilaraay along the Gwydir River were the same as those carried out at Myall Creek six months

---

54 Ibid., 81.
55 Ibid., 78.
56 Quoted in ibid., 101.
57 Ibid., 159.
58 Ibid, 183–190; Ryan L. 2003. 'Waterloo Creek, northern New South Wales, 1838', in *Frontier Conflict: The Australian Experience*, eds. B. Attwood & S. Foster. Canberra: National Museum of Australia, 33–43.

later. They included operating without any motive except to kill Indigenous people, tying up the victims beforehand, burning the bodies afterwards, and insisting on a code of silence in the aftermath.

The final massacre along the Gwydir River was recorded in August 1838 at Crawford's Station on Ardgowan Island, where nine Gamilaraay people were slaughtered, their bodies burnt and then buried in a shallow grave. Like John Henry Fleming, the leading assassin, Charles Eyles, was a settler who would also have a warrant issued for his arrest, only to escape, leaving his two convict stockmen to face arrest and charges of murder. In this instance, however, one of them committed perjury and the case was dismissed.[59]

The practice of frontier massacre in this period was marked by clear similarities. The most significant is that settlers and their workers in the Namoi and Gwydir valleys had no hesitation in calling on the Mounted Police to assist them in 'clearing' the land of its Gamilaraay owners, and the colonial government in Sydney was more than willing to oblige. The Mounted Police taught the stockmen the value of the bushwhack, a campaign of extermination conducted by a large group of horsemen that continued for several weeks, in which entire groups of Aboriginal people were tracked down and executed. The process included tethering the victims beforehand and burning the bodies in the aftermath. Finally, the close relationship that developed between the Mounted Police and stockmen in this period cannot be overemphasised. As demonstrated by the two joint operations with the military, it is clear that they took place at a critical moment in the expansion of the sheep and cattle industries and provided stockmen with critical techniques of Aboriginal extermination, including the daylight raid, the bushwhack and the opportunity massacre.

Frontier massacres, 1839–1848

Despite the Myall Creek trials in November and December 1838 and the proclamation issued by the governor in April 1838 that any suspicious Aboriginal death be investigated, civilian extermination of Aboriginal people on the New South Wales frontier continued unabated.[60] Between 1840 and 1848 settler capitalists known as 'squatters' sought leasehold runs or stations in nine new pastoral divisions that comprised the colony's Northern Division. Much of the vast area is now part of southern Queensland and

---

59 Milliss, *Waterloo Creek*, 581–586.
60 *Historical Records of Australia*, Series I, vol. xix, Proclamation: *New South Wales Government Gazette*, 21 April 1838, Enclosure in Gipps to Glenelg, 27 April 1838, 397–398.

CHAPTER 5: Establishing a Code of Silence

covers the homelands of the Anawan, Bigumbal, Banjalaung, Gamilaraay, Gumbaynggir and Mandandanji nations, as well as the Waiwan, Kooma and Ngarabal nations in present-day New South Wales, with a combined population estimated at more than 20 000.[61]

Each pastoral district was managed by a Crown Lands Commissioner, assisted by a detachment of border police. The commissioners exercised the powers of a magistrate and, in keeping with the requirements of the Colonial Office in London, they were also the Protectors of the Aboriginal people.[62] They were expected to annually visit every pastoral leasehold or run in their jurisdiction to assess its grazing capacity and to ensure that the annual licence fee of leasehold occupation was paid. In their role as Aboriginal Protector, they were also expected to investigate incidents of frontier violence and report them to the authorities in Sydney for further action. Their reports provide details of some of the best-known instances of frontier massacre in this decade.

The massacre map project records 29 instances of frontier massacre in the Northern Division during this period, that is, nearly three per year. They include ten instances in the Clarence River pastoral district, three in the Gwydir and New England pastoral districts, six in the Moreton Bay and Darling Downs pastoral districts, three in the Bligh district and seven in the Maranoa pastoral district, for a combined total of more than 700 Aboriginal deaths and the loss of 20 settler lives.[63] This tally is an underestimate, for in ten cases the exact number of deaths was not provided, so the minimum number of six has been recorded — in keeping with the methodology of the massacre map project. In five of these cases, less than one quarter of the known incidents overall, the perpetrators were led by government forces, such as a detachment of Mounted Police, and in others by the Crown Lands Commissioner with a detachment of border police. In each case they appear to have acted in response to civilian calls for assistance.

One of the more complex instances of frontier massacre in this decade relates to a joint operation between civilians and the Mounted Police that occurred in contravention of government policy. In October 1841 settler William Lee at Bathurst sent his overseer Andrew Keir and a group of stockmen with a large herd of cattle to the Bogan River, north-west of Mount Harris, in the Bligh pastoral district, to establish a pastoral

---

61 Population estimate is derived from Belshaw, 'Population distribution', 77–78.
62 For a discussion of the contradictory role of the commissioners, see Woollacott, *Settler Society*, 161.
63 'Colonial Frontier Massacres in Central and Eastern Australia 1788–1930'.

131

CIVILIAN-DRIVEN VIOLENCE AND THE GENOCIDE OF INDIGENOUS PEOPLES

run. Lee should have known better. The area was in drought, and on the advice of Francis Allman, the Crown Lands Commissioner, Governor Gipps had declared the river off limits to settlers to ensure sufficient water was available for Waiwan Aboriginal people in the region. Lee appears to have acted in defiance of the declaration, and when Keir and his party arrived at the river and began watering cattle, a party of Waiwan warriors that had followed the party for 16 days suddenly killed three of the stockmen. Keir rode off to seek help — not to the nearest settlement, at Wellington, where Allman was stationed — but to Bathurst, several hundred miles further south, where his employer, William Lee, resided. Lee alerted the magistrate Major James Morisset about the killings. Morisset lost no time in ordering the local detachment of Mounted Police to the Bogan River to arrest the culprits. However, the detachment's senior officer Lieutenant Nicholson was absent. Morisset instructed the detachment to proceed to Wellington, where they were to place themselves under Allman's command and then ride to Lee's Station and arrest the culprits. The detachment ignored Morisset's instructions and proceeded directly to Lee's Station with Keir as their guide. Along the way they killed a number of Aboriginal people, and when they arrived at Lee's Station they shot 12 more and captured 3 others identified as the killers of the three stockmen, only to have one of them escape. At that point Allman arrived with a detachment of border police and took the two Waiwan men into custody. When they were brought before the circuit court in Wellington in March 1842, he ensured that they were discharged for lack of evidence. According to Allman, the killing of the three stockmen arose from the Waiwan 'seeing their water drank up by those white men and their cattle, they turned to defend their water supplied to them by nature, as who would not — man or beast!' He also recommended that Lee's application for a pastoral licence for the station be withheld.[64]

By far the greatest number of frontier massacres in this period, 21 in all, were carried out by settlers and their employees. Of these, four were cases of deliberate poisoning of food given to Aboriginal people. The best known is the Kangaroo Creek poisoning of 1847, because it was reported to the Attorney-General's office in Sydney. According to historian Jane Lydon, settler Thomas Coutts occupied the Kangaroo Creek Station of 53 760 acres in the country of the Gumbaynggir people in the Clarence River pastoral district in 1845–1846. Kangaroo Creek was estimated by the Crown Lands Commissioner to have a grazing capacity of 560 cattle and 7 500 sheep. In

---

64 A complete account of the incident was reported in the *Sydney Morning Herald*, 24 August 1842.

CHAPTER 5: Establishing a Code of Silence

November 1847 the run comprised a head station and several outstations with hutkeepers, shepherds, stockmen and dray drivers and at least one Aboriginal worker, a man named Jemmy. The Gumbaynggir regularly visited the run for food rations as recompense for the loss of their hunting grounds, and Coutts often employed them to weed the station garden. The station workers also made friends with several of them, but Coutts appears to have decided they were a nuisance. On 28 November 1847 he offered 23 of them flour laced with arsenic. Their bodies were found not far away, and a few weeks later at least two station workers reported the crime to the police at Grafton, the nearest town. The Crown Lands Commissioner Oliver Fry visited the site in January 1848, and after taking samples of the bodies and the flour scattered nearby, he arrested Coutts. He charged him with wilful murder and committed him for trial in Sydney. After long deliberation, the Attorney-General decided not to proceed on grounds of insufficient evidence although he was in 'no moral doubt' that Coutts was guilty.[65] Three other cases of poisoning in the Northern Division were also reported, but no one was arrested, let alone charged with the offence.

The requirement that a magistrate should hold an inquest into every suspicious Aboriginal death was one possible reason for settlers operating in secret and taking the law into their own hands. Others could be attributed to the prolonged drought, which prompted a contest for control of the waterholes, and the economic recession of the 1840s, which triggered a collapse in the price of raw wool. Geographer Ian Clark notes that similar conditions prevailing in the Port Phillip district at the time also resulted in an increase in frontier massacres by colonists.[66]

Frontier massacres, 1849–1859

In 1848, settlers on the far reaches of the Northern Division petitioned Governor Charles Fitzroy for the establishment of a native police force to protect them from Aboriginal attack. Known as the 'Roman method' of deploying colonised peoples against one another, the settlers noted that native forces were deployed in this way across the British Empire, including the Port Phillip district, the Cape Colony, Ceylon, India and New Zealand.[67]

---

65 Lydon J. 1996. "'No moral doubt": Aboriginal evidence and the Kangaroo Creek poisoning, 1847–1849'. *Aboriginal History*, 20, 151–175.
66 Clark, *Scars in the Landscape*, 1–10.
67 In promoting a native police force in the Port Phillip District in 1837, Captain Alexander Maconochie referred to the 'Roman method'. See Maconochie. 1838. 'Extracts from the observations on the treatment of the Aboriginal inhabitants of NSW', *S.A. Gazette and Colonial Register*, 4 September 1838. See also Nettelbeck A. & Ryan L. 2018. 'Salutary

In response, Fitzroy authorised the formation of a mounted native police force for the Northern Division on condition that the settlers agreed to pay a levy to help support it and appointed Frederick Walker, then aged 28, as the first commandant.[68] According to Leslie Skinner, the historian of the force, the governor believed that it 'would not only have the effect of checking the collisions' between the Aboriginal landowners and the settlers, but would also act as a 'civilising measure' for Aboriginal recruits. By 1859 more than 175 Aboriginal men had served in the force. Led by white officers, they wore distinctive uniforms, carried double-barrelled carbines, swords and pistols, and operated in detachments of ten to twelve troopers. They would prove very successful in suppressing Aboriginal resistance, often with the assistance of settlers and stockmen.[69]

From the beginning of 1849 to December 1859, 21 incidents of frontier massacre were recorded in the Northern Division, with the estimated loss of about 700 Aboriginal, and at least 50 settler, lives.[70] This tally, however, is an underestimate because seven of the reports failed to provide a precise number of casualties. Instead, the minimum number of six has been used, in keeping with the massacre map project's methodology. Eight of the incidents were perpetrated solely by the Native Police, four of them were joint operations by settlers and Native Police, and seven were by settlers alone. In other words, the Native Police were involved in more than half of the reported incidents. The two incidents that were not perpetrated by settlers or Native Police, however, are the best remembered. These were the massacres of colonists by Aboriginal warriors; the killing of one white woman and five men at Mount Larcomb Station in 1855, and the killing of eight men and three women at Hornet Bank Station in 1857. These massacres are a stark reminder that the settlers' fear of the Aboriginal people in the region was well founded. In the massive retribution for the Hornet Bank killings by settlers and Native Police, some of which were joint operations, it is estimated that in the three months following the massacre, up to 300 Aboriginal people were slaughtered.[71]

A typical settler massacre of the period took place in 1849, when about

---

lessons: Native Police and the "civilising" role of legalised violence in colonial Australia'. *Journal of Imperial and Commonwealth History*, 46, no.1, 46–68.

68 *Historical Records of Australia*, Series I, vol. xxvi, Fitzroy to Grey, Despatch no. 180, 12 August 1848, 559.

69 Skinner, *Police of the Pastoral Frontier*, 12, 26–27, 386–395.

70 The map records 728 casualties from frontier massacres in the Northern Division 1849–1859. See https://c21ch.newcastle.edu.au/colonialmassacres.

71 Ibid. For the loss of several hundred Aboriginal lives in the aftermath of the Hornet Bank massacre, see Reid, *Nest of Hornets*, ix.

CHAPTER 5: Establishing a Code of Silence

40 Aboriginal people from the Mandandanji nation were killed near Mount Abundance Station in the Grafton Range in the Maranoa pastoral district. Allan Macpherson, the young settler who led the operation, was accompanied by Crown Lands Commissioner John Durbin and a small detachment of Mounted Police. Macpherson was in the process of abandoning the station he had established two years earlier and was seeking retribution for the killing of four of his station workers and the loss of several thousand head of cattle. News of the massacre soon reached Sydney, where his father, William Macpherson, was Clerk of the Legislative Council. Deeply anxious that his son could be arrested for murder, he was reassured by Allan who told him that on the frontier, 'the majesty of the law is entirely powerless'.[72]

Another typical engagement by the Native Police took place in May 1849 at Carbucky Station on the Macintyre River in the Gwydir pastoral district. According to a witness, William Butler Tooth, the commandant found Aboriginal men killing Tooth's cattle and a 'fight ensued. The blacks were so completely put down on that occasion and terrified at the power of the Police, that they never committed any more depredations near there. The place was quiet at once, and property became fifty per cent more valuable'.[73] In this massacre, it is estimated that at least 100 Aboriginal people were slaughtered.

By 1855, when the Colony of New South Wales achieved self-government, the settler-dominated legislature tried to ignore Lord Grey's policy that pastoral leases were not intended to deprive the Aboriginal owners of the right to hunt and reside on their homelands; that where they had been driven off, small Aboriginal reserves for agriculture and the distribution of rations should be established; and that an Aboriginal Evidence Bill should be introduced. In the case of Aboriginal evidence, however, the colony waited until 1876 to do so.[74] With the settlers in charge and a Native Police force patrolling the northern frontier, Aboriginal people's rights as British subjects were simply ignored. Skinner considers the Native Police force as 'tangible evidence of the final bankruptcy of frontier policy'.[75] A majority of settlers disagreed. When Queensland was established as a separate colony in 1859, they took over the Native Police force. For the next four decades

---

72 Foster S. 2010. *A Private Empire*. Sydney: Pier 9 Books, 241–245.
73 Quoted in Skinner, *Police of the Pastoral Frontier*, 30.
74 *Historical Records of Australia*, Series I, vol. xxvi, Grey to Fitzroy, Despatch No. 24, 11 February 1848, 223–228.
75 Skinner, *Police of the Pastoral Frontier*, 13.

the Native Police gained a fearsome reputation for clearing the frontier of Aboriginal people.[76]

Conclusion

Between the first recorded frontier massacre in 1794 to the end of 1859 the massacre map project has recorded 73 instances of frontier massacre in New South Wales.[77] Of these, 45 were perpetrated by civilians, 17 by military and police forces, nine were joint operations by civilians and military, and the remaining two incidents were Aboriginal massacres of settlers. Thus, it is clear that civilians were responsible for more than half of the massacres overall, and more than two thirds of the Aboriginal death toll of more than 2 000, with the loss of fewer than 100 lives among the colonists. The figure of 2 000 should, however, be considered a very conservative estimate, for there are several cases where the precise number of deaths was not recorded and the minimum number of six was substituted.

If we exclude the two massacres of colonists by Aboriginal people and divide the estimate of 2 000 Aboriginal deaths by the remaining 71 massacres, an average of 28.2 people killed per massacre results. The mortality rate is significantly higher than the average of 14 Aboriginal deaths in 25 frontier massacres recorded in Tasmania during the Black War between December 1826 and January 1832.[78] It is also higher than the average of 17.2 Aboriginal people killed in 68 frontier massacres in the Port Phillip district between 1836 and 1851.[79] The statistic for New South Wales is, however, based on a much longer period, over a far greater area, and a higher Aboriginal population. It is also worth noting the role of joint operations between settlers and soldiers in the three jurisdictions. In Tasmania, joint operations were the norm, accounting for more than 75 per cent of the massacres overall, whereas in the Port Phillip district they were responsible for about 25 per cent, with most of them occurring in the 1840s. In New South Wales they accounted for a little more than 12 per cent of the massacres.

Of the 45 massacres perpetrated by civilians in New South Wales, 21 were carried out in the decade following Myall Creek. There are two

---

76 Richards J. 2008b. *The Secret War: A True History of Queensland's Native Police*. Brisbane: University of Queensland Press.

77 This is the number recorded by the massacre map project at 10 October 2018.

78 The average for Tasmania is based on the statistics in Ryan L. 2012. *Tasmanian Aborigines: A History since 1803*. Sydney: Allen & Unwin, 142–145.

79 The average number for the Port Phillip District is based on the statistics in Ryan L. 2010. 'Settler massacres in the Port Phillip District, 1836–1851'. *Journal of Australian Studies*, 23, no. 3, 264.

CHAPTER 5: Establishing a Code of Silence

possible explanations for the escalation. First, in keeping with the policy of treating Aboriginal people as British subjects that was implemented in 1838, the colonial government was reluctant to authorise the Crown Lands Commissioners and the Mounted Police to carry out frontier massacres, although, as has been shown, some certainly did. Rather, the colonial government considered their role as preventing frontier 'collisions'. Secondly settlers were prepared to take the law into their own hands, as demonstrated by instances of poisoning and the actions of particular settlers in carrying out their own search-and-destroy operations.

By contrast, most of the 17 recorded instances of state-sanctioned massacre, together with the nine joint operations, were carried out in the first and fourth periods, when the colonial government took responsibility for policing new frontiers. Government forces played a critical role in 'training' settlers and stockmen to carry out frontier massacres. For example, the search-and-destroy operations, known as bushwhacks, that were conducted by Temple and Nunn in 1836 and 1838 established the tactics for frontier massacre that would continue in the decade following the Myall Creek massacre, and were then taken up by the Native Police in the 1850s. The only form of mass killing of Aboriginal people that was considered completely unacceptable by the colonial government was that of poisoning.

Thus, it would appear that as a massacre perpetrated by civilians, Myall Creek was not out of the ordinary. The culprits were experienced in the technique of frontier massacre, with each of them involved in at least one previous instance, and used swords and cutlasses as weapons of choice. That the incident took place in daylight as a pre-emptive strike, or opportunity massacre, was also not unusual. Indeed, the massacre map project indicates that once horses began to be used, daylight massacres became the norm. It was not unusual for the victims to be tied up beforehand and led to the site where they would be slaughtered, and for their bodies to be burnt. Nor was it unusual for a settler to lead the massacre. What was unusual about Myall Creek was that the massacre was reported, that the government took notice, that the perpetrators were arrested, and that witnesses spoke up. Above all, it was the fact that the victims were elderly men, women and children, rather than 'warriors', that prompted Attorney-General Plunkett to send a magistrate to track down the assassins and bring them to justice.

Can we consider the 71 recorded instances of civilian and military massacre an expression of genocide? Mark Tedeschi is in no doubt that the Myall Creek massacre was an act of genocide in that the assassins sought to eliminate the Wirrayaraay people entirely.[80] In this context, the bushwhacks

---

80 Tedeschi, *Murder at Myall Creek*, 269.

against the Gamilaraay people leading up to Myall Creek were also acts of genocide. What, then, of the other incidents recorded after Myall Creek? The project demonstrates that these massacres were also acts of genocide in that each was carefully planned, and that it is immaterial whether they were perpetrated by civilians or military and police forces. They all operated with the same outcome in mind — the elimination of Aboriginal people. And although it is possible to argue that, in the decade following Myall Creek, the colonial state put administrative changes in place, such as the appointment of Crown Lands Commissioners to prevent or curtail frontier massacres, it never acknowledged the rights of Aboriginal people to their lands and never held the Crown Lands Commissioners to account when they killed Aboriginal people. Very few of them took their duties as Aboriginal protectors as seriously as Francis Allman did at Wellington. Rather, they were more like John Durbin, who in 1849 assisted Allan Macpherson in the massacre of at least 40 Mandandanji people in the Maranoa pastoral district.

The establishment of the Native Police force in 1848, was a joint venture between settlers and the colonial state to suppress Aboriginal resistance. This would suggest that civilians and the colonial state bear joint responsibility for the outcome. From the 1840s onwards settlers and the state adopted the view that the Aboriginal people were destined to die out. Wrapped up in this new ideology, they could ignore the widespread practice of frontier massacre over such a long period of time. But the mass destruction of the Jiman people in the aftermath of the Hornet Bank massacre in 1858 would suggest that they match Semelin's concept of ethnic cleansing.[81]

What is remarkable about the New South Wales frontier massacres is that some of the Aboriginal victims did survive and would relate their experiences to their children and grandchildren, while some of the perpetrators would experience anguish and reveal their involvement in particular incidents several decades later in memoirs, breaking the code of silence that prevailed during the frontier phase. It would be another 150 years, however, before these kinds of evidence would be accepted as part of historical methodology — particularly in the massacre map project — and the extent and impact of frontier massacre would be revealed.

---

81 Semelin, *Purify and Destroy,* 345–346.

CHAPTER SIX

'Pale Death ... around our Footprints Springs':[1] Assessing Violent Mortality on the Queensland Frontier from State and Private Exterminatory Practices

Raymond Evans and Robert Ørsted-Jensen

> *When I ask them what they learn in Modern History, students disclose that it was ... very much about wars. When I ask whether this included the frontier wars, many respond with 'Huh? What are they?'*
>
> Elaine Laforteza, 27 April 2018[2]

> *Who, after all, speaks today of the annihilation of the Armenians?*
>
> Adolf Hitler, 22 August 1939[3]

History is invariably harsh. Yet, in Australia, there has been, for the most part, a marked divergence between the harshness of its past and the anodyne responses of much of its written history. This may partially be explained by its location within 'the consciousness of the West' as a self-declared 'superior' cultural and political formation, despite a long history of imperial intervention, dispossession and colonisation; its local allegiance to a white, nationalistic mode of analysis that serves to smooth away rough and difficult patches as so-called blemishes; and a shying away from a past that, in its actual founding, is inured with some remarkably cruel and violent

---

1   Forster W. 1877. 'The brothers', quoted in Evans R. 2007. *A History of Queensland*. Melbourne: University of Cambridge Press, 74. Forster, of Gin Gin Station, was a leading Queensland pastoralist who helped organise reprisal raids against Aboriginal peoples in the Burnett and Wide Bay region in the 1850s. In 1859–1860, he was premier of New South Wales.

2   Laforteza E. 2018. 'Teaching nationhood: An Asian Australian story'. Kardla (Fire)/ News/Symposia, 27 April. Australian Critical Race and Whiteness Studies Association. Available at https://acrawsa.org.au/2018/04/27/teaching-nationhood-an-asian-australian-storyteaching-nationhood-an-asian-australian-story/, accessed 30 October 2019.

3   Quoted in Lockner L. 1942. *What About Germany?* New York: Dodd, Mead, 4.

tendencies. The Australian frontier story *is*, in effect, such an origin story par excellence, and is saturated with incidents of 'systematic destruction of Indigenous societies through massacre, enslavement, dispossession, forced migration, confinement to marginal living conditions, abduction of children, the suppression of language, religion, cultural practice, and political and economic institutions'.[4] And in Queensland it is also a story in which state-led and civilian-driven violence are intimately intertwined.

The degree of lethal violence lodged in such processes is only just beginning to be academically appreciated and understood. It is still avoided in the research of many, and in the wider society is angrily denied by many others. It remains a contentious topic of debate and disputation within the nation's central institutions. The interlocking tendencies of violent commission and convenient omission of reportage have been embedded together throughout the entire historical process. Like the violence itself, the degree of persistent cover-up has been underrated. As Gideon Scott Lang, a leading Maranoa pastoralist, who was himself both a participant and observer of the brutal frontier activities, told a Melbourne audience in 1865: 'The number [of Aborigines] killed is not mentioned. They are never counted and in fact never looked for ... the usual course is not to look down so as to see the dead; *not one in twenty is ever reported*; neither is mention made of wounded or prisoners ...'[5]

Subsequent attempts to assess frontier mortality rates by way of guesses, estimates and ratios or by confining significant killings to groups of six or above, listed upon apparent 'massacre sites', seem doomed to partiality and error due to the fog of denial, suppression and obfuscation surrounding the vast range of individual, small-group and larger mass killings that occurred. Only the tip of the iceberg is ever likely to be discerned here, serving merely to confront those still believing that very little of this sort of thing ever happened in sunny Australia. Such endeavours will never uncover the true dimensions of the human wastage that occurred.

In this chapter, therefore, we shall attempt to slice through this Gordian knot by applying a mathematical model to the interpretation of available data, gathered here as a very cautiously estimated sample of

---

4 Powell C. 2011. *Barbaric Civilization: A Critical Sociology of Genocide*. Montreal: McGill-Queen's University Press, 129, 135; Evans R. 2013. 'Foreword', in Bottoms T. 2013. *Conspiracy of Silence: Queensland's Frontier Killing Times*. Sydney: Allen & Unwin, xvii–xviii.

5 Collins P. 2002. *Goodbye Bussamarai: The Mandandji Land War, Southern Queensland, 1842–1852*. St Lucia, Brisbane: University of Queensland Press, 150–154; Ørsted-Jensen R. 2011. *Frontier History Revisited: Colonial Queensland and the 'History War'*. Brisbane: Lux Mundi Publishing, 2 (emphasis added).

CHAPTER 6: 'Pale Death ... around our Footprints Springs'

known frontier cases. In this manner, we will arrive at a defensible and transparently constructed figure, representing the combined death toll of state-sanctioned Native Police killings, of complimentary, unprosecuted private colonists' assaults, as well as the violent deaths of the colonisers themselves at the hands of Aboriginal resisters. The colony of Queensland has been chosen for this assessment as it is the premier locale for researching frontier conflict in Australia. Queensland was one of those unique places where white settlement thoroughly pervaded the tropical zone, doing so at a time when Western weapons technology achieved a new peak in destructive efficiency. Simultaneously, Western racial theories that provided impetus and intellectual permission for destructive dispossession were burgeoning in their certitude and persuasiveness.

Queensland was one of those rare colonies where pastoral, mining, crop farming, timber, maritime and plantation frontiers were all concurrently advancing across First Nation lands and waters, exacerbating tendencies for violent extremes. Though pastoral frontiers were the most geographically extensive and ultimately devastating, gold-mining frontiers, opening from the 1850s and culminating in intensity during the 1870s, were also highly destructive, due to the sudden high influxes of feverish populations, high levels of environmental spoliation and, usually, a triangulated degree of racial conflict between Aborigines, Europeans and Chinese. Techniques of land theft and frontier devastation had already been well honed and rehearsed in the southern colonies of Tasmania, Victoria and New South Wales — and Queensland settlers benefited accordingly from such expertise. The colony's metropolitan centre, located in its far south-east, was incapable of maintaining control over this vast British imperial outpost, an immense area of 1 727 000 square kilometres and a coastline 4 000 kilometres in length. Of all the Australian colonies, Queensland thus possessed the largest territory for conversion to pastoral pursuits and crop farming, while simultaneously being of such an unwieldy size that it was difficult to oversee, service and control administratively. A tendency towards regional excess in the process of land seizure thus prevailed.[6]

Most significantly, the Queensland area, prior to first contact, was in the possession of the largest number of First Nation peoples, sustained by bountiful tropical and subtropical environments, even though they were eventually hit by smallpox epidemics that had ravaged populations further south. Robert Ørsted-Jensen, using proportional colonial estimates of pre-

---

6   Evans R. 2007. *History of Queensland*. Cambridge: Cambridge University Press, 2–3, 268–269.

CIVILIAN-DRIVEN VIOLENCE AND THE GENOCIDE OF INDIGENOUS PEOPLES

contact population sizes — compiled by Alfred Radcliffe-Brown in 1930, Noel Butlin in 1983, Malcolm Prentis in 1988 and the Australian Institute of Aboriginal and Torres Strait Islander Studies in 1994 — has calculated that the population in the Queensland area prior to 1788 was somewhere between 34.2 and 38.2 per cent of the overall Australian total, containing around 140 of the 407 known tribal groupings and upward of 250 000 people. This is in stark contrast to Tasmania, with only between 0.6 and 2 per cent of the entire population, to New South Wales with 10.3 per cent, or to Victoria with around 5.7 per cent. Hence, in Queensland, Aboriginal resistance, buoyed by higher numbers and a later contact chronology, was more robust, skilled and prolonged than elsewhere, and in the process of wresting the largest arable territory from the largest number of First Nation hands, the devastation became far more extensive and intense in this northern colony.[7]

The onslaught began with soldiers and convicts in the mid-1820s and extended, especially from the 1840s onwards, into the twentieth century as the pastoral frontier moved from the south-east in northerly and westerly directions. The colony of Queensland, which was separated from New South Wales in 1859, had originated as a brutal secondary punishment centre for twice-convicted convicts, established at Moreton Bay, later the capital city of Brisbane, between 1824 and 1842. It then expanded westward and northward with enormous pastoral stations, first for sheep and later cattle, into the adjacent Darling Downs, the Maranoa, the Dawson district and Wide Bay. It was all part of one of the largest and most rapid and relatively unregulated land-grabs in colonial history. By 1859, when Queensland achieved self-government, it was fast extending itself into the tropical zone. With separation came the power to control the Native Police force, previously organised by New South Wales in 1848–1849 to provide a buffer between white incomers and resistant Aboriginal populations. Yet, because the armed squads of Aboriginal troopers, recruited from distant tribal territories, and white officers only attacked local Indigenous clans and never policed violent white colonists, it rapidly assumed the character of a lethal organisation that rode shotgun beside the pastoral advance, cutting a violent swathe through First Nation populations. This process became even more concerted in intensity once Queensland pastoralists, elected and nominated to the new, bicameral parliament, assumed control of the expansion process in their immediate material self-interests.

Ongoing violence by this government-run Native Police force and private killings by settlers coexisted on the same lethal trajectory of human

---

7   Ørsted-Jensen, *Frontier History*, 9–15.

CHAPTER 6: 'Pale Death ... around our Footprints Springs'

and environmental wastage. The colonial state was funded by land taxes, garnered from First Nation estates relabelled Crown Land. Expansion was stimulated by the many and various, but principally pastoral, economic imperatives of the settler establishment, whose leading and wealthiest members dominated a parliament, ultimately administering frontier dispersals. These men, who formed the colony's ruling class, were the main beneficiaries of profit from the stolen lands. The entire process was murkily disguised. An official publication, *Our First Half Century*, produced in 1909, described colonial Queensland as 'a huge sheep and cattle farm with contributive industries', built upon 'almost tenantless ... and limitless' grasslands — 'the principal denizen of the lonely land being the timid kangaroo'![8]

Private citizens' forays against Aborigines received tacit official approval from a process that eschewed any consideration of land rights, sovereignty or evolving human or property rights before the law for Indigenous peoples, while reducing them to an unprotected, perpetually subhuman status. The British legal system, for the most part, averted its gaze as both Native Police squads and settler vigilante posses accomplished the violent deaths of tens of thousands of people, nominally defined as 'British subjects'. There were virtually no effective prosecutions at law as redress for exterminatory practices.[9]

Thus, an imperilled and socially exposed population was delivered up for carnage, as Aboriginal peoples were attacked and dispossessed within the context of an illegal and undeclared war. All around, the cultural and political resources of the usurping society were mobilised, both to deny and normalise violence, and to defame the victims uniformly as a kind of *ferae naturae* (wild in nature) in order to legitimate the forceful and extensive dispossession and transformation of the land.[10] State and private patterns of dispossession were thus tightly imbricated with overt racism in this saga of human annihilation and environmental transmission. Just how much human wastage this prolonged historical trend entailed will now be examined.

---

8   Anon. 1909. *Our First Half-Century: A Review of Queensland Progress*. Brisbane: Anthony J. Cumming, 97–99.

9   Evans R. 2008a. 'Done and dusted'. *Griffith Review*, 21, 192; Evans, *History of Queensland*, 74; Evans R. 2010. 'The country has another past: Queensland and the history wars', in *Passionate Histories: Myth, Memory and Indigenous Australia*, eds. F. Peters-Little, A. Curthoys & J. Docker. Canberra: ANU Press, 23; Ørsted-Jensen, *Frontier History*, 31–32.

10 Evans R., Saunders K. & Cronin K. 1988. *Race Relations in Colonial Queensland: A History of Exclusion, Exploitation and Extermination*. St Lucia: University of Queensland Press, 75–79.

'I cannot say the numbers that were killed':[11] Assessing violent mortality on the Queensland frontier

Attempts to assess Queensland's frontier mortality rate due to interracial violence date back to early colonial times. Though it was always easier to keep track of non-Aboriginal casualties, the Aboriginal death rate remained something of a convenient mystery. There was, however, a general impression that this figure must be large, given the reality of a 'never ceasing war', prosecuted with unflagging zeal by white colonists. During the 1860s, before the conflict peaked, colonial observers agreed that 'hundreds and hundreds were shot every year'. By the 1870s, they were speaking in terms of 'thousands'.[12]

Impressions grew hazier in the early twentieth century as the frontier experience faded from mass consciousness and Australian nationalism demanded a cleaner slate. Nevertheless, in 1935, the eminent social anthropologist Radcliffe-Brown estimated that, during the early colonial years, the Aborigines of southern Queensland had suffered 'an enormous mortality ... as the result of massacres by settlers and police'. 'There is abundant evidence,' he wrote, 'that many thousands were shot in order that the white man might enjoy undisturbed their tribal lands.'[13]

The first attempt to place an actual figure on the carnage, however, did not occur until 1972, when Henry Reynolds, writing in *Meanjin*, an Australian literary journal, provided a 'conservative' guesstimate of 5000 Queensland Aborigines as having died violently. Such was the infancy of the debate at this point that Raymond Evans in 1975 described this figure as 'sufficiently startling'. Yet he went on to suggest that, based upon his own empirical research, his 'calculated guess' would be a death rate of 'almost double' this. By the early 1980s, after Noel Loos had determined a rough total of 1000 non-Aborigines killed in Queensland frontier conflict, the well-known 10:1 mortality ratio was suggested by Reynolds and soon became the new consensus. Queensland Aboriginal deaths from frontier

---

11 These are the words of Sri Lankan ex-convict George 'Black' Brown, who was present at a Yuggera encampment near the Darling Downs in October 1841 when it was surrounded and attacked by white squatters and their workforce and a massacre occurred. See Evans R. 2008b. '"On the utmost verge": Race and ethnic relations at Moreton Bay, 1799–1842', *Queensland Review*, 15, no. 1, 23–29.

12 *Brisbane Courier*, 25 March 1865; *Queensland Parliamentary Debates*, 15 January 1868, 21 July 1875; *Port Denison Times*, 1 May 1869; *Rockhampton Bulletin*, 30 May 1865; Wills K. 1895. 'Reminiscence', Brandon Papers 75/75/3, Oxley Memorial Library, 106–107.

13 Radcliffe-Brown A.R. 1935. 'Black sunset', *Sunday Mail Magazine*, 8 September 1935.

CHAPTER 6: 'Pale Death ... around our Footprints Springs'

violence were now set at 10000 — half the agreed Australia-wide figure of 20000 killed from 1788 to 1930.[14]

Although Reynolds was at pains to emphasise that this estimate was both 'little better than an informed guess' and an irreducible minimum, it began to be widely quoted either as a maximum figure or a barely debatable constant. It is instructive to ask why a 10:1 ratio was so unproblematically accepted, given that other colonial assessments were also on record. For instance, in 1870, colonial commentator A. Carr claimed that, for every infraction against whites, Queensland Aborigines were 'hunted like wild beasts ...[and] decimated by being shot down by twenties or fifty at a time.' Writing in 1889, Archibald Meston, soon to become Southern Protector of Aborigines, concluded, after interviewing members of 60 to 70 'tribes', that the kill ratio was 'at least' 50:1. Why were such ratios never considered? Too far-fetched, perhaps? Well, we shall see.[15]

In 1982, Loos, echoing the impression of the Reverend Julian Tenison Woods from a century earlier, stated that the 10:1 ratio for North Queensland was 'so conservative as to be misleading'. And, tellingly, when Reynolds in 1987 advanced the Australian settler mortality total to 3000 killed and 3000 injured, the associated Aboriginal casualty rate remained stubbornly fixed at 20000. It was not accordingly calibrated upward to 60000 dead and wounded. Richard Broome's influential overview, *Aboriginal Australians*, published in multiple editions from 1982 onwards, would also help to cement the 20000 figure into an almost fixed state in general consciousness.[16]

---

14 Reynolds H. 1972. 'Violence, the Aboriginals and the Australian historian' *Meanjin*, 31, no. 4; Evans et al. *Race Relations*, 128; Loos N. 1982. *Invasion and Resistance: Aboriginal-European Relations on the North Queensland Frontier 1861–1897*. Canberra: Australian National University Press, 189–248; Reynolds H. 1987. *Frontier: Aborigines, Settlers and Land*. Sydney: Allen & Unwin, 29–30, 50; Reynolds H. 1981. *The Other Side of the Frontier*. Townsville: James Cook University Press, 99–100; Loos N. & Reynolds H. 1976. 'Aboriginal resistance in Queensland'. *Australian Journal of Politics and History*, 22, no. 2, 214–226.

15 Reynolds, *Frontier*, 50; Carr A. 1870. *Where not to Immigrate: Queensland as it Is*. London: T. Cooper, 24–25; Meston A. 1889. 'Report on the government scientific expedition to the Bellenden-Kerr Range (Wooroonooran), North Queensland', *Queensland Legislative Council Votes and Proceedings* II, 1213. See also J.C. Byrne's assessment of 'at least fifty natives [killed] for every white man that falls' in New South Wales, including the Moreton Bay region, in Byrne J.C. 1848. *Twelve Years Wandering in the British Colonies 1*. London: Richard Bentley, 276, as well as the *Port Denison Times*, 2 March 1867, advocating that for every white killed 'we take, say, fifty?'

16 Broome R. 2010. *Aboriginal Australians: A History Since 1788*. Sydney: Allen & Unwin. See also *Queenslander*, 25 February 1882; Loos, *Invasion*, 190. Interestingly, Richard Broome gives a ratio of between 12 and 17 Aborigines killed for every white in Victoria, as well as 40:1 for the Gippsland region, while arguing that this colony's frontier was 'arguably less violent than some'. Nevertheless, he still stays with the ratio of 10:1 for the

CIVILIAN-DRIVEN VIOLENCE AND THE GENOCIDE OF INDIGENOUS PEOPLES

Yet it was eventually challenged as being, in Reynolds' words, 'thought too high by some, too low by others'. Among the former, surprisingly, was Aboriginal academic Gordon Briscoe, who, in an extraordinary article published in the prestigious British *History Workshop journal* in 1993, claimed only 404 non-Aboriginal fatalities on the Queensland frontier, offset by 'approximately [*sic*] 381' Aboriginal deaths. Historians who alleged 'exaggerated ... widespread killings', Briscoe maintained, in an arresting precursor to Keith Windschuttle's approaching pre-emptive strike, were simply 'political opportunists', promoting a deluded myth about frontier 'wars'. Such intense reductionism reached its absurdist peak in 2000, when Windschuttle himself charged that Reynolds could only show five actual Aboriginal deaths at the hands of the Queensland Native Police. On the other hand, David Day, in his race-based, general Australian history, *Claiming a Continent*, argued that the 20 000 benchmark 'stretched credulity to the limit', considering that only around 60 000 Aborigines, which included people of partial Aboriginal descent, had survived dispossession by Federation in 1901, out of an estimated original population of 750 000 to 1.5 million. He concluded that a 'guesstimate' of 'somewhat more than 50 000' deaths Australia-wide — a figure approaching that of Australians killed in the First World War — 'might be more accurate', though still conservatively drawn. Finally, in 2003, Evans suggested that the national 20 000 figure could 'possibly' be accounted for by Queensland's frontier violence alone.[17]

Where do all these guesstimates leave us? Frontier records are so purposefully incomplete as to render an overall body count impossible, and the 10:1 ratio is so malleable and questionable as to be severely flawed.

---

whole of Australia. Broome R. 2003. 'Statistics of frontier conflict', in *Frontier Conflict: The Australian Experience*, eds. B. Attwood & S. Forster. Canberra: National Museum of Australia, 90, 95–96.

17 Reynolds, *Frontier*, 30, and *Other Side*, 100–101; Broome R. 1982. *Aboriginal Australians: Black Response to White Domination*. Sydney: Allen & Unwin, 55. Nevertheless, Broome again writes that although he was placing Aboriginal violent frontier deaths at 'about 20 000, yet it could be much more'. He also calculates the national European death rate at a low 1 000 to 1 500; Briscoe G. 1993. 'Aboriginal Australian identity: The historiography of relations between indigenous ethnic groups and other Australians', *History Workshop Journal*, 36, 136, 145–146. Briscoe accuses 'three writers in particular' who have promoted false ideas, that is, the 'myth' of a 'frontier war', namely, 'Reynolds, [Charles] Rowley and Loos'. Reynolds H. 'The perils of political re-interpretation', *Sydney Morning Herald*, 25 September 2000; Day D. 1997. *Claiming a Continent: A New History of Australia*. Sydney: Angus & Robertson, 130; Evans R. 2003. 'Across the Queensland frontier', in Attwood & Forster, *Frontier Conflict*, 73, 75; Evans R. 2004. '"Plenty shoot 'em": The destruction of Aboriginal societies along the Queensland frontier', in *Genocide and Settler Society: Frontier Violence and Stolen Indigenous Children in Australian History*, ed. A. Moses. New York: Berghahn Books, 167; Ørsted-Jensen, *Frontier History*, 253–256.

CHAPTER 6: 'Pale Death ... around our Footprints Springs'

Furthermore, crucial Native Police files, dealing with field activities, have been culled. They have mysteriously gone missing from the Queensland Police Department archives where they should have been stored and retained.

How do we know this? Early official procedural records indicate a rigorous system of reportage of Native Police activities. On several occasions, orders were issued that field officers were to provide continual 'collision reports', detailing circumstances of any frontier clash in which their troopers engaged. Additionally, from the mid-1860s, printed and leatherbound operational diaries were issued to each subinspector, who was required at regular intervals to forward details, along with monthly and quarterly enumeration reports, to police headquarters in Brisbane, including the calculated number of casualties.[18]

Accumulated from scores of Native Police barracks across many decades of patrolling, this archive of monthly reports and diary extracts must have been immense. Yet numerous searches for these elusive documents by historians have proven largely fruitless. It would appear that this vast repository was never transferred by the Queensland Police Department to the Oxley Memorial Library, the State Library or the Queensland State Archives. What actually exists, in the form of 'Native Police records' in the latter repository is a residue of around ten per cent of the files, including relatively innocuous procedural staffing materials. There is no sign that anyone outside the force has ever seen the remainder of the data. What remains for public view are scattered, seemingly copied, and probably abbreviated versions of the original correspondence, requested at times by other ministerial arms of government, often during periods of controversy. These were generally handwritten copies that were quite likely and easily sanitised. Most of the original documents have vanished.

What became of them? This has remained a mystery until quite recently, when first Ørsted-Jensen and then Ray Kerkhove discovered press accounts written by the veteran *Sydney Morning Herald* journalist and Alexander Vindex Vennard, subsequent owner of the *Townsville Daily Bulletin*. Prior to March 1940, Vennard wrote to the Queensland Police

---

18 Ørsted-Jensen, *Frontier History*, 95–98, 100–101, 253–256; Public Records Office, Kew, London, Executive Minutes EXE/E2/60/56, Lieut. R. Morisset to Queensland Colonial Secretary, January 1861; Queensland State Archives (hereafter QSA), Colonial Secretary's Department (hereafter COL) A13/1666 Native Police Officer Instructions, February 1861; QSA Queensland Police Commissioner's Office (hereafter QPC) POL/4/249 Native Police Officer Instructions, 15 May 1867; QSA QPC POL/ 12M/78/100 Native Police Office Instructions, 13 April 1878.

147

CIVILIAN-DRIVEN VIOLENCE AND THE GENOCIDE OF INDIGENOUS PEOPLES

Department requesting access to the official records of 'the Black Police on the Palmer field' from the 1870s. This frontier was well-known for its racial violence due to private miner and Native Police assaults and spirited First Nation resistance. Vennard was officially informed, however, that 'such records, which were in their [the Police Department's] possession, had been destroyed sometime previously', possibly late in 1939. Vennard published this intelligence on three known occasions — first in the *Townsville Daily Bulletin* on 14 March 1940, then in the *Northern Miner* on 22 April 1943, and once more in the *Daily Bulletin* on 28 March 1946, leaving little doubt that this exchange referred to the deliberate destruction of the Queensland Native Police files.[19]

Yet all is not lost and a more exacting methodology is still possible. For surviving Queensland Native Police material on the duration of the major camps, the regularity of patrols and reported violent encounters, surviving in other places, does provide us with a framework that is far more dependable than mere guesswork and ratios. The exhaustive archival research of Jonathan Richards to locate extant official documentation, outlined in his doctorate of 2005 and his 2008 publication, *The Secret War*, has allowed for a coherent understanding of the Native Police as an institutional force. Richards lists 85 Native Police barracks established at different times between 1859 and 1898 across the vast expanses of Queensland as the colonial frontier advanced.[20] By 1869 such establishments, begun in the late 1840s, had spread from Sandgate in the south to Burketown in the north. During the 1860s there were 25 in existence and, as the frontier spread into Cape York and the far west in the 1870s, that number almost doubled to 42. These operational epicentres, moving across the colony in tandem with the expanding frontier, were augmented by other campsites, utilised when the trooper squads, along with their white officers, were on regular patrol, leading to a known

---

19 *Townsville Daily Bulletin*, 14 March 1940; *Daily Bulletin*, 28 March 1946; *Northern Miner*, 22 April 1943.

20 Richards J. 2005. 'A Question of Necessity: The Native Police in Queensland'. PhD dissertation, Griffith University; Richards J. 2008b. *The Secret War: A True History of Queensland's Native Police*. St Lucia, Brisbane: University of Queensland Press, *passim*. An assessment is possible, notwithstanding the recent opinion by the same author that 'there is too little systematic data to draw much more than speculative conclusions as to the scale and incidence of killing and other violence'; Finnane M. & Richards J. 2010 'Aboriginal violence and state response: Histories, policies, legacies in Queensland 1860–1940'. *ANZ Journal of Criminology*, 43, no. 2, 442; Evans, 'The country has another past', 29.

CHAPTER 6: 'Pale Death ... around our Footprints Springs'

total of 'nearly 200 Native Police campsites across Queensland' — obviously startling evidence of a massive and prolonged paramilitary presence.[21]

As the camps expanded, so too did the firepower of an increasing number of Aboriginal troopers and white officers. Breech-loading Snider rifles, supplied from 1873, multiplied by a factor of five to ten the firepower of the previous muzzle-loading Yeomanry Pattern carbines issued from 1848, as well as the Cape Mounted Corps double-barreled carbines in use from 1859, and the more efficient Terry's breech loaders, widely used in the Maori Wars of the 1860s and introduced later in the decade. The Snider, with its .577 calibre cartridge, capped with a soft leaden head, could, to quote historian Tony Roberts, 'kill an elephant'.[22] During the 1880s, there were still 30 barracks in operation, mostly in the far north and the Gulf country as, from 1882–1883, troopers were increasingly armed with the more effective Martini-Henry rifle, a weapon of 'unusual flexibility' that outperformed the Snider. By the 1890s, there were only 20 barrack-like camps, shrinking to 6 in the Cape York Peninsula by 1898 as the frontier wound down.[23]

Most crucially, Richards has also supplied, in an appendix to his thesis, duration dates for each camp. A minority of these, such as at Laura, Kirkleton, Nigger Creek and Turn-off Lagoon in North Queensland, were operational for two decades or more. Yet, in composite, Richards' 84 camps, in existence between 1859 and 1897, cover an aggregate period of 596 years, or around 7 years per camp. Writing in the 2010 anthology, *Passionate Histories*, Evans married these statistics to intelligence about the force's monthly patrols, conducted to pre-empt or avenge alleged Aboriginal depredations within

---

21 Richards J. 2005. 'Native Police camps and stations by date of opening', in 'A Question of Necessity', 353–354. This source lists 85 camps, even though Richards' location map at 355 positions only 74. We have removed the Frome camp from our calculations as it was established in 1898, leaving 84 camps within our sample here. For the 200 identified camps, see Wallis L. et al. 2016. *Rewriting the History of the Native Mounted Police in Queensland*. Nulungu Publication Series, Nulungu Insights No. 1. Broome: Nulungu Research Institute, University of Notre Dame Australia. See also Anon. 2017. 'Outback search for Native Mounted Police camps', Flinders University Newsdesk, 12 June. Available at https://news.flinders.edu.au/biog/2017/06/12/native-mounted-police-camps,/ accessed 30 October 2019.

22 Evans, *History of Queensland*, 96; S. Whiley to R. Evans, private correspondence, 8 May 1995. Ørsted-Jensen, *Frontier History*, 37–38; Evans et al., *Race Relations*, 57, 129. For Martini-Henry, see https://firearms.net.au/military/index,php?option=com_content&view, accessed 15 August 2018; Roberts T. 2009. 'The brutal truth', *The Monthly*, November, 48. Roberts also notes: 'British .577 calibre Snider military rifles ... fired a massive lead bullet designed to mushroom upon impact, leaving a gaping hole. The bullet had a hollow internal chamber in the nose and would therefore be illegal in modern warfare.' Roberts T. 2005. *Frontier Justice: A History of the Gulf Country to 1900*. St Lucia: University of Queensland Press, 13.

23 Richards, 'Native Police camps', 64; Whiley to Evans, 8 May 1995.

their geographical ambits. In purely mathematical terms, this creates a total of 7152 patrols. In order to account for periods of illness, climatic disasters, trooper desertions and other disruptions, he cautiously stripped this figure back to 6000 patrols, an average of ten per year. This is a conservative assessment, especially if one takes into account that from many barracks two or even three patrols might at times be conducted in some months or, in periods of crisis, continual patrolling by so-called flying detachments might be also instituted.[24]

The next thorny question involves the average number of collisions with Aborigines inflicted by each patrol. Assessing this is, of course, highly problematic for, as we have seen, most of the routine monthly reports and officer diaries have gone missing, and are probably destroyed. Yet, handwritten copies of reports and even diary extracts have occasionally survived in holdings other than the Police Department — for instance, in the files of the Colonial Secretary, Governor, Attorney-General or Colonial Office. In 2010, Evans was able to locate only 22 of these documents, but since that time he and Ørsted-Jensen have assembled a more robust and dependable sample of 111 monthly patrol accounts from both official and press sources. From this substantially larger sample, facilitated by the early research of amateur historian Alan Hillier, we are able to construct a more nuanced interpretation of the dispersal rate per patrol. Evans' 2010 sample produced an average of 2.6 dispersals per circuit, or 57 dispersals overall. In order to proceed cautiously, he then stripped that average back to two collisions per patrol. Yet the later compilation has shown that figure to be inflated. We now have compiled a new aggregate of 85 dispersals across the 111 patrols, or an average of 0.78 per patrol. Yet we believe that this assessment is probably still too high.[25]

This becomes clear when the sample is divided into 86 sequential reports, those available across more than one month consecutively, and 25 non-sequential reports, consisting of stand-alone files lifted from an unknown sequence of monthly totals. The contrast between the two series is stark. For the more normative sequential reports, the collision average is 0.36; yet for the non-sequentials it rises sharply once more to almost two dispersals per patrol. Clearly, the latter reports, although indicating some of

---

24 Evans, 'The country has another past', 30; Richards, *Secret War*, 17; Hillier A. n.d. "'If you leave me alone, I'll leave you alone", Biographical Sketches: Reports and Incidents from the Myall Wars of the Queensland Native Mounted Police Force, 1860–1885', unpublished manuscript, 263.

25 Evans, 'The country has another past', 30–31; Hillier, 'If you leave' me alone, *passim.*; Ørsted-Jensen, computer file archive of frontier conflict (in possession of that author).

CHAPTER 6: 'Pale Death ... around our Footprints Springs'

the more ferocious peaks in Native Police violence, are the more exceptional ones. They reflect the kind of murderous frenzy that usually erupted around such events as the Wills party massacre in 1861; the killings of Native Police officers Acting Sub-Inspector Cecil Hill in 1865, Sub-Inspector Henry Kaye in 1881, and Cadet Marcus Beresford in 1883 by resisting Aborigines; the *Maria* shipwreck tragedy of 1872; the Palmer gold rush of 1873–1876; the Strau, Conn and Molvo group killings of 1874, 1875 and 1878, respectively; and the violent deaths of pastoralists James Powell and Edmond Watson, which led to massive reprisals against the Kalkadoons in 1884 and 1889.[26]

The more exceptional non-sequential reports, which can register as many as five or seven dispersals per patrol, deal with only a fraction of such events, as the official censorship of excessive reprisals has been substantial. Yet, if we stick with what we know, and incorporate these 25 reports as special cases, we can use them to plot a mean average between our overall dispersal estimate of 0.78 monthly and our sequential report estimate of 0.36. This averages out at a more conservative 0.57 collisions per patrol. So, we now have a most cautiously determined 6000 patrols with 3420 dispersals.

How many Aboriginal people on average died violently during each dispersal? Of course, we again have only the numbers provided by white contemporaries, usually Native Police officers themselves, to assess this, and these are usually hesitantly or modestly given. Nevertheless, we have still endeavoured to proceed prudently here, particularly where differing assessments of casualties are provided and where the actual number of different dispersals per campaign also becomes problematic. The following two pertinent examples of cautious proceedings in this matter should suffice to illustrate the judicious methodology we have employed.

Manumbar Station, 10 February 1861

Shortly before sunset on this Sunday, a detachment of troopers from Maryborough, who were bringing up horses from Brisbane to Rockhampton, opened fire on a body of Aborigines on Manumbar Station in the South Burnett district. The corpses of eight victims were afterwards located by the station owner, John Mortimer, and his stockmen — four on the Manumbar run and the other four on neighbouring Yabba Station. Mortimer additionally examined several gunshot wounds on two injured survivors. These were

---

26 Bottoms, *Conspiracy of Silence*, 1–2, 108–109, 124, 134–135, 147–148, 162–164; Ørsted-Jensen, *Frontier History*, 37, 50–51, 55–57, 199–200; Evans et al., *Race Relations*, 44, 52–53; Hillier, 'If you leave me alone', 20–21, 142–143, 157–175, 192–194, 230; Richards, *Secret War*, 22–23, 25–26, 61–62; Armstrong R. n.d. *The Kalkadoons: A Study of an Aboriginal Tribe on the Queensland Frontier.* Brisbane: William Brooks, 168–172.

CIVILIAN-DRIVEN VIOLENCE AND THE GENOCIDE OF INDIGENOUS PEOPLES

people who, he wrote, had 'been in our employment ... for the last eight or nine years' and who had 'never been charged with a crime of any kind'. The Aborigines who guided Mortimer to the bodies wished to show more of them nearby, but Mortimer stated he had seen enough. He afterwards added that he was nevertheless 'convinced there were many more'. So, we may be dealing with between 12 and 20 casualties on these two properties alone.[27]

Yet no official investigation was ever ordered. Mortimer's figure of eight dead was later accepted by a government retreating from closer examination. Further research, however, suggests that the eight killed marked merely the tail end of several dispersals. Rudolph Morisset, the Native Police Commandant, himself revealed that these deaths were related to a wider series of episodes. He had 'found the blacks collected in several places in very large numbers', he wrote, and had opened fire on them 'on two or three occasions'. Albert Tyrer, the Yabba storekeeper, further swore that he knew of Aborigines also having been shot on Imbil Station, owned by the Lawless Brothers, some 30 kilometres south-east of Manumbar. This was corroborated by the co-proprietor of Kenilworth Station, who had been informed by a 'blackboy' who arrived from Imbil of 'a great noise' between the Native Police and 'the blacks' at Walleraine, an Imbil outstation. A leading article by the meticulous *Brisbane Courier* editor, Theophilus Pugh, maintained that 'five and thirty blacks are said to have been ruthlessly massacred and among the number slain were women and children, and natives well-known in the neighbourhood'.[28]

So, the possibility certainly remains that the number slain was as high as 35, and that we may indeed be dealing with two separate dispersals — the one at the Manumbar and Yabba stations and the one at Imbil — averaging about 17 dead per incident. For the sake of scrupulously protecting the integrity of our statistical sample from overstatement or undue inference, however, we have counted a mere 10 deaths in a single incident in this case.

Raglan Creek, November 1860

A punitive expedition against 'a large number of blacks' was mounted following the rape and murder of white bar worker, Fanny Briggs, at

---

27 *Moreton Bay Courier*, 16 March 1861, 28 March 1861, 4 June 1861, 6 September 1861; *Argus*, 13 July 1865; *Select Committee into Native Police*, 1861, 101–108; Ørsted-Jensen, *Frontier History*, 40–41.

28 QSA, Col A14/945, Lieut. R. Morisset Official Report, 3 April 1861; A14/61/794 A14/61/908 and A 14/61/945, Lieut. R Morisset Official Reports, 14 April 1861; *Select Committee into Native Police* 1861, 24–25; *Moreton Bay Courier*, 16 April 1861.

CHAPTER 6: 'Pale Death ... around our Footprints Springs'

Gracemere Station near Rockhampton. The suspected Aborigines were violently evicted, even though the culprits were later discovered to have been the Native Police troopers who were conducting the 'eviction'. Once more, the sparse surviving records do not allow us to know what this 'large number' actually was. Quite likely it was more than 30 or so. The expedition was led by Chief of Police and Native Police Commandant Edwin Morriset himself, accompanied by three white officers, the four guilty troopers and a local grazier.[29]

Although Morisset later reported that 'no indiscriminate slaughter took place' and that there were only two Aboriginal casualties, his assurances tend to contradict the fevered preparation for wholesale killing among local colonists and Native Police from the day that Briggs' body was found. More than 140 years after the event, the handwritten eyewitness account of a pioneer, a German bushman named Konrad Nahrung, has recently surfaced in a private family archive that supports this conclusion. Nahrung recounts how, while he and his mates, German Joe and Jim Cassidy, were taking a bullock dray loaded with wool bales from Walloon Station to Rockhampton, they suddenly came upon a most 'gruesome sight': 'a mob of blacks' had been 'camped in a patch of scrub' at Raglan Creek and 'nearly all were shot'. The 'avengers had not been particular in burying the bodies', Nahrung writes, and the 'corpses were lying everywhere'.[30]

Again, there is no attempt here to give any enumeration of the dead, but contemporary correspondents to the *Brisbane Courier* further reinforce the impression of substantial killings. As one wrote in early April 1861, the Rockhampton area had 'witnessed scenes in the neighbourhood which one hardly dare relate ... the bloodiest of murders committed upon the innocent natives'. And, as the writer noted, there was an accompanying conspiracy of silence: 'the greatest solicitude upon the part of those who saw the deeds that they should not be talked about'. Aborigines were being shot down 'like dogs', another added four days later. Then, in early May, a Port Curtis correspondent, belying Morisset's exculpatory phrase, referred directly to 'the "indiscriminate" slaughters after the murder of Fanny Briggs — those foul ones around Maryborough, Gladstone, Rockhampton and those places; all of which have been hushed up by the government'. It seems fairly clear, therefore, that many had been killed here in pogrom-like fashion extending

---

29 *Moreton Bay Courier*, 24 January 1861; Macdonald L. 1981. *Rockhampton: A History of City and District*. St Lucia: University of Queensland Press, 188–189.

30 Nahrung K. c. 1900. 'My life' (unpublished manuscript in possession of authors), 39–40.

CIVILIAN-DRIVEN VIOLENCE AND THE GENOCIDE OF INDIGENOUS PEOPLES

across a wide region. In the light of such evidence, we have estimated a conservative total of 20 deaths associated with the Raglan Creek episode.[31]

Evans's 2010 chapter in *Passionate Histories* provided the questionably low summation of only two killed during each Native Police clash, arriving nevertheless at the arresting estimate of 24 000 killed by this organisation alone under Queensland colonial jurisdiction between 1859 and 1897. Further consideration of a much wider database has now found these figures to be too low. Ørsted-Jensen has compiled a range of accounts of 75 official dispersals where a numerical total of Aborigines killed is specifically provided. Such mortality numbers range from one to 60, averaging 12.7, more than six times higher than Evans had allowed. If we again pare that number back to 12 killed per patrol, we arrive at the sobering total of 41 040 Aborigines killed during 3 420 official frontier dispersals across almost forty years of conflict.[32]

'Our revenge, though complete, had been rather too heavy':[33] Assessing combined frontier casualties from state-led and private assault

The mortality figure of roughly 41 040 is a mathematical and statistical projection of the fragmentary evidence left to us about the severe degree of state-sponsored destruction accompanying the long-term project of land dispossession in colonial Queensland. It is not, and can never be, a precisely accurate figure, nor is it an absolute or maximal one. Indeed, it approximates towards its opposite, a minimal estimate. The overall number will never be known. Perhaps, if Aboriginal people had really been treated as other 'British subjects' were, and each massacre site, killing field or individual murder location treated as a conventional crime scene, evidence to secure convictions assiduously gathered, and the contemporary legal documentation had all managed to survive, we now might have the kind of evidence that could 'stand up in court'. But these mass killings were wanton, furtive and unprosecuted. No perpetrator, either official or private, ever paid the full penalty for killing an Aborigine in Queensland frontier conflict. Indeed, paramilitary state functionaries, designated loosely as 'police', were

---

31 *Brisbane Courier*, 2 April 1861, 6 April 1861, 30 May 1861.
32 Evans, 'The country has another past', 31; Ørsted-Jensen, *Frontier History*, 16–21.
33 *Queenslander*, 20 April 1901.

CHAPTER 6: 'Pale Death ... around our Footprints Springs'

the actual perpetrators of a good deal of the slaughter. No wonder the story and the statistics have lain fallow for so long.[34]

Such estimations no doubt also appear radical and iconoclastic — even extreme to some. They certainly debunk the consensual 20000 Australia-wide figure, roughly assessed over 140 years of conflict. They also shred the aforementioned estimates that the Queensland Aboriginal total of those killed by Native Police, or anyone else, was 24000, 20000, 10000, 5000, 381 or five. Yet the methodology employed here has been deliberately understated throughout, built upon the truncated base of surviving documentation and the proclivity of perpetrators normally to mask the full death toll and report lower destruction yields than in reality. As Gideon Scott Lang commented in 1865: '"One I think was shot" says a report — I suspect there were a good many more' Each potentially reduced estimate in the compilation has then been further assiduously pruned and discreetly diminished statistically. So, however startling it may at first appear, this is a careful, minimal assessment rather than one that is excessive or capriciously assembled.[35]

Furthermore, let us be entirely clear about what we are claiming here. The 41040 death rate does not represent anywhere near a full quotient of those who fell on the Queensland frontier. It relates only to Native Police activity from 1860 to the mid-1890s and does not even cover, at this point, official dispersal activities by the same force during the preceding decade (1849–1859). How many may have died at the hands of the Native Police in the Queensland zone in the decade when it was still controlled by New South Wales? Writing in 1975, L.E. Skinner enumerated at least 25 different Native Police camps operating at various times across almost eleven years of frontier activity. He tabulated around 55 white personnel involved as officers and, in 1854, around 120 Aboriginal troopers; in 1856, 72 troopers and in 1859 between 80 and 90 of them. It does not seem too ambitious to suggest that this force, ranging in monthly patrols between Goondiwindi in the south-west and Rockhampton in the north-east, accounted for another 3000–4000 frontier deaths, or 300–350 per annum, especially as the massive bloodletting that followed the Fraser family massacre at Hornet Bank

---

34 For colonial suppression of frontier conflict, see Harris J. 2003. 'Hiding the bodies: The myth of humane colonization of Aboriginal Australia'. *Aboriginal History*, 27, 79–104; Evans, 'Done and dusted', 183–198.

35 Scott G.S. 1865. *The Aborigines in Australia: In their Original Conditions and their Relations with the White Men*. Melbourne: Wilson & McKinnon, 45–46.

CIVILIAN-DRIVEN VIOLENCE AND THE GENOCIDE OF INDIGENOUS PEOPLES

Station in 1857 would be included in this total. In that year the nominal annual average would have been met within a few weeks.[36]

Nor does it yet include 'invader casualties', which Ørsted-Jensen has recently calculated to be in the vicinity of 1500. His total includes 800 mainland European deaths from Aboriginal resistance, another 235 or so of their Aboriginal assistants and bonded workers, around 230 non-European fatalities, including Chinese, Melanesians and other migrants, and a further, quite conservatively calculated, 223 deaths in Torres Strait conflicts. Nor does our progressive total include any incorporation of non-lethal casualties, as other war statistics invariably do. As Stephen Gapps notes in *The Sydney Wars*, a ratio of 3.5 wounded for every frontline death is conventionally accepted for historical European military conflicts. Even if this ratio is stripped back to a very low 1:1 parity, one would need to double the overall casualty figure we are fast approaching in this chapter to arrive at a complete sense of the human destruction inflicted. And, most importantly, the calculation does not as yet cover any of the Aboriginal casualties during private vigilante actions by settlers. Such figures began to mount in the Queensland region from the 1820s.[37]

It is again impossible to provide an accurate head count of these latter casualties — undoubtedly a great number — as once more the process was secretive and unprosecuted. We can, however, find numerous contemporary assertions that suggest a rough equivalence between private and state-led casualties. Some prominent observers even suggest that private parties killed more Aborigines. Let us therefore further explore some of this potent, impressionistic evidence.

The Scottish squatter Jacob Low, of Welltown Station, near Goondi-windi had a reputation, along with others, such as Jonathan Young and Augustus Morris, for protecting Aborigines from the depredations of surrounding pastoralists in the Macintyre district in south-western

---

36 Skinner L.E. 1975. *Police of the Pastoral Frontier: Native Police 1849–59.* St Lucia, Brisbane: University of Queensland Press, 374–379, 383–395. Other works detailing the frontier mayhem of this decade include: French M. 1989. *Conflict on the Condamine: Aborigines and the European Invasion.* Toowoomba: Darling Downs Institute Press; Reid G. 1982. *A Nest of Hornets: The Massacre of the Fraser Family at Hornet Bank Station, Central Queensland 1857, and Related Events.* Melbourne: Oxford University Press; Collins, *Goodbye Bussamarai*; Evans R. 2009. 'Queensland 1859: Reflections on the act of becoming'. *Queensland Review*, 16, no. 1, 1–14; Evans, *History of Queensland*, 70–75; Coffey R. 2010. 'Frontier Violence at Gin Gin'. BA (Hons) thesis, University of Queensland; Ørsted-Jensen, *Frontier History*, 114–116; Bottoms, *Conspiracy of Silence*, 12–45.

37 Ørsted-Jensen, *Frontier History* 16–21, 187–251; Gapps S. 2018. *The Sydney Wars: Conflict in the Early Colony, 1788–1817.* Sydney: NewSouth Books, 266.

CHAPTER 6: 'Pale Death ... around our Footprints Springs'

Queensland. This was a region of intense and prolonged conflict during the 1840s and 1850s. Yet, as a member of the Queensland Legislative Assembly in 1875, Low admitted that, despite his benign reputation, he had 'killed many blacks himself' on several occasions. He then asserted that private vigilante settlers were responsible for 'more bloodshed' than were Native Police patrols. Private involvement in quasi-military raids on Aboriginal encampments, usually under cover of night, appears to have been ubiquitous, either as independent grassroots mobilisations or in illegal combination with Native Police assaults.[38]

Even celebrated pioneering families with a traditional reputation for humane forbearance were caught up in the bloodshed. David McConnell of Cressbrook Station in the Brisbane Valley wrote privately to his brother Frederick about putting 'terror into their [the Yuggera's] hearts ... people living in England think it is a great crime to hurt a poor black fellow but ... many of us think it is wiser to shoot any of them that we meet & any number, anywhere beyond the settled districts, until they are thoroughly pacified'. According to Mary McConnell, a greatgrandchild, Cressbrook was a pastoral property 'founded on the fear of God'.[39]

Similarly, in addressing the Queensland Parliament in 1880, a German merchant Albrecht Feez, recalled how in 1858 he had met the Archer brothers, William and Colin, at the head of 'a large escort' in the vicinity of Gracemere Station, later Rockhampton. 'Mr. Archer' told him that the posse was 'going to punish the blacks for depredations they had committed'. An estimated 14 Aborigines were shot as a result at the Fitzroy River. Even though Gracemere was founded with the help of Native Police, this family too has retained a reputation for progressive views and benevolent actions.[40]

Other apparently less culpable squatters, such as Donald Gunn of Pikedale Station near Stanthorpe, remembered later just how commonplace it was to gun down Aborigines — 'in many instances' simply because they were 'a nuisance' to cattle. Frederick Bell, grandson of pioneer pastoralist James Bell of Jimbour Station, near Dalby, recounted to the Royal Historical Society of Queensland in 1947 that, at stations such as Mount Playfair, one of the methods used to stop 'thieving' by the Goorang Goorang people 'was to put strychnine in the flour' given to them — a common frontier

---

38 *Queensland Parliamentary Debates*, 21 July 1875; Collins, *Goodbye Bussamarai*, 52.
39 David McConnell to William McConnell, 22 May 1844, quoted in Conners L. 2017. 'Uncovering the shameful: Sexual violence on an Australia colonial frontier', in *Legacies of Violence: Rendering the Unspeakable Past in Modern Australia*, ed. R. Mason. New York: Berghahn Books, 36–37.
40 *Queensland Parliamentary Debates*, 1880, XXXII, 673.

157

practice from the late 1830s. At Camboon and nearby stations, '[t]here were hundreds of these blacks shot and left to rot like cattle where they fell, or snigged away with a horse if too close to camp. Willie [Walsh] often found and picked up skulls and placed them at night on stumps around the camp'. In one incident alone, a combined body of troopers and pastoral workers 'rounded up and shot about 40' at the MacKenzie Range after two shepherds and two hurdle makers were speared at Camboon's Nine Mile outstation.[41]

The famed pastoralist Robert Christison of Lammermoor Station south-east of Hughenden in the Flinders district, has been lauded for his 'justice and kindness' in dealings with the Dalleburra people, largely due to a hagiographical biography of 1927, written by his daughter, Mary M. Bennett, 'an agitator for reform on Aboriginal policy' in Western Australia during the 1930s. Bennett extols her father's peaceful coexistence with the local clans, a positive interaction devoid of violence and once more presented in stark contrast to the exterminatory behaviour on surrounding stations. Yet this is belied by a startling entry in Christison's own private diary from mid-1869: 'I have made up my mind to treat them like wild animals, kindness is no use. The better they are treated the worse they are — war to the knife for the men and the whip to the boys ... they will soon find out what bitter enemies we are when forced to punish them.'[42]

Low, McConnell, the Archers, Gunn, Bell and Christison comprise a roll call of allegedly compassionate frontier practitioners in Queensland historiography. Yet all were mired to a considerable degree in the massive swathes of racial violence that swirled around them — either as participants or laconic observers, uttering no apparent public protest as Aboriginal peoples were cut down in scores and hundreds. An exterminatory cultural *Zeitgeist* enveloped them all, providing permission and excuse for unrestrained assault. It is chilling testimony to both the enormity and the casual banality of this pervasive, eradicative impulse that has left behind, most commonly, only vague, generalised traces in the primary records. As the *Queenslander* noted in 1875, North Queensland colonists felt it 'their duty to shoot every nigger they meet'.[43]

Looking back over almost a prior century of racial conflict in 1901, Brisbane journalist and local councillor Ebenezer Thorne, author of

---

41 Gunn D. 1937. *Links with the Past*. Brisbane: John Mills, 16; Bell F.M. 1947. 'Camboon reminiscences'. *Royal Historical Society of Queensland*, IV, no. 1, 58.

42 *Argus*, 24 December 1927; Bennett M.M. 1927. *Christison of Lammermoor*. London: Alston River; Cryle M. 2009. 'A fantastic "adventure": Reading *Christison of Lamermoor*'. Brisbane: UQ eSpace, 228.

43 *Queenslander*, 30 October 1875.

CHAPTER 6: 'Pale Death ... around our Footprints Springs'

the migrant-attracting tome, *Queen of the Colonies* (1876), also frankly summarised the history of southern Queensland as one of unrelenting ethnic cleansing:

> [W]e have managed, in one way or another, to gradually clear a large portion of [Queensland's] coloured owners, and have at the same time contracted the habit of thanking God we are not as other men—those rascally Spaniards for instance— and we have no sense of shame ...
>
> It is recorded by the biographer of the discoverer of the Mississippi, Hernando de Soto, that 'he joyed in the hunting of savages'. The same may be said of nearly everyone of the old race of Queensland squatters. But perhaps they 'joyed' as much in surrounding them in their camps at night and exterminating all the tribe—excepting the younger women—at a blow, as they did in hunting them ... Others again looked on poison as a better plan for clearing the country ... I once traveled through a beautiful plain, on one side of which lay the whitening bones of a whole tribe who had thus been disposed of, with the exception of one lad ... One could fill pages with pleasant stories of this sort. Those [killers] were the earliest labourers on behalf of a 'White Australia'. They had the same thoroughness that characterizes their successors of today ...
>
> A gentleman now residing a few miles from Brisbane ... used to tell how he was once taken to task by his employer when, as a very young man, he had taken part in his first battue because he had not killed a picaninny which [*sic*] he said he had seen crawl into a bunch of long grass. He was told, with a directness which would do credit to the most cold-blooded of other nationalities, that he must remember in future that he had to kill the nits as well as the lice.[44]

So, bearing such arresting images in mind, was private vigilantism by white settlers from the 1840s into the twentieth century less lethal than the killing capacity of continual Native Police patrols from 1849? Did it represent a roughly equivalent onslaught, or was it perhaps even more devastating in its overall impact? A series of credible witnesses before the 1861 Select Committee into the operations of the Native Police, such as pioneer squatter Thomas Petrie, the explorer and pastoral advocate Augustus Gregory, the Parliamentary Sergeant-at-Arms Captain Richard Coley, and leading pastoralist and premier-in-waiting Robert MacKenzie, all supported the proposition that the settlers killed more than the troopers. James Kerr

---

44 Thorne E. 1901. 'A "white Australia": The other side'. *United Australia*, 2, no. 4, 11.

Wilson, the founder of Callandoon Station on the MacKenzie River near the Queensland border, testified that whites would shoot 'five or six *whenever they met them*' and poison them wholesale. Similarly, John Watts, Member of the Legislative Assembly for Drayton and Toowoomba — a squatter from Eton Vale on the Darling Downs — added in the parliament of 1861 that 'hundreds' of Aborigines had been murdered 'in cold blood by giving them arsenic and strychnine in their food'. Other colonists, 'armed to the teeth ... tended much more to the destruction of the blacks' than did the Native Police force, he concluded. Writing to the *Queenslander* in September 1867, a pastoralist on the Burnett River, near Bundaberg, reported:

> [M]en, women and children were slaughtered indiscriminately during the settlement of the Darling Downs ... I have often heard men who call themselves gentlemen [other squatters] advocate the shooting of the gins [Aboriginal women]. I could also point to instances where gins have actually been shot when the police were accompanied by a number of white men. It is because the [native] police can be controlled in this respect and white men cannot.[45]

How do we navigate this maelstrom of private violence, actually burgeoning in its vehemence during the 1870s and 1880s? Realistically speaking, so many instances occurred covertly. Many others left either no documentary residue or produced accusatory whistle-blower accounts that were sometimes later destroyed or left unsupported by corroborative testimony. The best we can now offer are the surviving archives of frontier incidents and to calculate once more what these reveal as a plausible mathematical sample. Such data, considering the strongly denialist atmosphere in which it was produced, should be seen once more as a most conservative accounting of the violent instances that occurred during the process of dispossession. Ørsted-Jensen has compiled a surviving archive of 644 frontier collisions of all types in Queensland, whether official or private, based upon many years of painstaking collation. Some 275 (or 43 per cent) of these incidents are settler attacks and 369 (or 57 per cent) involve troopers. Allowing this again to be a representative sample, we can suggest that, if the aforementioned 3 420 Native Police collisions equate to 57 per cent of the total, then the settlers' 43 per cent can approximate to another 2 580 attacks, leading to a mathematical total of 6 000 assaults overall.

---

45 *Select Committee on Native Police, 1861,* 19, 72, 116, 135, 138, 151; *Brisbane Courier,* 27 July 1861; *Queenslander,* 21 September 1867. See other reports: *Brisbane Courier,* 7 September 1867, 12 September 1867; *Queenslander,* 12 February 1876. (emphasis added).

CHAPTER 6: 'Pale Death ... around our Footprints Springs'

The average number killed per private assault is 8.3, based on figures provided in 113 settler accounts. If we again scale this back to an average of eight, it provides us with the tentative figure of another 20 640 violent deaths at private hands. This average is feasible, if not once more understated, given the settlers' notorious reticence in reporting their illegal dispersal activities, as well as a high level of attacks, as also recorded recently by Timothy Bottoms in *Conspiracy of Silence*. Together, then, our two totals of Native Police and settler inflictions amount to 61 680 in some 6 000 attacks, each of which averages out in numbers killed to 12 and 8, respectively, considerably higher than the figure of five or six presently used to indicate an Aboriginal 'massacre'.[46] So, were there nominally around 6 000 'massacres' of Aborigines in frontier Queensland? How could any 'massacre map' ever accurately incorporate this massive number? There would certainly be little cartographical breathing space left.

Adding in an estimated figure of 3 500 deaths associated with Native Police activity in the 1850s, as well as the 1 500 enumerated 'invader' deaths, we arrive at an aggregate of 66 680 people killed overall. This provides us with a rough, yet defensible tally of lethal human destruction from both sides of the frontier in colonial Queensland. Incidentally, it also provides us with a cautious ratio of Aboriginal to settler deaths of around 44:1, indicating that contemporary reporters, such as Carr, Meston and his Aboriginal informants were a lot closer to the mark than historians have been. Additionally, if the wounded were considered, as is the case when assessing the destructive impacts of conventional warfare, on the most stringently cautious of ratios of 1:1, this number would double to roughly 133 000 Aborigines and settlers dead and wounded.

Conclusion

Scholars of the First World War will also notice that the figure of 66 680 is remarkably close to, though larger than, the full Australian combat death toll of 62 300 in that war — and all this in just one of the six Australian colonies. Queensland, with the largest total of pre-contact Aboriginal peoples — between 34 and 38 per cent — and the largest habitable territory to be usurped — around half the size of the present-day European Union — clearly must be viewed as the core territory for Australian frontier conflict. The bulk of the casualties occurred here. Yet, if the mortality

---

46 Ryan L. 2016. 'Frontier massacres in the Australian colonies'. Interview, University of Newcastle; Dovey C. 2017. 'The mapping of massacres', *The New Yorker*, 6 December 2017.

figures across the other five colonies and one territory — presently assessed at a very low 10 000 killed and another 10 000 wounded — are added, the total death rate for all the Australian frontiers would rise even further above that of the Great War and move inexorably towards the aggregate number of Australians killed in all foreign wars — presently 102 846. Of all the historians making earlier 'guesstimates', it would seem that David Day was the one closest to the truth. Significantly, too, this figure returns us to the veracity of land-taker and ethnographer Edward Curr's 1887 claim that '[f]ifteen to twenty–five per cent fall by the rifle'. Curr had extensive pastoral frontier experience from Tasmania to Queensland and had corresponded with fellow squatters across all the colonies. As Reynolds concludes: '[He] ... probably knew as much as anybody about conditions all over Australia.' If we take the Aboriginal mortality figure of 65 180 as a percentage of the estimated original pre-contact population for Queensland of between 250 000 and 300 000, we arrive at a range of 22 to 26 per cent killed, very close to Curr's original estimate.[47] This human wastage does not, of course, include the many others who died as a result of starvation and disease due to violent dispossession, or those who suffered the effects of child theft, sexual exploitation or forced labour that accompanied the overall devastation.

We are fully aware of the contemporary implications of our findings. We have been conducting this research incrementally during a time when conscientious historians have been pilloried for even suggesting that extensive mass killings once occurred across Australia. We are acutely sensitive to the wider denialist mood persisting in some sectors of Australian society and its mainstream media. The prevailing consensual image in Australia's collective mind of itself as the 'fair-go society', a 'quiet continent' hosting the 'good nation' of 'mates' and 'good blokes', operates to frustrate forthright recognition of its manifold killing fields and to render dispossession a kind of *tabula rasa*. It does not allow for assessments that see both the state and private colonial populations in a kind of prolonged and collusive death dance with the original peoples — a macabre process in which both official and civilian bodies apparently contributed almost equally to the annihilation. And so, we proceed always with caution and moderate assessment, even as we wear the derisively placed 'black armband' tag with conviction. We research, calculate and write in order to return to history the full ledger of those who, long ago, died protecting their sovereignty, their cultures, their homelands and their peoples, but whose deaths were more often hidden

---

47 Bottoms, *Conspiracy of Silence*, passim.; Curr E. 1886. *The Australian Race: Its Origins, Language, Customs*. Melbourne: John Ferres, 209.

CHAPTER 6: 'Pale Death ... around our Footprints Springs'

than acknowledged by a society that made guile and secrecy its watchwords. Our allegiance is towards identifying, as best we can, historical precision and accuracy, however disturbing this may be, rather than polishing the national escutcheon to an ever-gratifying sheen.[48]

We appear to be looking at an important series of prolonged wars fought against the hundreds of Aboriginal First Nations. They were admittedly unusual wars, where the winning side managed to define both protagonists as 'British subjects' in order to avoid officially the very definition of warfare; where there were no declarations of hostilities, no agreed rules of engagement, no careful body counts of dead or wounded, no conventions for the treatment of prisoners, no precise points of closure, no armistice, no surrender, no settlements, no treaties, indemnities or reparations and, afterwards, no recognition of a gallant foe. They were largely unpublicised wars against an opponent whose land rights, humanity and sovereignty were negated, and they were fought without 'the more defined, structured pattern of the clash of conventional armies'. Their 'arbitrariness was monumental'. And when the struggle was over, the account of only one side was recorded, as much of the carnage was swept under a thick carpet of denial. Imagine attempting to understand the Pacific War of 1941–1945 with only uncontested Japanese documentation, or the Western Front from only German military accounts.[49]

Yet, as Reynolds has recently pointed out, these were also a set of 'singularly Australian wars' about 'purely Australian questions' — primarily control of land and territorial sovereignty. 'So if we are talking about war,' Reynolds surmises, 'it was clearly one of the few significant wars in Australian history and arguably the single most important one. For Indigenous Australia, it was their Great War. How could any other compare?'[50]

The statistical contribution we make here to the debate concludes that for all participants, this was also, in immediate terms, *our* (that is, every Australian's) Great War, a war for both the defence and conquest of Australia. As Mark McKenna pertinently states:

> Unlike any other nation, Australia has embraced a legend of national birth that takes place 16 000 kilometres offshore ... By doing so, we've

---

48 Evans R. 1995. 'Blood dries quickly: Conflict study and Australian historiography', in *Historical Disciplines in Australasia: Themes, Problems and Debates*, ed. A. Moses. Special issue of *Australian Journal of Politics and History*, 41, 80–102; Reynolds H. 2013. *Forgotten War*. Sydney: University of New South Wales Press, 122.

49 Evans R. 1999. *Fighting Words: Writing about Race*. St Lucia: University of Queensland Press, 23–24.

50 Reynolds, *Forgotten War*, 248, 254.

> turned our eyes from the true site of melancholy, loss and 'birth' in our history ... Our excessive emotional investment in Anzac Day ... points yet again to our inability to mourn the dispossession of Aboriginal people. In a very real way, we have continued to circumvent the heart of the matter.[51]

Though the Australian War Memorial presently evades the issue with an ideological obduracy, it must eventually be faced. For only then, armed with an encompassing empathy and integrity, can we move forward to a process of nation-building that is ethically based rather than being, as it is at present, merely ethnically constructed.

---

51 McKenna M. 2018. 'Moment of Truth: History and Australia's Future'. *Quarterly Essay*, 69.

CHAPTER SEVEN

'There Cannot be Civilisation and Barbarism on the Island': Civilian-driven Violence and the Genocide of the Selk'nam People of Tierra del Fuego[1]

Alberto Harambour

As the winter of 1899 was approaching, Moritz Braun, the managing director of the Sociedad Explotadora de Tierra del Fuego (Company for the Exploitation of Tierra del Fuego) wrote to the company's president, Peter McClelland, regarding 'an Indian girl you wished to be sent to you'.[2] Braun wrote that he had tried, to no avail, to get one from the Salesian missions at Dawson Island and Rio Grande, where the company deported most of the Selk'nam who had survived its raids. However, since winter was near, it was likely that Indian hunters would try to steal stock from one of the company's sheep stations. As the station labourers were killing guanacos, a type of wild llama, by the thousand, the few remaining free Selk'nam would be forced to try and plunder some animals from the ranches. Then, Braun promised, 'I will try and have a girl kept to send you' to Valparaiso, where McClelland also acted as head of the powerful Duncan and Fox conglomerate, which controlled the Explotadora, as well as other Chilean firms. Two years earlier, Braun had sent McClelland another Selk'nam girl.[3]

---

1   This article was first conceptualised towards the end of the Fondecyt research project 'Colonization and nomadism in the making of popular experience in Southern Patagonia (Argentina and Chile), 1843–1923', and was completed thanks to the support of Fondecyt research project no. 1181386 'State and market in the frontiers of civilization: Transnational histories of postcolonial colonialism in South America, 1870s–1940s'. I thank Stefy Torrejón, Mario Azara and Nicolás Toledo for their research assistance, Ivette Martínez and Carlos Vega for enriching conversations, and Sebastián Hurtado and Mohamed Adhikari for assistance with translation and useful commentary.
2   Unless otherwise noted, all translations from Spanish are my own.
3   Archivo Mauricio Braun, Museo Regional de Magallanes (hereafter AMB-MRM), Correspondencia despachada, 1899, Director-Gerente Mauricio Braun to Peter McClelland, President of the SETF, 2 June 1899; Correspondencia recibida, 1897, McClelland to Braun, 11 September 1897.

CIVILIAN-DRIVEN VIOLENCE AND THE GENOCIDE OF INDIGENOUS PEOPLES

According to *The Pastoral Review* of 1920, the Sociedad Explotadora was 'possibly the largest sheep owning company in the world'.[4] It was founded after the Chilean state granted a local businessman, the Portuguese merchant and moneylender José Nogueira, almost 1.5 million hectares of land on the northern shore of the Big Island of Tierra del Fuego in 1890.[5] As was the case with most southern Patagonian land concessions, the state had only vague knowledge of the terrain, and networks of corruption informed its decision. Nogueira quickly transferred over 100 000 hectares to two British firms, the Patagonian Sheep Farming Company and the Philip Bay Sheep Farming Company, as well as to the Sociedad Ganadera Gente Grande, owned by the Hamburg-based Wehrhahn Brothers Company. In 1893, after Nogueira died, his son-in-law Moritz Braun met Peter McClelland, who contributed capital, breeding stock, managers and know-how to develop the Explotadora. By then, four companies controlled the northern half of the Big Island, having introduced thousands of sheep raised north of the Strait of Magellan or in the Falkland Islands. In less than a decade, the Explotadora would come to control all the other companies mentioned above. Once that was achieved, the only obstacle to extensive sheep ranching on the model of Australia and the Falkland Islands was a final solution to the 'Indian problem'.

According to Nicos Poulantzas, 'genocides are the elimination of those who come to be "foreign bodies" in the national territory and history, exclusions out of space and out of time'.[6] Up to 1881, neither Argentina nor Chile had settled their territorial claims over Tierra del Fuego, South America's southern-most archipelago, measuring roughly 50 000 square kilometres in area, where the 'most important division is topographical and diametrically opposed to that made by [Western] man', as the artist-explorer Charles Wellington Furlong described it. While 'the northern half is practically an open, flat or undulating country ..., the southern half is mostly bog-lands, screened by thick woods and impenetrable forests, while range upon range of

---

4   According to the *Pastoral Review*, 16 December 1920, XXX, no. 7, 915, by 1920, the Explotadora 'owns 1,656,775 sheep. Its capital is £1,800,000, and its various reserve funds amount to £1,906,076 .... During the year the lambing amounted to 92.47 per cent ... and totaled 9,115,422 lbs., realizing £1,203,909. Profit for the year was £1,225,415. The taxation is infinitesimal'.

5   Archivo Histórico Nacional (Santiago) (hereafter AHN). Fondo Gobernación de Magallanes (hereafter FGM), Vol. 9, 1888–1892, Presidential Decrees, 22 April 1889; 15 November 1889; 9 July 1890.

6   Poulantzas N. 1991 [1978]. *Estado, Poder y Socialismo*. Mexico City: Siglo XXI, 136.

CHAPTER 7: 'There Cannot be Civilisation and Barbarism on the Island'

impassable, snow-capped mountains swing across it, west to east'.[7] This was the land of the Selk'nam, or Ona as they were also known, while the south-eastern extreme was the domain of the Haush, a kindred ethnic group. After Argentina and Chile resolved their diplomatic dispute over Tierra del Fuego in 1881 and offered land to export-oriented companies, all of the Indigenous peoples were erased from their ancestral territory.

Tierra del Fuego had been the epitome of no-man's land in the European imagination since the passage of Magellan in 1520. That image was entrenched by the derogatory comments of Robert FitzRoy and Charles Darwin about its soil, coastal waters and native peoples, especially in Darwin's influential book, the *Voyage of the Beagle*. Describing it as inhabited by 'the most abject and miserable creatures I anywhere beheld', and as a place 'where death and decay prevail', Darwin thought of Tierra del Fuego as if it would remain a wasteland for centuries to come.[8] He was proven wrong in only a few decades, however. After the late 1870s these southern territories, which up to then had remained out of the reach of both state authority and markets, were integrated into the world economy, with devastating consequences for their Indigenous peoples. 'The intentional physical destruction of a social group in its entirety', or at least the 'annihilation of such a significant part' that it was no longer able 'to reproduce itself biologically or culturally', to borrow Mohamed Adhikari's definition of genocide, describes the fate of the Fuegian Indigenous peoples. This genocide was state authorised, but perpetrated by civilians.[9]

This chapter analyses the interaction of political, economic and religious forces that produced the colonial genocide of the Selk'nam. First, I address the place of the island in the context of late-nineteenth-century Argentinian and Chilean geopolitical expansion, the juridical dispute between the two nations and its eventual settlement. Then, I address the decision-making process concerning that age-old American question: 'What do we do with the Indians?' Throughout the Americas, agreements between governments and religious agents led to final solutions in which forced removal or extermination was justified in the name of progress. I go

---

7   Furlong C.W. 1909. 'Into the unknown land of the Onas'. *Harper's Magazine* (August), 443–454.

8   Darwin C. 1839. *The Voyage of the Beagle*. London: Henry Colburn, 235, 605; FitzRoy, R. 1839. *Narrative of the Surveying Voyages of His Majesty's Ships Adventure and Beagle between the Years 1826 and 1836*. London: Henry Colburn.

9   Adhikari M. 2014. '"We are determined to exterminate them": The genocidal impetus behind commercial stock farmer invasions of hunter-gatherer territories', in M. Adhikari, ed. 2014. *Genocide on Settler Frontiers: When Hunter-Gatherers and Commercial Stock Farmers Clash*. Cape Town: UCT Press, 2.

CIVILIAN-DRIVEN VIOLENCE AND THE GENOCIDE OF INDIGENOUS PEOPLES

on to describe the implementation of policies of eradication in Tierra del Fuego, contrasting recently discovered testimonies of shepherd-hunters with the absence of Indigenous voices. Finally, I point to the global relationship between capital and state forces and its particular role in the making of this frontier genocide.

The abject peoples of the Land of Fire

When the Spanish expedition of 1520, led by the Portuguese explorer Ferdinand Magellan, encountered the strait named after him, the crew thought that these southern lands were part of a different continent, the *Terra Australis Incognita*. In 1578, Francis Drake's expedition navigated the strait, as well as the western and southern coasts of the Big Island of Tierra del Fuego, initiating a violent encounter between Fuegians and European sailors.[10] As Magellan had done with Patagonians — the name he assigned to the natives of the region — Drake kidnapped Fuegian natives, a practice that continued right up to the mid-twentieth century.[11] It was as specimens for exhibition in human zoos, and as interpreters, forced labourers and sexual slaves, that Fuegians entered European imaginaries of savagery and as the inhabitants of the southern-most part of the earth. These representations were reinforced in the late 1820s by British expeditions to the southern channels led by Philip Parker King and Robert FitzRoy, with Charles Darwin becoming their most famous populariser.[12]

After Darwin, the Patagonian Missionary Society initiated an unprecedented venture by establishing permanent outposts along the Beagle Channel in the far south. Their aim was to persuade the Yaganes, the nomadic canoe people of the southern channels, to settle down as shepherds and farmers.[13] Their experiences contributed to the colonists' differentiation between the canoe peoples — the Yaganes and Kawésqar, together also

---

10 Chapman A. 2012. *Yaganes del Cabo de Hornos: Encuentros con los Europeos Antes y Después de Darwin*. Santiago: Pehuén-Liberalia, 39–47.
11 Harambour A. & Barrena J. 2019. 'Barbarie o justicia en la Patagonia occidental: Las violencias coloniales en el ocaso del pueblo kawésqar, finales del siglo XIX e inicios del siglo XX'. *Historia Crítica*, 71 (forthcoming).
12 Alvarado M., Odone C., Maturana F. & Fiore D., eds. 2007. *Fueguinos: Fotografías Siglos XIX y XX. Imágenes e Imaginarios del Fin del Mundo*. Santiago: Pehuén.
13 Bridges T. 2001. *Los Indios del Confín del Mundo: Escritos para la South American Missionary Society*, trans. A. Canclini. Ushuaia: Zagier & Urruty. See also Gardiner A. 1896. *Records of the South American Missionary Society, or Fifty Years Work of the Church of England in South America (British Guiana Excepted)*, 4 ed. London: South American Missionary Society; Young R. 1905. *From Cape Horn to Panama: A Narrative of Missionary Enterprise among the Neglected Races of South America, by the South American Missionary Society*. London: South American Missionary Society.

CHAPTER 7: 'There Cannot be Civilisation and Barbarism on the Island'

referred to as Alacalufes—and the warrior-like hunter-gatherers of the island, the Selk'nam.[14] Because the Anglican outposts concentrated on the channels and the southern part of Tierra del Fuego, the missionaries had infrequent contact with the Selk'nam, whom they feared. While whalers, explorers and missionaries entered into both commercial and violent contact with the nomads of the sea, the Selk'nam remained a largely unknown part of the 'Fuegian races'.

It was late 1879 when the first-ever official reconnaissance expedition crossed the Strait of Magellan to the Big Island. The Chilean navy officer Ramón Serrano Montaner led a small party through its north-western region, under constant surveillance from different groups of Selk'nam. Early on, he categorically stated that 'you cannot but think that of all the savages [of Patagonia], these are the most backward. Forced to travel constantly in search of their food, they sleep where the night surprises them'.[15] Montaner's party had a friendly encounter with the single group of Selk'nam that dared approach them. A few days later, however, while the horses grazed unattended, six animals were killed or wounded by arrows. After that, the soldiers opened fire on any Indian they saw. An Argentinian military contingent did the same a few years later, in the north-eastern portion of the island. Captain Ramón Lista, who led that expedition through the 'Country of the Onas', asserted that there, the 'human species' was 'still sunk in the Stone Age'. The party, which included the Italian Catholic priest Giuseppe Fagnano, first encountered a group of Indians who retreated and took up a defensive position. Twenty-eight of them were killed; those wounded and captured were retained as guides. Nine of them were sent to Buenos Aires. In the following weeks, Captain Lista had a peaceful encounter with another Selk'nam group and did recognise their humanity. He judged them inferior to men of European ancestry, but superior to the canoe Indians of the Patagonian channels.[16]

These early expeditions established that Tierra del Fuego was suitable as pasture for the thousands of sheep that grazed across the Strait, in the continental grasslands. They also spread rumours about the existence of

---

14 For an up-to-date introduction to the earlier population and group differentiation in Fuegia, see Prieto A. 2011. *Arquería de Tierra del Fuego*. Santiago: Cuarto Propio, 31–39.

15 Serrano R. 1929. 'Diario de la escursión a la isla grande de la Tierra del Fuego durante los meses de enero i febrero de 1879 por el Teniente 2 de la Armada de Chile Ramón Serrano Montaner', in *Exploraciones y Estudios Hidrográficos: Contribución de la Armada de Chile a la Exposición de Sevilla*. Santiago: Imprenta de la Armada, 386.

16 Lista R. 1887. *Viaje al País de los Onas: Tierra del Fuego*. Buenos Aires: Establecimiento Tipográfico de Alberto Núñez 27, 72–74..

CIVILIAN-DRIVEN VIOLENCE AND THE GENOCIDE OF INDIGENOUS PEOPLES

gold deposits. Meanwhile, Argentina and Chile resolved their competing territorial claims over the island. The treaty of 1881 juridically defined their territorial sovereignties by tracing a north–south line straight down the island, with the eastern third assigned to Argentina. This resolution had little impact on state-led settlement, but opened up substantial opportunities for the expansion of highly profitable sheep farming. In the 1850s the London-based Falkland Islands Company initiated its operations in the South Atlantic with sheep brought from the British Isles, South Africa and Australia. Between 1877 and 1885, both the Argentinian and Chilean authorities, whose actual control over the territory was very limited, succeeded in attracting capital from the Falkland Islands for investment in the southern-most tip of the continent. After the 'Falklander invasion', as Moritz Braun called it, and in the context of the international delimitation of the Big Island being settled, as well as the information provided by the Serrano and Lista expeditions, the time had arrived for global capitalism to cross the Strait of Magellan and for settlers to advance into Selk'nam territory. Tierra del Fuego was seen as a no-man's land, inhabited by half-naked savages.

The gold rush and predatory colonialism

Well before the Chilean and Argentinian governments undertook any action on the distribution of land, rumours about the existence of gold deposits attracted several hundred prospectors to the southern coast of the Strait of Magellan after 1880, and later through the Fuegian archipelago to the Beagle Channel.[17] By and large, miners resorted to violence upon any contact with Selk'nam people. This conflict was not mediated in any way by state authority, which was nominal throughout the region. The bows and arrows of the Selk'nam were no match for the repeating rifles of colonists and miners, whose use of horses also gave them a huge military advantage. Foreigners generally killed men, children and elders, but captured women as sexual slaves.

The most famous of the gold prospectors was Julius Popper, who established himself along the north-eastern Atlantic coast around San Sebastian Bay. In 1886, he undertook a major expedition through Tierra del Fuego, surveying mineral deposits through most of the watercourses of

---

17 Martinic M. 2003. 'La minería aurífera en la región austral americana (1869–1950)'. *Historia*, 36, 219–254; Spears J.R. 1895. *The Gold Diggings of Cape Horn: A Study of Life in Tierra del Fuego and Patagonia*. New York: G.P. Putnam's Sons. See also Penrose R. 1908. 'The gold regions of the Strait of Magellan and Tierra Del Fuego'. *The Journal of Geology*, 16, no. 8, 683–697.

170

the island. He envisioned introducing sheep-farming settlers to the island, and presented plans to the Argentinian government for a port around what is now the town of Río Grande. Popper's expedition also produced his notorious photographic album,[18] which includes infamous pictures portraying the killing of Selk'nam hunters, whose corpses lie on the ground while his paramilitary group aim their rifles at new victims. Though Popper's gold-mining expedition was short-lived, lasting between 1887 and 1889, he has often been charged as being mainly responsible for the persecution of the natives. He was also a controversial figure because he was involved in conflict with other prospectors, as well as with the Chilean and Argentinean authorities. Popper's gruesome photographs, grandiloquence, the military paraphernalia, coins and stamps he issued to his multinational band of adventurers, and the utopianism of his projects transformed him into a legendary figure — the 'king of Patagonia'. In the end, his impact on colonisation and the destruction of the Selk'nam was quite minor, especially in comparison with the second wave of foreigners that entered the Big Island in the 1890s. Popper died in 1893 at the age of 35 while in Buenos Aires.[19]

Although the gold rush opened the way for sustained violence against the Selk'nam, the brief boom did not transform it into the main catalyst of genocide, as happened from the late 1840s in California, where gold diggers led the genocidal impulse.[20] According to the memoir of James Radburne, a young English shepherd who landed on the northern coast of Tierra del Fuego in 1892:

> The miners camped on the island also raided the Indian camps for their women, and after the usual scrubbing they lived with them until they'd made their 'pile' [of gold] and left the island; or until the women were so notoriously pregnant that they should be left ... Once, all of the women of a mining camp, but one, fled. The men shared her until she was expelled when almost ready to give birth.[21]

---

18 The original copies of Popper's *Album in Tierra del Fuego* can be found at the Museo del Fin del Mundo, in Ushuaia. See also Popper J. 1887. *Exploration of Tierra del Fuego: A Lecture Delivered at the Argentine Geographical Institute on the 5th of March, 1887.* Buenos Aires: L. Jacobsen & Co.; and Popper J. 2003. *Atlanta: Proyecto para la Fundación de un Pueblo Marítimo en Tierra del Fuego, y Otros Escritos.* Buenos Aires: Eudeba.

19 The literature on Julius Popper is extensive. A good starting point would be Ansel B. 1970. 'European adventurer in Tierra del Fuego: Julio Popper'. *Hispanic American Historical Review,* 50, no. 1, 89–110.

20 Madley B. 2016. *An American Genocide: The United States and the California Indian Catastrophe, 1846–1873.* New Haven: Yale University Press.

21 Childs H. 1997 [1936]. *El Jimmy: Bandido de la Patagonia*, trans. E. Pisano. Punta Arenas: Ediciones de la Universidad de Magallanes, 52–53.

Jimmy's use of 'also' refers to the practice he and other employees of sheep-farming stations would later indulge in. There are multiple, though scattered, traces of the miners' violence against the Selk'nam, who practised a hit-and-run strategy of resistance against the invaders. Most of the reports dwell on the kidnapping and sexual exploitation of women and girls, and the brutal killing of men.[22] Alluvial mining operations relied on the northern port of Porvenir, to which the Chilean state granted the status of 'town' in 1894. For the only newspaper of the colony, published in Porvenir, achieving this new standing signalled 'the ultimate triumph of civilisation against barbarianism in its last and southernmost trenches, and the acquisition of new and powerful elements of wealth for the nation'.[23] These 'new and powerful elements' consisted of bare land suitable for sheep farming.[24] On the southern end of the island, prospectors arrived later, only in the early 1890s. Their predatory behaviour was already well known to locals. Lucas Bridges, third son to missionary Thomas Bridges and one of the first Europeans to be born in Tierra del Fuego, explains in his memoirs that they 'had read and heard about their conduct'; however, 'those men coming from everywhere in the world, from Alaska to Australia' created a good impression among the former Anglican missionaries. Furthermore, they were 'sent from heaven, as the Bridges family sold them meat and other supplies'.[25] They thus benefited the colonial outpost in the Beagle Channel as consumers, although they had little contact with the Indigenous peoples.

The first wave of colonists in Tierra del Fuego, despite the persistence of private violence, did not produce a systematic campaign of extermination against the native population. The number of prospectors, their dispersal in small parties and their limited economic capacity did not have the magnitude of the second wave, which was led by export-oriented British sheep farmers. It was with the establishment of the first sheep-farming stations that the genocidal impulse against the Selk'nam materialised. It was the privatisation of the land in Tierra del Fuego that led to the eradication of its native population, flora and fauna.

---

22 Harambour A. 2016. *Un Viaje a las Colonias: Memorias de un Ovejero Escocés en Malvinas, Patagonia y Tierra del Fuego (1878–1898)*, trans. M. Azara & A. Harambour. Santiago: DIBAM-Centro de Investigaciones Diego Barros Arana; Bascopé J. 2010. 'El oro y la vida salvaje en Tierra del Fuego, 1880–1914'. *Magallania*, 38, no. 2, 5–26.

23 'Puerto Porvenir. La nueva población', *El Magallanes*, 29 July 1894.

24 The article was critical, though, of the concentration of landownership as it would impede the settlement of more colonists and the expansion of the town, which was surrounded by large sheep stations. In the following decades, the limitations to the growth of the town of Porvenir was a contentious matter.

25 Bridges L. 1948. *Uttermost Part of the Earth*. London: Hodder & Stoughton, 175–177.

Sheep farming and genocidal colonialism

Both the treaty of 1881 and the official expeditions, reinforced by private ventures such as that of Popper, allowed Argentina and Chile to declare their respective claims to Tierra del Fuego as part of the state, and to incorporate them as 'national territories'. This concept was based on the Constitution of the United States and meant the incorporation of those lands and peoples, both immigrant and indigenous, as part of their respective nations, and subject to the discretionary power of the national presidents, who appointed local governors. As a result, the governors were given direct powers to make land grants to private businessmen, avoiding any accountability or restrictions regarding extensions, terms or procedures. This created fertile conditions for corruption. The system benefited intricate networks in Buenos Aires and Santiago, consisting of politicians, business interests and Patagonian land brokers.[26] Land grants, supporting the global expansion of capitalism, favoured European subjects almost exclusively, while the Indigenous population, ranked among the lowest in the racial hierarchy, was left in a limbo of juridical exception, with no defined legal status.

No formal categorisation of Patagonian inhabitants was ever produced by the two governments. They were not classed as colonial subjects, and they were not foreigners, let alone citizens.[27] They were devoid of any legal consideration by the state. Government consideration did not advance much beyond the northern half of the island, which is better for sheep farming than the forested and mountainous southern half. By 1884, the Argentinian Southern Naval Expedition displaced the Anglican mission, based at Ushuaia since 1869, and established a penal colony in the Beagle Channel. There was no similar attempt in the northern region. On the contrary, both states relied on private companies for the occupation of the land and allowed them a monopoly of violence. As in the Falkland Islands, and thereafter in continental Patagonia, sheep stations, or *estancias*, operated as nodes of colonial control. In practice, the colonisation of Tierra del Fuego occurred through these stations, and the fate of the Selk'nam people was decided there.

What to do with the Indians? Almost every state agent envisioned a destiny of displacement, confinement or eradication for the Selk'nam.

---

26 Harambour A. 2017. 'Soberanía y corrupción: La construcción del estado y la propiedad en Patagonia austral (Argentina y Chile, 1840s–1920s)'. *Historia*, 50, no. 2, 555–596.

27 We have recently analysed the legal status of the Kawésqar population in Chilean legal practice, which was extended to the Selk'nam; see Harambour & Barrena, 'Barbarie o justicia'.

CIVILIAN-DRIVEN VIOLENCE AND THE GENOCIDE OF INDIGENOUS PEOPLES

Lieutenant Serrano concluded that they would be 'easy to civilise' if they could be attracted to 'the advantages of commerce' by priests and soldiers tasked with looking after the natives.[28] Captain Lista thought of 'changing their barbarous customs and their nomadic lifestyle for the advantages of civilised life around the centres of population that will surge in the desert'.[29] Some governors imagined policies of indigenous sedentarisation around forts, settling missionaries among them, or 'extracting' them all to some enclosed location.[30] The proposals for civilisation had little effect, however, as the resolution of the Indian question was privatised, along with the land. By 1893 all of the Chilean land was occupied by four companies, which soon became three, and then, in the 1910s, by a single firm, the Explotadora. By 1896, the senior partners of these companies had acquired most of the land across the as-yet-unmarked boundary between Argentinean and Chilean Tierra del Fuego.

In contrast to non-settler colonial formations, as Patrick Wolfe has asserted, 'settler colonies were not primarily established to extract surplus value from indigenous labour'.[31] The sheep-farming industry required access to extensive empty lands for grazing large numbers of sheep. It needed the space to be fenced and cleared of competing grazing animals. It also required only a few reliable, multitasking workers, able to build fences, drive off intruders, herd sheep and exterminate the guanacos that consumed grass reserved for sheep. Farm owners found what they needed in a mostly European labour force, who did not even have to learn Spanish to conduct their daily business. There was no need to exploit Indian labour or to incorporate Argentinian or Chilean workers. The legal transfer of Selk'nam land to foreign companies was paralleled by the land grant of Dawson Island, in the southern half of the Strait of Magellan just across Useless Bay, to the Salesian order, led by Giuseppe Fagnano. It was close to the spot where the Sociedad Explotadora set up its beachhead, Caleta Josefina, named after Josefina Menéndez, wife of Moritz Braun and daughter of José Menéndez. The land grant decree signed by Chilean president José Manuel Balmaceda in June 1890 was based on four considerations, namely: 'the convenience for

---

28 Serrano, 'Diario de la escursión', 427.
29 Lista, *Viaje al País*, 57.
30 See Señoret M. 1895. *Memoria del Gobernador de Magallanes: La Tierra del Fuego i sus Naturales*. Santiago: Imprenta Nacional; Guerrero M. 1897. *Memoria que el Delegado del Supremo Gobierno en el Territorio de Magallanes don Mariano Guerrero Bascuñan presenta al señor Ministro de Colonización*. Santiago: Imprenta i Librería Ercilla.
31 Wolfe P. 1999. *Settler Colonialism and the Transformation of Anthropology: The Politics and Poetics of an Ethnographic Event*. London: Cassell, 1.

CHAPTER 7: 'There Cannot be Civilisation and Barbarism on the Island'

the State to favor and stimulate enterprises whose object is the civilisation of the indigenous peoples of Tierra del Fuego'; the humanitarian duty to civilise them; the national colonisation of 'such faraway territories'; and the use of private means that would not cost the state anything.[32]

Coinciding with the start of large-scale sheep farming on the Big Island in the early 1890s, the Salesians began to set up the San Rafael Mission on Dawson Island. It attracted some canoe Indians, for whom contact with navigators already had a long history of sexual violence and murder. The mission also maintained relations with Anglican missionaries settled in Ushuaia.[33] At this point, there was no missionary activity specifically directed at the Selk'nam. Between 1889 and 1894, San Rafael preferred to minister to the canoe people. Up to two hundred Indians, mostly Kawésqars, resided at the mission or passed through it. Between 1895 and 1901, however, the composition and condition of the inmates at San Rafael changed radically. Many Selk'nam were taken on because the sheep stations had implemented a policy of forced removal and killing of the Selk'nam, among whom losses were significant. The Indians rarely attacked colonists, who were mounted and equipped with repeating rifles. The Selk'nam did, however, sabotage the flocks by driving them into swampy areas, cutting their leg tendons, and killing them in other ways. They also damaged fences, which took a great deal of time to repair.

The decision regarding a final solution to the problem of Selk'nam resistance came in mid-1895. In a private letter sent from Valparaíso to Punta Arenas, the president of the Explotadora, McClelland, explained to Braun that they had received a request from Padre Fagnano 'to give £1 sterling for each Indian sent over to Dawson Island ... [as] the cheapest way we can get rid of them, short of shooting them, which is rather objectionable'.[34] McClelland trusted that Braun would approve the request. In Braun's memory, however, the idea was his own. He decided to meet with Fagnano once again, suggesting that 'with our contribution in money and materials they would build everything necessary for installing the indigenous families, whose shipment we would do ... I was not thinking of anything other than getting the Ona off me'. 'My thesis,' he explained, 'was that there was no space for civilisation and barbarism on the island'.[35]

---

32 Guerrero, *Memoria que el Delegado*, 156.
33 Bridges, *Uttermost Part*, ch. XXIX.
34 AMB-MRM, Correspondencia Recibida, 1895, Peter McClelland to Moritz Braun, 1 June 1895. Also quoted in Martinic M. 1973. 'Panorama de la colonización en Tierra del Fuego entre 1881 y 1900'. *Anales del Instituto de la Patagonia*, IV, no. 1, 73.
35 Braun M. 1985. *Memorias de una Vida Colmada*. Buenos Aires: Autoedición, 135–136.

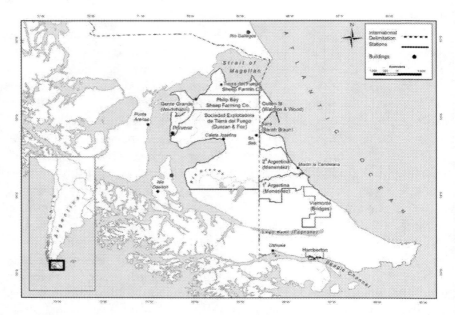

Figure 7.1: Main colonial outposts and sheep-farming stations in Tierra del Fuego, c. 1895

The solution offered by Fagnano was not quite original, although the dispute over the originality of the idea was further discussed. According to Punta Arenas priest Maggiorino Borgatello, he had discussed the issue with Lieutenant Colonel Daniel Cruz Ramírez, 'one of the chiefs of the Sociedad Esplotadora' in early 1895: 'He promised me that the Government would help, and also the Society.' He would meet Fagnano in Santiago and the Salesians would 'accept the Indians the Sociedad Esplotadora would send them'. According to Maggiorino Borgatello, Cruz talked to Chilean president Jorge Montt, Fagnano and the directors of the Explotadora, which agreed, as McClelland had indicated, to send 'all of the Indians found on their property ... to save them from extermination'. The Salesians later confirmed the deal.[36] As a result, between 1890 and 1895, the number of Indigenous persons confined at the Dawson Island mission increased from 97 to 215. Most of them were Kawésqar, who were relatively free to come and go as they pleased. By 1895, the missionaries started talking about internees, or deported Selk'nam, who became a large majority at the mission station. In 1896 there were 270, in 1897 about 400, and in 1898 the inmates reached

---

36 ANH-FGM, Maggiorino Borgatello's Judicial Declaration, 11 January 1896, *Sumario sobre Vejámenes Inferidos a Indígenas de Tierra del Fuego*, Leg. 75, 119–121.

CHAPTER 7: 'There Cannot be Civilisation and Barbarism on the Island'

a peak of 550. Attrition rates were exceptionally high, with reportedly as many as one out of five ending in a mass grave in most years between 1896 and 1908. Luis Carnino, a Salesian priest who arrived at the Dawson mission in 1896 and became its director in 1910, claimed that in some years the death rate was as high as 40 per cent. By 1911 there were a mere 36 survivors at the mission station.[37] As Casali et al. demonstrate for the mission of La Candelaria, a second Catholic mission on the Atlantic coast, tuberculosis was the main cause of death, with infection spreading through overcrowding and sharing of infected clothes.[38] According to Braun, with 'my ships' and 'with no harm', he did 'transfer some seven hundred Onas [in less than a decade], everything done with my sympathetic friend Fagnano and his Meritorious order'. The Explotadora paid 'one pound sterling for every Indian, being man, woman or child'.[39]

Of hunters, gatherers and hunter-gatherers

In a well-known alternative rendering of settler Indian-hunting practices, station managers paid 'one pound for each pair of Indian ears' produced.[40] Instead of glorifying the civilisational role of the sheep-farming companies, a critical narrative tradition focuses on their cruelties in the settlement of Tierra del Fuego. Specialised hitmen were brought in from abroad to round up Selk'nam on the plains and to shoot them. According to long-standing rumours, some men even poisoned beached whales.[41] The Selk'nam and canoe Indians would gather around the carcass for a feast, and harvest oil and fat for future use. There is no proof of the use of this method of killing, though. Likewise, there is also no proof of the piece-rate deal for severed ears.[42] On the contrary, there are unequivocal references in official, business

---

37 Aliaga F. 2000. *La Misión Salesiana en Isla Dawson*. Santiago: Salesianos, 130. See also García-Moro C. 1992. 'Reconstrucción del proceso de extinción de los Selknam a través de los libros misionales'. *Anales del Instituto de la Patagonia*, 21, 33–46.

38 Casali R., Fugassa M., & Guichón R. 2006. 'Aproximación epidemiológica al proceso de contacto interétnico en el norte de Tierra del Fuego'. *Magallania*, 34, no. 1, 87–101.

39 Braun, *Memorias de Una Vida*, 135–136.

40 'A story, widely circulated and still current, tells that certain of the newcomers were paid a pound a head for every Indian killed', explained Bridges in 1948: 'Personally I believe this to have been done by one individual only ... He was not in the service of anyone who owns lands at the present'. Bridges, *Uttermost Part*, 265.

41 Furlong, 'Into the unknown', 443; Borrero J.M. 1989 [1928]. *La Patagonia Trágica*. Ushuaia: Zagier & Urruty, 21–22. The story of the poisoned whale was criticised by Braun, *Memorias de Una Vida*, 137: according to him, there was not enough strychnine to cause such a massive poisoning.

42 According to Bridges, *Uttermost Part*, 269. the pound-for-ears deal applied to just one case, which he does not identify.

CIVILIAN-DRIVEN VIOLENCE AND THE GENOCIDE OF INDIGENOUS PEOPLES

and Salesian sources of the salaried, daily routine of Indian-hunting by workers on sheep ranches. Even managers took part in the killing and capture of Selk'nam. Most of the captured were shipped to Dawson Island in the Strait of Magellan or sent on foot to La Candelaria on the Atlantic coast, where they were confined. Most died sooner rather than later.

Indian hunters from sheep stations and the Indian gatherers from mission stations played differentiated though complementary roles in the destruction of Selk'nam society. While the former practised direct physical violence, the latter worked on the deportees' minds and souls in the short time between their arrival at the mission station and when most succumbed to infectious diseases.[43] The routines of the human hunters and the human gatherers differed greatly, with the former operating in terms of commercial timing and the latter through self-regulated Catholic routines. Both were free of any form of state regulation. Nor were station workers constrained by any protocol but those of their managers, which were broadly defined by the interests of the Punta Arenas-Valparaíso business axis. More than professional assassins, which they were, the workers deployed a regime of violence against a naturalised enemy they regarded as the incarnation of primitiveness, alien to notions of God, property and government. The hunters and captors of humans were 'neither criminals nor mad men', as critics sometimes claimed.[44] On the contrary, they were contract workers who, for the most part, stayed for a few years, made some money, and went back home or found new, more attractive destinations, usually within the British Empire. A few of them stayed, became independent farmers, and founded new ranches on the Big Island or in southern Patagonia. In the last few years, written accounts of some of their experiences have emerged.

One such man, Charles Finger, a young socialist born near London, arrived in Tierra del Fuego in 1890. He was 20 and 'burning with the hope to be first man somewhere'.[45] Another, James Radburne, 18, escaped from legal trouble in Berkshire. He landed in early 1893 at Springhill, and was hired by Waldron and Wood, a Falkland Islands company linked to the Explotadora.[46] William Blain was older. At 39, he was a veteran shepherd,

---

43 For a comprehensive epidemiologic history of one of these mission fields, see Casali R. 2013. *Conquistando el Fin del Mundo: la Misión La Candelaria y la Salud de la Población Selk'nam (Tierra del Fuego 1895–1931)*. Rosario: Prohistoria.

44 Levi P. 2017 [1958]. *Si Esto es un Hombre*, trans. P. Gómez. Buenos Aires: Ariel, 107.

45 Finger C. 1968 [1936]. *Valiant Vagabonds*. New York: Books for Libraries Press, 203.

46 Childs, *El Jimmy*. 'Jimmy, the outlaw of Patagonia', was the title of the first biography of a labourer who hunted Selk'nam, and was based on extensive conversations with James Radburne in the Andean lakes of the Santa Cruz National Territory, where he had a small ranch and raised a family with a Tehuelche woman.

CHAPTER 7: 'There Cannot be Civilisation and Barbarism on the Island'

born in the Scottish Lowlands, who had migrated to the Falklands in 1878. He was part of the continental 'invasion' and crossed the Strait with the first flocks in early 1881.[47] Blain served as subadministrator of the Tierra del Fuego Sheep Farming Company at Springhill. Finger and Radburne, in contrast, were day labourers. The three of them arrived, having heard terrifying stories about the 'Onas' or 'Oonas' of *Terra del* — as they called the island — who were portrayed as cannibals ready to attack whites. The three of them took part in the harshest years of the repression and were part of a largely British colonial enterprise that produced wool exclusively for the London market. They were paid in pounds sterling and were part of the new racial elite introduced by the sheep industry.

At Springhill, Blain was in charge of organising the daily routines of men, such as Radburne and Finger, and worked under the guidance of Ernst Wales, a senior manager and important stockholder. 'He gave me strict orders not to allow the men to mistreat the Indians,' Blain explained in his memoirs. But the Indians could not be caught. So, Wales hired two men only known as 'The Devil' and 'Buffalo Bill'. 'I got them mounted on two good horses, well-armed, with three days provisions turned them adrift to clear the camp around of man, woman and child but not shed human blood. But in self-defense.' Dogs belonging to natives 'they were to destroy without reserve'.[48] The technique worked. The hunters kept going out and bringing women and children, though rarely any men. They usually came back with bows, something very unlikely to have been taken from a living Selk'nam man. Soon, the raids involved more men. 'Indian-hunting was not as romantic as I had imagined, and I could not admire the system that was freeing the island of natives, but it was part of my job and, at the same time, more exciting than anything I done before,' said Radburne, according to his biographer.[49] His chief, Wales, also took part in the hunting. Radburne explained that 'no Indian, with no consideration of age or sex, would escape

---

47 Harambour, *Un Viaje a las Colonias*.
48 National Records of Scotland, William Blain, Memories of Tierra del Fuego, GDI/987/9, 12. The expression 'well armed' did not appear in the first transcript of these documents, 'The journal of William Blain, shepherd in Tierra del Fuego, 1891–98', by Arnold Morrison. See, http://myweb.tiscali.co.uk/scotsinargpat/blain.htm, accessed 19 June 2018. Nor does does it appear in its first translation into Spanish, published by Mateo Martinic in 1999 as 'Diario de vida de William Blain. Ovejero en Tierra del Fuego (1891–1898). *Magallania*, 27, no. 1, 199–222. The full version of these memoirs was published in Harambour, *Un Viaje a las Colonias*.
49 Childs, *El Jimmy*, 29.

CIVILIAN-DRIVEN VIOLENCE AND THE GENOCIDE OF INDIGENOUS PEOPLES

alive if the bosses were present'. The 'relentless' Sam Hyslop allowed the elders to flee 'if the boss was not there'.[50]

William Blain's memoirs, however, make no mention of Wales' or Hyslop's murders or orders to perpetrate them, as Radburne had done.[51] Nor did Charles Finger, who worked at the neighboring Gente Grande Station under the command of the Scot, John McRae, one of the partners of the German Wehrhahn Brothers Company. 'A very rough kind of communism seems to prevail here,' noted Finger, referring to the relative equality among Europeans in Tierra del Fuego. 'Several whites have been shot at with arrows,' he was told. And he added in a footnote, quoting Darwin: '[N]ature by making habit omnipotent, and its effects hereditary, has fitted the Fuegian to the climate and the productions of his miserable country'. Once he landed at Gente Grande, he was surprised to find many men of many nationalities and very few natives. After a few weeks, he wrote that it was 'the first time' he had 'missed the Socialist Commune Celebration ... When I come to think of the scarcity of all forms of law in this part of the world, and note how happiness, plenty and good-fellowship prevails, I feel more anarchistically inclined than ever'.

This communism and anarchism applied only to colonists and was not extended to Indians, as the two groups were seen as belonging to radically different conditions of humanity. As the de facto sovereign over more than 123 000 hectares, McRae had complete freedom to carry out his Indian-hunting practices. Indeed, McRae became the first Chilean authority on the island when he was appointed ad hoc local authority.[52] The sovereignty of capital and the sovereignty of the state coincided and became entangled in his person.[53] Finger noted this, but wrote nothing about the destruction of Selk'nam sovereignty. South of Gente Grande, and ten times larger, was Caleta Josefina, which belonged to the Explotadora and was administered by a New Zealander Alexander Cameron. There are neither diaries nor memoirs regarding the doings of the workers on Caleta Josefina.

---

50 Ibid., 52.
51 I have compared Blain's and Radburne's narratives of killings in Harambour A. 2015. 'El ovejero y el bandido: Trayectorias, cruces y genocidio en dos relatos de viaje británicos en Tierra del Fuego (década de 1890)'.*Anales de Literatura Chilena*, 16, no. 24, 163–182.
52 McRae was appointed 'subdelegado' (subdelegated) from at least 1892. Martinic M. 1981. *La Tierra de los Fuegos*. Porvenir: Municipalidad de Porvenir, 74.
53 The entanglement and differentiation of powers in the colonial process is the central theme of my 2012 PhD dissertation, 'Borderland Sovereignties: Postcolonial Colonialism and State Making in Patagonia, Argentina and Chile, 1840s–1922'. Department of History, Stony Brook University, New York.

CHAPTER 7: 'There Cannot be Civilisation and Barbarism on the Island'

Cameron and McRae, their superiors Braun, Stubenrauch and Wales, and dozens of station personnel were to testify in an extensive trial about 'humiliations against the Indians of Tierra del Fuego'.[54] It began in late 1895 and was a milestone in confirming the deployment of the combined forces of religion, capital and state in the eradication of the natives of Tierra del Fuego. The trial was the result of a press campaign in central Chile, most likely initiated by Salesian priests, against an order of the liberal Chilean governor, the naval captain Manuel Señoret. The governor was involved in a long-running dispute with the Italian missionaries over the final destination of captive Selk'nam. He thus decided to redirect a group of 165 Selk'nam, whom the Explotadora administrator Alexander Cameron was deporting to Dawson Island, to Punta Arenas instead, as a way of accelerating their 'civilisation'. He wanted the children to be distributed among the principal families and to force the adults to perform manual labour. This deeply annoyed the Dawson Island community, which lost the largest human shipment it would ever have received, and the Salesians instituted legal proceedings against the governor. For a year, before the trial was suspended for almost a decade, a parade of men from the sheep-farming industry described the well-known, but rarely depicted, practices of Indian-hunting, forced removal, execution of men, appropriation of children and sexual slavery.

McRae was fingered as a confiscator and distributor of Indigenous children, besides being responsible for killings, illegal captures and assassinations, as were Cameron, Mont Wales and a number of their workers. Braun, Stubenrauch, Heede, Wood and other entrepreneurs were identified as appropriators of minors, all of them female, and as carrying overall responsibility for the mandate to 'clean' the fields of Indians.[55] Despite the barbarism described in the testimony, and their responsibility for the alleged crimes, the final verdict delivered was:

> That it is public knowledge that the indigenous people of Tierra del Fuego were living in a state of barbarism; that they had no law of territorial property, and that they were nomadic, feeding themselves through hunting and, mainly, with the sheep they came across;

---

54 ANH-FJM, *Sumario sobre Vejámenes Inferidos a Indígenas de Tierra del Fuego*, Leg. 75. The full transcript of the trial is available at Aike. Biblioteca Digital de la Patagonia. See http://www.bibliotecadigital.umag.cl/bitstream/handle/20.500.11893/487/1895.%20 Sumario%20sobre%20vej%C3%A1menes%20Tierra%20del%20Fuego.pdf?sequence= 1&isAllowed=y, accessed 18 June 2018.

55 For some of the most notorious denunciations, see *Sumario sobre Vejámenes*, 60, 82, 180, 182.

> That regarding these indigenous people, there is no provision for defining their legal status; That the preceding ... do not allow for criminal prosecution of any person for the humiliations that are said to have occurred against the indigenous tribes that have lived in Tierra del Fuego and adjacent islands.[56]

As the judge sanctioned the extra-legal status of the Selk'nam, and perpetrators went unpunished, the civilian-driven final solution to the Selk'nam problem was legalised and legitimised. Wales and Cameron were acquitted, as were four employees of the Explotadora, whose bail costs were paid by Braun.[57]

The agreement between the Salesians and sheep farmers was subsequently renegotiated, and hundreds of Selk'nam were deported to mission stations in the next few years. In 1897, a Special Commissioner sent from Santiago to investigate irregularities in land transfers took the opportunity to make further recommendations to the government. In talks with Moritz Braun of the Sociedad Explotadora, Ernesto Hobbs of the Sociedad Ganadera Gente Grande, Mont Wales of Philip Bay Farming Company and Rudolph Stubenrauch of Wehrhahn & Company, all expressed their willingness 'to provide the horses and employees to capture and deport the Indians, and to contribute an annual sum' to maintain the deported families under the rule of the Salesian missions. The Indians could be confined on Dawson Island, the islands of Navarino or Wollaston south of the Beagle Channel, or anywhere else in the western Patagonian channels. Company shepherds would carry out the raids, accompanied by Catholic missionaries, a guard or a special agent, to 'avoid any useless violence'. The raids would be conducted two or three times a year, preferably in summer and timed to prevent overcrowding of mission stations.[58] The government would subsidise transportation costs with an annual payment of six thousand pesos to the Salesian order. According to the Special Commissioner, in a short time the Selk'nam 'race' would be 'lending its support to the development and prosperity of the territory which, until recently, was the theatre of their savage devastation'. As planned by the sheep-farming companies, the Catholic order and the state authorities, this would be the final solution to 'the struggle between civilisation and barbarianism' in Tierra del Fuego.[59]

---

56 Ibid., 198.
57 Ibid., 376.
58 Guerrero, *Memoria que el Delegado*, 138, 140.
59 Ibid., 153–155.

CHAPTER 7: 'There Cannot be Civilisation and Barbarism on the Island'

Incursions by shepherds through 'the country of the Onas' proceeded rapidly in the following years, moving southward as ethnic cleansing emptied the northern plains of indigenes. Displaced Selk'nam moved towards the southern forests and the Atlantic coast, where Sociedad Explotadora stations were set up in 1896 and 1897. There they encountered some of the more infamous Indian hunters, such as Norman Wood of San Sebastián, and Alexander McLennan, the manager of Primera Argentina.[60] The newly established Argentinean police force in the area contributed to the persecution of the Selk'nam, and they also started to capture and deport Indigenous families to La Candelaria. According to Ramón Lucio Cortés, the first Argentinean sheriff on the Atlantic coast, Wood's men 'were occupied exclusively with the hunting of Indians, in both Argentinian and Chilean territory'.[61]

Persecution also increased intra-ethnic violence, as displaced Selk'nam groups were pushed into contact and conflict with each other. The memoirs of Lucas Bridges confirm this: 'Under the increasing pressure from the north,' he recalled, Selk'nam visits to the southern-most ranches increased, and 'the parties from farther afield grew more numerous'.[62] They were 'being pushed off the edge of the world', explained Furlong.[63] The scarcity of animals to hunt and the decimation of Selk'nam bands led in some cases to the amalgamation of groups, and the tendency to congregate near white settlements. This led to disputes over women and fights over resources. According to Bridges, he witnessed intense intergroup conflict, some of which lasted for years and had mortal outcomes. As a result, both families and individuals sought the protection of the Salesian mission in San Sebastián Bay, where some of the biggest sheep stations were located. There, new forms of resistance and conflict emerged under new conditions of the marginal incorporation of Selk'nam men into the colonial economy as labourers and of women as servants, or as sexual slaves and partners.[64] Evidence of their experiences barely exists in the historical record as a result

---

60 See Marchante J.L. 2014. *Menéndez, Rey de la Patagonia*. Santiago: Catalonia, 165–156, 200–204. The infamous McLennan appears as The King of Tierra del Fuego in Bridges' *Uttermost Part*, which used a pseudonym, McInch, so as not to offend his descendants by telling of his horrendous crimes.

61 Belza J.E. 1975. *En la Isla del Fuego. Vol. II. Colonización*. Buenos Aires: IIHTF, 203. Belza's works are by far the main ones quoted by Inda E. 2008. *The Extermination of the Onas*. Buenos Aires: Cofomar.

62 Bridges, *Uttermost Part*, 269–270. See also 383–387.

63 Furlong C. 1910. 'The vanishing people of the land of Fire: *Harper's Magazine* (January), 217–229.

64 Casali, *Conquistando el Fin*, 191–235.

CIVILIAN-DRIVEN VIOLENCE AND THE GENOCIDE OF INDIGENOUS PEOPLES

of the forced assimilation of survivors into a colonial society deeply marked by racism. There are a small number of Selk'nam testimonies and family histories that have survived, which may help to rebuild some sense of this past and of their survival.[65]

In La Candelaria, the official number of Selk'nam was 163 in 1899, 133 in 1901, 35 in 1904, and 27 in 1906.[66] At the Dawson Island mission, the Selk'nam made up a majority of the inmates for the first time in 1896. There were about 300 in 1896, 400 in 1897, and 550 in 1898. According to Salesian data, the death toll for the five years to 1900 were devastating: 115 died in 1896, 145 in 1897, 110 in 1898, 95 in 1899, and 80 in 1900. Thereafter, the number of inmates dropped to 205 in 1900. By 1911, the Salesians considered the mission no longer necessary, as only 36 internees survived. Of this group, 25 were transferred to La Candelaria, Argentina, three dying en route. The number of internees at La Candelaria rose to 34. By 1925 the Salesians considered this station no longer viable and closed it down. Officially, 862 Indians had died at the Dawson station.[67]

Lucas Bridges, a settler sympathetic to the Selk'nam, had visited Dawson Island in 1894. There he met Hektliohih, a big man he had known a few years earlier in Ushuaia where he arrived after his capture in the northern part of the island. Eventually, Hektliohih was able to escape to the forest and join other unknown survivors. They were recaptured and sent to Dawson Island, from where there was no possibility of escape. He wore Western rags, and he did not speak of any maltreatment. Instead, he said to Bridges, 'Shouwe t-maten ya' (The nostalgia is killing me). This is one of the very few Selk'nam statements to have survived. 'And so it was,' added Bridges, 'he did not survive much longer.'[68] Bridges became honorary commissioner of

---

65 See the interviews with Angela Loij, Federico Echeuline, Alfredo Rupatini, Enriqueta Varela and Luis Garibaldi Honte in Chapman A. 2002. *Fin de un mundo: Los Selk'nam de la Tierra del Fuego*. Santiago: Taller Experimental Cuerpo Pintados. A relatively well-known history of Selk'nam resistance is that of the so-called guerrilla fighter Capelo, included in Bridges' book and in different versions by Belza. See especially Belza J.C. 1973. 'Capelo, el Ona Guerrillero'. *Karukinka*, 5 (July), 17–32. There is a general discussion on resistance and accommodation in Casali R. 2008. 'Contacto interétnico en el Norte de Tierra del Fuego: Primera aproximación a las estrategias de resistencia Selk'nam', *Magallania*, 36, no. 2, 45–61. See also Moreno M. 2017. 'Estado, soberanía y resistencia indígena: La colonización ovina de Tierra del Fuego y la resistencia Selk'nam, 1881–1911', in *Seminario Simon Collier*. Santiago: Instituto de Historia P. Universidad Católica de Chile, 129–153.
66 Casali, *Conquistado el Fin*, 107.
67 Aliaga, *La Misión Salesiana*, 130. For amazing testimony on the supposed happiness of Indians at the Salesian missions, see Borgatello M. 1920. *Florecillas Silvestres*, trans. G. Roca. Turin: Scuola Tipográfica Salesiana.
68 Bridges, *Uttermost Part*, 270–271.

CHAPTER 7: 'There Cannot be Civilisation and Barbarism on the Island'

the area on the southern tip of the Big Island, and the Selk'nam survivors he used as labourers built the first roads between his sheep stations. For the Argentinean Ministry of the Interior, this demonstrated 'the ease of attracting them [Indians] to work and, thus to civilisation'.[69] On the Explotadora's biggest station, Caleta Josefina, in late 1898, its administrator, Alexander A. Cameron, proudly communicated to Peter McClelland that 'the Indian problem is almost solved.[70]

Conclusion

The Selk'nam of Tierra del Fuego were virtually exterminated by pastoral settlers in the first decade after the landing of sheep. In Tierra del Fuego there were no national armies that led the Euro-American conquest of the territory. As indicated by the South African historian Nigel Penn, 'settler colonialism could only triumph or enter its eliminationist phase where or when it was able to impose its will absolutely'.[71] In Tierra del Fuego it did not depend on the will or the active policy of states, as in south-central Argentina and Chile. Laissez-faire was structurally constitutive of settler colonialism in Tierra del Fuego, and the privatisation of land involved the privatisation of genocide.

The incorporation of Tierra del Fuego into global circuits of capitalist production was so devastatingly successful that there is no written word left by any one of the Indigenous peoples of that country. There is no single testimony of Selk'nam interned in the mission camps. The civilising process wiped out the names and persons of the Big Island. A population estimated at between three- and four thousand hunter-gatherers had been reduced to a few hundred by the end of the 1890s. By 1919, the surviving Selk'nam numbered barely 7 per cent of their original population estimate.[72] The production of wool for export and the occupation by tens of thousands of sheep had reconfigured their land; most of those deported died on isolated mission stations; and the Argentinean and Chilean states had appropriated their sovereignty.

---

69 Departamento de Interior. 1901. *Memoria del Departamento del Interior Correspondiente al año 1900*. Buenos Aires: Imprenta de Tribuna, 80–81.

70 Letter of 15 September 1898, as quoted in Marchante, *Menéndez*, 225.

71 Penn N. 2014. 'The destruction of hunter-gatherer societies on the pastoralist frontier: The Cape and Australia compared', in *Genocide on Settler Frontiers: When Hunter-Gatherers and Commercial Stock Farmers Clash*, ed. Adhikari M. Cape Town: UCT Press, 174. In the Chilean conquest of Arauco and the Argentinean occupation of the Pampas and northern Patagonia between the 1860s and the 1880s, the process was led by the national armies.

72 García-Moro, Reconstruccion, 33–46.

CIVILIAN-DRIVEN VIOLENCE AND THE GENOCIDE OF INDIGENOUS PEOPLES

'To talk about the benefits Monsignor Fagnano contributed to the culture of the Indians and the civilised in Magallanes, would occupy many volumes,' a local newspaper claimed in 1924.[73] In 1945 missionary Pedro Giacomini was of the opinion that in the Salesian missions 'the Indians found bread, peace and Paradise'. Yet, by then, there were barely 20 Selk'nam left alive and were ready to 'disappear for ever from the face of the Earth'.[74] In 2011, according to Mateo Martinic, a renowned and prolific historian of Patagonia:

> [T]he Salesians put in that admirable work all the goodwill they could, with self-sacrificing and total dedication, motivating spiritual fervour, and with an incredible determination for the salvation and well-being of the Selk'nam and Kawésqar aboriginal peoples. If things did not go as well as they thought, it was not their responsibility, and posterity understood and still understands it thus.[75]

In this kind of narrative, very influential in current Patagonian politics of identity, 'the extinction of aboriginal peoples' appears as one of the 'collateral phenomena of progress'.[76] In this manner, the commemoration of Selk'nam spirituality, which has become fashionable, is based on the Catholic ethnography of Martin Gusinde of the 1910s and 1920s. Strengthened by the global spread of ethnic tourism, it appears to be a celebration of native prehistory. What remains, however, are colonial and national histories.[77]

If 'modernity can be defined as compulsive modernisation',[78] the sheep-farming companies' extermination of these hunter-gatherers, with the active participation of the Salesians and backed by the Chilean and Argentinian states, should be considered its agents. British and multinational subjects replaced the Selk'nam, and flocks of sheep took the

---

73 'Los Salesianos y Chile', *La Unión*, Punta Arenas, 9 June 1924, 12–14.
74 Giacomini P. 1945. 'Prólogo', en Massa S.S., Lorenzo Revdo. Padre', in *Monografía de Magallanes. Sesenta años de Acción Salesiana en el Sur – 1886–1946: Recuerdo del Noveno Congreso Eucarístico Nacional de Magallanes. 6 al 10 de Febrero de 1846.* Punta Arenas: Escuela Tipográfica del Instituto Don Bosco, 9.
75 Martinic M. 2011. 'Centenario del cierre de la misión de Dawson: Reflexiones sobre un esfuerzo admirable e infructuoso'. *Magallania*, 39, no. 2, 97–103.
76 Martinic M. 2015. Review of *Menéndez, rey de la Patagonia. Magallania*, 43, no. 1, 328–330.
77 For entanglements between traditional historiography and the current politics of identity in Chilean Patagonia, see Harambour A. 2018. 'Los prohombres y los extintos: Patrimonio, identidad e historiografía regional en Magallanes'. *Cuadernos de Historia*, 48, 57–88.
78 Bauman Z. 2000. 'The duty to remember: But what?', in *Enlightenment and Genocide, Contradictions of Modernity*, eds. J. Kay & B. Strath. Brussels: Presses Interuniversitaires Européennes & Peter Lang, 38.

CHAPTER 7: 'There Cannot be Civilisation and Barbarism on the Island'

place of guanaco herds, which Furlong described as 'the barometer of the Indians' existence'.[79] Aboriginal dogs and native rodents were exterminated too. Imperial expansion and colonialism erased ten thousand years of indigenous socio-ecological history by incorporating Tierra del Fuego into the circulation of British capital and, thereafter, into the realm of national states, through a private policy of forced removal in which actors from religious, economic and political spheres converged. In Pierre Bourdieu's words, the state operates as a sort of metacapital, able to distribute and redistribute capital.[80] By granting lands they barely knew for exploitation by commercial enterprises, and by excluding the people who inhabited these lands from any legal standing, the Argentinean and Chilean states privatised the monopoly of violence through their policy of laissez-faire. By doing so, they freed the forces of racial extermination practised mostly by British subjects in an informal, entrepreneurial and imperial setting.

The privatisation of killing involved the transfer of the historical responsibility for genocide, with the states transferring it to sheep-farming companies, and entrepreneurs to shepherds. Gold prospectors played an independent part. The emerging public discussion about how to deal with the Selk'nam genocide is an open matter in which past, present and future merge in the continuum of coloniality, framed by the termination of the Selk'nam existence.

---

79 Furlong 'Vanishing people', 217–229.
80 Bourdieu P. 1999. 'Rethinking the state: Genesis and structure of the bureaucratic field', in *State/Culture: State-Formation after the Cultural Turn*, ed. G. Steinmetz. Ithaca: Cornell University Press, 53–75.

CHAPTER EIGHT

Missionaries, Agents, Principals and Teachers: Civilian Complicity in the Perpetration of Genocide in Indigenous Boarding Schools in New Mexico and Manitoba, 1879–1975[1]

Andrew Woolford

In the late nineteenth century, a confluence of factors created conditions for a different approach to civilian- and state cooperation in the commission of genocidal violence in North America. The costs and bad publicity of Indigenous massacre in the United States made warfare a less attractive option for addressing the so-called Indian problem.[2] The continued push for western lands — whether for agriculture, resource extraction or railroads — limited forced removal as a viable strategy, though some continued to press for segregating Indigenous peoples onto still smaller tracts of land.[3] Moreover, the devastating toll of disease, demise of the fur trade and starvation that came with territorial and species losses, together weakened Indigenous societies. This opened political space for more assertive settler colonial practices of dispossession.[4]

Under these conditions, governments in both Canada and the United States turned toward assimilative education as their favoured strategy for solving the 'Indian problem'. In the US, the federal government managed

---

1   The research presented in this chapter was made possible by funding from the Truth and Reconciliation Commission of Canada and a Fulbright Visiting Scholar Fellowship. I am also pleased to acknowledge the generous financial support of the Social Sciences and Humanities Research Council of Canada through the Manitoba Research Alliance grant: Partnering for Change – Community-based Solutions for Aboriginal and Inner-city poverty. Thanks to Theodore Fontaine, Mary Courchene, David Rundle Sr., Daniel Highway, Caroline Perreault, William Morriseau, Purvis Fontaine and Betty Ross for the knowledge they have shared with me over the years. Any errors presented are the responsibility of the author alone.

2   Laderman S. 2002. '"It is cheaper and better to teach a young Indian than to fight an old one": Thaddeus Pound and the logic of assimilation'. *American Indian Culture and Research Journal*, 26, no. 3, 85–111.

3   Walker F.A. 1874. *The Indian Question*. Boston: James R. Osgood and Company, 66; Otis E.S. 1878. *The Indian Question*. New York: Sheldon & Company, 133.

4   Nichols R.L. 1998. *Indians in the United States and Canada: A Comparative History*. Lincoln: University of Nebraska Press, 241–284.

CHAPTER 8: Missionaries, Agents, Principals and Teachers

the Indigenous education system, though it was put into effect by civilians. In Canada, the day-to-day operation of the system was placed largely in the hands of Catholic, Anglican, Methodist and Presbyterian missionaries, with the government primarily in charge of funding and general oversight of schools. These schools have been described as institutions of 'cultural genocide',[5] or simply as genocide.[6] I will not here engage the debate over whether or not these actions constitute genocide in a legal or sociological sense, as my views on this topic are covered elsewhere.[7] Instead, I examine the roles of civilian workers in fostering, and occasionally disrupting, group destruction at the Santa Fe (SFIS) and Albuquerque (AIS) Indian Schools in New Mexico, and at the Fort Alexander (FAIRS) and Portage la Prairie (PLPIRS) Indian Residential Schools in Manitoba. In so doing, I seek to complicate the relationship between state- and citizen-driven aspects of genocidal violence by focusing on the relational dynamics of destruction in a manner that situates genocide participation and complicity within collective action frames that permit diverse motivations, intents, practices and engagements to coalesce across varied temporal and spatial scales. The notion of the collective action frame will be used not only to connect civilian-driven violence to broader state strategies of Indigenous elimination, but also to show how civilian actors both internalise and negotiate these strategies in ways that are not always straightforward and often add distinct local dimensions to a genocidal project.

Settler agency and claims of benevolence

Guenther Lewy makes the argument that neither the US nor Canadian governments actively sought the destruction of Indigenous groups as such.[8] The harms resulting from government policy and settler actions, according

---

5 Truth and Reconciliation Commission of Canada. 2015. *The Final Report of the Truth and Reconciliation Commission of Canada. Vol. 6: Reconciliation: Canada's Residential Schools.* Montreal: McGill-Queen's University Press.

6 See in general Bischoping K. & Fingerhut N. 1996. 'Border lines: Indigenous peoples in genocide studies'. *Canadian Review of Sociology and Anthropology*, 33, no. 4, 481–506; Chrisjohn R. & Young S. 1997. *The Circle Game: Shadows and Substance in the Indian Residential School Experience.* Penticton, BC: Theytus Books; MacDonald D.B. & Hudson G. 2012. 'The genocide question and Indian residential schools in Canada'. *Canadian Journal of Political Science*, 45, no. 2, 427–449.

7 Woolford A. 2009. 'Ontological destruction: Genocide and Aboriginal peoples in Canada'. *Genocide Studies and Prevention*, 4, no. 1, 81–97; Woolford A. 2015. *This Benevolent Experiment: Indigenous Boarding Schools, Genocide and Redress in North America.* Lincoln and Winnipeg: University of Nebraska Press & University of Manitoba Press.

8 See Lewy G. 2007. 'Can there be genocide without the intent to commit genocide?', *Journal of Genocide Research*, 9, no. 4, 661–674.

to his view, were largely compelled by a misguided benevolence. In less redemptive versions of the same argument, rampant desire for Indigenous territories, rather than an explicit effort to eliminate Indigenous peoples, drove settler colonial eliminationism.[9] In other instances, the move to forcibly assimilate Indigenous children through boarding schools is described as emanating from humanitarian motivations to provide assistance to Indigenous peoples, who were struggling with group-threatening situations, such as the loss of the bison as a source of subsistence on the prairies.[10] Such explanations are self-serving, since the historical record shows no single motivation for sequestering Indigenous children within assimilative boarding schools. For some advocates, boarding schools were the last hope of transferring acquisitive individualism to a backward race, while for others it was a chance to direct Indigenous people toward menial employment. Still others saw the schools as a means to save the souls of Indigenous children by ridding them of the corrupting influences of home and community, or as a means to push them along an evolutionary course toward a more civilised position.[11] Such diverse motives were common among colonisers. As Cooper notes:

> Among colonizing elites—even if they shared a conviction of superiority—tensions often erupted between those who wanted to save the souls or civilize natives and those who saw the colonized as objects to be used and discarded at will. Among metropolitan populations, colonized people sometimes provoked sympathy or pity, sometimes fear—as well as the more complex sentiments that emerged during the actual encounters and political struggles in the colonies themselves.[12]

The organisation of group destruction, it will be argued, does not require that these diverse perspectives be distilled into a single ideology, so long

---

9   See for example Trevithick, S. 1998. 'Native residential schooling in Canada'. *Canadian Journal of Native Studies*, 18, no. 1, 68.

10 On the impact of bison destruction, see Daschuk J.W. 2013. *Clearing the Plains: Disease, Politics of Starvation, and the Loss of Aboriginal Life*. Regina: University of Regina Press, 102–126.

11 For a good overview of these competing viewpoints, see Hoxie F. 1983. *The Final Promise: The Campaign to Assimilate the Indian, 1880–1920*. Lincoln: University of Nebraska Press, 1–40.

12 Cooper F. 2005. *Colonialism in Question: Theory, Knowledge, History*. Berkeley: University of California Press, 24.

CHAPTER 8: Missionaries, Agents, Principals and Teachers

as they cohere around a common collective action frame that enables coordinated rather than completely haphazard interventions.[13]

If the colonial elites differed with respect to their motives for assimilative schooling, what about those who worked in the schools? The documentary evidence shows that many who worked in the schools were cruel, abusive or indifferent to the children placed in their care.[14] However, what about those teachers, principals and other staff members who on occasion showed kindness in their interactions with Indigenous students, or who even assisted Indigenous peoples in their resistance to assimilation?[15] The outpouring of horrific tales from Canadian residential schools has provoked a defence from those who feel there is 'another story' to tell, such as Eric Bays, former Bishop of the Diocese of Qu'Appelle in southern Saskatchewan, who suggests:

> I think all those who have written historical accounts of the schools would admit that there were, in some schools and in some eras, good staff people who were doing their best for the students under their care. Unfortunately, the story reported in recent years has often lumped all residential schools together, putting all the schools, at all times, under suspicion of wrongdoing.[16]

It has never been the case, though, that perpetrators need to be uniform in their actions for genocide to be committed. Christopher Browning, for example, compares the men of Police Battalion 101, who participated in some of the most horrific killings in Poland in the early stages of the Nazi Final Solution, with the guards of Philip Zimbardo's Stanford prison experiment, who were each described as falling into one of three groups: guards who sought to ease the suffering of inmates to the extent possible in existing structural conditions; guards who followed orders, but were not excessive in their cruelty toward prisoners; and guards who were devious

---

13 See Snow D.A. & Benford R.D. 1988. 'Ideology, frame resonance and participant mobilization'. *International Social Movement Research*, 1, 197–217.

14 Truth and Reconciliation Commission of Canada, *Final Report*, 107–112.

15 See for example the essays collected in Haig-Brown C. & Nock D.A., eds. 2006. *With Good Intentions: Euro-Canadian & Aboriginal Relations in Colonial Canada*. Vancouver: University of British Columbia Press; and Trafzer C.E., Keller J.A. & Sisquoc L., eds. 2006. *Boarding School Blues: Revisiting American Indian Educational Experiences*. Lincoln: University of Nebraska Press.

16 Bays E. 2009. *Indian Residential Schools: Another Picture*. Ottawa: Baico Publishing, 161. See also Niezen R. 2013. *Truth & Indignation: Canada's Truth and Reconciliation on Indian Residential Schools*. Toronto: University of Toronto Press, especially ch. 4.

and creative in the cruelties they imposed on prisoners.[17] This division of the guards is, of course, a simplification of the diverse ways in which people participate in the suffering of others, but it captures how those who provide human labour power within genocidal spaces are not necessarily themselves full embodiments of a genocidal ideology. They are instead agents within a larger collective project, who seek lines of action that reflect, and are consistent with, their personal dispositions and orientations.

Following on the diversity of dispositions and actions within a genocidal context, it can be argued that intent is not reducible to the thoughts or practices of a single individual, or to an overarching deadly ideology. Intent is negotiated under structural and discursive conditions — dominant patterns of seeing and acting within the world that shape our social relations. These conditions can coalesce into a collective action frame, a 'schemata of interpretation', that allows actors to find common meaning in a complex world.[18] Such a frame is the product of social interactions, as well as a force that textures these same interactions. A collective action frame is thus a shared way of understanding the world through which we make sense of it and the challenges we face therein. It makes collective action possible by lending coherence to what might otherwise be seen as chaotic. Under the guidance of a collective action frame, institutional and personal interventions into the lives of others are made possible, but not without degrees of freedom that allow for individual negotiation of the collective action frame, that is, for specific adaptations and motivations to arise in particular settings. The collective action frame is not an ideological straitjacket; instead, it contours and suggests action through the way it defines the social situation. A collective action frame is not simply an ideology either; ideologies are more rigid systems of ideas intended to communicate more specific courses of action. In contrast, collective action frames are a set of shared assumptions that help coordinate interpretations of specific events.[19]

---

17 Browning, C. 1998. *Ordinary Men: Reserve Police Battalion 101 and the Final Solution in Poland*. New York: Harper Perennial, 168.
18 Goffman E. 1974. *Frame Analysis: An Essay on the Organization of Experience*. Cambridge, MA: Harvard University Press, 21. Goffman's approach to framing has subsequently influenced work in communications, social movements, public policy and other fields examining how general understanding of social phenomena emerge and gain coherence. See for example Snow & Benford, 'Ideology, frame resonance and participant mobilization'; Snow D.A. & Benford R.D. 1992. 'Master frames and cycles of protest', in *Frontiers in Social Movement Theory*, eds. A.D. Morris & C. McClurg Mueller. New Haven: Yale University Press, 133–155.
19 Oliver P. & Johnston H. 2000. 'What a good idea! Ideologies and frames in social movement research'. *Mobilization: An International Quarterly*, 5, no. 1, 37–54.

CHAPTER 8: Missionaries, Agents, Principals and Teachers

The case studies presented in this chapter illustrate that civilian complicity in genocide need not follow from a strong ideological authoritarianism, since the collective action frame provides sufficient regularity of practices while also allowing civilians to bring their own motivations to their common purpose. Sociologically speaking, then, intent in genocide is often more generalised than the product of *dolus specialis*, or specific intent. Thus, collective action that aims at the destruction of another group is made possible through a combination of broad social pressures and widely circulating discourses, as well as by immediate situational factors such as the institutional organisation of destruction, patterns of fear of the other, desire for the land or resources possessed by the other, and a multiplicity of interests or concerns.[20]

In short, the generalised intent identifiable in a collective action frame sets the course for destruction and makes possible instances of specific intent among individuals, but it is not necessary that specific intent be observable in all participating actors, since this generalised collective action frame can have a momentum of its own that carries along with it actors not fully conscious of, or willfully blind to, their roles in genocide, or even those who find novel and unexpected ways to adapt themselves to this collective action frame in order to subvert it or lessen its impact.

To this extent, our ability to think through relations between elite- and local-level perpetrators of genocide has been hamstrung by the framing of perpetration in terms of specific intent.[21] While elite-level planners may formulate ideologies, drawing from a broader collective action frame in order to plan a programme of destruction, most foot solders of genocidal violence commit their acts 'at a distance' from centres of formulation and articulation.[22] A sociologically enriched understanding of human action at the micro level takes into account the collective action frames that provide the analytical tools that make genocide thinkable, alongside the meso-level institutions that provide the resource networks necessary for carrying out

---

20 See Barta T. 2008. "'They appear actually to vanish from the face of the earth.' Aborigines and the European Project in Australia Felix'. *Journal of Genocide Research*, 10, no. 4, 519–539.

21 Williams T. & Pfeiffer D. 2017. 'Unpacking the mind of evil: A sociological perspective on the role of intent and motivations in genocide'. *Genocide Studies and Prevention*, 11, no. 2, 72–87.

22 Latour B. 1987. *Science in Action: How to Follow Scientists and Engineers through Society*. Cambridge, MA: Harvard University Press, ch. 6; Miller P. & Rose N. 1990. 'Governing economic life'. *Economy and Society*, 19, no. 1, 1–31.

CIVILIAN-DRIVEN VIOLENCE AND THE GENOCIDE OF INDIGENOUS PEOPLES

group destruction.[23] It is within the context of these broader frameworks that individuals manifest genocidal action, whether in the form of direct participation, indirect facilitation or silent complicity in group destruction.[24]

The criminological language of 'perpetration', while providing a sense of moral gravitas for the wrongness of participation in genocide, obscures the complex nature of engagement in such action. The perpetrator, as a master status, reduces inconsistency of action into a single state, that of the individual bent on genocidal destruction. Though such zealous individuals do exist, what we more commonly find are individuals who are habituated to specific institutional orders and who are interpreting a variety of frameworks and preferring potential lines of action. Certainly, they may possess a racial animus, murderous self-interest or some other motivating characteristic that propels their participation. But it is also the case that, immersed in genocidal circumstances, they may be active participants in some moments, complicit bystanders in others and sources of resistance and disruption in still others. This is often true for the civilian actors I discuss below. What matters is that the bulk of their actions contributed to the maintenance, extension and application of a genocidal collective action frame. In general, they accept a definition of the situation that contributes to the destruction of the target group. Though they may at times divert from the overarching genocidal frame, perhaps offering concern or support to a particular targeted individual, the balance of their action contributes to the project of destruction.

Thus, typecasting terminology that speaks to roles of beneficiaries, perpetrators, bystanders, upstanders, accomplices and the like are simply that — analytical tools for simplifying a complex social reality. At the micro-sociological level, actors can take on, and even simultaneously occupy, multiple roles. Their contribution to genocide stems from the coherence given to these diverse roles and practices by the overarching genocidal frame.

Thus, while it is important to address the role of civilian-driven violence in genocidal contexts, this violence cannot be disconnected from the macro-level, and often state-driven, collective action frames that make

---

23 Meso-level institutions are medium-sized organisations that operate between larger national and international or (macro-level) systems and the smaller or (micro-level), systems of everyday life. The meso level includes organisations, such as regional school boards, police forces, health systems and other such collective actors. These institutions are typically charged with organising and implementing policies created at the macro level, so they take effect on the micro-level activities of individuals, families and small communities.

24 See Woolford, *This Benevolent Experiment*, 21–46, for a broader explication and application of these ideas.

CHAPTER 8: Missionaries, Agents, Principals and Teachers

such violence thinkable and actionable. But we should not mistake this for a unidirectional transfer of collective action frame to civilian and military participants in genocidal violence. The discursive flows of the settler colonial world in which assimilative boarding schools were situated did not solely originate at the higher echelons of society, nor at the local levels. They reverberated and fed back, looping between societal levels. In the case of assimilative violence in Canadian and US settler colonialism, local adaptations to the genocidal collective action frames resulted in unexpected mutations within the project of Indigenous group destruction.

Indigenous boarding schools in Canada and the US

The origins of the boarding school system, in both the US and Canada, are at times attributed to Lieutenant Richard Pratt, who began his experiment in Indigenous education in the late 1870s, with 72 captured Cheyenne, Arapaho, Kiowa, Comanche and Caddo at the Fort Marion prison in Florida.[25] Pratt would later hone his methods at the Carlisle School in Pennsylvania, drawing Indigenous children from across the American West and forcibly educating them in proximity to 'civilisation.' Pratt's invention had a longer lineage, going back to practices of juvenile reform in institutions, such as Mettray in France, as well as to the history of missionary schooling in North America, to name just two influences.[26]

What is evident is that Pratt's approach, not to mention his efforts at self-promotion, were timely. As the nineteenth century approached its close, news of slaughter and barbarity from the so-called Indian Wars had greatly upset groups of Indian reformers in the eastern United States. These well-positioned individuals influenced the US government to reconsider its more violent policies toward Indigenous groups. Their efforts were enhanced by criticisms from prominent figures, such as US Representative Thaddeus Pound, that the results of the Indian Wars were extremely counterproductive given the costs of these ventures.[27] They, too, pointed toward assimilation and segregation as alternatives to physical destruction. In this political climate, Pratt's model inspired the creation of many similar schools, as well

---

25 Adams D.W. 2005. *Education for Extinction: American Indians and the Boarding School Experience, 1875–1928*. Lawrence: University Press of Kansas, ch. 2; Fear-Segal J. 2007. *White Man's Club: Schools, Race, and the Struggle of Indian Acculturation*. Lincoln: University of Nebraska Press, 1–18.

26 Truth and Reconciliation Commission of Canada, *Final Report*, McGill-Queen's University Press, 135.

27 Laderman, 'It is cheaper and better to teach a young Indian', 85–111. See also in general Walker, *The Indian Question*; Otis, *The Indian Question*.

CIVILIAN-DRIVEN VIOLENCE AND THE GENOCIDE OF INDIGENOUS PEOPLES

as a system that would move Indigenous children through local day schools and on to boarding schools located either within or far from their home communities to hasten their assimilation.[28]

In the same year that Pratt opened his school at Carlisle in 1879, Nicholas Flood Davin was despatched by the Canadian government, at the time led by Conservative Prime Minister John A. Macdonald, to review Indigenous education in the US. Davin's travels brought him to Washington and Minnesota, not to Carlisle. He nonetheless returned to Canada impressed by the US move toward an industrial-style education in which Indigenous children were removed from their home communities to boarding schools, where they spent part of their day in work training and part of their day in formal education. Davin recommended that such schools be systematically deployed in Canada. He argued that Canada, because of the isolation of many Indigenous communities in the country, should operate its system through missionary societies that already had a foothold in these communities.[29] By the early 1880s, three industrial-style boarding schools were established in the Canadian West, where the need was determined to be greatest.

By the turn of the century, Indigenous boarding schools were well established in each country as a means to 'Kill the Indian in him, and save the man'.[30] Both systems moved toward compulsory assimilative education and sought to overcome the resistance of parents to sending their children to these schools. A collective action frame thus took shape whereby Indigenous children were viewed as the best targets for resolving the so-called Indian problem. By forcibly assimilating these children, the fiscal and political challenges of massacre and forced removal, as well as the moral discomfort with permitting the ravages of disease and starvation to eliminate Indigenous peoples, could be overcome without straying from the goal of destroying Indigenous societies. Assimilation, and the notion of uplifting Indigenous peoples to share in civilisation, thus provided a collective action frame that united multiple actors in a common project.

This project, however, eventually took divergent paths in the US and Canada. Between 1885 and 1888, under the leadership of Commissioner John Atkins, the US Bureau of Indian Affairs (BIA) reduced funding to

---

28 Adams, *Education for Extinction*, ch. 2.

29 Davin N.F. 1879. *Report on Industrial Schools for Indians and Half Breeds*. Ottawa, 14 March, 12.

30 Pratt R.H. 1973 [1892]. 'The advantages of mingling Indians with whites', in *Americanizing the American Indians: Writings by the 'Friends of the Indian' 1880–1900*, ed. F.P. Prucha. Cambridge, MA: Harvard University Press, 261.

CHAPTER 8: Missionaries, Agents, Principals and Teachers

mission-based contract schools and instead concentrated its resources on federal boarding schools.[31] No such move occurred in Canada, leaving school administration in the hands of Christian denominations. This resulted in different staffing and disciplinary regimes in the two countries. For example, many early superintendents of US boarding schools were former military men, whereas in Canada missionaries were the predominant recruits for both leadership and teaching positions. The professional orientations of the principals and superintendents influenced everyday life at the schools. In the US, military drills and regimentation were common, while the pulse of Canadian schools kept time with a more monastic pattern. However, in Canada, monastic discipline lasted longer than military discipline in the US, in part because the religious denominations in Canada had deeper roots in the Canadian system, giving them greater clout.[32]

The institutional configuration of boarding schools in Canada also resulted in a less dynamic school system. While in the US the schools went through dramatic changes depending on prevailing political and economic conditions and changes in the leadership of the BIA, Canada's system saw few major changes from its beginnings until the 1950s.[33] For example, the context of New Deal America opened space for Indian Commissioner John Collier to implement transformation that sought to empower Indigenous communities to gain greater control over their lives and preserve their cultures.[34] No such softening of policy was felt in Canada until much later.

Canada did, however, undergo one significant change in the early twentieth century. And this change, too, resulted in some variance with the US system. After Wilfred Laurier's Liberals defeated the Conservative Party in 1896, they re-examined the costs of large industrial-style boarding schools, turning their attention to smaller, reserve-based residential schools. Reserve-based residences also existed in the US, but were more strategically integrated into a system meant to move Indigenous children gradually from community schools to industrial schools near urban centres. This path was not followed in all circumstances and some US Indigenous children entered industrial boarding schools at very young ages. Canada's system was even more haphazard, with no clear logic as to why or when a student might be

---

31 Prucha F.P. 1984. *The Great Father: The United States Government and the American Indians, Vols. I & II*. Lincoln: University of Nebraska Press, ch. 3.

32 Woolford, *This Benevolent Experiment*, 140–159.

33 Titley, E.B. 1986. *A Narrow Vision: Duncan Campbell Scott and the Administration of Indian Affairs in Canada*. Vancouver: UBC Press, 75–93.

34 Szasz M.C. 1999. *Education and the American Indian: The Road to Self-determination since 1928*. Albuquerque: University of New Mexico Press, 37–49.

CIVILIAN-DRIVEN VIOLENCE AND THE GENOCIDE OF INDIGENOUS PEOPLES

placed in a day school, reserve residential school or distant industrial school other than space being available at the time the student sought placement.[35]

In both the US and Canada, many students suffered during their boarding school years. Loneliness and homesickness were common ailments, while epidemics of tuberculosis, flu and other diseases wrought havoc on the student population at various times and in various places. The spread of disease was facilitated by overcrowded conditions, poor ventilation, inadequate health care and poor nutrition. Students also experienced physical, sexual and cultural violence during their time at school. As a captive population, the children were vulnerable to a variety of predators, and teachers responded to what they perceived to be the abjectness and obstinacy of certain students with physical punishment. Moreover, children's traditional world views and values were also under persistent attack, with Indigenous cultures denigrated and belittled so as to disconnect these young people from their origins.[36]

Assimilative boarding schools began to fall out of favour in both countries by the late 1960s, when integration of Indigenous students into public schools became the dominant philosophy. Some assimilative schools, however, continued to operate after this point, while others were transferred to Indigenous school boards.[37] It would be some time before the horrors of these schools were confronted in either Canada or the US. In Canada, survivor-led class action lawsuits initiated in the 1990s and the 1996 Royal Commission on Aboriginal Peoples brought greater attention to the abuses in the residential schools. Legal and public pressure eventually culminated in the signing of the Indian Residential School Settlement Agreement of 2007, which included a lump-sum compensation programme. The programme was based on actuarial assessment of abuses suffered, and instituted a Truth and Reconciliation Commission, among other provisions.[38] This resulted in more and more of the violence in residential schools being revealed, and in fewer voices defending this system. A similar process has not yet occurred in the US and there is less oral evidence of the everyday assault on Indigenous cultures within these schools. Nonetheless, we do have enough archival, oral, diary and other resources available in both countries to provide basic insight into the roles played by civilians in the project of aggressive civilisation.

---

35 Woolford, *This Benevolent Experiment*, 74.
36 Woolford, 'Ontological destruction', 92.
37 Woolford, *This Benevolent Experiment*, 88–95.
38 For a broad overview of redress policy in Canada, see Miller J.R. 2017. *Residential Schools and Reconciliation: Canada Confronts its History*. Toronto: University of Toronto Press.

Missionaries, agents, principals and teachers in Manitoba and New Mexico

Given this basic outline of the North American Indigenous boarding school systems, how might we understand the participation of various civilian actors in the violence wrought through these schools? In what follows, emblematic examples of civilians engaged in assimilative schooling in New Mexico and Manitoba are considered. Both New Mexico and Manitoba represent regions where the respective federal governments felt a particular need for assimilative schooling, given their sizeable Indigenous populations. Likewise, the schools under consideration here, Fort Alexander and Portage la Prairie in Manitoba, and Santa Fe and Albuquerque in New Mexico, were close enough to their catchment communities to allow parents and community leaders some opportunity to see how children were being treated, though the schools were still largely closed to adult members of local Indigenous communities. Because of this influence, one sees instances where civilian actors needed to adjust their adherence to the settler colonial collective action frame in a manner that responded to local considerations.

Missionaries

Missionaries brought the idea of assimilative schooling to North America. The first permanent mission was established in what is now the state of New Mexico in 1598.[39] At such missions, Indigenous peoples were gathered to live within mission compounds under the direction of missionaries, but little in the way of formal education took place in these spaces.[40] For example, Jesuits in what is now Quebec established a seminary for Indigenous students around 1638. The six young students who were enrolled abided by a schedule that included mass, prayer, catechism, reading and writing. Two of the six died of disease and another left prior to graduation.[41] Similar efforts were made by Protestant missionaries, such as John Eliot, Thomas Mayhew Jr. and Eleazor Wheelock, who sought to convert and enlighten Indigenous youths in the US through Christian teaching. Eliot set up 14 'praying towns' between 1651 and 1674, and some of the Indigenous inhabitants of these towns were instructed in reading and writing in their native languages, as well as in English, so that they

---

39 Reyhner J. & Eder J. 2004. *American Indian Education: A History*. Norman: University of Oklahoma Press, 23.
40 Ibid., 19–28.
41 Ibid., 23.

CIVILIAN-DRIVEN VIOLENCE AND THE GENOCIDE OF INDIGENOUS PEOPLES

could teach others. The inhabitants were also encouraged to change their appearance and dispositions to European norms.[42]

In what is now Canada, the Récollets, an order of Franciscans, established the first known boarding school for Indigenous children in 1620. The goal of their short-lived seminary was to convert Indigenous children, who would proselytise within their own communities. As the Récollets faded in their educational efforts, Jesuits, who in 1633 began their own movement toward seminary-style schooling for Indigenous children, replaced them. Under their model, Indigenous children were removed from the influence of their families, provided a Christian education, and sent back to their communities to convert others.[43]

Without the support of colonial governments, this early attempt at assimilative schooling failed and was largely abandoned by the 1680s. It was beset by multiple challenges: parents were reluctant to hand over their offspring; the children resisted the restraints of formal schooling; and Indigenous peoples refused to relinquish their cultures for the allegedly superior European equivalent. J.R. Miller adds: 'A major reason that the experiment in residential schooling failed in New France was that an assimilative educational programme made no sense in an extractive colonial economy or in a world where northeast woodlands people were excellent warriors and allies just as they were.'[44] With only spiritual suasion, albeit often aggressive, at their disposal to induce parents to send their children to school, and no laws requiring compulsory education, the early missionaries in both Canada and the US were hard-pressed to populate their schools.

For example, as settlers came to the Red River area in what is now Manitoba, the Hudson's Bay Company began to see promise in allowing 'civilising agents' to enter the territory freely. This began with an 1818 invitation to the Catholic bishop of Quebec to provide missionaries. That summer, Joseph Provencher led three Roman Catholic secular priests from Quebec to Red River, where, after six months, they established a Métis day school, as well as another at Pembina. But the Métis were invested in hunting and trapping and therefore less interested in the agricultural instruction offered at these schools. Wesleyan missionaries entered the picture in the early 1840s, as they sought to establish missions and offer education beyond Red River. The man leading the Wesleyan efforts, James Evans, however, ran

---

42 Ibid., 28–37; Szasz M.C. 1988. *Indian Education in the American Colonies, 1607–1783.* Albuquerque: University of New Mexico Press, ch. 4.
43 Miller J.R. 1996. *Shingwauk's Vision: A History of Native Residential Schools.* Toronto: University of Toronto Press, 39–40.
44 Ibid., 60.

CHAPTER 8: Missionaries, Agents, Principals and Teachers

afoul of both the Hudson's Bay Company and Indigenous groups, as he was accused of meddling in company affairs and fondling children. He left the region and returned to England in 1846.[45]

Thus, missionaries guided by moral certainty and proselytising zeal- were unable to bring about the demise of Indigenous spiritualties. They operated within a collective action frame that privileged the Christian faith. This did not in all cases necessitate the destruction of Indigenous culture, as missionaries located within Indigenous communities on occasion permitted, or even encouraged, a degree of syncretism to gain traction within communities. Where missionaries had a more debilitating impact was as a conduit for the transmission of European diseases though trade networks and warfare, which ensured the spread of pathogens across North America. Missionaries, whose presence in Indigenous communities was often demanded as a condition for continuing trade, also brought these deadly illnesses to the Indigenous people whose souls they sought to save.[46]

By the twentieth century, the role of missionaries would shift in both countries. Because the Canadian system relied upon missionary societies to administer Indigenous boarding schools, the efforts of missionaries in Canada will partly also be discussed in the sections on principals and teachers below. Missionaries, however, also played a part at other levels in the system. In the first half of the twentieth century, this role entailed preserving the boarding school system and resisting government proposals to secularise it or place it under more immediate government oversight. For example, in 1905, Samuel H. Blake from the Mission Society of the Church in Canada, a body of the Anglican Church, wrote to the Deputy Superintendent of Indian Affairs that, based on conferences between Anglican, Presbyterian and Methodist dominations, it was clear that the objectives of Indian education were not being fully achieved. To remedy the situation, he recommended that Indian day schools be dispensed with, and that more resources be directed toward boarding and industrial schools. He also recommended that Indian youths be provided with a portion of land, as well as support to start farming after their education was completed, so that they would not

---

45 Carney R. 1995. 'Aboriginal residential schools before Confederation: The early experience'. *CCHA Historical Studies*, 61, 13–40; Enns R.A. 2009. '"But what is the object of educating these children, if it costs their lives to educate them?" Federal Indian education policy in Western Canada in the late 1800s'. *Journal of Canadian Studies*, 43, no. 3, 101–123.

46 Trigger B.R. 1985. *Natives and Newcomers: Canada's 'Historic Age' Reconsidered.* Kingston: McGill-Queen's University Press, 226–272.

CIVILIAN-DRIVEN VIOLENCE AND THE GENOCIDE OF INDIGENOUS PEOPLES

simply return to the reserve or 'hunting lodge'.[47] This was a common refrain among missionaries, calling for more control over Indigenous children to be handed to the churches, and for Indigenous children to have less contact with their families and communities. This is not to suggest that there was uniformity among members of the various denominations on the running of schools. Indeed, one also sees moments of criticism emerging.[48]

In the US, missionaries were largely pushed out of the boarding school system by 1900, partly to limit Catholic influence over Indigenous children.[49] In New Mexico, this did not mean the disappearance of missionaries from assimilative education. Despite the withdrawal of federal funds, the St Catherine's School, a Roman Catholic organisation, continued operating thanks to the personal wealth of Katherine Drexhall, who brought a considerable inheritance with her when she joined the order of nuns. This allowed St Catherine's to act as both competitor and co-conspirator in Indigenous assimilation. In the former role, St Catherine's had an advantage over federal schools, such as SFIS, because many of the local Pueblo communities were syncretically Catholic. Thus, on a September 1891 visit to Taos Pueblo, SFIS superintendent Samuel M. Cart found the community unwilling to send their children to any but a Catholic school, and he learnt that the superintendent of St Catherine's had visited Taos before him to encourage the Pueblo to maintain this view.[50]

Whether as system gatekeepers in Canada, or as competitors and co-conspirators in the US, missionaries outside of formal boarding school institutions continued to invest in the idea of assimilative education and the collective action frame that Indigenous lives and cultures were problematic and therefore in need of transformation. While some missionaries forged bonds with Indigenous communities and were influenced to look critically at the assimilative project, most continued to perceive their role as divinely ordained to overcome savagery.

---

47 Library and Archives Canada (hereafter LAC), RG 10, vol. 6001,file 1-1-1, part 1, Letter from S.H. Blake, Mission Society of the Church in Canada, to the Superintendent of Indian Affairs, Indian Affairs.
48 Miller, *Residential Schools and Reconciliation*, 121–150.
49 Keller R.H. 1983. *American Protestantism and the United States Indian Policy, 1869–82.* Lincoln: University of Nebraska Press, 208–209.
50 Bureau of Indian Affairs, Records Created at Santa Fe Indian School, State Archives and Library, Santa Fe, New Mexico (hereafter SAL), Press Copies of Miscellaneous Letters Sent, RG 75.20.36, reel M1473, roll 1, v. 1–2, Superintendent S.M. Cart to Commissioner of Indian Affairs, 11 September 1891.

CHAPTER 8: Missionaries, Agents, Principals and Teachers

Indian agents

Another set of actors working outside the schools, but in close cooperation with them, were Indian agents. These individuals mediated the interests and influences of a variety of actors, including Indigenous groups, governments, churches and missionary societies, as well as business and corporate entities. They were in frequent communication with superintendents and principals at Indigenous boarding schools, often serving as intermediaries between government and the schools, as well as between schools and communities. Indian agents also played a role in providing inducements for children to attend boarding schools, either through threats, such as the withdrawal of rations, or the promise of rewards, such as touting the health benefits of attending school. In addition, they assisted with evaluating children applying for admission to school as well as helping with their travel arrangements.[51]

In Canada, the *Field Manual for Agency Superintendents* described their responsibilities in relation to residential schools as follows: '[t]o assist in every way, the Principal of the residential school in the performance of his duties. He should co-operate with the principal in matters of repair and maintenance of the school, the attendance of children at the school, and the general administration of the educational unit.'[52] The agent could also suggest that poorly performing teachers be relieved of their duties, and had oversight over student admission and dismissal at schools. The agent's actions were, however, tempered by the influence of other parties involved in schools. In Canada, for example, the Catholic Church sought to influence the choice of the Indian agents near their schools for fear that Protestant agents would favour sending children to Protestant schools. Moreover, even when agents were aware of physical and sexual abuse within schools, and were inclined to intervene, they found themselves up against church authorities who preferred to handle such matters internally, and a Department of Indian Affairs that ignored reports of harm done to children.[53]

For example, in 1937 the Indian agent played a key role in assessing the applications of Dorothy and Isabel Cameron, aged seven and nine, from Swan Lake, Manitoba. Their father, Sam, who signed their application forms,

---

51 Jacobs M.D. 2009. *White Mother to a Dark Race: Settler Colonialism, Maternalism, and the Removal of Indigenous Children in the American West and Australia, 1880–1940.* Lincoln: University of Nebraska Press, 149–192.

52 Quoted in Satzewich V. & Mahood L. 1995. 'Indian agents and the residential school system in Canada, 1946–1970'. *Historical Studies in Education*, 7, no. 1, 54.

53 Ibid., 56–60. For a general discussion of the role of Indian agents, see also Brownlie R.J. 2003. *A Fatherly Eye: Indian Agents, Government Power, and Aboriginal Resistance in Ontario, 1918–1939.* Toronto: Oxford University Press.

CIVILIAN-DRIVEN VIOLENCE AND THE GENOCIDE OF INDIGENOUS PEOPLES

requested that they be admitted to PLPIRS. Both girls up to that point had attended the Swan Lake day school. Dorothy had minor trachoma and a slightly cold temperature, but was otherwise described as healthy and well-nourished, while Isabel was reported to be fully healthy. However, Philip Phelan, chief of the training division, wrote to Indian agent Joseph Waite on 7 January 1938 that he was unsure why these girls should be admitted, since their parents were alive and they were already attending day school. The agent responded that there was no special reason why the girls should be admitted to residential school, and their applications were rejected.[54] However, Waite wrote to the Secretary of Indian Affairs on 22 November 1938 to say that the situation in the home of Dorothy and Isabel Cameron had changed, and that their mother, who had tuberculosis, needed to be shipped to a sanatorium, leaving their father to care for three small boys. Therefore, he recommended that the girls be admitted to PLPIRS. Phelan responded favourably, but also noted that the grant for PLPIRS would not be extended beyond 90 pupils.[55] A few years later, Isobel and Dorothy Cameron were both attending PLPIRS, as were two of their brothers. By this point, their mother had died and their father had enlisted in the army and was fighting in France. Isobel was due to be discharged, but principal John A. McNeill wrote to the government, saying that he would like to keep her for longer, since there was no one to care of her other than her aged grandparents.[56] The government agreed, and the extension was approved. Throughout this conversation the Indian agent maintained an active intermediary role.

The Indian agent in the US was directed to encourage so-called progressives within Indigenous communities so that more traditional forces would not obstruct the progress of civilisation. In the regulations for the Indian service it was recorded: 'The chief duty of an agent is to induce his Indians to labor in civilized pursuits. To attain this end every possible influence should be brought to bear, and in proportion as it is attained, other things being equal, an agent's administration is successful or unsuccessful.'[57]

In addition to encouraging Indigenous persons to adopt agricultural and other means of livelihood, as well as discouraging behavior, such as gambling and alcohol consumption, Indian agents fulfilled this requirement

---

54 LAC, RG 10, vol. 6275, file 583-10, part 1, Philip Phelan, chief of the training division, to J. Waite, Indian agent, 7 January 1938.
55 LAC, RG 10, vol. 6275, file 583-10, part 1, J. Waite, Indian agent, to the Secretary of Indian Affairs, 22 November 1938.
56 LAC, RG 10, vol. 6275, file 583-10, part 1, McNeill, principal PLPIRS, to J. Waite, Indian agent, 30 October 1944.
57 1884 regulations quoted in Prucha, *The Great Father*, 645.

CHAPTER 8: Missionaries, Agents, Principals and Teachers

by influencing parents to send their children to day or boarding schools, and by rounding up those children who played truant or refused to attend school.[58] Margaret Jacobs details how Indian agents used a variety of inducements to encourage children to attend school. These included bribery, coercion, threats, trickery, claims of obligation, moral suasion and the withholding of rations.[59]

For example, around 1884, a group of Ute from the northern part of New Mexico came to AIS to see their children. Erna Fergusson, a writer and reporter for the *Albuquerque Herald*, speculated that many were drunk and reported that they proceeded to occupy the dining room of the school in order to demand better quarters for their children. The Indian agent from Santa Fe, who happened to be at AIS at the time, jumped onto a table and addressed the men in Spanish, explaining to them that he represented the government and the government would do terrible things to them if they did not cease their protest.[60] The threat of government violence was of real consequence to the Ute, who were locked in conflict with the US government between 1849 and 1923. At the time of their protest at AIS, they were still under close scrutiny in the aftermath of the 1879 killing of Indian agent Nathan C. Meeker in White River, Colorado, who had threatened to call in the army on the Ute unless they submitted to assimilation.[61] The words of an Indian agent from Santa Fe thus possessed real force for the Ute.

Indian agents were powerful actors with respect to Indigenous communities. They were civilian government employees, but were positioned as primary enforcers of the eliminationist collective action frame. They existed on the front lines of settler colonialism and were responsible for quelling Indigenous resistance to forced assimilation. Indian agents were selected, because they were known to be amenable to church and government objectives. While they on occasion exhibited concern for the experiences of Indigenous peoples under their charge, most in this survey held true to the collective action frame of Indigenous assimilation with little adaptation.

---

58 Child B.J. 1996. 'Runaway boys, resistant girls: Rebellion at Flandreau and Haskell, 1900–1940'. *Journal of American Indian Education*, 35, no. 3, 49–57.

59 Jacobs, *White Mother to a Dark Race*, 165, 170.

60 Fergusson E. 'Old Albuquerque: Do you remember the first Indian school?', *Albuquerque Herald*, 9 July 1923.

61 See Athearn F.J. 1976. *An Isolated Empire: A History of Northwest Colorado*. Denver: Department of the Interior, Bureau of Land Management, Colorado Division, 43–54.

Principals and superintendents

Paige Raibmon uses the example of George Raley, principal at Coqualeetza Indian Residential School in British Columbia, to demonstrate that principals in Canada possessed a degree of autonomy in administering their schools, allowing them to control the intensity of assimilation. Raibmon writes:

> Raley's attempts to improve the institutional environment at Coqualeetza are evidence of the considerable, although not unlimited, room to maneuver within the parameters of the social values of the day and of the Canadian residential school system. Still more significantly, Raley's actions demonstrate that the way an individual used this latitude made a great deal of difference to the children with whose residential school experience he was entrusted.[62]

However, even seemingly gentle principals, or superintendents as they were called in the US, were not necessarily operating in a manner that countered the overriding collective action frame of Indigenous destruction.

Pratt, for example, presented himself at Carlisle as a kind, but firm, father figure. In some instances, assimilation was also presented as a benevolent alternative to the ravages of disease. One of the first superintendents at AIS, Richard W.D. Bryan, described the plight of the Pueblo school as follows:

> These Pueblo Indians had been living for centuries in the midst of a Spanish civilization and their improvement was scarcely appreciable. They were being rapidly surrounded by an aggressive American civilization and without the help of Christian education their extinction was inevitable [...] It is impolite for a superior race to allow an inferior one to die out in their midst and it is unchristian in the extreme.[63]

The frontier myth of a clash between backward and civilised peoples thus provided the ideational backing for legitimating assimilation as benevolence.

But how to get parents to send their children to school? This was a question faced by principals and superintendents in Canada and the US before assimilative education was made mandatory in both countries in the 1890s. Samuel Cart, the first superintendent at SFIS, communicated frequently with Indian agents to try to secure students for his school. he

---

62 Raibmon P. 1996. "'A new understanding of things Indian": George Raley's negotiation of the residential school experience'. *BC Studies*, 110, Summer, 96.

63 Center for Southwest Research, University of New Mexico, Albuquerque, New Mexico (hereafter CSR), Richard W.D. Bryan Family Papers 1844–1939, MSS 1BC, box 1, folder 1, Bryan Family Papers, Superintendent Bryan, 15 September 1884.

CHAPTER 8: Missionaries, Agents, Principals and Teachers

faced resistance in many communities. The Jicarilla Apache, for example, were unwilling to send their children to the school until they could be sure that the children would be safe from smallpox while there.[64] In seeking to convince Indigenous families to send their children to SFIS, Cart argued it should be impressed upon parents —

> that this is a Government school and that the Indians should send their children here as a duty to the Government .... They should educate their children as a duty they owe to them; that they are better fed and clothed and cared for than they possibly could be at home; that they should patronize this school because it is a training school, where their children can learn a useful trade and acquire the habits and customs of American citizens; I have offered to pay them for bringing in their children (and in some cases have done so) at the same rate it would cost the Govt. by regular modes of travel; have invited the parents to visit the school, and have treated them kindly when they came; have pointed out the advantages that certain educated and trained Indians had over others in the way of earning a better living &c; have shown them the climate in Santa Fe is very healthful.[65]

In this instance, the government's investment in Indigenous children, and Indigenous peoples' position as wards of the state, overrode the wishes of Apache parents that their children be allowed to remain home. Such power struggles between school staff and Indigenous communities were not infrequent in the late nineteenth century, and even erupted occasionally in the twentieth century, as superintendents confronted these communities and sought to recruit more Indigenous students.[66]

Superintendents at AIS and SFIS soon learnt that they had to be more flexible in their negotiations with Pueblo communities and parents if they wanted to ensure a steady stream of Pueblo enrolments. Despite government efforts to make schooling compulsory, Pueblo parents would not send their children unless superintendents accommodated their requests. For this reason, superintendent Rueben Perry at AIS, and various superintendents at SFIS, learnt to be more accommodating with respect to matters such as student home visits. Indeed, a particularly urgent demand was made by Pueblo parents that they be permitted to see their children, and early

---

64 SAL, RG 75.20.36, Reel M1473, roll 1, v. 1–2, Superintendent S.M. Cart to Commissioner of Indian Affairs, 14 January 1891.

65 SAL, RG 75.20.36, reel M1473, roll 1, v. 1–2, Superintendent S.M. Cart to Commissioner of Indian Affairs, 1 April 1891.

66 Gram J. 2012. 'Education on the Edge of Empire: Pueblos and the Federal Boarding Schools, 1880–1930'. PhD dissertation, Southern Methodist University, 5–6.

on SFIS superintendent Cart allowed parents to visit their children at the school. Both Cart and Perry used promises of summer vacations spent at home as a means to entice Pueblo students to join their schools. Such vacations were largely available only to Pueblo students, had to be funded by parents, and were allowed on condition that students returned to the school at the start of the fall semester.[67] Later, at SFIS, superintendent Clinton J. Crandall began his 12-year tenure by trying to limit summer vacations for students, only eventually to concede the matter under pressure from the Pueblo communities.[68]

Such concessions, however, should not be taken as evidence that Crandall or other superintendents completely relented in their pursuit of assimilation. Throughout his career, Crandall was consistent in his view that Indigenous children needed to adapt to Euro-American society. For example, in a 1924 discussion with SFIS superintendent John DeHuff concerning the latter's desire to transfer a few Santo Domingo boys to AIS, Crandall, by then superintendent for the North Pueblos, commented that 'Santo Domingo is a reactionary pueblo. It will take fifty or one hundred years under our present process to bring this people up to any degree approaching the standard of our American civilization'.[69] Instead, Crandall and his ilk often adapted, using the degrees of freedom available within their collective action frame to accommodate Indigenous demands so as to ensure that the greater goal of assimilation could continue unhampered despite Indigenous resistance.

In some instances, experiences drawn from the schools influenced progressive changes in Indigenous educational policy, such as when SFIS superintendents John DeHuff and Chester Faris, inspired by the artistic efforts of their students, encouraged the government to make more space for Indigenous arts within the curriculum.[70] DeHuff, who was superintendent at SFIS from 1916 to 1924, and who was influenced by his wife, Elizabeth, who possessed a keen interest in Indigenous arts, was able to allow practices, such as Pueblo dancing, on campus for many years before his superiors took

---

67 Ibid., 55.
68 Ibid., 67–68.
69 Records of the Bureau of Indian Affairs, National Archives and Records Administration, Rocky Mountain Region, Denver, Colorado (hereafter NARA), RG 75, Northern Pueblos Agency, General Correspondence and Reports, 1877–1934, box 23, folder 424, Superintendent C.J. Crandall, Northern Pueblos Agency, to Superintendent J.D. DeHuff, SFIS, 27 May 1924.
70 Meyn S.L. 2001. *More Than Curiosities: A Grassroots History of the Indian Arts and Crafts Board and its Precursors, 1920–1942*. Lanham: Lexington Books, 65–66.

notice.[71] However, one cannot say that DeHuff used his autonomy solely to soften the schooling experience for students, since he was also quite liberal with his use of the strap, especially when students were discovered to have engaged in romantic trysts. On several occasions in his journals, DeHuff recounts how he administered severe beatings to male students who violated the sexual mores of his school, despite government circulars prohibiting corporal punishment in boarding schools.[72] DeHuff could be a stern and punitive superintendent in certain circumstances, while at other times doubting the efficacy of the boarding school system. On 31 March 1919, DeHuff included in his journal entry a reflection on Francis Saunders' 1912 book, *The Indians of the Terraced Houses*, in which the author criticised US government policy toward the Pueblo, questioning how 'large boarding-schools are maintained and paid for by the taxpayers of the United States, where white education, in part literary and in part industrial, is crammed down the young Pueblo throat in steam-heated rooms and in an atmosphere often foul to suffocation.'[73] Although DeHuff did not agree with Saunders' arguments in their entirety, he noted: 'I too have been thinking for some time past that perhaps the boarding school, like the one of which I am superintendent, has some seriously objectionable features, although there is much to recommend it.'[74] Such ambivalence and self-doubt from the leader of a boarding school suggests that his commitment to the settler colonial project wavered at times. Indeed, in 1924, DeHuff was dismissed, in part for allowing Indigenous dancing, when the BIA, under the leadership of Commissioner Charles Burke, resumed a strict assimilationist posture.

By the 1930s, conditions at SFIS had improved noticeably. Under superintendent Chester E. Faris, a Quaker from Indiana, greater effort was put into working with Pueblo communities to shape the school. Of his approach, Faris stated: 'I always made a rule never to tell an Indian what to do ... I waited until he told me what he wanted, and then I helped him get it.'[75] Under Faris, military drills were abolished and a high-school programme was started. Vocational trades were expanded to include building trades

---

71 For further discussion of Pueblo Indian dance controversy and the moderate role of the DeHuffs therein, see Wegner T. 2009. *We Have a Religion: The 1920s Pueblo Indian Dance Controversy and American Religious Freedom.* Chapel Hill: University of North Carolina Press, ch. 3.

72 CSR, MS 99 BC, Elizabeth Willis DeHuff Family Papers, J.D. DeHuff Diary.

73 Saunders F. 1912. *The Indians of the Terraced Houses.* New York: G.P. Putnam's Sons, 256–257.

74 CSR, J.D. MS 99 BC, Elizabeth Willis DeHuff Family Papers, J.D. DeHuff Diary.

75 Hyer S. 1990. *One House, One Voice, One Heart: Native American Education at the Santa Fe Indian School.* Santa Fe: Museum of New Mexico Press, 31.

CIVILIAN-DRIVEN VIOLENCE AND THE GENOCIDE OF INDIGENOUS PEOPLES

and auto mechanics, while topics such as Indian arts, culture and history were increasingly taught. But this would not last, and by the 1950s efforts to 'terminate' Indigenous identity became policy across the US.

In the Manitoba schools, one sees less variance among principals with regard to the collective action frame of Indigenous destruction. In June 1930, in *The Missionary Monthly*, PLPIRS principal William A. Hendry published an article titled 'An Indian training ground'. In it he wrote: 'Our chief recruiting ground is the Long Plain Reserve which is sixteen miles to the west of the school. More than half of our pupils come from this reserve. The Indians of the Sioux village are being moved to it, which will make it the largest reserve in southern Manitoba.' He also spoke of the advances made in Indian education at his school, suggesting that most Indian students were able to speak English and were learning to farm. But, he added: 'If we continue giving to him, ever giving, we may be working toward an ever-fading objective, and at the same time creating in the Indian what is sometimes called "lethargy of expectancy."' In short, the Indian as a problem for 'civilisation' framed his concerns for the school, and he took his project to be that of making the Indian into an independent and resourceful actor who would need less from the government.[76]

Later principals at PLPIRS would prove even more intolerant. In a 1949 statement, former student Rowena Smoke said of Mrs Ross, the school matron, and Mr Jones, the principal:

> Mrs Ross hits us on the head with her fists ... We ran away because we do not like Mrs Ross ... Mr Jones cut my hair off last year because I ran away. I ran away last year because I was treated badly by Mrs Ross. Mr Jones whips us when we say anything back to Mrs Ross.[77]

Several other girls complained of their treatment at the hands of Ross and Jones, and gave this as the reason they ran away from school. Mrs Ross responded by pointing out that she sometimes pulled hair and rapped the girls on the head with her knuckles, though not out of anger.[78] Jones requested through the Indian agent that he be permitted to punish one of the girls further, by cutting her hair, so that she might serve as an example

---

76 LAC, RG 10, vol. 6001, File 1-1-11, part 2, Headquarters – Schools – General, 1904–1928, Reverend W.A. Hendry, 'An Indian training ground', *The Missionary Monthly*, June 1930.

77 LAC, INAC – Resolution Sector – Indian Residential Schools Historical Files Collection – Ottawa file 501/25-1-067, Vol. 1, Statement from R. Smoke, Long Plain Sioux to Department of Indian and Northern Development.

78 LAC, INAC – Resolution Sector – Indian Residential Schools Historical Files Collection – Ottawa File 501/25-1-067, vol. 1, M.B. Ross, Matron.

CHAPTER 8: Missionaries, Agents, Principals and Teachers

to the other students. Indian Affairs, however, reined him in and he was told to practise punishment as if he were 'a kind, firm and judicious parent in his family'.[79] Jones would later be removed as principal of PLPIRS.[80]

The principals at Roman Catholic schools were also strongly committed to an assimilative line of action. During the 1920s, a period when superintendents Perry (AIS) and DeHuff (SFIS) called upon the BIA to be more tolerant of Indian dances and fiestas, the principals of Roman Catholic boarding schools demanded that the Canadian government remain vigilant on the prohibition of Indian dancing:

> Several people have desired us to countenance the dances of the Indians and to observe their festivals; but their habits, being the result of a free and easy mode of living, cannot conform to the intense struggle for life which our social conditions require. This has to be kept in mind for the training of new generations.[81]

They were consistent in their commitment to assimilation and saw themselves as the primary vehicles for achieving this end. In this respect, in 1964, the federal government requested changes to religious instruction at FAIRS. In response, principal Jalbert took issue with the notion that the period of catechism should be moved from 9:00 a.m. to 3:00 p.m. at the end of the school day, so that it would not interfere with the hours of education. He argued: 'Religion is the most important subject in the school programme. It should get priority. The Department stresses the need of vocational guidance. This is good. But vocational guidance without a good religious foundation produces people who evaluate everything in dollars and cents.'[82]

Superintendents and principals thus navigated between the demands that they attract students to ensure the continued success of their school, and the requirement that they transform Indigenous pupils into assimilated colonial subjects. These two tasks at times contradicted one another, and sparked innovation with respect to government policy, negotiating

---

79 LAC, RG 10, vol. 6275, file 583-10, part 2, B. Neary, Superintendent of Indian Education, to inspector A.C. Hamilton, 25 February 1949.

80 The Children Remembered. Residential School Archive Project of the United Church of Canada, 'Portage la Prairie Indian Residential School.' Available at http://thechildrenremembered.ca/school-locations/portage-la-prairie/, accessed 9 August 2018.

81 LAC, RG10, Vol. 6041, file 160-5, part. 1, Reverend J.B. Blanchin and Reverend F. Beys, Outline of resolutions of a 1924 convention of Indian Catholic school principals.

82 LAC, Deschatelets Archives, Oblates of Mary Immaculate, Ottawa HR 6681.C73R 99, Jalbert, Rev. L., O.M.I., principal, FAIRS, Pine Falls, Manitoba to M. Rehaluk, supervising principal, Clandeboye Indian agency, Selkirk, Manitoba.

CIVILIAN-DRIVEN VIOLENCE AND THE GENOCIDE OF INDIGENOUS PEOPLES

these adaptions within the overarching collective action frame. But much depended on the context in which they operated. While the US federal model of assimilative education gave superintendents some degree of freedom in how they ran their schools, the institutional influence of missionary societies tended to restrict adaptation in Canada.

Teachers

Education at Indigenous boarding schools in many cases lasted only half the day. Nonetheless, teachers had great influence on student experiences of assimilative education. On occasion, a teacher resisted the collective action frame of assimilation. In the 1930s and 1940s, SFIS gained a reputation as an Indian arts school.[83] This was made possible by the leadership of commissioner John Collier in reducing the intensity of the assimilative frame. Also, the 1932 hiring of Dorothy Dunn contributed greatly to this reputation. Dunn encouraged students to take pride in their cultures while she sought to guide them in further developing the artistic skills and crafts of their home communities.[84] Funding for such programmes was cut after the outbreak of the Second World War, when policy reverted to an assimilationist stance.

More often than not, teachers were found to be incompetent, abusive or driven by an unyielding belief in the need for assimilation. A petition from the chief and councillors of the Peguis, Fisher River, Berens River and Bloodvein First Nations in Manitoba was sent on 27 January 1919 to the 9th Duke of Devonshire, Victor Cavendish, who was then serving as Governor General of Canada. In the petition, concerns were expressed about how boarding school funding arrangements produced conflict between churches, which competed with each other for converts. Such competition, it was suggested, caused division within communities. Also, the control that religious denominations had over the hiring of teachers was felt to result in the hiring of incompetent teachers who 'do as they like'. The petition recommended that education be handled entirely by the government, which would be in keeping with treaty promises.[85]

Overall, J.R. Miller writes of 'a tendency to use the residential schools as a dumping ground for missionary workers who were a problem for

---

83 For more discussion of arts and crafts among the Pueblo, as well as at SFIS, see Meyn, *More Than Curiosities.*

84 Hyer, *One House, One Voice, One Heart.*

85 LAC, RG 10, vol. 6001, file 1-1-11, part 2, Headquarters – Schools – General, 1904–1928, Petition from the chief and councilors of Peguis, Fisher River, Berens River and Bloodvein to His Royal Highness, Victor Christian William, 27 January 1919.

CHAPTER 8: Missionaries, Agents, Principals and Teachers

evangelical bodies'.[86] Up to the 1950s, the churches were responsible for hiring teaching staff. The Catholic Church, for instance, typically hired teachers from female religious orders, 'whose recruits were often young women from rural backgrounds'.[87] Examples of incompetence are common in the Truth and Reconciliation Commission of Canada (TRC) testimony of former students from PLPIRS and FAIRS. In contrast, the federal archival record is a poor source of information on teaching staff at these schools. For example, criticism of teaching staff at FAIRS is rare in Canadian government records. Nonetheless, one does on occasion see mild concern by inspectors that certain teachers lacked the skills or training to fulfil their positions.[88] This is in stark contrast, however, to survivor testimony provided to the TRC, which bears witness to a very violent school, where extreme physical and sexual abuse was not uncommon.[89]

In the US, the 1920 AIS annual report noted: 'The best people are not attracted by the meagre salaries offered while the best employees in the service are constantly resigning to accept better positions outside.'[90] David Wallace Adams writes more generally of the teachers who were hired to work in US Indigenous boarding schools:

> The average teacher appears to have been a single woman in her late twenties. Between 1892 and 1900, out of 550 teachers, assistant teachers, and kindergartners appointed under civil service rules, some 312, a modest majority, were women. A dramatic shift was taking place, however, and by 1900 the Indian Office reported that of the 347 teachers employed, 286 were women.[91]

After an initial period in which men and women were hired in near equal numbers to teach, the turn of the century saw a turn away from men, often former soldiers, to lower-waged young women. Some of the latter proved to be caring and helpful toward their students. It was indeed sometimes the case that the young women recruited brought their own proto-feminist beliefs, whether maternal, anti-modernist or liberal in orientation, to their

---

86 Miller, *Shingwauk's Vision*, 320.

87 Truth and Reconciliation Commission of Canada. 2012. *They Came for the Children: Canada, Aboriginal Peoples, and Residential Schools*. Winnipeg: Truth and Reconciliation Commission of Canada, 71.

88 For example, see LAC, RG 10, vol. 8448, file 506/23-5-019, Philip Phelan, chief of training division, to Reverend J.O. Plourde, OMI, 5 July 1938.

89 Fontaine T. 2012. *Broken Circle: The Dark Legacy of Indian Residential Schools, A Memoir*. Victoria: Heritage House; Woolford, *This Benevolent Experiment*.

90 NARA, AIS, M1011, Superintendents' Annual Narrative and Statistical Reports from Field Jurisdictions of the Bureau of Indian Affairs, 1907–1938, 1920 Annual Report.

91 Adams, *Education for Extinction*, 82.

interactions with students in the schools.[92] And some teachers served as an inspiration and source of cultural affirmation for students. The aforementioned Dorothy Dunn at SFIS is an example of a teacher who was reluctant to embrace the broader assimilative project of the school system. A student from SFIS recalled:

> Well, Dorothy didn't actually interfere with the culture of the Indian people. She was very careful not to pressure anybody into painting what their elders didn't want them to paint. She just told us we had freedom of our own thoughts, and whatever we painted was all right with her as long as it was pertaining to learning and also a few rules in the lessons that she put out and guidelines.[93]

US schools, however, also featured their share of teachers willing to use violence to advance assimilation among the student body. Under the relatively enlightened BIA commissioner John Collier, warnings were issued to teachers for abusing students. On 16 August 1934, Secretary of the Interior Harold Ickes felt it necessary to circulate a letter on school punishment to all superintendents, principals and teachers at Indian schools. He wrote: 'Commissioner Collier has called my attention to a number of incidents which indicate that mediaeval forms of discipline have not yet been done away with in some Indian schools.' He listed such abuses as beatings, hours of kneeling on concrete floors and standing one quarter of a day with eyes fixed upon a wall, and noted that Collier had filed charges against five teachers who had been suspended, and two others who were dismissed from the service.[94] The fact that such a reminder was needed demonstrates the gap between federal policy and its application on the ground, and the time lag experienced in attempts to reform Indigenous schooling.

The role of teachers varied between harsh and cruel disciplinarians to supportive allies in resisting the assimilative pressures of the schools. Teachers could be both the fiercest enforcers of group-destroying violence ,and central figures in subverting the collective action frame of Indigenous destruction.

---

92 Jacobs, M.D. 1999. *Engendered Encounters: Feminism and Pueblo Cultures, 1879–1934.* Lincoln: University of Nebraska Press.
93 CSR, Santa Fe Indian School, The First 100 Years Oral History Interviews by S. Hyer & P. Velarde (Santa Clara), interviewed 2 October 1986.
94 SAL, John Collier Papers, Secretary Ickes letter on Indian school discipline, 16 August 1934.

Conclusion

From this brief overview of the roles of missionaries, Indian agents, principals and teachers in four Indigenous schools in New Mexico and Manitoba, it is evident that these actors did not work uniformly or fully in concert to impose settler colonial ideals on their societies. Instead, they approached their jobs from different starting points and were informed by varying dispositions and points of view. Nonetheless, they found in the collective action frame of Indigenous destruction, as captured in the notion of the 'Indian problem', a means for coordinating their actions. They accepted assimilation as the most viable solution to the problem, even if they did not always act in similar ways.

Missionaries and Indian agents each had more direct contact with Indigenous communities. While this contact could at times enlighten these actors and lead to their seeking, at least on a modest level, to understand Indigenous perspectives on the value of their cultures and their views on appropriate education, in most of the cases examined here these individuals tended to be firm adherents of a settler colonial collective action frame that prioritised assimilation. Missionaries often did so through the moral certainty of their religious standpoint, while the power of the Indian agent over the Indigenous community in his charge, and the effort that went into selecting individuals who supported the assimilative project, often provoked a paternalistic authority in such individuals. In addition, in Canada, connections between the missionaries and the Indian agent often helped coordinate their shared interest in preserving practices of assimilation.

The differences that divided early school principals in Manitoba and New Mexico led to greater diversity in the dispositions of these actors. In the US, superintendents, such as Bryan, Perry and Cart, came from a military background. Given that their schools were federal-run institutions, staffed by many who had experience with Indigenous communities through the Indian Wars, they often brought their military experience to bear upon the schools they directed. Thus, military drills, uniforms, parades, practices of comportment and the like were common fare at these institutions. For these principals, such strategies, as introduced by Lieutenant Richard Pratt at Carlisle, were obvious ways of addressing what they believed to be the problem with the 'Indian' — their backwardness and lack of civilisation. For them, military discipline was the main means for Indigenous transformation. Even as these military methods fell out of favour at New Mexico schools when official policy changed, they emerged in other aspects of school life. Such was the case with the 'health inspections' that replaced military drills at

CIVILIAN-DRIVEN VIOLENCE AND THE GENOCIDE OF INDIGENOUS PEOPLES

AIS in the early 1930s.[95] Nonetheless, the principals also needed to populate their schools, and even with compulsory schooling laws in place, they found they had to appeal to Indigenous parents in order for the latter to send their children.

In contrast, early principals at FAIRS and PLPIRS referenced monastic rather than military values when training Indigenous students for assimilation. For FAIRS, a Catholic school run by the Oblates of Mary Immaculate, the Durieu system often directed their efforts. As Miller describes this system:

> This regime, named after Oblate Paul Durieu, employed methods of total control over mission Indians for the purpose of effecting a permanent conversion to Christian religious values and practices. The Durieu system aimed at eradicating all unchristian behaviour by means of strict rules, stern punishments for transgressors, and use of Indian informers and watchmen as proctors to ensure conformity and inflict punishments as necessary.[96]

Prayer and confession were regular markers of the passage of time at these schools, and silence was expected of the students, as they were meant to engage in quiet spiritual reflection rather than interact with their classmates.

Yet other influences could lead to different emphases among Indigenous boarding school staff in trying to fit their activities into an assimilative collective action frame. Superintendent DeHuff at SFIS was a firm moralist when it came to governing sexual behaviour on his campus, but his exposure to Indigenous culture, through the interests of his spouse, led him to be more permissive when it came to cultural dances and festivals.

Teachers, too, varied in their adherence to the assimilative collective action frame. While some were tough and violent in their efforts to 'correct' Indigenous children away from their cultures, others used gentler techniques. More radically, the artistic inclinations of a teacher, such as Dorothy Dunn, in some ways disrupted the assimilative force of the school through outright encouragement of Indigenous arts. For the most part, the collective action frame that presented Indigenous lifeworlds as a problem to be combated through assimilation and civilisational uplift resulted in varied efforts to understand Indigenous cultures, and to act upon Indigenous young people, through this lens. But the framework was not an ideological

---

95 NARA, RG 75, Albuquerque Indian School, General Correspondence Files 1917–1936, 001-003, entry 29, box 30, file 670, Superintendent Perry, AIS, to Commissioner of Indian Affairs, 18 October 1932.
96 Miller, *Shingwauk's Vision*, 91.

216

absolute. Some, such as Dunn, did resist its interpretive force. Nonetheless, this frame offered a powerful narrative that made possible the coordination of assimilative activities across two countries.

Civilian-driven violence thus took shape in a world in which a dominant collective action frame operated to present the Indian as a problem in relation to settler colonial ambitions, and as a problem that could be resolved through forced assimilation. However, such violence is intertwined with state-driven strategies, meso-level institutional practices and the dispositions held, and everyday challenges faced, by the civilian actors. In most instances, adaptations under the collective action frame served to advance the objectives of Indigenous destruction locally, but on occasion subversive interventions took shape that contributed to the preservation of Indigenous cultures.

CHAPTER NINE

'Little Kings': Farmers' 'Erasive' Practices in German South West Africa

Robert Gordon

During the South African military occupation of German South West Africa (GSWA) between 1915 and 1918 there were a number of spectacular trials of German farmers accused of murdering Bushmen, later known as San.[1] While much has been written about the causes of genocide, the literature on how genocides end is sparse. The chief of staff of the German army considered *vernichtungspolitik* (extermination politics) impractical, while Chancellor Von Bülow was concerned about its economic, humanitarian, political and diplomatic consequences.[2] The protests of civilians, most prominently a few missionaries[3] and a scattering of experts, but also, more importantly, established settlers who were concerned that their source of cheap labour was being eradicated, played an important part in ending the 1904–1908 wars. Yet, five years later, settlers themselves engaged in what Haussler has termed 'erasive practices.'[4] This chapter explores the skeins of relevance in the dissonance between this public rhetoric and ground-level practice.

Recent scholarship has conceptualised the colonial state that was GSWA as 'weak',[5] 'improvisational'[6] or 'ceremonial'.[7] In such situations, Radcliffe-Brown's insight, namely that the state as a 'fiction' does not exist as an entity over and above society, is relevant. Rather it was an organisation,

---

1 Gordon R.J. 1992. *The Bushman Myth and the Making of a Namibian Underclass.* Boulder: Westview, 77–81.
2 Hull I. 2003. 'Military culture and the production of "Final Solutions" in the colonies: The example of Wilhelmian Germany', in *The Specter of Genocide*, eds. R. Gellately & B. Kiernan. New York: Cambridge University Press, 157.
3 Pool G. 1979. *Die Herero-Opstand, 1904–1907.* Cape Town: HAUM, 257.
4 Haussler M. 2013. '"Kultur der Grausamkeit" und die dynamik "eradierender Praktiken": Ein Beitrag zur Erforschung extremer Gewalt'. *Sociologus*, 63, 147–169.
5 Zollmann J. 2010. *Koloniale Herrschaft und ihre Grenzen: Die Kolonialpolizei in Deutsch Südwest-Afrika.* Göttingen: Vandenhoeck & Ruprecht.
6 Muschalek M. 2014. 'Everyday Violence and the Production of Colonial Order: The Police in German Southwest Africa 1905–1915'. PhD dissertation, Cornell University.
7 Gordon R.J. 2009. '"Hiding in full view": The forgotten Bushman genocides in Namibia'. *Genocide Studies & Prevention*, 4, 29–58.

CHAPTER 9: 'Little Kings'

'a collection of individual human beings connected by complex relations and these individuals had different roles and held different positions of power or authority'.[8] An important segment of one such collection consisted of settler farmers in GSWA, who defined themselves as 'the backbone of the country' despite being a numerical minority and an insignificant contributor to national income. Farmers played a key role in facilitating Bushman genocide. This created a conundrum: while genocidal practices facilitated the acquisition of land, farmers could not survive without cheap labour, of which the Bushmen formed an important part.

Genocide, the organised, unilateral, intentional mass killing of a social group, can also be practised by collections of people beyond the formal sanction and policies of the state. The ambience of an 'improvisational' state pushes to the fore the role of genocide as a means to eliminate a population regarded as deviant.[9] Social control entails how and why people define and respond to deviant behaviour. In this case, settlers defined indigenes and especially Bushmen as deviant — not being able to distinguish between 'mine and thine', being untrustworthy, treacherous, 'worse than jackals' and 'vermin'. In short, they informally replicated the Roman legal maxim of *communis hostis omnium* (the common enemy of all).[10] But, as social control, the maxim impacts on both victim and victimiser.

What was it in this milieu that tolerated, indeed encouraged, 'erasive' actions by settler-citizens? In a companion paper, I have analysed how the Bushmen were 'tamed' rather than erased during the interwar period in Namibia, when the civil service was reduced to less than a quarter of its size during the German era. This occurred despite the structural continuities between the German colonial and mandatory eras.[11]

Given the weak, improvisational and ceremonial nature of the colonial state, I suggest that structurally the situation was one of neo-feudalism, in which colonial power was to be found in towns, police and military outposts, and farmsteads, which were linked by patrols and visits, a veritable 'rag rug of islands of colonial power'.[12] The conceptual utility of feudalism has largely been ignored, but, as Eric Wolf pointed out, feudalism is a recurrent and

---

8 Radcliffe-Brown A.R. 1940. 'Preface', in *African Political Systems*, eds. M. Fortes & E.E. Evans-Pritchard. London: Oxford University Press, xxiii.

9 Campbell B. 2009. 'Genocide as social control'. *Sociological Theory*, 27, no. 2, 150–172.

10 Heller-Roazen D. 2009. *The Enemy of All: Piracy and the Law of Nations*. New York: Zone Books.

11 Gordon R.J. 2017. '"Taming" Bushman farm labour: A villeinous era in neo-feudal Namibia?'. *Anthropology Southern Africa*, 40, no. 4, 261–275.

12 Cited in Zollmann J. 2011. 'Communicating colonial order: The police in German South-West Africa'. *Crime, History & Societies*, 15, no. 1, 38.

not a universal constellation, which can occur either in the course of state formation or as a result of political devolution and breakdown.[13] In my analysis, I use a framework derived from the Weberian notion of villeinage and Agamben's idea of besiegement.[14] The similarities with villeinage are striking. A 'villein' was a person legally tied to the lord of the manor and who occupied an interstitial social space between a 'freeman' or peasant and a slave, in a situation of 'relative servitude'. The manorial system was highly decentralised and relatively isolated. Villeins could not leave the land without the landowner's consent, worked on the lord's estate at the will of the lord, and had minimal control over goods and property. Here, villeinage is used as a heuristic guide, not as empirical or historical fact. Weber's analysis of agrarian society offers a more complex and multidimensional picture of agrarian social and material conditions by arguing that the material world is not only economic, but geographic as well. In contrast to earlier writers who saw feudalism as an objective legal system, Weber saw it as essentially a personal, non-objective relationship entailing intuitive understanding of the 'living reality'. He concluded that the 'structure of domination ... affected the general habits of people more by virtue of the ethos which it established'.[15]

A Weberian perspective thus offers the possibility of understanding how the Bushmen were 'tamed' or 'eradicated' on levels of both cause and meaning. In the realm of meaning, appearances can be deceptive. In threatening environments and situations of extreme uncertainty, where social and political life was under threat, a 'paranoid ethos' emerged within settler society characterised by suspicion, sensitivity to others' motives and malice thought to be omnipresent.[16] Settler *Umwelt*, the social environment from which cause for alarm arises, created the dominant ethos of 'besiegement', an imaginary state of siege felt by settlers, and provided a moral language to justify actions and behaviour. This heavily patriarchal symbolic universe was structured around ideas of conquest, technology, the threat of indigenes and firearms. In an effort to provide farm labour, the authorities passed several laws and ordinances designed not only to tie indigenes down, but also to ameliorate settlers' sense of besiegement. This was done by unofficially devolving authority to farmers. The result was a socio-cultural milieu in which farmers could rule their farms as petty fiefdoms.

---

13 Wolf E. 1982. *Europe and the People Without History*. Berkeley: University of California Press, 404.
14 Agamben G. 2005. *State of Exception*. Chicago: University of Chicago Press.
15 Radkau J. 2011. *Max Weber: A Biography*. New York: Polity, 419–420.
16 Schwartz T. 1973. 'Cult and context: The paranoid ethos in Melanesia'. *Ethos*, 1, no. 2, 153–174.

CHAPTER 9: 'Little Kings'

Despite the dreams of Germany's influential and enthusiastic colonial lobby to recreate the *Heimat*, a New Germany, to rival New France and New England, their efforts were not exactly successful. Recovery from the disastrous 1904–1908 wars saw a large increase in the number of settlers, from 4 640 in 1903 to 7 110 in 1907, and 14 830 in 1913. The 1913 census revealed that of the 14 830 whites in GSWA, 12 292 were German citizens — including 3 058 females and 1 587 listed as farmers — the equivalent to a small town in Germany. [17]

Compared to the 1911 census, the significant changes were the downsizing of the military and police by some 250 personnel, while the number of farmers increased by approximately 200. [18] The most prominent feature of this post-war period was the dramatic expansion of settler farms, from 458 in 1904 to 1 331 in 1913. In the Grootfontein District, the epicentre of the Bushman genocide, the number of farms increased from 25 in 1904 to 173 in 1913. [19]

Even before the 1904–1908 wars, members of the Schutztruppe (colonial army) were encouraged to take up farming after demobilisation. Governor Theodor Leutwein argued that their —

> already acquired knowledge of the country alone is worth several thousand Marks. They also did not have to pay the costs of emigrations and could make the selection of their plots during their service time, also cost-free. Furthermore, for a certain time before leaving the colonial army they were permitted to watch their own cattle posts, so that in references to purchasing breeding stock they could ascertain the best prices as well as the most practical opportunities. [20]

Farming was promoted by Leutwein as a means of upward mobility, as in Germany they would have remained propertyless.

With dispossessed land readily available as a result of the 1904–1908 wars, the administration offered generous terms to attract settler farmers who would, they felt, also provide a bulwark against potential Indigenous uprisings. The authorities signalled their intent to pursue settlement aggressively with the appointment in 1905 of Friedrich von Lindequist, the first civilian governor, and a vociferous proponent of smallholders. Generous terms, coupled with the lavish compensation paid to established

---

17 Walther D. 2002. *Creating Germans Abroad*. Athens: Ohio University Press, 26.
18 Leser H. 1982. *Namibia*. Stuttgart: Ernst Klett, 30; Gann L. & Duignan P. 1987. *Rulers of German Africa*. Stanford: Stanford University Press, 13.
19 Gordon, *Bushman Myth*, 202.
20 Walther, *Creating Germans*, 14.

farmers, resulted in a surprisingly rapid recovery of the agricultural sector.[21] Particularly magnanimous terms were offered to those thought to be good citizens: ideally, someone who would be hard-working, self-reliant and not cohabit with Indigenous women. Cheap land confiscated from indigenes was offered at half price to discharged troops and government officials. Interest-free government loans of 6000 marks were available to German citizens, repayable in ten annual payments after ten years. Certain conditions were stipulated. To prevent speculation, applicants had to start developing their farm within six months and were not allowed to sell it for ten years. Apart from settlement subsidies, there were fencing bonuses, generous borehole and dam subsidies, and free livestock inoculation — as well as boarding school subsidies for children.

Empowering farmers

Settler politicisation was largely stimulated by the destructive policies of Lothar von Trotha, the former governor and military commander during the 1904–1908 wars. Arguing that the authorities had enticed them to settle in GSWA by guaranteeing the security of their lives and property, farmers insisted on compensation. So much support did they have in Germany that they managed to persuade the *Reichstag* to increase the budgeted two million marks compensation to 10.5 million marks, but in the process managed to antagonise the *Reichstag*, the Colonial Office and the local administration, who increasingly resented the way the farmers accessed state coffers.

In late 1906 Lindequist instituted a *Gouvernmentsrat*, an advisory board, consisting of eleven civilians and seven officials, which most notably discussed the Native Ordinances. Finally, in January 1909 a new system of government was instituted, consisting of three tiers — municipal, district and territorial. The last-mentioned, known as the *Landesrat*, met for the first time in 1910. Half the members were elected directly by district advisory councils and were usually farmers or businessmen, while the other half, appointed by the governor, were typically members of the administration or the military, as well as a number of settlers whose interests or professions the governor felt were not represented. This was done to counter the 'crude despotism of numbers'.[22] Moreover, as Governor Schuckmann observed, there was a lack of 'social unity'. Settlers had a 'materialistic streak' with everyone wanting

---

21 Von Weber O. 1982. *Geschichte des Schutzgebietes Deutsch-Südwest-Afrika*. Windhoek: SWA Wissenschaftlichen Gesellschaft, 17.
22 Bley H. 1971. *South-West Africa under German Rule*. Evanston: Northwestern University Press, 191.

CHAPTER 9: 'Little Kings'

'to get rich as quickly as possible'. They anticipated automatic 'government help', expecting 'a full bottle of milk held to their lips'.[23] Initially the *Landesrat* was simply an advisory board, but gradually settler demands led to their being given power to modify the governor's decisions concerning agriculture, health, roads, wildlife and, most importantly, labour.[24]

The purpose of this realignment was ostensibly educational, to make settlers responsible for developing economic self-sufficiency. Settlers, however, saw it as an opportunity to access and allocate *Reichstag* funds that they felt they deserved as war compensation. Moreover, being 'the men on the spot' they knew better than Berlin how to allocate the funds.[25] In this debate there was a 'great disparity between the fervour of their arguments and the speed with which they changed their demands'.[26] The unreality of their claims was frequently remarked upon by officials, who noted that as late as 1914 only about 2 000 of the nearly 7 000 male settlers were entitled to vote in local elections.

Farmers also realised that as the settler population grew, they would lose political influence if decisions were made by simple majority, and so suggested that the governor appoint members according to *stand*, that curious German word referring to occupation, status and class. When this appeal failed, they attempted a compromise, proposing that constituencies be based on town and rural areas, only to be met again with failure. As a sop, governors appointed nominated farmers to the *Landesrat*. Until the First World War, farmers generally constituted two-thirds of its membership. Despite deriding the *Landesrat* as a *Hilfsparliament* — an auxiliary parliament or mere 'debating chamber' — farmers engaged in aggressive debates in the *Landesrat*, claiming that their interests should be the sole criterion for policy-making. They complained that the administration was doing 'nothing' — clearly an exaggeration, given the already generous assistance provided. Farmers launched impassioned press campaigns around the issue of how the revenue windfall arising from the 1908 discovery of diamonds should be spent. They argued that agriculture should benefit as the mineral industry would be short-lived, while agriculture was sustainable over the long term. Farmers framed the argument rather ominously, saying that they constituted the 'productive element', while shopkeepers, tavern licensees

---

23 Ibid., 192.
24 Du Pisani A. 1985. *SWA/Namibia: The Politics of Continuity and Change.* Johannesburg: Jonathan Ball.
25 Wildenthal L. 2001. *German Women for Empire, 1884–1945.* Durham: Duke University Press; Bley, *South-West Africa*, 185–195.
26 Bley, *South-West Africa*, 194.

and the like were 'not being usefully productive. They merely consume what others have produced'.[27] This dispute was significant, noted Bley, because it was a defence prompted by the settlers' failure to achieve their utopian dream of being unrestricted masters of GSWA.[28]

The dominant influence of farmers after the 1904–1908 war was not a sudden phenomenon. It had received strong support in Germany before then, largely from a small group of professional patriots organised around the Pan-German League and the German Colonial League, who promoted German colonialism for reasons of international prestige. At the inaugural meeting of the *Farmerbund* (Farmers' Union) in early 1904, they resolved to send two delegates to Germany to seek affiliation to, and support from, the national German Farmers' Union, and managed to obtain an audience with the Kaiser, which undoubtedly inflated their sense of self-importance. In 1907 farmer societies from a number of districts united to form the *Deutsch-Südwestafrikanischer Farmerbund.* But during 1910 and 1911 interpersonal rivalries came to the fore and three regional associations were formed — North, South and Central. Even the Central association threatened further fission, making for confusion. Apart from controlling the largest newspaper in the territory, farmers promoted their own visibility by organising Farmer Days or agricultural shows in Windhoek and in outlying towns. In 1912, they managed to set up an Agricultural Bank, supported by funds from the German lottery. And in 1913, on Berlin's instructions, an Agricultural Council was created to advise the governor. They were clearly skilled political organisers.[29]

Apart from various pressure groups, farmers had support within government. Significant in this regard was Lindequist, who first came to the *Schutzgebiet* (Protectorate) in 1894 as a judge, and in 1898 initiated its first farmer organisation. From 1900 to 1903 he served as German consul-general in Cape Town before returning to GSWA as the first civilian governor from November 1905 to May 1907, when he was promoted to Deputy Secretary in the *Reichskolonialamt* (Imperial Colonial Office) until 1910, when he was appointed Secretary of State for Colonies. Another influential supporter was Oskar Hintrager, who had served as a volunteer in the Anglo-Boer War (1899–1902). Posted to GSWA in 1905, he remained there as deputy governor until 1914, and thus through sheer longevity became highly

---

27 Ibid., 198.
28 Ibid., 199.
29 Halenke H. 1985. 'Farmvereine und Genossenschaften', in *Vom Schutzgebiet bis Namibia, 1884–1984*, eds. H. Becker & J. Hecker. Windhoek: Interessengemeinschaft Deutschsprachiger Südwester, 119–124.

CHAPTER 9: 'Little Kings'

influential. Like Lindequist, he continued his interest in promoting German settler colonialism after the Great War.[30]

The first item of business at the inaugural *Landesrat* session concerned 'Native Labour'. The series of draconian ordinances issued by Lindequist in August 1907 to facilitate the 'internal' labour supply were judged to be inadequate. These ordinances allowed indigenes to be stripped of their property, largely land and livestock. Deprived of their 'traditional livelihood', it was assumed that they would be forced into the colonial workforce. Indigenes had to apply to the governor for permission to own livestock. Another set of regulations sought to control the movement of indigenes through pass laws. People had to wear brass tokens around their necks, a central register of natives was to be developed, and work contracts were regulated. Settlers were given the right to engage in 'fatherly chastisement' of their workers. Lastly, and ominously for the Bushmen, indigenes could be punished as 'vagrants' if they were found 'loitering' or could not demonstrate a means of support. These three sets of regulations locked together in mutually supporting ways to force indigenes into the settler-controlled economy. Commenting on the ordinances, the mouthpiece of organised farmers, the *Windhuker Nachtrichten* of 19 September 1907 claimed: '[T]he native must be made aware that he has a right to exist only in direct dependence on the territorial authorities; without this, he is in a certain sense an outlaw: a livelihood outside of working for whites is not available to him.' Directly and indirectly, this legislation facilitated the genocide of Namibian Bushmen communities, as their mode of existence was defined by the state as vagrant or outlaw.[31]

The war had decimated the workforce and the labour shortage was aggravated by the expansion of farming, railway construction and, most importantly, the discovery of diamonds in 1908. So desperate was the situation that, despite the draconian ordinances, the administration considered importing labourers from China, India and Germany's other African colonies. Instead they made do with more than 6 400 workers from the Cape Colony in 1911 alone.[32] To remedy the situation, a full-time Native Commissioner was appointed with three main priorities, namely, to develop effective methods to control indigenes, to facilitate the labour

---

30 'Dr Oskar Hintrager', in Dierks K. 2003. *Biographies of Namibian Personalities*. Available at http://www.klausdierks.com/Biographies/Biographies_H.htm, accessed 31 October 2019.

31 Gordon R.J. 1998. 'Vagrancy, law and "shadow knowledge": Internal pacification 1915–1939', in *Namibia under South African Rule: Mobility and Containment*, eds. P. Hayes, J. Silvester, M. Wallace & W. Hartmann. Windhoek: Out of Africa, 51–77.

32 Stoecker H., ed. 1986. *German Imperialism in Africa*. London: Hurst, 138.

supply, and, almost as an afterthought, to improve Indigenous living conditions.

The state provided resources, both instrumental and symbolic, to settlers. Given its weak infrastructure, it was especially its ceremonial role that empowered settlers. This was not restricted to pageantry, largely manifested in public displays on commemorative occasions such as agricultural shows and the Kaiser's birthday, but was also applied to police and military patrols to remind the inhabitants of the power of the state.

One of Bismarck's greatest legacies, apart from uniting Germany, had been the creation of a new form of bureaucratic organisation. Taking his cue from the well-organised and efficient Prussian military, he militarised the civil service, insulating it from the swing of politics and giving its officials an incremental career path with military norms of 'fraternity, authority and aggression' embedded in a pyramidal command structure. In this model, as Sennett points out, one was not rewarded for doing more than expected but rather punished for stepping out of line. Bureaucrats lived in a Weberian 'iron cage'. This mindset is important for understanding the genocides committed in GSWA.[33]

Until 1905, most colonial officials in GSWA were military personnel on secondment. Planners imagined creating a state-like structure that would mirror their European experience. Colonial legislation was directly linked to the administrative branch of government in an effort to exclude the German parliament, thus creating a *Verordnungstaat*, in which rule was by decree, rather than a *Rechtstaat* (constitutional state). In Namibia, Schwirck concluded, 'a whole legal discourse and law itself enabled rather than restrained colonial abuse'.[34] While in a *Rechtstaat* one can demand that a right be implemented and challenge a judgment, in a *Verordnungstaat* ordinances are top-down and enforceable by punishment. Moreover, the judiciary was organised on the consular system in that there was no distinction between legal and administrative systems, which clearly increased the powers of officialdom.

The police

The key agency charged with implementing ordinances was the Imperial Mounted Police, founded in 1907. While controlled by the civil administration, it was organised along military lines and indeed drew

33 Sennett R. 2006. *The Culture of the New Capitalism*. New Haven: Yale University Press.
34 Schwirck H. 1998. 'Violence, Race and the Law in German South West Africa, 1884–1914'. PhD dissertation, Cornell University, 23.

most of its personnel from the military. Most of the non-commissioned officers, the mainstay of the force, came from the lower middle class or *Altmittelstand*, that is, of small peasant farmer, artisanal or lower clerical origin. Non-commissioned officers were perhaps the most important cog in the Wilhelminian system, having attended a special *Unteroffiziersschule* (non-commissioned officers' school) for three or four years and, unlike officers, tended to stay in the same place for longer periods and did not aspire to officerhood. Wherever they went they brought with them *haltung*, a certain physical and moral bearing.[35] Outside the towns and garrisons, they constituted the eyes, ears and face of the colonial state.

The police underwent rapid growth from 84 Europeans at 32 stations in 1907, to 28 sergeant-majors, 532 Europeans, mostly sergeants, and 370 Indigenous police servants at 111 stations in 1913.[36] It was nevertheless chronically underfunded and understaffed, as it was originally planned to have 720 German non-commissioned officers by 1913.[37] As factotums of the state, the police undertook various duties, ranging from census-keeping and stock inspection to erecting road signs — activities frequently done on their monthly mounted patrols by horse or camel. However, in GSWA, police and settlers saw their primary role as controlling indigenes by enforcing the 1907 ordinances, and by combatting stock theft and banditry. In this, their African assistants were indispensable. Not only did they accompany patrols, and were allowed to carry firearms and to ride, but also their local knowledge was crucial. Assistants were frequently called upon to do the 'dirty work', such as flogging, and when they killed presumed thieves or bandits, or took the law into their own hands, there were usually no repercussions. This practice carried over into the South African era. In 1917 in the Grootfontein district, former assistant, then constable, Bushman Jacob Hybeb shot and killed fellow Bushman Fritz while the latter was stealing *mielies* (maize). Magistrate Brownlee informed the inquest, 'Fritz is a well-known stock thief, two charges of theft having already been laid against him', while Constable Hybeb 'is a Kalahari Bushman and has been very useful in rounding up Bushmen thieves on previous occasions'. Despite this staunch support, the Secretary for the colony responded that he should be prosecuted, but there is no record of this happening.[38]

---

35 Gann & Duignan, *Rulers of German Africa*, 5.
36 Stals E.L.P. 1984. *Duits-Suidwes-Afrika na die Groot Opstand*. Pretoria: Government Printer, 66.
37 Zollmann, 'Communicating colonial order', 37.
38 National Archives of Namibia (hereafter NAN), ADM 3768, Prosecuting officer to magistrate, Grootfontein, 17 February 1917.

CIVILIAN-DRIVEN VIOLENCE AND THE GENOCIDE OF INDIGENOUS PEOPLES

Visitors from South Africa, such as prospector Jack Cornell and anthropologist Winifred Hoernlé, were impressed by the experience and professionalism of the police.[39] Nevertheless, the police faced a constant barrage of criticism from farmers in the press and the *Landesrat*. This climaxed when a Bushman killed Sergeant Alefelder outside Grootfontein in 1911. The farming lobby goaded the government into forceful action. Given that Bushmen used poisoned arrows, a decree was issued allowing firearms to be used if Bushmen were believed to be attempting to resist arrest, while in cases of stock theft or banditry collective liability was to be applied to the settlement where the stolen items were found and all Bushmen in the locality were to be arrested. Encouraged, one official asked if women could also be shot as they 'were just as dangerous as the men'.[40] This decree was later made applicable to all indigenes, but as Muschalek notes, these decrees simply provided de jure justification for a de facto situation.[41] Perhaps a more significant consequence was that the military was now to be utilised in anti-banditry and stock-theft patrols as well. Indeed, the administration was so acutely aware of the ineffectiveness of the police that they planned to create a gendarmerie and combine it with the military in 1915.

The 1913 *Landesrat* sitting saw heated discussion and agreement that it was impossible to habituate Bushman adults to sedentary labour, and thus training for labour should begin with children. This inaugurated a policy of forcefully separating children from their families. Adult males were sent to the diamond mines at Lüderitzbucht, their families to the Warmbad district in the south, and many children allocated to local farmers.[42]

Franchising violence: Fatherly chastisement

The 1907 ordinances facilitated two outcomes. First, they franchised coercive power to settlers, while at the same time empowering them psychologically. The ideological edifice of the state was used to condone and justify everyday violence by settlers. Rohrbach, formerly settlement commissioner for the colony, complained: '[T]he conviction has gained ground that without the formality of the law and the juristic atmosphere of our high Prussian-

---

39 Cornell F.C. 1986 [1920]. *The Glamour of Prospecting*. Cape Town: David Philip, 219; Hoernlé A.W. 1987. *Trails in the Thirstland: The Anthropological Field Diaries of Winifred Hoernlé*, eds. P. Carstens, G. Klinghardt & M. West. Cape Town: University of Cape Town, 41. Hoernlé was bothered that at the outstations unmarried police kept young Indigenous girls, who did their laundry and provided sexual gratification.
40 NAN, WII, 2043, Buschleute, 1895–1915.
41 Muschalek, 'Everyday violence', 294.
42 NAN WII, ZBU 2043, rough draft, Govt. Whk. to District Office Gobabis, November 1913.

CHAPTER 9: 'Little Kings'

German officials, nobody can administer anything.'[43] Such formality was a crucial factor in giving settlers self-confidence, which, Rohrbach believed, rendered them 'spiritually more effective than any average million of people at home'.[44]

If there was one practice that characterised settler–Indigenous relations, it was the quasi-legal right of *vaterliches zuchtigungsrecht*, or fatherly chastisement, inevitably a flogging, by the *dienstherr* (employer), a family member or a white employee. This right was clearly illegal, as there was no statute that granted employers the right to discipline workers physically. Instead it was treated as a 'customary right', necessary as an educational tool given that indigenes were regarded as children. As with children, punishment had to be administered as soon as possible and thus one could not wait for officials to arrive. Nevertheless, in court records, farmers emphasised that flogging was for disobedience, never mentioning educational motives.

Because such punishment was uncodified, it meant that the chastiser determined the severity of punishment inflicted for a variety of alleged wrongs, such as 'idleness', neglect of duty, 'cheekiness' or insubordination. No trial was required, and indigenes had no opportunity to refute the charge. To do so would risk additional lashes for impudence. While workers were supposedly protected by the decrees and could complain to authorities about mistreatment, this was almost impossible, as they had to obtain a pass from the employer to travel to the nearest official, and then the complaint would in all likelihood be dismissed as frivolous.

To be sure, some officials complained that every dispute with natives seemed to lead to excessive paternal discipline, but such concerns were papered over with the argument that the colonial state had not yet reached a level of development that allowed it to mediate such conflict.[45] Even Hintrager was forced to concede:

> We can now generally observe that offences committed against the natives seldom meet with appropriate punishment. The natives are deprived of nearly all rights from the outset by the fact that most courts are only prepared to believe the statements of natives about white men

---

43 Rohrbach P. 1915. *German World Politics*. New York: Macmillan, 152.

44 Ibid., 137.

45 An excellent discussion of this topic is to be found in Schwirck H. 2002. 'Law's violence and the boundary between corporal punishment and physical abuse in German South West Africa'. *Akron Law Review*, 36, 81–113; and Muschalek M. 2019. *Violence as Usual: Everyday Police Work and the Colonial State in German Southwest Africa*. Ithaca: Cornell University Press, 129–150.

> if these statements are confirmed by other evidence. On account of the paternal right of corporal punishment that legal practice grants to every white employer, and pleading self-defence, the accused very frequently secure their acquittal .... It is to the leniency of the courts that I attribute the marked increase in the number of cases of ill-treatment of the natives, of which missionaries and native affairs commissioners complain.[46]

Of course, fatherly chastisement, with all its biblical undertones, did not emerge overnight. Francis Galton, he of eugenics fame, travelled through Namibia in the 1850s and wrote a best-seller, *The Art of Travel*, largely based on his adventures. In general, and in accordance with the prevailing theories of the Victorian era, indigenes were simply seen as adults with childish minds. The chapter 'Management of savages' contains advice such as the following:

> Bearing towards natives—A frank, joking, but determined manner, joined with an air of showing more confidence to the savages than you generally feel, is the best. It is observed, that a sea captain generally succeeds in making a very good impression on natives; they thoroughly appreciate good practical common sense, and are not half such fools as strangers usually account them. If a savage does mischief, look on him as you would on a kicking mule or a wild animal whose nature it is to be unruly and vicious, and keep your temper quite unruffled.[47]

Another precolonial Namibian traveller, Thomas Baines, also wrote a travel manual. Sometimes, he wrote, colonists are forced to take the law into their own hands as for example:

> A native servant having transgressed in this manner, the people of the farm were assembled, and he was put upon his trial; the evidence was against him, and he was asked, 'Will you be taken before the magistrate? Will you receive forty lashes at the waggon wheel, or will you be shot? They generally,' said our informant, 'choose to take the flogging offhand'. 'But how,' said we, 'if some cunning fellow should choose to be shot?' 'Oh,' said he, 'that is not very likely; but a man once did so, and he was allowed to run a hundred yards, when a bullet was fired past him, but sufficiently near to let him hear the singing of it.'[48]

He also advised that in disputes with indigenes, rituals mimicking colonial

---

46 Stoecker, *German Imperialism*, 209.
47 Galton F. 1855. *The Art of Travel*. London: John Murray, 60–61.
48 Lord W.B. & Baines T. 1871 *Shifts and Expedients of Camp Life, Travel and Exploration*. London: Horace Cox, 705–706.

CHAPTER 9: 'Little Kings'

courts, entailing the hearing of evidence to demonstrate a 'love of fair play', be enacted, unless it was a 'case of gross and insolent disobedience, which it is necessary to chastise with a strong hand upon the spot'.

Galton's metaphor of 'shipboard discipline' is apt. Indeed, flogging was so pernicious in the navy and especially in schools that the French referred to it as the 'English vice'. In order to discipline the mind, it was necessary to discipline the body, the rationale went. Flogging was common practice in most settler colonies and especially in Natal and Kenya where, like their German confrères, settlers argued for the right to administer 'rough justice'. Complaining about inefficient police and administrators generated a sense of settler identity based on tough masculinity.[49]

Little kings

In 1914 a local newspaper reported a telling exchange in the *Landesrat* between farmer Blank and the governor. Blank was reported as saying: 'On his farm he was master and not the police. If the police wanted to play master he would throw them out. We will not have our freedom meddled with.' The governor responded that 'freedom was not possible without law ... [and after quoting Goethe, continued] the farmer feels as if he is a little king on his farm, but the law stands over him. And when you toss out the police officer, Mr. Blank, then I say to you get out of here'.[50]

Grootfontein district, where three police sergeants and one farmer were killed by Bushmen between June 1911 and May 1913, was the vortex of the Bushman genocide and provides a glimpse of how this played out at the local level. At the April 1912 meeting of the *Farmerbund* a motion was carried, with only three dissenting votes by missionaries, that captured Bushmen be tattooed; that all Bushmen be deported to a large reservation on the eastern side of Omuramba Omatako; and that those captured outside this reserve be deported to the Lüderitzbucht diamond mines. These demands received much public support in the press.[51] The following year, over 250 Bushmen were incarcerated.[52] The relatively benign district Hauptmann, Von Zastrow, proposed dealing with Bushmen by issuing identity discs and rewarding

---

49 This was exacerbated by the fact that most of the soldiers had been volunteers who were largely motivated to 'prove themselves' as 'real men'.

50 *Deutsche Südwest-Afrikanische Zeitung*, 11 March 1914, cited by Zollmann, *Koloniale Herrschaft*, 280.

51 *Deutsche Kolonial Zeitung* 1911, 17, 73; 1912, 463–464; 1913, 88; 'Farmer-Verein Grootfontein', *Deutsche Südwest-Afrikanische Zeitung*, 27 April 1912, 13.

52 Köhler O. 1957. 'Dokumente zur Enstehung des Buschmannproblems in Südwestafrika', in *Afrikanischer Heimatkalender*, 52–64.

CIVILIAN-DRIVEN VIOLENCE AND THE GENOCIDE OF INDIGENOUS PEOPLES

them with food and tobacco if they kept the discs for extended periods. Bushmen who settled on mission stations were granted immunity from legal prosecution as long as they remained on mission land. Von Zastrow explained:

> I know that the farmers who need workers will be angry with the mission as well as the administration ... but especially the new farmers are not yet ready to teach the Bushmen. This is why the Bushman always runs away from the farms. I am rather for winning a lot of workers through a slow process of understanding than having a few farmers happy for a short time.[53]

The authorities also commissioned a special expedition led by Hauptmann Müller to investigate the feasibility of a reserve. Müller concluded that this was impractical.[54] Farmers, however, remained unpersuaded. Von Zastrow would attend many of these meetings, arguing that these proposals were impractical and uneconomical, and reminding farmers that they were contributing to the problem by not employing Bushmen as herdsmen but rather hiring them to hunt full-time. He argued that the system of mobile police stations was achieving increasingly satisfactory results. Ignoring Von Zastrow, farmers gave credence to wild rumours that Bushmen were engaging in cannibalism and had sworn to kill every white farmer. Farmers engaged in acts of violent self-help, often in the form of retributive commandos, killing many Bushmen.[55] Other farmers found it more rewarding, at least financially, to hand over captured Bushmen to the police for 30 marks per head. The neighbouring Gobabis district chief, Graf Von Schwerin, noted that this 'borders on trade in human beings'.[56] He also noted that a proposal to allow farmers the same power as police when accompanying patrols was unnecessary since farmers already felt free to take the law into their own hands, and if charged were generally treated liberally.[57] While large military and police patrols accompanied by farmers were involved in 'Bushman hunts' in Grootfontein, Von Schwerin discouraged this practice in his district as it exacerbated the situation. He only sent out patrols to investigate reported cases of stock theft and

---

53 Cited in Gordon, *Bushman Myth*, 72.
54 Müller concluded his report with: 'I have never heard of anyone successful at driving jackals before dogs.' See Muller, Hauptmann, 'Die Buschleute im Kauakauveld', *Deutsche Südwest-Afrikanische Zeitung*, 13 August 1912; 16 August 1912.
55 *Deutsche Südwest-Afrikanische Zeitung*, 24 December 1913.
56 NAN, ZBU 2043, W11, rough draft, Govt. Whk to District Office Gobabis, November 1913.
57 NAN, ZBU 2043, Bezirksamt Gobabis to Government; ZBU WII O.2, 8 December1911.

232

CHAPTER 9: 'Little Kings'

banditry, while Bushmen transgressing the pass or hunting laws were left alone.[58]

How did farmers come to see themselves and behave as little kings? Boosters of settlerdom proclaimed that there was such a positive spirit among settlers that class distinctions, as found in Germany, were non-existent, and hospitality was so exemplary that one could travel through the country without a pfennig in the pocket.[59] A more sober assessment suggests otherwise. 'It is awkward having anything to do with the Germans because rank counts so much and one can't get at the individual direct,' Hoernlé complained.[60] Windhoek boasted a discriminating social life based on the social hierarchy of a provincial German town, and by 1914 had more than 24 cultural associations ranging from shooting clubs to gymnastics and choral societies. Nevertheless, the industrialist Walther Rathenau, who visited GSWA in 1908 with Colonial Secretary Bernhard Dernburg, found the colony 'a land of small people, of limited means and narrow vision'. He noted that the 8 000 settlers were involved in over 8 000 lawsuits annually, including over 3 600 prosecutions for trespassing! Later Dernberg claimed that the crime rate for settlers was four times higher than in Germany, and was mostly blamed on foreigners.[61] The brutal racism shocked him:

> It is unpleasant and humiliating for strangers to observe how these [indigenes] timidly and with the expression of poor sinners press themselves to one side at the approach of a European, and submissively doff their caps in front of every white man. Nowhere are the innocent cheerfulness and trust, which are characteristic of natives in English colonies, to be seen. It has the outward appearance of slavery, as seen in the beer-dreams of the petty philistine.[62]

Then there was alcohol. The value of annual alcohol consumption was in excess of a staggering 600 marks per person, with the tax on spirits the state's only receipts worth mentioning until the discovery of diamonds. Others complained that farmers would consume champagne at the slightest occasion, despite paying 20 marks a bottle. Long-term settler

---

58 NAN, ZBU 2043, W11, rough draft, Govt. Whk to District Office Gobabis, November 1913.

59 Reiner, O. 1924. *Achtzehn Jahre Farmer in Afrika*. Leipzig: Paul List, 211.

60 Hoernlé, *Trails in the Thirstland*, 41.

61 Aitken, R. 2007. *Exclusion and Inclusion: Gradations of Whiteness and Socio-economic Engineering in German Southwest Africa 1884–1914*. Oxford: Peter Lang, 81.

62 Rathenau W. 1985. *Walther Rathenau: Industrialist, Banker, Intellectual and Politician: Notes and Diaries, 1907–1922*, ed. H. Pogge von Strandmann. Oxford: Oxford University Press, 83, 89, 84.

CIVILIAN-DRIVEN VIOLENCE AND THE GENOCIDE OF INDIGENOUS PEOPLES

Clara Brockmann suggested that many smallholders failed not because of 'inactivity' and 'stubbornness', but by 'playing the great gentleman' and 'drinking themselves to ruin by buying rounds of champagne'.[63] In 1911 there was a tavern for every 109 colonial males, and Windhoek alone had 18.[64] The largest employer after government was by far hotels. Just over a quarter of all employees, including a third of all whites and coloureds, worked in such establishments.[65]

Given this milieu, how did farmers, largely ignorant of local farming and cultural practices, maintain such eminence despite leading a precarious, isolated existence, constrained by unstable climatological and ecological conditions, and lacking a ready market and transport? Moreover, farmers resented being financially under-resourced, without fixed income, and often forced to sell cattle to pay off debt.[66] Between 1907 and 1913 cattle herds quadrupled in size, which put severe ecological pressure on rangeland. Farmers struggled as the price of cattle dropped from 250 to 300 marks in 1907 to 100 to 150 marks in 1911.[67]

One option for struggling farmers was to leave. Official records show that in 1910 there were 5766 immigrants and 4835 emigrants, an extraordinary ratio of out-migration given all the official inducements.[68] Those who remained, tended to engage in a rich fantasy world, imagining themselves as tough and manly. There were several structural features shaping this fantasy world, apart from excessive alcohol consumption. Violence was almost inevitable given the concentration of single males, their socio-economic backgrounds and desire for upward mobility. Also, their lives were shrouded in uncertainty, as settlers were thin on the ground and rumours proliferated of the dangers posed by indigenes.[69] Even close allies were seen as potential threats. In 1905, for example, rumours that the Boers were secretly planning a putsch enjoyed wide publicity.[70] Some officials were aware of this settler fantasy world; thus, Von Zastrow, instructing troops about to go out on an anti-Bushman patrol, advised: 'The people out there will have some gruesome stories to tell you but only half of them are true.'[71] The situation undoubtedly bred a remarkable paranoia, which manifested

---

63 Brockmann, C. 1912. *Briefe Eines Deutschen Mädchen aus Südwest*. Berlin: E.S. Mitler, 171.
64 Walther, *Creating Germans*, 90.
65 Great Britain, 1920. *Peace Handbooks*, vol. XVIII. London: H.M. Stationery Office, 82.
66 Bley, *South-West Africa*, 193.
67 Von Weber, *Geschichte des Schutzgebietes*, 180.
68 Walther, *Creating Germans*, 25.
69 These structural conditions are discussed in Gordon, 'Hiding in full view'.
70 *Deutsche Kolonial-Zeitung* 1905, 'Buren planen einen Putsch', 431.
71 NAN, G. Walbaum Diary, 38

CHAPTER 9: 'Little Kings'

itself in subtle ways. While the laws were draconian, their effectiveness was in doubt, and attempts to ensure greater effectiveness of the plethora of rules and regulations controlling indigenes served to exacerbate the situation. The administration realised this, as one of its memoranda admitted: 'It will frequently be found that natives who are actually vagrants are in possession of registration badges, these are obtained from other natives or stolen. Care should therefore be taken that proper proof of employment is produced and that the native is in possession of his own registration badge.'[72]

Farmers attributed their insecurity to inadequate policing. They loudly proclaimed that the police were undermining their authority and were ignorant about 'native character', while farmers based their authority on their daily experience of dealing with Indigenous peoples. They often justified their insecurity by inventing threats.[73] Although Zollmann concluded that the police almost never had a moderating effect on farmers,[74] the situation was more nuanced. As representatives of the state, the police controlled access to state resources. More immediately, they largely controlled the flow of labour to farmers. In addition, given their multiple functions, covering both policing and administration, they had much informal power exercised as 'discretion' and clothed in the rhetoric of the rigorous application of the law. Local police power was further enhanced by the high turnover of more senior officials. Unlike their metropolitan counterparts, colonial civil servants lacked tenure and thus were not encouraged to question or take a stand against abuses, or to criticise their superiors, for fear of losing their jobs.[75] Indeed, while farmers might deny it, they were 'dependent masters' and this heightened their sense of injustice, as Albert Memmi recognised in his classic *The Colonizer and the Colonized*.[76] The dominant impression, though, is that policy was largely reactive to settler demands. Some settlers did their best to tone down the more extreme demands, for fear of a public outcry in Germany.

---

72 NAN, SWAA 2/14/2. Native Affairs. Memoranda and Reports 1916. Paranoia about Bushmen has a long history extending up to the current period. See Gordon, *Bushman Myth*.
73 Lantian A., et al. 2017. '"I know things they don't know!": The role of need for uniqueness in conspiracy theories'. *Social Psychology*, 48, 160–173.
74 Zollmann, *Koloniale Herrschaft*, 281.
75 Gann & Duignan, *Rulers of German Africa*, 88.
76 Memmi A. 1968. *The Colonizer and the Colonized*. Boston: Beacon Press.

235

The *Platzgeist* fantasyland

In 1907 a young political economist, Moritz Bonn, visited GSWA and had an epiphany. He realised that colonialism was not only racist, exploitative and uneconomical, but also ridiculous, and he became one of the first scholars to plead the necessity of decolonisation.[77] To Bonn, the notion of 'ethnographically' recreating a *Heimat* was not only absurd, but also the justifications put forward by its proponents were easily refuted. Citing national statistics, he effortlessly dispelled the notion that Germany needed colonies for its surplus population.

Bonn's first-hand description was salutary in its portrayal of the settler *Platzgeist* (spirit of the place) He found that 'a feeling of frustration, of pettiness and of meanness pervaded the colony'.[78] Europeans 'glared and stared at us, full of suspicion. One evidently did not expect anybody to come to this part of the world without sinister intentions'.[79] Despite a government circular instructing officials to advise and help him, cooperation was virtually non-existent: 'Most of the junior officials were scions of the Prussian nobility who had not learned much and who were suspicious of every kind of learning. They had come out to Africa because it offered them a chance of bossing on a scale no longer available even in darkest Pomerania. All of them looked upon me and especially my wife as undesirable intruders.'[80] In 1914 he was more explicit:

> Though the country has regularly been called a white man's country, most manual work is carried out by native labour ... [t]he real problem ... has always been not only how to find the white man to settle the country, but quite as much how to find coloured labourers to support them when settled.[81]

Bonn recognised the neo-feudal nature of the colony:

> In South-West Africa, we have created a kind of manorial system with a European lord of the manor and an African serf ... you quickly drift into European problems ... but whatever you do on African soil; will always be

---

77 Gordon R. 2013. 'Moritz Bonn, Southern Africa and the critique of colonialism'. *African Historical Review*, 45, no. 2, 1–30.

78 Bonn M.J. 1948. *Wandering Scholar*. New York: John Day, 140.

79 Ibid., 134. Cornell also found German officers to be overbearing and swashbuckling. They greeted him with 'scowls and surly demeanor' and drank to excess in the presence of their men. He dismissed them as 'contemptable bullying cads' living in a 'detestable junkerdom of this "Kolonial" edition of Prussianised Germany'. See Cornell, *Glamour of Prospecting*, 37, 39, 315, 316.

80 Bonn, *Wandering Scholar*, 135.

81 Bonn M.J. 1914. 'German colonial policy'. *United Empire*, 5 (2 February), 129.

> merely 'semi-European'. The democracies you create are not a people, but merely a class, whose progress, existence and safety depends on the services of a subject race which they cannot amalgamate, but which they must rule. There lies ... the labour foundation of the African society ... Whatever you do, you will rule [the native] as a foreigner ... and you will always rule him however just your government may be, by the point of the sword.[82]

This generated a peculiar form of nationalism among the settlers, whose largely unrealistic expectations were nurtured on the stories of Fennimore Cooper and Karl May. Later, Bonn was to expand on this point: 'The pride of the self-made man who glorifies his achievement has given way to the boast of ancestry. All-embracing nationalism has limited his knowledge of the outer world which is now "merely a stage on which great deeds can be accomplished."' Here they 'dream of endless spaces, room to breathe and unemployment is unknown. They know very little about economic facts and care less for economic argument, though poverty and penury have influenced their attitude.'[83] It was not only popular writers who shaped colonial consciousness. On the contrary, '[Colonial] Power was dressed up by poets and philosophers in the stirring garments of their own imaginations.'[84] At the same time, referring to GSWA, the settler notion of *Deutschtum*, or national consciousness, gave them the self-assigned right to ask the Motherland to pay for development and security in the colony, and if this was refused, to feel ill-treated.[85] They were indeed 'dependent masters' (*abhängige Herren*). Ironically, 'this idea in its most trite form proclaims the master position of the white race, by which the German *Spiesse* [philistines], who are excited about colonialism, willingly seeks to prove that he has

---

82 Ibid., 135.

83 Bonn M.J. 1938. *The Crumbling of Empire: The Disintegration of World Economy*. London: Allen & Unwin, 336.

84 Ibid., 141. His perspective on colonialism being ridiculous led to this insight: he described Von Trotha as a 'theatrical' general who tried to act like a 'native potentate' and concluded a newspaper polemic thus: 'What Herr von Trotha labels a law of nature, as the result of his long-term study of colonial policy, is therefore not only wrong, it is nowadays much more dangerous than his actions in South West. No arguments will ever undo the extermination of the Herero. But as long as there are people who consider such a policy as necessitated by a law of nature, there is the danger that it may also be used elsewhere. If the mistakes of Trotha's colonial policy lend themselves to theoretical transfiguration, nothing will protect us from their repetition.' See *Frankfurter Zeitung*, 14 February 1909.

85 Bonn M.J. 1910. 'Siedlungsfragen und Eingeborenenpolitik II: Die Entstehung der Gutsherrschaft in Südafrika'. *Archiv für Sozialwissenschaft und Sozialpolitik*, 31, 24–25.

CIVILIAN-DRIVEN VIOLENCE AND THE GENOCIDE OF INDIGENOUS PEOPLES

captured the quintessence of modern colonial problems.'[86] Significantly, colonials also developed a biological nationalism, epitomised by the slogan that it was a 'natural law' that indigenes would die out when brought into contact with superior 'races'. This meant that imperialism was no longer based on an ideology of uniting diverse 'races' in a common bond of imperial statehood, but instead assumed unchangeable biological characteristics unless miscegenation occurred.[87] The German word *Spiessburger* is notoriously difficult to translate but, roughly, means an upwardly aspiring narrow-minded philistine, or what Nietzsche termed a *Bildungsphilister* — a dogma-prone newspaper reader with cosmetic exposure to high culture. After reading relevant court cases from this era, as far as I could ascertain, all the accused settler farmers were clearly members of the *Spiessburgertum*.

Several factors contributed to this fantasy-like *Platzgeist*, with its genocidal overtones ranging from the explicit racism prevalent in Germany to the backgrounds of the intrepid settlers. In a study of the rise and fall of schools of philosophy, Collins singled out two key factors: networks and the seminar. Modified to fit the colonial situation, one could argue that *Platzgeist* cohesion was facilitated by this settler network, which, because of its vast geographical stretch, meant that when farmers met they were inclined to hold intense discussions resembling seminars in the local taverns or while imbibing. The excessive use of liquor was believed by several officials to be the cause of sadistic practices toward indigenes.[88] While intoxication was not a prerequisite for 'erasive' practices, the role of alcohol abuse, especially its ritual and celebratory uses, constitute an important, if under-researched, element in genocide studies. Alcohol consumption served several purposes: incentivising and rewarding violence; relaxing inhibitions to killing; and as a coping mechanism.[89] Along with alcohol consumption, another important mode of expressing settler virility was excessive swearing, leading one official to complain that settlers used every opportunity to make indigenes feel despised by using 'picturesque and powerful swearwords'.[90] Swearing and flogging served as visual displays of settler masculinity and dominance, not only to indigenes, but to fellow settlers as well.

---

86 Bonn M.J. 1910b. 'Siedlungsfragen und Eingeborenenpolitik III: Die Entstehung der Gutsherrschaft in Südafrika', *Archiv für Sozialwissenschaft und Sozialpolitik*, 31, 830. [author's translation].
87 Bonn M. 1932. 'Imperialism', in *Encyclopaedia of the Social Sciences*, eds. E. Seligman & A. Johnson. New York: Macmillan, 610.
88 Zollmann, *Koloniale Herrschaft*, 284.
89 Westermann E. 2016. 'Stone-cold killers or drunk with murder?: Alcohol and atrocity during the Holocaust.' *Holocaust and Genocide Studies*, 30, no. 1, 1–19.
90 Stals, *Duits-Suidwes-Afrika*, 113–114.

Conclusion

When South Africa took over administration of the territory under a League of Nations mandate, a large-scale farming scheme for poor Afrikaners was set up in the same areas where the Bushman genocides had occurred. Despite being subject to the same structural conditions of under-capitalisation, distant markets and an unpredictable ecology — the situation exacerbated by a greatly reduced civil service — no genocidal actions occurred, despite Afrikaner settlers being just as racist as their German predecessors.

What had changed was the *Platzgeist*. What created and sustained the 'erasive' ethos were interactive ritual chains that bridged segments of the social world. These rituals required physical co-presence in an encounter in which participants felt a sense of privileged inclusiveness and shared a 'common mood or emotional experience'.[91] These ritual encounters, Collins claims, generated emotional energy that served to 'temporarily reinforce the identities of group members and motivate them to act in accordance with what they take to be the group's values ... even when the group is not gathered together'.[92] Taking the situation rather than the individual as starting point, Collins suggests that ideology was relatively unimportant, as people commonly joined social movements before they acquired clear beliefs about issues, but then provided ex post facto rationalisations when challenged on their membership or actions. He asserts that 'when a particular belief becomes entangled with an identity — when it becomes, in other words, a focus in some chain or linkage of successful interaction rituals circulating as a marker of membership in some group — it becomes more or less immune to rational argument'.[93] It also led to 'deviance amplification'. In sum, rather than emphasise ideology, the nature of ritual interactions has to be brought to the fore. Perhaps one of the most prominent features of the copious German settler literature is the prominence given to *Gemütlichkeit* (geniality) towards insiders. Given their isolation, when settlers met, they typically engaged in heavy drinking in which emotional intensity was fuelled by bravado. It was in such charged, ritualised situations that participants developed 'typification schemes' and 'sense-making'.[94]

---

91 Collins R. 2004. *Interaction Ritual Chains*. Princeton: Princeton University Press, 48.

92 Marquez X. 2013. 'Engines of sacrality: A footnote on Randall Collins' *Interaction Ritual Chains*'. Blog post, Abandoned Footnotes, 14 April. Available at http://abandonedfootnotes.blogspot.co.uk/2013/04/engines-of-sacrality-footnote-on.html, accessed 31 October 2019.

93 Ibid.

94 Berger, P. & Luckmann T. 1966. *The Social Construction of Reality*. New York: Vintage. Typification schemes refer to the means whereby people perceive and structure their

CIVILIAN-DRIVEN VIOLENCE AND THE GENOCIDE OF INDIGENOUS PEOPLES

In contrast to German farmers, dominant network nodes of mandate-era Afrikaner farmers were not the tavern, but rather the church. Most of them belonged to the strict, conservative Dutch Reformed Church. Thus, while they were racist, and sometimes brutal, they were not genocidal. Ironically, while in German times Bushmen sought protection from farmers by working for policemen, in the mandate era Bushmen sought protection from the police by working for farmers.[95]

This chapter has dealt with a conundrum: farmers' criticisms of the excesses of Von Trotha's infamous genocidal activities in 1904–1905 were one of the major factors leading to his recall, yet five years later farmers were calling for, and actively participating in, the now almost-forgotten genocides of those labelled Bushmen. The focus has been on how, in a state that is precariously organised, a collection of settler farmers who defined themselves as 'the backbone of the country' exercised influence beyond their limited numbers and minor contribution to the economy. The key interpretive dimension emphasised is how these self-styled 'hardy pioneers' imagined 'Bushmen' within the organisational scaffolding provided by the colonial state. Newly arrived farmers from Germany, whose fantasies were cultivated by writers such as Karl May, found their imaginations running wild when it came to the Bushmen. They also imagined themselves as feudal lords, and I have suggested that, given the sparseness of officials and state infrastructure, the situation did indeed resemble one of neo-feudalism. Conjointly, while the 'state' knee-haltered their imaginations, the actions inspired by their fantasies served to modify the state. The major constraint on their activities was not so much moral decency as fear of embarrassment both locally and, especially, in the metropole.

---

world through typologies. It is an essential and intrinsic aspect of the ways in which actors orient themselves to situations.

95 Zollmann, *Koloniale Herrschaft*, 2, 91.

CHAPTER TEN

Settler Genocide in Rwanda? Colonial Legacies of Everyday Violence

Susan Thomson

In August 2006, Thomas told me that he considered his detention to be bogus.[1] How could he, a poor subsistence farmer with many Tutsi friends and neighbours, be accused of acts of genocide? Thomas's refrain was one I had heard often throughout my 2005–2006 research in Rwanda.[2] I was not surprised to hear Thomas explain his imprisonment as a form of wrongful persecution. Most of the prisoners I met, men and women alike, offered carefully worded sermons of Tutsi hatred for Hutu to explain their innocence — sermons that mirrored the anti-Tutsi rhetoric of both the late 1950s and early 1990s. Among the 36 prisoners I consulted, all but 2 insisted that they could not have committed acts of genocide, as the crimes they perpetrated were instead forms of self-defence in the context of the civil war that began in October 1990. Thomas lamented this legal bind by explaining that he could not be guilty, even though he had confessed to killing three Tutsi:

> Killing was the law.[3] We had to kill or suffer ourselves! Hutu killed Tutsi but Tutsi also killed us. There was a civil war, you see! We knew our enemy was Tutsi. I killed. Yes, but I was also following orders. It was an

---

1   Not his real name. All names used in the text are pseudonyms.
2   I describe my research design and methodology in Thomson S. 2013b. *Whispering Truth to Power: Resistance to Reconciliation in Post-genocide Rwanda*. Madison: University of Wisconsin Press, 28–46; Thomson S. 2013a. 'Academic integrity and ethical responsibilities in post-genocide Rwanda: Working with research ethics boards to prepare for fieldwork with "human subjects"', in *Emotional and Ethical Challenges for Field Research in Africa: The Story Behind the Findings*, eds. S. Thomson, A. Ansoms & J. Murison. London: Palgrave Macmillan, 139–154; and Thomson S. 2010. 'Getting close to Rwandans since the genocide: Studying everyday life in highly politicized research settings'. *African Studies Review*, 53, no. 3, 19–34.
3   Straus corroborates Thomas's perception that Hutu perpetrators killed Tutsi because it was the law of the land, citing the authority of the state, a culture of obedience, and a broader climate of insecurity. Straus S. 2006. *The Order of Genocide: Race, Power and War in Rwanda*. Ithaca: Cornell University Press, 227–239.

CIVILIAN-DRIVEN VIOLENCE AND THE GENOCIDE OF INDIGENOUS PEOPLES

extreme time and some of us did extreme things.[4] I admit to that. But we cannot forget that the RPF [Rwandan Patriotic Front] are foreigners and they killed our president![5] They came from outside to oppress Hutu. That cannot be overlooked. Tutsi leaders have always oppressed Hutu like me. This issue of ethnic groups cannot be swept away. Now the government is made up of extremist Tutsi who say ethnicity doesn't matter![6] But people, so we Hutu suffer as killers, rotting in prison while Tutsi who killed are outside, living free. That's what you outsiders don't understand. There was war and some of us did things to win the war.[7] It wasn't genocide, it was a way to save Rwanda for Hutu like me.[8]

Thomas's soliloquy in the open courtyard of his prison just outside Huye town speaks to more than the civilian-driven nature of Rwanda's 1994 genocide.[9]

---

4 On the climate of fear and uncertainty from 1990 to 1994, cited by Thomas as 'extreme things', see Thomson S. 2018a. *Rwanda: From Genocide to Precarious Peace.* New Haven: Yale University Press, 17–32. To compare anti-Tutsi rhetoric in the 1950s and 1990s, see Newbury C. 1998. 'Ethnicity and the politics of history in Rwanda'. *Africa Today*, 45, no. 1, 14–18.

5 On 6 April 1994, President Habyarimana was assassinated when his aircraft was shot down on its approach to Kigali International Airport. The president was returning from peace talks with the Rwandan Patriotic Front (RPF) in neighbouring Tanzania. Habyarimana's supporters blamed the assassination on the RPF, a rebel group led by minority Tutsi rebels. By 7 April 1994, Hutu hardliners within the presidential camp had moved to eliminate the leadership of the more moderate and largely Hutu political opposition, and within three days they had out manoeuvered Hutu moderates within their party to install a new government of hardliners. Des Forges A. 1999. *Leave None to Tell the Story: Genocide in Rwanda.* New York: Human Rights Watch, 144–175.

6 On the current government's policy of ethnic unity since 1994, see Purdeková A. 2015. *Making* Ubumwe: *Power, State and Camps in Rwanda's Unity-Building Project.* New York: Berghahn Books; and Thomson, *Whispering Truth to Power*.

7 To contextualise Thomas's statement about the role of civil war in legitimating the killing of Tutsi, see Fujii on individual motivation and method to commit acts of genocide. Fujii L.A. 2009. *Killing Neighbors: Webs of Violence in Rwanda.* Ithaca: Cornell University Press, 76–102.

8 Fieldnotes, August 2006. I distinguish between 'fieldnotes' and 'interviews' in data collection. The material gathered in formal interviews, defined narrowly to include only the stories and observations of research participants, usually in the presence of a translator and in full view of family, neighbors and even local government officials, are cited as 'interviews'. The experiences and observations in my everyday interactions with Rwandans from all walks of life — rural farmers and elites alike — that I inscribed every evening in the format of 'fieldnotes' are cited that way. Thomson, *Whispering Truth to Power*, 26.

9 I regularly spent time with Thomas while waiting to meet the prison warden, so I could officially receive permission to interview prisoners in Huye prison in South province. Thomas worked for the warden three afternoons a week helping, as best I could tell, with receiving visitors. This sometimes included obviously foreign researchers like myself, but usually Thomas oversaw the long queues of family members who visited prisoners they personally knew — relatives and friends — to augment meagre meal portions provided by the prison.

CHAPTER 10: Settler Genocide in Rwanda?

His words confirm the scholarly consensus on the structural factors that drove the genocide — an intense civil war, launched by the now ruling and Tutsi-dominated RPF in October 1990, the authority of the state and ethnic classifications of Tutsi and Hutu as in- and out-group political categories. Thomas also makes reference to the idea of ethnic Tutsi as foreigners, an idea that has received relatively little attention in the literature on the causes of the 1994 Rwandan genocide.[10] Instead, scholars, policy-makers and journalists have largely focused on the role of Rwandan state institutions in orchestrating popular participation in the murder of at least 500 000 ethnic Tutsi in just 100 days, from April to July 1994.[11] This literature analyses the role of ethnic Hutu hardliners in eliminating moderate Hutu military and political leaders to clear a path for genocide, while assessing the ability of state agents — military and paramilitary units, as well as local government officials — to mobilise ordinary people to the project of eliminating Tutsi.[12]

While scholars, such as Fujii and Straus, have richly theorised the reasons why Hutu killed Tutsi during the 1994 genocide, these studies do not explicitly address the everyday forms of violence that made killing one's neighbour, relative or colleague a legitimate choice for ordinary people in 1994.[13] In contrast to genocide scholars, such as Fein and Valentino, who concern themselves with the drivers of genocidal violence, and unlike scholars of political violence, such as Kalyvas, who generally concern themselves with modes and variance of violence in war, this chapter analyses everyday forms of violence as a root cause of mass violence, such as genocide.[14] It is motivated by a larger, overarching question be-

---

10 Fujii L.A. 2004. 'Transforming the moral landscape: The diffusion of a genocidal norm in Rwanda'. *Journal of Genocide Research*, 6, no. 1, 99–114; Reyntjens F. 2018. 'Understanding Rwandan politics through the *longue durée*: From the precolonial to the post-genocide era'. *Journal of Eastern African Studies*, 12 no. 3, 514–532; and Straus, S. 2015. *Making and Unmaking Nations: War, Leadership, and Genocide in Modern Africa*. Ithaca: Cornell University Press, 276–292.

11 Des Forges, *Leave None to Tell the Story*, 15–16; Guichaoua A. 2015. *From War to Genocide: Criminal Politics in Rwanda, 1990–1994*, trans. D. Webster. Madison: University of Wisconsin Press, 143–292; Kimonyo J-P. 2014. *Rwanda's Popular Genocide: A Perfect Storm*. Boulder, CO: Lynne Rienner.

12 For research summaries of the historical causes of the 1994 genocide, see Longman T. 2004. 'Placing genocide in context: Research priorities for the Rwandan genocide'. *Journal of Genocide Research*, 6 no. 1, 33–39; Thomson, S. 2016. 'Genocide in Rwanda', in *Oxford Bibliographies in African Studies*, ed. T. Spear. New York: Oxford University Press.

13 Fujii, *Killing Neighbors*; Straus, *The Order of Genocide*.

14 Compare, for example, Fein H. 1990. *Genocide: A Sociological Perspective*. London & Newbury Park: Sage Publications; Valentino, B.A. 2004. *Final Solutions: Mass Killing and Genocide in the Twentieth Century*. Ithaca: Cornell University Press; Kalyvas S. 2006. *The Logic of Violence in Civil War*. New York: Cambridge University Press.

CIVILIAN-DRIVEN VIOLENCE AND THE GENOCIDE OF INDIGENOUS PEOPLES

yond the well-documented and empirically rich studies about what made genocide the choice of Hutu political and military leaders. Instead, I ask how an ideology of genocide, infused with everyday forms of violence, led ordinary Rwandan civilians to act on the call to kill their Tutsi brethren.

As such, I use the idea of Tutsi as a monolithic class of foreigners to frame the 1994 genocide as an example of settler genocide. Thinking about Tutsi as settlers provides a novel analytical avenue to understand and explain the logic of genocide as something that needs to be cultivated in society. In Rwanda, this means the diffusion of a genocidal norm rooted in an ideology that framed *all* Tutsi as a threat to Hutu survival.[15] As Adhikari explains, genocide 'cannot happen accidentally'.[16] Said differently, genocidal violence must be taught. To prime civilians for the grisly task, political leaders cannot assume their participation. There must be the intent to exterminate an entire group of people because of some innate and immediate threat posed by the group. In pre-1994 Rwanda, the message of ethnic Hutu hardliners was that genocidal killing was normal insofar as it was an acceptable and legitimate course of action during Rwanda's civil war and genocide. The process of killing one's neighbour is rooted in the crafting of a genocidal norm that takes root long before the call to action is made.

I contend that the process of normalising genocidal violence is rooted in the presence of everyday forms of violence in society. These norms emerged in an extended period of state-building that was well under way before the first contact with European colonists, as I illustrate below. An understanding of this history matters, as it illustrates how colonial contact formalised the ethnic categories of Hutu, Tutsi and Twa, which would later serve as identity markers for the 1994 genocide. This is not to suggest that Rwandans are culturally or historically programmed to commit genocide. Quite the opposite. An analysis of precolonial history lays the groundwork for an understanding of how the transition from precolonial to colonial and later postcolonial rule reveals structural continuities in the political salience of ethnicity, and how the centralisation of state power made genocide an option.[17] This continuum provides a basis for understanding the process by

---

15 Des Forges A. 1995. 'The ideology of genocide'. *Issue: A Journal of Opinion*, 23, no. 2, 44–47; Fujii, 'Transforming the moral landscape', 102–103.

16 Adhikari M. 2010. *The Anatomy of a South African Genocide: The Extermination of the Cape San Peoples.* Cape Town: UCT Press, 12.

17 Desrosiers M.E. 2014. 'Rethinking political rhetoric and authority during Rwanda's First and Second Republics'. *Africa*, 84, no. 2, 119–225; Newbury D. 2012. 'Canonical conventions in Rwanda: Four myths of recent historiography in central Africa'. *History in*

CHAPTER 10: Settler Genocide in Rwanda?

which civilians are capable of reducing the politically or socially 'other' into expendables, providing the licence to kill.

Moreover, an empirical analysis of precolonial history further illustrates how postcolonial elites employed myths of history about the precolonial period to justify the physical violence against Tutsi as foreigners intent on oppressing Hutu.[18] This historical analysis paves the way for an assessment of the various forms of structural and symbolic violence that preceded or coexisted with the state-sanctioned goal of killing one's neighbour, as was the case in 1994. I then theorise everyday forms of violence, to focus on the long shadow of state-sanctioned dehumanising, scapegoating, marginalising and social exclusion that produced the fear, anger and uncertainty that in turn led some Rwandans — ordinary men like Thomas — to commit acts of genocide.[19]

Next, I demonstrate that postcolonial Rwandan society was characterised by these latent and pervasive forms of everyday violence rooted in social and cultural norms that normalised physical violence against Tutsi before and during the 1994 genocide. The rhetoric of ethnic Hutu postcolonial presidents, namely Grégoire Kayibanda (1962–1973) and Juvénal Habyarimana (1973–1994), framed all Tutsi as more than the beneficiaries of Belgian colonial rule between 1916 and 1962. They also painted the minority Tutsi as arrogant and wily invaders who sought to dominate the majority Hutu, stripping them of the rightful ownership of *their* Rwanda. In tracing the institutional and ideological legacy of everyday forms of ethnic violence, this chapter re-evaluates the 1994 genocide as an example of postcolonial settler genocide and illuminates the everyday processes that made genocide a viable political goal that put the dirty work of killing in the hands of civilians.

Africa, 39, no. 1, 41–76; Reyntjens, Understanding Rwandan politics through the *longue durée*'; Twagiramungu N. 2010. 'The anatomy of leadership: A view-from-within of postgenocide Rwanda'. Unpublished paper presented at the 53rd Annual Conference of the African Studies Association (in possession of the author).

18 Newbury, 'Ethnicity and the politics of history in Rwanda', 9–10; Newbury, 'Canonical conventions in Rwanda', 46–57.

19 Scheper-Hughes N. 1993. *Death Without Weeping: The Violence of Everyday Life in Brazil.* Berkeley: University of California Press, 216–233; Thomson S. 2017. 'The long shadow of genocide in Rwanda'. *Current History*, 116, no. 790, 183–188. See also Lindner E.G. 2004. 'Genocide, humiliation, and inferiority: An interdisciplinary perspective', in *Genocides by the Oppressed: Subaltern Genocide in Theory and Practice*, eds. N.A. Robins & A. Jones. Bloomington: Indiana University Press, 138–158.

A case of settler genocide

In a collection about civilian-driven settler genocides, Rwanda appears at first glance as an outlier. As Veracini explains, settler colonialism is analytically and practically distinct from colonialism.[20] Colonies are political entities that are both dominated by a foreign power and seek to impose foreign power structures on the local entity. This process is also characterised by conquest, meaning that the colonisers are the founders of political systems and social orders, which they then use to govern and control the local population. Settler colonisation differs as a political project that intends to replace the local population with a new society of settlers. As such, violence against local populations, whether through assimilation or, in extreme cases, extermination, is part and parcel of settler colonial projects. A defining feature of settler colonialism are ideologies of racial superiority, with white settlers from European countries at the helm. In other words, settlers come to stay, to permanently occupy new homelands, carving up land to dispossess local populations in order to assert their ownership of place while also creating a culture of settler domination.[21]

The Rwandan case is not a classic case of settler colonialism. Neither the Germans (1897–1916) nor the Belgians (1916–1962) sought to settle in Rwanda permanently or to fully dominate the Indigenous population.[22] There was no mass migration of Germans or Belgians to the territorial entity that is today known as Rwanda. At the time of colonial contact, in 1892, when representatives of the German government first arrived to assess what use they might make of the place and its people, present-day Rwanda did not exist.[23] When the Germans made contact with representatives of the royal court of the day, the kingdom was in turmoil, following a series of internal coups that would do as much to shape modern Rwanda as would the presence of colonial power.[24] The presence of European colonisers would result in two key political outcomes that would later inform the implementation of the 1994 genocide. The first was the classification of Hutu and Tutsi into monolithic political categories, and the second

---

20 Veracini L. 2010. *Settler Colonialism: A Theoretical Overview*. London: Palgrave Macmillan 2–15.
21 Ibid., 68–69.
22 Vansina J. 2010. *Being Colonized: The Kuba Experience in Rural Congo, 1880–1960*. Madison: University of Wisconsin Press, 35–57; Veracini, *Settler Colonialism*, 3–4.
23 Vansina J. 2004. *Antecedents to Modern Rwanda: The Nyiginya Kingdom*. Madison: University of Wisconsin Press, 176.
24 Newbury D. 'Introduction', in Des Forges A. 2011. *'Defeat is the Only Bad News': Rwanda Under Musinga, 1896–1931, ed*. D. Neubury Madison: University of Wisconsin Press, xxiii–xxxi.

CHAPTER 10: Settler Genocide in Rwanda?

was the creation of a centralised and hierarchical socio-political structure designed for control. As Vansina explains, contemporary Rwandan society is 'built on the economic, social and political foundations encountered by the first colonials' in present-day central Rwanda.[25]

The 'settlers' in the Rwandan case are elite Tutsi, a minority within a minority, as members of the royal court of the day, who would soon come to see themselves as outsiders, to accord with European ideas about racism at the moment of colonial contact in the late-nineteenth century. There is no doubt that the arrival of colonisers in Rwanda was part and parcel of the process by which European power came to dominate much of the world outside Europe and North America.[26] A key difference from the ways in which most of Africa came under colonial dominion was 'a great and unsung collaborative enterprise' between Tutsi royal elites of the day and the newly arrived Europeans.[27] The racist ideas of Rwanda's colonists would initially benefit the ruling Tutsi, while also later having enormous impact on the ideas and practices of Rwanda's political elite, ideas that would lay the ideological foundation for the 1994 genocide.

Rwandan Tutsi became settlers through the introduction of the so-called Hamitic hypothesis, a racist idea rooted in the presumed superiority of Europeans. The hypothesis valued most those Africans who appeared physically and geographically proximate to Europeans. The colonists saw themselves in the tall, elegant, fairer-skinned Tutsi with narrow, northern European-type facial features. As such, Tutsi became 'white Africans', who had surely brought the sophisticated social and political structure of the Tutsi royal court from the Roman colonies of North Africa.[28] In contrast, the Europeans saw Hutu as natural cultivators, evidenced in their short, husky builds, dark skin and broad, flat facial features. In sustained efforts to rationalise their own biases, the Europeans ignored racial aberrations that did not accord with their notion of sophisticated Tutsi and hard-working, but simple, Hutu. Tutsi were regarded as natural leaders, given their innate intelligence, while Hutu, given their submissive and good-natured dispositions, were obvious subjects. This framing effaces the fact that signifi-

---

25 Vansina, *Antecedents to Modern Rwanda*, 3.

26 Wolfe P. 1999. *Settler Colonialism and the Transformation of Anthropology: The Politics and Poetics of an Ethnographic Event* London: Cassell; Young C. 1994. *The African Colonial State in Colonial Perspective*. New Haven: Yale University Press.

27 Des Forges, 'Ideology of genocide', 45.

28 Ibid., 44. Des Forges also explains that the Germans saw the toga-wearing Tutsi royalists as proof of ties to Roman colonies. Images of members of the court in togas and colonial military garb are available in her 2011 book, *Defeat is the Only Bad News*, 70, 98, 156, 212.

CIVILIAN-DRIVEN VIOLENCE AND THE GENOCIDE OF INDIGENOUS PEOPLES

cant numbers of Tutsi and Hutu lived similar lifestyles, keeping cattle and cultivating their fields. Many Hutu in precolonial Rwanda owned cattle, and many Tutsi practised agriculture.

This framing did more than accord with the racist worldview of the colonisers. It also meant that regional and class distinctions between and among Hutu and Tutsi were ignored. Both Hutu and Tutsi soon became, in the eyes of Europeans, homogeneous categories, inscribed with innate intellectual and moral qualities. Of course, elite Tutsi were politically astute by training and experience, not by birth, a fact that few royalists would remember as they exploited the racial prejudices of Europeans for their own benefit.[29] This notion of innate Tutsi superiority and right to rule would become a founding myth worth defending, whatever the cost. Ironically, the myth that legitimated Tutsi rule at the time of the colonial encounter would ultimately be turned against them to justify their massacre in 1994.

When the colonisers established indirect rule in the central region of Africa, it coincided with a period of intense internal military and political wrangling in Rwanda.[30] Royal court lore, however, presented Europeans with the image of a peaceful society politically unified in custom and devoid of divisive distinctions of race and class. In the telling of court oral historians — later bolstered by European anthropologists — the kingdom was able to maintain peaceful coherence through occupational categories of Tutsi and Hutu that defined social life.[31] Tutsi pastoralists, who had recently immigrated from the north, found the agricultural Hutu and forest-dwelling Twa living precariously on what their limited resources could provide. Tutsi royalists explained that it was the political power of kingship, and the social institution of cattle-sharing called *ubuhake*, that tied Rwandans together.[32] The practice involved the transfer of a cow from a Tutsi patron to a Hutu client. According to this instrumental view, the utility of controlling cattle was so crucial to social and political harmony that Hutu willingly subordinated themselves to Tutsi. In turn, Hutu owed labour and produce to their patrons. And, since all cattle were the property of the king, Hutu became royal subjects.

---

29 Vansina, *Antecedents to Modern Rwanda*, 174–175.

30 By 1913, Rwanda was home to only five German administrators and 41 missionaries. Newbury D. & Newbury C. 2000. 'Bringing the peasants back in: Agrarian themes in the construction and corrosion of statist historiography in Rwanda'. *American Historical Review*, 105, no. 3, 845.

31 For example, Maquet J.J. 1961. *The Premise of Inequality in Ruanda: A Study of Political Relations in a Central African Kingdom*. London: Oxford University Press.

32 Newbury C. 1988. *The Cohesion of Oppression: Rwanda, 1860–1960*. New York: Columbia University Press, 140–141.

CHAPTER 10: Settler Genocide in Rwanda?

By 1916, when the Belgians gained control of Rwanda under a League of Nations mandate, a single intellectual and ideological image of precolonial Rwanda was already entrenched, that of a homogeneous Rwandan culture and history, and of Tutsi rulers and Hutu supplicants.[33] The image of a peaceful Rwanda, willingly stratified by ethnic hierarchy, was one that 'met the goals of the colonial administration as well as those of the Court and justified the parameters of colonial rule'.[34] It also masked the political violence of the day as the court sought brutally and forcibly to incorporate land, pasture and people into its dominion. The key point is that colonial rule did not create state domination and Hutu-Tutsi inequality. What mattered was the way colonialism extended the reach of the state, the forms of domination and the nature of political competition. In the long run, these socio-political transformations helped to generate the conditions for widespread rural discontent after the decision in 1957 that Rwanda would be granted independence, which in turn mirrored the rhetorical and physical violence of the early 1990s.[35]

State-building is a violent process, and modern Rwanda is no exception to this rule.[36] Since the end of the eighteenth century, warring was the 'main instrument of power of the Nyiginya kingdom'[37] When the colonists arrived, processes of political centralisation, exploitation of the population and local skirmishes were well under way.[38] Institutionalised physical violence in the context of state-building were staples of everyday life. Disappearances and detention, but also beheadings for treason, death by poisoning for friends turned foes, rape and torture were also common during

---

33 Thomson, *Rwanda*, 41–43.
34 Newbury in Des Forges, *'Defeat is the Only Bad News'*, xxxvi–xxvii. Several prominent authors emphasise the peaceful and harmonious unity of Rwandans prior to the arrival of the Europeans and have contended that ethnic identity was a colonial creation, and that this creation is a primary cause of the 1994 genocide. See, for example, Gourevitch P. 1998. *We Wish to Inform You that Tomorrow We Will Be Killed with Our Families: Stories from Rwanda*. New York: Farrar Straus & Giroux; Mamdani M. 2002. *When Victims Become Killers: Colonialism, Nativism and the Genocide in Rwanda*. Princeton: Princeton University Press. The current government has also adopted this perspective, claiming that the terms 'Hutu' and 'Tutsi' had no significant meaning in precolonial Rwanda and blaming Rwanda's divisions primarily on the Germans and Belgians. See for example, Republic of Rwanda. 1999. *The Unity of Rwandans: Before the Colonial Period and under the Colonial Rule under the First Republic*. Kigali: Urugwiro Village/Office of the President.
35 Newbury, 'Ethnicity and the politics of history in Rwanda', 10.
36 Tilly C. 2003. *The Politics of Collective Violence*. Cambridge: Cambridge University Press; Young, *African Colonial State*.
37 Vansina, *Antecedents to Modern Rwanda*, 182.
38 Ibid., 180–194.

paramilitary raids to acquire cattle, which were needed in large numbers to allow the court to enter into *ubuhake* contracts. Denunciations and accusations soon became the order of the day, as warriors and courtiers alike sought the king's favour, often at the expense of ordinary people. Public executions for those individuals who sought to challenge the court or the diktats of the king were commonplace.[39] Cycles of revenge rooted in the righting of past wrongs soon characterised the politics of the day, a trend that persists in Rwandan political culture.[40]

In March 1897, German officials proposed, in the nick of time, a military alliance with the royal court. In November 1896, Yuhi Musinga had acceded to power following a coup d'état intended to maintain the power and authority of the illustrious Nyiginya kingdom.[41] Musinga's father, Kigeri Rwabugiri, had ruled for almost 30 years between 1867 and 1895, in a near-constant mobilisation for war. Rwabugiri's warmongering was rooted in cattle ownership and control of land. Tutsi pastoralists looked down on Hutu cultivators who worked the land, assured of their own superiority. Before the colonisers arrived, the categories of Tutsi and Hutu already existed as occupational categories. Rwabugiri's warring saw him reach into regions dominated by Hutu cultivators. By making alliances with local Hutu and Tutsi leaders, Rwabugiri took into his service sizeable numbers of men from outside the traditional royal elite in order to increase his power. Martial ability and experience, the traits most useful to Rwabugiri's expansionist politics, would soon come to define both Hutu and Tutsi lineages.[42]

At the time of Rwabugiri's death in 1895, lineage heads of the regions occupied by his armies rejected the legitimacy of the Nyiginya court, setting in motion Musinga's ascension to the throne, in a period of great uncertainty marked by military struggle and shifting political loyalties among competing non-royal Hutu and Tutsi lineages.[43] When the Germans

---

39 Ibid., 179.
40 Thomson, *Rwanda*, 123–130.
41 Des Forges, *'Defeat is the Only Bad News'*, 3–24.
42 During his reign, Rwabugiri initiated numerous military campaigns to extend the scope and reach of his power through conquest to the south, the south-west, the west, the north-west, the north and the south-east. See Vansina, *Antecedents to Modern Rwanda*, 156–161. In the process, Rwabugiri made increasing demands for food, livestock and people in the regions under attack, in efforts to bring these outlying regions under his political and military control.
43 Vansina, *Antecedents to Modern Rwanda*, 33–35.

CHAPTER 10: Settler Genocide in Rwanda?

arrived at the court to declare their intention to maintain a military presence and pursue trade, the new king greeted them with open arms.[44]

Musinga and the Germans struck a deal that would shape the form and function of the modern Rwandan state. German military advantage gave Musinga's court the means necessary to incorporate restive outlying areas into the Nyiginya administrative grid, even as German-sponsored missionaries helped local populations resist court expansion.[45] Soon, the political and military goals of the Musinga court and the colonial vision of expanding German influence in Africa would converge in mutually beneficial ways. In areas outside the authority of the court, German colonial power would bring these regions to heel. At the same time, German authorities extended their influence through the expansion of court institutions, laying the foundations of the modern Rwandan state.

This brief historical detour explains how the ideologies of racial difference helped to normalise everyday forms of violence, starting at the moment of colonial contact in 1892. Everyday forms of violence help to foster and maintain a broader climate of fear and uncertainty in which civilians expect impunity for political and military crimes. As many scholars have explained, hundreds of thousands of ordinary citizens have died in Rwanda over the course of various intense struggles over power carried out by their leaders to control labour, land, pasture and crops.[46] As such, this imprecise understanding of Rwandan history has had immense political ramifications for civilians, including, but not limited to, those who took up the call to commit genocide in 1994.[47]

Everyday forms of violence

This section focuses on everyday forms of violence to understand how killing Tutsi became normalised in a context of fear, insecurity and confusion that made the call to genocide a legitimate social act.[48] This is not to suggest that

---

44 Musinga was not the heir-designate to Rwabugiri. In a period of extended turmoil, Musinga deposed his half-brother Rutarindwa, who had succeeded his father at the time of his death in September 1895. He acceded, following the political machinations and military manoeuvres of his mother, Kanjogera, and her warrior brothers of the Bakagara lineage of the royal Bega clan. See Des Forges, 'Defeat is the Only Bad News', 10–14; Vansina, Antecedents to Modern Rwanda, 165–191.

45 Des Forges, 'Defeat is the Only Bad News', 45–70.

46 Des Forges, Leave None to Tell the Story; Fujii, Killing Neighbors; Newbury, 'Ethnicity and the politics of history'; Straus, The Order of Genocide; Straus, Making and Unmaking Nations.

47 Newbury, 'Canonical conventions in Rwanda', 68–72.

48 The concept of 'the everyday' allows analysts to identify and theorise the unwritten and informal rules of everyday life. For a summary of the concept as employed by social

251

Rwandans who committed acts of genocide did so blindly or without a sense of personal responsibility. Indeed, scholars have documented that Hutu who killed Tutsi did so for various reasons beyond ethnic enmity, such as greed or revenge, even as they saved Tutsi they personally knew.[49] The literature on motivation for civilian participation also finds that state officials — military and political leaders alike — used their power and authority to incentivise people who were poor, giving them licence to loot and promising them the land and businesses of victims. I contend that the weight of the state and the power of economic incentive provided the impetus for ordinary Hutu to heed the call to commit acts of genocide. A focus on everyday forms of violence, notably their structural and symbolic forms, provides an avenue to think through how normalised, everyday forms of violence beget genocidal violence.

Violence is a slippery analytical concept. It is at once nonlinear, productive, destructive and reproductive insofar as violence gives birth to itself. Given this slipperiness, anthropologists and sociologists analyse violence along a continuum of harms, arguing that the violence of the everyday provides the necessary environmental conditions for genocidal violence when the social and political contexts are conducive.[50] In other words, mass killing campaigns have their roots in less dramatic everyday acts: exploitation, marginalisation, powerlessness and cultural imperialism.[51] Indeed, social scientists have demonstrated that domestic abusers and those who commit sexual assault are often themselves victims of beatings at home.[52] They have also documented the ways in which repressive political regimes resting on physical violence of torture, terror and other human

---

theorists, see Kalekin-Fishman D. 2013. 'Sociology of everyday life'. *Current Sociological Review*, 61, nos. 5–6, 714–732.

49 Fujii, *Killing Neighbors*; Straus, *The Order of Genocide*; Jefremovas V. 1995. 'Acts of human kindness: Hutu, Tutsi and genocide'. *Issue: A Journal of Opinion*, 23, no. 2, 28–31.

50 See for example Jones A. 2009. '"When the rabbit's got the gun": Subaltern genocide and the genocidal continuum', in *Genocides by the Oppressed*, 185–207; Kesselring R. 2017. *Bodies of Truth: Law, Memory, and Emancipation in Post-apartheid South Africa*. Stanford: Stanford University Press; Scheper-Hughes, *Death Without Weeping*.

51 Young I. 2004. 'Five faces of oppression', in *Oppression, Privilege, & Resistance: Theoretical Perspectives of Racism, Sexism and Heterosexism*, eds. L. Heldke & P. O'Connor. Boston: McGraw-Hill, 37–62.

52 Hudson V., et al 2014. *Sex and World Peace*. New York: Columbia University Press. For Rwanda-specific examples, see Burnet J.E. 2019. 'Rwanda: Women's political representation and its consequences', in *The Palgrave Handbook of Women's Political Rights*, eds. S. Franceschet, M.L. Krook & N. Tan. London: Palgrave Macmillan, 563–576; Burnet J.E. 2012b. 'Sexual violence, female agencies, and sexual consent: Complexities of sexual violence in the 1994 Rwandan genocide'. *African Studies Review*, 55, no. 2, 97–118.

CHAPTER 10: Settler Genocide in Rwanda?

rights abuses reproduce the violence that brought them to power in the first place.[53] Even as the victors proclaim peace, everyday forms of violence persist, and are often made more pointed in society through a series of 'little' violences found in the structures, habits and mentalities of everyday life, of what Mbembe calls 'the intimacy of tyranny'.[54] Thomas speaks to this intimacy in recounting the violence inherent in his everyday life in the distribution of food in his community:

> You see, before the genocide, we shared with our neighbours. It didn't matter who was Tutsi or who was Hutu. When there was a good harvest, we all ate. When there wasn't, we all went hungry. If someone broke with this idea of sharing, we would beat them into submission. If that person continued to steal, then they could experience a lot of pain. A pain I think they truly deserved. It was a form of justice for people like us [subsistence farmers].
>
> Elders would decide that someone had taken more than their share, so they would be called to account, and to make reparations. If they didn't come, or if they declined responsibility, then we knew they were not one of us. Rejecting to participate in community life could result in different kinds of punishment. In many cases, that person would get burned.[55] It was a way of maintaining harmony in our community. If you didn't share, or took more than you deserved, you would get excluded, beaten or burned. I remember being a young kid and seeing the father of one of my friends get burned. He died and no one talked about it because the punishment was said to be fair. I understood then,

---

53 Bourgois P. 2001. 'The power of violence in war and peace: Post-Cold War lessons from El Salvador'. *Ethnography*, 2, no. 1, 5–34; Fanon F. 1963. *The Wretched of the Earth*. New York: Grove Press, 254–261. For Rwanda-specific examples, see De Lame D. 2005. *A Hill among a Thousand: Transformations and Ruptures in Rural Rwanda*, trans. H. Arnold. Madison: University of Wisconsin Press.

54 Mbembe A. 1992. 'The banality of power and the aesthetics of vulgarity in the postcolony'. *Public Culture*, 4, no. 2, 22. See also Arendt H. 1969. *On Violence*. New York: Penguin Books, 35–56; Bourdieu P. & Wacquant L. 1992. *An Invitation to Reflective Sociology*. Chicago: University of Chicago Press, 167–173.

55 Thomas is referring to an extrajudicial form of mob justice known as 'necklacing', in which a redundant car tyre filled with gasoline is placed around the victim's arms and chest and set alight, resulting in death. In speaking about the necklacing incidents he witnessed as a child, Thomas is sanguine: 'Seeing someone get burned to death is a good form of justice because the punishment is quick and it is permanent. I'm glad the [current] government is not practising permanent justice as genocide is more complicated to understand than stealing food. If I killed to save myself and my family, should I burn? I know killing is bad, and is different than stealing food, but I was following orders! If you are told to kill or get killed, what are your choices, really? I wonder about this everyday as I sit and rot in this prison.'

> even as a young kid, what was expected of me to be a member of our community.[56]

Everyday violence situates acts of genocide on a continuum of harms that denies the humanity of a socially constructed other in so-called times of peace. The intellectual tie is in recognising the links between the violence of everyday life and explicit political terror or state repression.[57] The link is made through an appreciation of structural forms of violence — the violence of humiliation, exclusion, hunger and poverty — that act as the springboard for physical violence entailing bodily harm.[58] In turn, structural forms of violence produce and reproduce symbolic violence, that is, the violence embedded in modes of action and cognition, in which the individual internalises a feeling of being lesser than or undeserving.[59] Symbolic violence is also found in the social practice of accepting one's marginality or powerlessness as representative of the way society is structured, of accepting one's status 'as the way it has always been', in the way, for example, teenage sexual assault is often explained away as 'boys will be boys'. Taken together, symbolic and structural forms of violence assure individual and collective modes of submission or deference, imposing a measure of legitimacy on the social order of everyday violence as accepted and 'normal', for example the normalcy of labelling Tutsi as foreigners who do not deserve to be full members of Rwandan society in the postcolonial period, and the labelling of Hutu as simple, but good-natured, individuals who accepted their own lesser-than status as the natural order of things in the precolonial and colonial periods.

Everyday forms of violence operate on a continuum of normalised harms, rooted in a system of domination that links the rulers to the ruled through a sociality of intimacy that normalises class, gender and racial inequalities.[60] These inequalities manifest in society as family violence,

---

56 Fieldnotes, July 2006. Thomas was around eight years old in 1982 when he witnessed his first public necklacing. This means he was around 19 or 20 years old in 1994 when the genocide started.

57 Bourdieu & Wacquant, *Invitation to Reflective Sociology*; Taussig M. 1992. *The Nervous System*. New York: Routledge, 29–35.

58 Farmer P. 1997. 'On suffering and structural violence: A view from below', in *Social Suffering*, eds. A. Kleinman, V. Das & M. Lock. Berkeley: University of California Press, 261–283. Galtung J. 1969. 'Violence, peace and peace research'. *Journal of Peace Research*, 6, no. 3, 167–191; Scheper-Hughes, *Death Without Weeping*, 286–296.

59 Bourdieu P. 2001. *Masculine Domination*. Stanford: Stanford University Press; Lindner, 'Genocide, humiliation, and inferiority'.

60 Mbembe 'Banality of power', 29 refers to normalised gender, race and class inequalities as 'a practice of conviviality' that asks analysts to 'be attentive to the myriad ways in which ordinary people bridle, trick, and actually toy with power instead of confronting

CHAPTER 10: Settler Genocide in Rwanda?

gender violence, hate crimes, racial violence, police violence, terrorism and war, all of which are sanctioned or supported by the state, and which exist in all societies.[61] In this way, the accepted, unquestioned 'normality' of these inequalities as a product of the political order is at the heart of the operation of everyday violence in any society.[62] In the Rwandan case, everyday forms of violence are the result of both the policy choices of elite Tutsi in the precolonial period and the decisions they made with European colonisers to assure their continued rule. The result, as we have seen, was the foundation of embedded unquestioned norms and habits about ruler and ruled, as well as the emergence of particular moral qualities of being Hutu or Tutsi that, in turn, were made real in the lives of civilians in the postcolonial period, as will be demonstrated in the next section.

As such, Tutsi-Hutu relations can be read as a mode of ruler-ruled dominion given the political, economic and cultural dominance of Tutsi elites. In this reading, Rwandan society is characterised by two ethnic classes: Tutsi oppressors and Hutu oppressed. This takes on a special salience given the minority status of Tutsi in Rwandan society. In the telling of postcolonial Hutu elites, ethnic Tutsi are settlers who gained control of the Rwandan state during the colonial period with the express purpose of subjugating the hard-working and earnest Hutu majority.[63] In response, postcolonial political and military elites kept on simmer the possibility that they could call upon their Hutu brethren to annihilate their Tutsi oppressors. This framing meant that all Tutsi, whether politically connected or not, became a common enemy when so labelled by the state. Regime rhetoric kept alive the idea that power-hungry Tutsi could once again try to oppress the Hutu majority to return them to precolonial forms of indentured servitude, when a capricious Tutsi royal court ruled.[64] And,

---

directly'; Mbembe. Scott takes a similar approach, focusing on the public performance of deference and loyalty of subordinate groups to understand how domination works in practice; see Scott J. 1990. *Domination and the Arts of Resistance: Hidden Transcripts.* New Haven: Yale University Press.

61 See Straus, *Making and Unmaking Nations*, 273–321, for an analysis of the conditions that make genocide the government policy of choice through his study of cases where political violence did not cascade to genocide. His study focuses on how political and military leaders frame threats and define goals to deal with those threats to the social order. I contend that this elite framing legitimises the presence of everyday violence in society. Indeed, all societies are beset by difference. What makes genocide possible is how these differences are made real in people's lives in a particular social and political context.

62 Mac Ginty R. 2014. 'Everyday peace: Bottom-up and local agency in conflict-affected societies'. *Security Dialogue*, 43, no. 3, 213–229.

63 Desrosiers, 'Rethinking political rhetoric', 199.

64 Based on identity-card data collected by the colonial administration, 16 per cent of Rwandans were Tutsi, 83 per cent Hutu and 1 per cent Twa at the end of colonialism in

CIVILIAN-DRIVEN VIOLENCE AND THE GENOCIDE OF INDIGENOUS PEOPLES

as Straus notes, the 1994 genocide was the choice of 'an outmaneuvered, vengeful and ideologically committed hardliner [Hutu] elite [in] response to their imminent defeat, their sense of betrayal, and their outrage at the killing of their leader'.[65]

What, then, are the forms of everyday violence that provided the fertile ground for genocide to be enacted? The Belgian anthropologist Danielle de Lame analyses how competing founding myths of Tutsi and Hutu are rooted in a long-standing culture of violence, focused on avenging the losses of one's lineage.[66] This right of revenge results in the omnipresence of fear shaped by a near-constant threat, including loss of life in both periods of peace and war. Public displays of power and dominance were informed by precolonial royal authority, as the authority and legitimacy of precolonial Tutsi kings was built on 'the right to kill and to enrich'.[67] The cycles of revenge that characterise the historical resolution of political conflict in Rwanda mean that those elites who employed violence to hold power feared later being targeted for death in response to the violence they ordered, putting those in their lineage at risk of retributional violence. Elite power struggles — shaped by winner-takes-all conflicts and the historical exclusion of the losers in politics and the economy — also have important implications for the security of ordinary people, for they live with the effects of elite decisions taken in their name. Both Hutu and Tutsi tie their emotional and physical security to a righting of past wrongs. History is cyclical, meaning Hutu elites are to revenge the hurts and losses of all Hutu, while Tutsi elites are to do the same for all Tutsi.

The result is an omnipresent threat of violence stemming from the highest levels of the state, with political and military elites dictating policy, programmes and practice down the hierarchy to local government officials, who then ensure that the rural masses carry out the orders as instructed. Local leaders, in turn, monitor the activities and speech of individuals within their bailiwick. Compliance with government directives is paramount, as is knowing and respecting one's place in the hierarchy. Respect for authority and hierarchy is everything. Those suspected of disrespecting authority, or of questioning 'how things are', can be beaten by neighbours, illegally sent to prison by an offended official, denied access to community spaces, such as church, through social shunning or rejection. Underpinning these

---

1962. Newbury, *Cohesion of Oppression*, 3.
65 Straus, *Making and Unmaking Nations*, 313.
66 De Lame, *A Hill among a Thousand*, 487.
67 Des Forges, *Leave None to Tell the Story*, 159.

CHAPTER 10: Settler Genocide in Rwanda?

everyday harms is a culture of individual humiliation and political exclusion rooted in the lesser-than status of non-elite ordinary Rwandans, whether poor urbanites or rural subsistence farmers, Hutu and Tutsi alike. Jean-Paul, a Hutu man accused of genocide and sentenced to life in prison in 2005, highlights this sense of humiliation and exclusion:

> You see, I am an unimportant person. I was born to poor parents without much land. I am barely educated and I'm not yet married. This means I will never be an important person, even if I try and try to lift myself up. When I met someone more powerful than me, I lower my head and try not to be seen. I say nothing, even when I feel bothered by what is being said. Why? Because it is a useless effort to even try when those of who want to do more or be different are targeted for trying to be something other than a farmer.

> When someone important, like, say, a police officer or my *conseiller* [local official], asks for community participation, I must go, otherwise I know I might get beaten up, or made to pay a fine or even put in jail for disobeying. It doesn't matter what I think, because I am only to listen and do what is told, not to think about the nature of the order or ask questions about why the decision was taken in this way or that way. Now, I killed Tutsi and even one Hutu who didn't believe that Tutsi wanted our land and our women. So I am guilty. But of what? Of being poor and unmarried and without hope in my life because of high politics. Leaders said very plainly, in speeches on the radio, that if we didn't kill Tutsi they will be the ones to cut our throats. I couldn't believe that my Tutsi neighbours would kill but then, over time, I began to wonder as there was less to eat, less to share and more demands from the authorities. What was I to think when I heard, over and over and over again, words about cutting throats?[68] In Rwanda, if you don't follow along, you can get into serious trouble. Now the [current] government is made up of Tutsi so Hutu like me will surely rot in prison. Rwanda is no longer for Hutu so I must shut up and accept my fate. What other choice do I have, really?[69]

For the average Rwandan, class status shapes the violence of daily life. As Jean-Paul's testimony illustrates, a person's class is informed by the degrees

---

68 Jean-Paul seems to be referring to the kill-or-be-killed language that framed government speeches during the civil war. Des Forges analyses the messaging of Tutsi vermin and scum and the need for Hutu self-defence. See *Leave None to Tell the Story*, 85–86. The radio was a crucial vector in framing all Tutsi as the source of Hutu insecurity. Radio made talk of killing Tutsi a popular topic of everyday conversation, shared through jokes, music and on-air banter. Des Forges, *Leave None to Tell the Story*, 70, 315–316.

69 Interview, April 2006.

of inequality experienced as a result of economic position, social status and access to networks of elite persons of prominence. Your location in the hierarchy further shapes how you are likely to exploit degrees of difference, giving local elites social and political power relative to their standing. Knowing your station in life and understanding who is more or less important than you is central to successfully navigating Rwandan social and political life. Lesser or low-status Rwandans understand 'being important' or 'being a high person' as code for people who are more powerful than they are, just as important people know their equals and superiors. Poor people — whether Tutsi, Hutu or Twa — call those in positions of power over them *abaryi* (eaters), highlighting their awareness that they are unable to make ends meet, while officials appear to get fat at the trough of government. Access to resources — economic, social and cultural — are further shaped by racism. Historically, the elite Tutsi sense of superiority to Hutu 'appears more elitism than racism'.[70] The attitudes and behaviour of both Hutu and Tutsi, regardless of economic class, are racist toward members of the minority Twa, representing historically and today just one per cent of the Rwandan population.[71] Hutu and Tutsi alike have systematically scorned Twa, based on their physical stature as forest-dwelling pygmies, denying them basic courtesies of community membership, such as sharing food and drink, participating in church life, or intermarriage.[72]

Given this structural environment, everyday violence takes multiple forms, shaped by one's ethnic and class position in society. The majority of rural poor, Hutu and Tutsi alike, struggle to make ends meet in day-labour jobs that are offered at the whim of local employers, who are often also local military officials or political leaders. These officials are armed, carrying guns, batons and other weapons, to remind the population of the ever-present possibility of state-sanctioned bodily harm.[73] Individual stresses about access to employment are shaped by lack of access to land, a process controlled by the leadership of the day. Young men engage in excessive drinking, sometimes leading to fist fights, which are tolerated by community members. These fights are sometimes the product of access to resources, including land, but also to things such as bicycles and building supplies. A

---

70 Des Forges, 'Ideology of genocide', 44.
71 Thomson, *Rwanda*, 24.
72 Des Forges, *Leave None to Tell the Story*, 69.
73 Wagner M.D. 1998. 'All the *bourgmestre*'s men: Making sense of genocide in Rwanda' *Africa Today*, 25, no. 1, 25–36.

CHAPTER 10: Settler Genocide in Rwanda?

Rwandan man cannot mature to social adulthood without founding a family.[74] Having a family means courting a wife and demonstrating the ability to provide for one's family. Fights over women are common, particularly among young men of marriageable age. The social and sexual behaviour of young women is monitored, mostly by older women — sisters, mothers and senior wives — but also by men, to ensure that they behave according to cultural codes of being quiet and submissive.[75]

The boundaries of social and political life, and the resulting culture of impunity, are in part created and maintained by the continuum of everyday violence, which operates from the micro and often private sphere of jokes, proverbs, vulgarities and folktales intended to humiliate, dehumanise or denigrate the other. Multiple examples are found in the register of Rwandan proverbs, riddles and poetry. Linguists have identified at least 2 500 proverbs, cataloguing them by theme, including political authority and power, ethnic relations, gender relations, policing sexual morality, elite and non-elite relations, justice, national unity and peace, to name a few.[76] For example, the proverb 'If you teach a Hutu to shoot a bow, he'll shoot an arrow into your stomach' highlights more than Tutsi distrust of Hutu; it is also used to justify the natural right of Tutsi to govern. Another example, 'In a court of fowls, the cockroach never wins his case', means that individuals of lesser status rarely receive justice because they lack the necessary political connections. Those who betray the political authority of the day can be labelled as 'dogs', worthy of death for the betrayal of their political masters. References to betrayal and dogs are both linked to proverbs that rationalise the presumed superiority of political elites over the rural masses. By communicating messages that cannot be expressed openly, proverbs are the underpinning of Rwandan political life. Proverbs set out the parameters of social behaviour, which in turn found fertile ground in the anti-Tutsi radio

---

74 Sommers M. 2011. *Stuck: Rwandan Youth and the Struggle for Adulthood*. Athens: University of Georgia Press, 25–30.

75 Jefremovas V. 1991. 'Loose women, virtuous wives, and timid virgins: Gender and the control of resources in Rwanda'. *Canadian Journal of African Studies*, 25, no. 3, 378–95. See also Burnet J.E. 2012a. *Genocide Lives in Us: Women, Memory, and Silence in Rwanda*. Madison: University of Wisconsin Press, 41–44; Thomson S. 2018b. 'Engaged silences as political agency in postgenocide Rwanda. Jeanne's story', in *Rethinking Silence, Voice and Agency in Contested Gendered Terrains*, eds. S. Parashar & J. Parpart. London: Routledge, 110–123.

76 Crépeau P. & Bizimana S. 1979. *Proverbes du Rwanda*. Tervuren: Musée royale de l'Afrique centrale.

CIVILIAN-DRIVEN VIOLENCE AND THE GENOCIDE OF INDIGENOUS PEOPLES

broadcasts, songs, editorials and cartoons that dominated Rwandan media between 1992 and 1994.[77]

Proverbs as an expression of political dominion are the gateway from speech to tolerated forms of private and public violence, as part of the continuum of everyday violence — from wife beating or child abuse in the privacy of the home to public violence, such as rape and physical assault, or extreme forms, such as necklacing. These tolerated and normalised forms of violence, are the backbone of pervasive and patterned acts of physical and sexual violence, sanctioned by the authorities of the day. In turn, these normalised patterns of atrocity, such as pogroms or massacres, prepare the ground for systematic campaigns of genocidal violence.[78] In Rwanda, contests over political power cultivated a dynamic of fear that put ordinary people in a defensive posture as political elites jockeyed for primacy in a state system designed for hierarchy and compliance.[79] As such, Rwandan political culture, as well as its top-down state system, made the transmission of a singular and all-encompassing directive for genocide possible and actionable. The substance of the message was made through norms of everyday violence that allowed for the othering of Tutsi, while also reminding Hutu, in particular ordinary men like Jean-Paul and Thomas, of their civic duty to commit acts of genocide. Everyday violence as the primary vector of civilian violence, infused with an ideology of Tutsi as wily foreigners, is what made genocidal violence not only thinkable, but also actionable in the Rwandan context.[80]

Putting ideology into action

In Rwanda, a genocidal message made the difference in prompting civilians to kill, often repeatedly. Understanding how ordinary men, such as Thomas, choose to kill requires an understanding of the broader context in which the genocidal message was received. As Fujii notes, 'people must be emotionally charged and psychologically prepared' for the work of killing neighbours. The primary prompt was the normalising of a collective sense of fear, as Hutu leaders employed tropes of Tutsi foreigners to both prompt a sense of duty and inculcate fear to incentivise civilian Hutu to kill. From 1990 to 1993, senior military officials oversaw the recruitment of Hutu civilians to

---

77 Taylor C. 2004. 'Visions of the "oppressor" in Rwanda's pre-genocidal media', in *Genocides by the Oppressed*, 122–137.
78 Baines E. 2003. 'Body politics and the Rwandan crisis'. *Third World Quarterly*, 24, no 3, 479–493; Burnet 'Sexual violence'.
79 Newbury, 'Ethnicity and the politics of history', 17.
80 Des Forges, 'Ideology of genocide', 45–46.

CHAPTER 10: Settler Genocide in Rwanda?

stage attacks against Tutsi in the form of practice massacres and the burning of Tutsi homes and other property.[81] These forms of violence are part of the continuum of everyday violence as ordinary indignities translate into accepted modes of political repression, sanctioned by the state.

Practice murders, then, provided a veil of legitimacy to the call to Hutu civilians to remain vigilant to the threat posed by Tutsi. They also allowed local officials to set up civilian defence militias, comprised of Hutu men, whose norms and practices had their origin in football clubs. The first to be trained were members of youth football leagues.[82] Soon, the clubs became militarised under the mentorship of government party loyalists and businessmen, particularly as the civil war intensified, morphing into a form of state-sanctioned and -funded civil defence patrols at local level and government militias at national level.

The practice of civil defence provided poorer, rural Hutu with the necessary training to kill. As Wagner explains, civil defence patrols helped to develop the shared vocabulary of a common Tutsi enemy, as well as the techniques for identifying and seeking out 'enemies of the [Hutu] people' and their 'accomplices'.[83] These state-sponsored practice murders taught civilians three important skills: how to kill on cue; that killing Tutsi was indeed a form of self-defence; and to reward, not punish, those who took part.[84] Wagner makes clear the ideological weight of this political environment for ordinary Hutu men, with their 'eyes cast downward — because looking out was dangerous — practising the survival tactic of not seeing and not feeling in a climate rife with insecurity, political violence, military invasion, aggression and fear'.[85] Jean-Bosco, a poor rural farmer who I interviewed in 2006, said the same: 'You see, normal relations of being neighbours had broken down. It became dangerous to think about anyone but yourself and your family. Sharing and other daily activities were monitored. Those who showed concern for Tutsi could end up in jail, or worse.'[86]

This broader climate of fear and insecurity was bolstered by the ideological dominance among the Hutu political and military elite of a hierarchical, nationalist 'founding narrative' that framed the civil war that preceded the 1994 genocide in identity terms.[87] The founding narrative is

---

81 Fujii, 'Transforming the moral landscape', 107.
82 Thomson, *Rwanda*, 266, n. 35.
83 Wagner, 'All the *bourgmestre*'s men', 30.
84 Des Forges, *Leave None to Tell the Story*, 89–90; Fujii, 'Transforming the moral landscape', 108.
85 Wagner, 'All the *bourgmestre*'s men', 30.
86 Interview, August 2006.
87 Straus, *Making and Unmaking Nations*, 275.

the Hutu social revolution. Drawing on the myths of history analysed above, this narrative held that since the majority Hutu have long suffered persecution at the hands of their Tutsi overlords, Hutu should organise themselves to prevent a return to Tutsi power and oppression of Hutu.[88] How then did a climate of fear catalyse genocide? The development of an ideology of genocide, in this case crafting a genocidal message that exploited Hutu-Tutsi relations, has been a common tactic of political elites when their rule is threatened.[89] Hutu elites employed a carefully elaborated myth of history to frame Tutsi as foreign invaders who had stolen Rwanda from its rightful inhabitants, the Hutu. As Hamites, Tutsi shared no natural kinship with Hutu, who were of Bantu origin. This historical narrative was broadcasted, mostly via radio, but also in the speeches of Hutu leaders to the Hutu masses. The language of genocide, of exterminating all Tutsi, regardless of occupation or class, became an everyday subject of conversation, and, as such, imaginable. This founding myth of Tutsi persecution as the cardinal source of Hutu oppression became a story of self-defence rooted in historical injustices, which are in turn recognisable as everyday forms of structural and symbolic violence.

Again, this is not to suggest that ordinary Hutu civilians in pre-1994 Rwanda were preprogrammed to commit acts of genocide. Conceptually, everyday forms of violence are linked to the militarisation of society, understood as war readiness characterised by a strong military capability used to defend or promote national interests. Rwanda's martial history of rewarding violence in pursuit of the interests of the state meant that ordinary people were predisposed to accepting a final solution of exterminating all Tutsi to solve the political problem of power-sharing with the RPF. But it does not explain the relationship between a climate of fear and popular civilian participation in the 1994 genocide. Genocide is a complex and sense-defying phenomenon. It is also an extreme form of violence, thankfully rare, and indeed a risky one for political and military leaders who make the call — and for men like Thomas, who find themselves on the losing side of elite decisions — to kill. Genocide is intentional and cannot be conjured out of thin air. The political and economic conditions must be ripe, in addition to there being an able and willing leadership and a compliant population. As genocide scholars have persuasively documented, the casual rule of thumb is 'no war, no genocide'.[90] The civil war launched by the rebel RPF

---

88 Thomson, *Rwanda*, 43–46.
89 Desrosiers, 'Rethinking political rhetoric', 219–220.
90 Straus, *Making and Unmaking Nations*, 34–53.

CHAPTER 10: Settler Genocide in Rwanda?

would fundamentally change the political and military climate in Rwanda. The RPF invasion from Uganda in October 1990 ended a period of relative calm and prosperity that many Rwandans — Tutsi and Hutu, rural peasant and urban elite — had enjoyed since the 1973 coup, when Habyarimana had taken power from Rwanda's first postcolonial president, Kayibanda.

By the late 1980s, Habyarimana's regime was reeling from multiple internal and external shocks. World prices for coffee and tea, Rwanda's primary exports, fell precipitously, resulting in famine, mass unemployment and a dramatic drop in government revenues.[91] At the same time, Western states adopted democracy as their new pet project, tying foreign aid packages to domestic political reform, as they continued to apply the bitter pill of structural adjustment.[92] With the RPF invasion, Habyarimana's one-party state had a full-fledged crisis brewing: a military war with Tutsi rebels, a political war with Hutu opponents clamouring for pluralism, less foreign aid, and an increasingly restive population worried about the source of their next meal. The civil war, initiated by a Tutsi-led rebel group, gave political entrepreneurs in Habyarimana's inner circle the cover to employ historical images of Tutsi as enemy, foreigner and oppressive overlord. It was easy to recover this perception of Tutsi masters, given that the Hamitic myth of the colonial period had long been packaged in classrooms across Rwanda, delivered by European or European-educated teachers.[93] Tutsi superiority over Hutu, and the utter dismissal of Twa, were staples of Rwanda's political history, understood through the lived experience of ordinary Rwandans, who knew first hand the repressive nature of Tutsi dominion during the colonial period.[94] Acute civilian insecurity, tied to a fear-based, all-consuming message about the looming threat Tutsi posed to Hutu as Rwanda's rightful inhabitants, created the conditions for the order of genocide to take effect, in an environment beset by symbolic forms of everyday violence: the distortions and political uses of history to create in- and out-groups of oppressed Hutu and oppressive Tutsi. The nationalist aspirations of Hutu hardliners were grafted onto *all* Tutsi, regardless of income, occupation or political affiliation.

When Habyarimana was assassinated on 6 April 1994, his supporters blamed the RPF and the Hutu political opposition for his murder. His death marked the moment at which Hutu hardliners took control of the govern-

---

91 Thomson, *Rwanda*, 64.
92 Uvin P. 1998. *Aiding Violence: The Development Enterprise in Rwanda*. West Hartford, CT: Kumarian Press, 40–50.
93 Des Forges, 'Ideology of genocide', 45.
94 Thomson, *Whispering Truth to Power*, 47–75.

ment, eliminating Hutu political opponents who sought to continue peace talks with the RPF.[95] In wresting control of the state from Hutu political moderates, political and military hardliners initiated their plan for genocide. It rested on an existing climate of fear of the Tutsi other. Hardliners — those bent on eliminating Tutsi and holding on to power — 'engendered the civilian administration and the civilian population to identify, sort and destroy Tutsi civilians across the small nation of some seven million inhabitants'.[96]

As Guichaoua makes clear in his research on the causes of the genocide, there was no sophisticated preplanning to methodically kill Tutsi.[97] Instead, he persuasively documents the gradual emergence of a genocidal policy instituted by Colonel Théoneste Bagosora and other Hutu hardliners around 12 April 1994. By this time, just one week after Habyarimana's death, it was clear that the Hutu hardliners, led by Bagosora and a handful of senior politicians from Habyarimana's own MNRD party, would be unable to end the civil war and stake their claim to State House. The rebel RPF, under Paul Kagame's military leadership, was simply too strong to be quickly and easily defeated. Genocide, as a political and military solution, became the strategy of choice, with civilians having long been primed to enact the goals of Hutu nationhood at the expense of Tutsi lives. When the genocide ended and the RPF finally took State House in late July 1994, some 175 000 to 250 000 ordinary Hutu civilians had acted on the call to commit genocide. The imperative to kill was rooted in Tutsi foreignness, as well as in economic deprivation, a point succinctly made by Jean-Bosco: 'I did not think the Tutsis would come to kill us to steal land, but when the government broadcast that the RPF came to take our land, steal our women, and would kill all Hutu, I got really scared. It was said over and over again — on the radio but also in speeches by officials. I really feared for me and my family.'[98] Jean-Bosco, Jean-Paul and Thomas, and thousands of Rwandans like them, acted on what they believed to be true and real. The result was a '"cottage-industry" genocide that reached out to all levels of the population'. [99]

Conclusion

Identifying continuums of everyday violence offers a systematic way to understand and explain the analytical link between often invisible yet

---

95 Straus, *The Order of Genocide*, 224–227.
96 Straus, *Making and Unmaking Nations*, 274.
97 Guichaoua, *From War to Genocide*, 143–292.
98 Interview, August 2006.
99 Des Forges, 'Ideology of genocide', 44.

normalised processes of exploitation, marginalisation and powerlessness that in turn legitimate state-led violence and repression. As such, structural and symbolic forms of routinised, bureaucratised and banal forms of racialised, classed and gendered violence lay the institutional groundwork for genocidal violence. Competing founding myths, of Tutsi as innately superior and Hutu as rightful inhabitants, provided the necessary fodder to frame the genocidal message of 1994 in historical terms. As such, Hutu hardliners were able to diffuse a genocidal norm that resonated with Hutu civilians, men like Jean-Bosco and Thomas, who, in their own telling, killed Tutsi in a kill-or-be-killed environment.

An analytical focus on the everyday forms of violence opens up the possibility of understanding and explaining why civilian Hutu perpetrated acts of genocide. It adds a layer of nuance to the idea that Hutu killed willingly or blindly, and situates state-led violence on a continuum that makes everyday forms of violence recognisable in times of so-called peace. As such, we see how individuals can be primed to kill, by linking the normalised violence of the everyday to abnormal times of war and genocide. In other words, to explain why ordinary civilians take up the call to genocide, we need to be able to understand the framework of everyday forms of structural and symbolic violence — of the less dramatic, permitted and even rewarded everyday acts that promote the possibility of participation in genocidal acts, given the right cocktail of political and economic conditions. The first step is to recognise that genocide, as a form of mass political violence, is part of a continuum of violence that is socially incremental and experienced by civilians — victims, perpetrators, rescuers and bystanders — as expected and routine, as embedded in everyday race, class and gender relations.

CHAPTER ELEVEN

Colonialism, Frontiers, Genocide: Civilian-Driven Violence in Settler Colonial Situations

Lorenzo Veracini

In *Hitler's Ostkrieg and the Indian Wars,* Edward Westermann observes that the US did not enact a policy of 'intentional genocide' in the nineteenth century, while Nazi Germany in the twentieth century obviously did. Westermann then concludes that this was because *at the centre*, that is, in Washington, DC, there was 'no consensus'.[1] Westermann acknowledges that, at the margins, away from the capital, there were frequent calls for extermination, but considers that the Indian reservations enabled survival, whereas this would not be the case in Eastern Europe for targeted populations. The relationship between settler colonialism as a mode of domination and genocide has been analysed in what is by now an important debate, and a similar discussion has addressed the relationship between American history specifically and genocide. I refer to a 2016 book, but historians have for some time extensively compared processes leading to the formation of the settler colonial polities with those of Nazi Germany.[2]

---

1   Westermann E.B. 2016. *Hitler's Ostkrieg and the Indian Wars: Comparing Genocide and Conquest.* Norman: University of Oklahoma Press.
2   Thornton R. 1987. *American Indian Holocaust and Survival: A Population History since 1492.* Norman: University of Oklahoma Press; Stannard D.E. 1992. *American Holocaust: The Conquest of the New World.* Oxford: Oxford University Press; Churchill W. 1997. *A Little Matter of Genocide: Holocaust and Denial in the Americas, 1492 to the Present.* San Francisco: City Lights Books; Moses A.D., ed. 2005. *Genocide and Settler Society: Frontier Violence and Stolen Indigenous Children in Australian History.* New York: Berghahn Books; Kiernan B. 2007. *Blood and Soil: A World History of Genocide and Extermination from Sparta to Darfur.* New Haven: Yale University Press; Moses A.D. & Stone D., eds. 2008. *Colonialism and Genocide.* Abingdon: Routledge; Alvarez A. 2014. *Native America and the Question of Genocide.* Lanham: Rowman & Littlefield; Anderson G.A. 2014. *Ethnic Cleansing and the Indian: The Crime That Should Haunt America.* Norman: University of Oklahoma Press; Woolford A., Benvenuto J. & Hinton A., eds. 2014. *Colonial Genocide in Indigenous North America.* Durham: Duke University Press; Madley B. 2016. *An American Genocide: The United States and the California Indian Catastrophe, 1846–1873.* New Haven: Yale University Press; Hasian M. 2019. *Debates on Colonial Genocide in the 21st Century.* Houndmills: Palgrave; Whitt L. & Clarke A. 2019. *North American Genocides: Indigenous Nations, Settler Colonialism, and International Law.* Cambridge: Cambridge University Press.

CHAPTER 11: Colonialism, Frontiers, Genocide

In my opinion, contributors to these needed and overdue debates have been getting the sequence wrong: it is not that settler colonialism is genocidal, it is genocide that is settler colonial. Patrick Wolfe's seminal article on the 'logic of elimination' argued that settler colonialism is not always genocidal.[3] The corollary to his intuition that settler colonialism eliminates in a variety of ways and not necessarily by physically exterminating Indigenous collectives — Wolfe had assimilation in mind — is that physical elimination is inevitably about the radical reconstitution of space. But the reconstitution of space — turning place into space and then into place again — in the specific context of the settler colonial frontier, the prospect of turning Indigenous place into settler place is inevitably settler colonial. Note, however, that a prospect is not an inevitability: what happens on the ground is rarely what happens in the representations of settlers.[4] One category is a subset of the other: genocide is one of the possible outcomes of settler colonial processes. Reflecting on the origins of genocide, Zygmunt Bauman famously noted that states are 'gardeners' and that they see the minorities under their control as 'weeds'.[5] But that this metaphor is settler colonial should be pointed out: the settler colonies, after all, were once called 'plantations'. Colonialism and genocide are related.

The first and second sections of this chapter proposes a heuristic framing for understanding colonialism as violence. On the basis of this understanding, the third section engages with the interventions collected in this book. Settler frontiers are sites that empires, states, their bureaucracies and their armies find hard to reach, even if often this disconnect is only temporary. Their power dissolves, exhausted by distance. When they reach, they rely on settler communities and follow their lead. Even if genocide is typically implemented by a state, as a massive literature has explored in regard to Europe and the twentieth century, genocides happen on settler colonial frontiers too. The characteristic determinants of genocidal circumstances are often there: motive, opportunity and radicalisation. When genocides occur on remote frontiers, they are likely to be civilian-driven.

---

3   Wolfe P. 2006. 'Settler colonialism and the elimination of the native'. *Journal of Genocide Research*, 8, no. 4, 387–409.
4   A related argument is offered in Short D. 2016. *Redefining Genocide: Settler Colonialism, Social Death and Ecocide*. London: Zed Books.
5   See Bauman Z. 1989. *Modernity and the Holocaust*. Cambridge: Polity Press, 92; and Moses A.D. 2008b. 'Genocide and modernity', in *The Historiography of Genocide*, ed. D. Stone. Houndmills: Palgrave Macmillan, 189.

What is colonialism?

I am a comparative historian of colonial phenomena. I teach an undergraduate course entitled 'Colonialism: A Global History'. It focuses heuristically on a succession of global expansionary 'waves' and defines colonialism as a relationship — an unequal one premised on displacement. There are, of course, many unequal relationships; they are all predicated on different vectors of difference — gender, religion, language, ability and many more. Displacement, a foundational displacement that establishes metropole and colony as co-constituting entities occupying separate locations, is one such vector among many, and they all mix on the ground according to shifting dynamics. In the global narrative developed in this course, settler colonialism constitutes a third wave that follows the initial colonial onslaught in the Americas and Indian Ocean, and the establishment of a slave-driven plantation economy in the Atlantic basin. Settler communities had been established already, but they were for a long time marginal, located in unpromising areas, supported by colonial upstarts, populated by generally 'disreputable' individuals, numbed by isolation, and far from their original cultural centres. It is only with what James Belich has called the global 'settler revolution' of the nineteenth century that settlers became central; the transport and the industrial revolutions had made the temperate prairies, for example, accessible, productive and profitable.[6] This is relatively late in the context of a global history that had begun three centuries earlier.

And yet, the global settler revolution reorganised space at a rapid rate. It resulted in several 'neo-Europes' firmly located where there previously were none — unavoidable geopolitical facts of the ground. The revolution had an ideological dimension too: it upended the relationship between metropole and periphery.[7] The centre now was at the margin. It was in the neo-Europes that new types of socio-political organisation were tested, and where allegedly better specimens of humanity were to reproduce, characterised by terms such as New Zealand's 'better Britons', Australia's 'coming man', or Zionist 'sabras'. Of course, this 'revolution' was global in the sense that it was operating simultaneously in all continents, but it only invested specific macroregions. Elsewhere, first- and second-wave colonialisms were subsumed by other colonial formations during the age of 'free trade impe-

---

6   Belich J. 2009. *Replenishing the Earth: The Settler Revolution and the Rise of the Anglo-World, 1783–1939*. Oxford: Oxford University Press.
7   'Neo-Europe' is Alfred Crosby's definition of settler society. See Crosby A. 2007. *Ecological Imperialism: The Biological Expansion of Europe, 900–1900*. 2nd ed. New York: Cambridge University Press.

CHAPTER 11: Colonialism, Frontiers, Genocide

rialism' — the fourth wave — before in turn being replaced by new colonial formations in a renewed mercantilist wave that accompanied and followed the imperialist 'scramble' — the fifth wave. Apart from affecting different regions at different times, first-, second- and third-wave colonialisms are distinct because they relied on different providers of colonial labour. The first relied on local subjugated labour; it found it *in situ*, partitioned it among the colonists — through, for example, the *encomienda* system — and consumed it at a fierce rate. The second imported labour from across the ocean as it organised the intensive production and commercialisation of colonial commodities. The third (settler colonialism), did not rely on colonised others, or aimed not to. In the imagination, even though very rarely in reality, the labour of the colonised was regarded as superfluous on settler colonial frontiers. On settler frontiers, wasting labour was not about dissipating a potential resource — it was a capital investment.

During the sixth global colonial wave, between the wars, many were aiming to combine selected elements of fifth- and third-wave colonialism. These are the settler projects that Susan Elkins and Caroline Pedersen have analysed in their seminal book on colonialism with settlers during the twentieth century.[8] The promoters of these colonial projects wanted the reorganisation of space that came with settlers. They wanted to establish communities of settlers — including the elimination of the native, or their permanent containment — but did not approve of the upending of the spatial relationship between metropole and periphery. The metropole remained central in their formulations. A note on containment as elimination: containment that is brought to its logical extreme is a nonrelation. Containment follows a logic of elimination that operates through space rather than time: from 'I do not entertain a relationship with you because you no longer exist', to 'I do not entertain a relationship with you because you are no longer here'. They are profoundly different stances, but when colonialism is understood as a relation it becomes clear that they follow the same logic.

Previously, third-wave colonialism (settler colonialism) had been an alternative to second- (mercantilism) or fourth-wave colonialisms (free-trade colonialism). Now fifth-wave colonialism (imperialism, Hobson style) was a prerequisite for sixth-wave colonialism (metropole-driven settler colonialism and associated projects of Indigenous containment). But colonialism with settlers is not settler colonialism. This undoing of displacement — according to this type of colonialism, metropole and settler colony

---

8   Elkins E. & Pedersen C., eds. 2005. *Settler Colonialism in the Twentieth Century: Projects, Practices, Legacies.* Abingdon: Routledge.

269

constituted a single political entity, for example France and Algeria — eventually reconnected and resubordinated the margins to the centre. Likewise, genocide — colonial genocide — was eventually brought back to Europe. It is in this context, of having to deal with irresolvable internal contradictions, that the conceptual separation between centre and periphery that is inbuilt in the colonial relationship — a separation that is typically demarcated by 'blue water', a non-space — was itself displaced in South Africa. Obsessively replicated on actually existing ground, which is space, it was added to the contradictions resulting from the need to reproduce and simultaneously limit the reproduction of colonised labour and contain it. Apartheid was indeed 'colonialism of a special type'.[9]

Which brings me to the other intervention I would like to offer: not only is genocide necessarily settler colonial (even though settler colonialism is not always genocidal or even successful — settlers often fail and not because they do not try). Westermann's distinction between centre and periphery as it pertains to settler frontiers gets the spatial relationship as well as the chronological sequence wrong. If one is looking at settler colonialism as a mode of domination, the centre is at the margin. In other words, settler colonialism is rhizomatic (a rhizome being a stem with multiple roots and shoots through which certain plants spread), whereas colonialism is arboreal (a plant that expands through a single trunk). Granted, colonialism and settler colonialism are equally violent modes of domination premised on unequal relationships and they are both predicated on displacement, but the former is centripetal, while the latter is dispersed, diffused, centrifugal.

This has important consequences as the state is unable or unwilling to reach remote frontiers because it is exhausted by distance. Since remote frontiers are defined negatively by the absence of the state, it is largely only civilians that are present; and when the representatives of the state are 101112in situ, they are often subordinate to settlers. Out there, the settlers effect the monopoly on force that elsewhere is held by the state; a monopoly

---

9   See Legassick M. & Wolpe H. 1976. 'The bantustans and capital accumulation in South Africa'. *Review of African Political Economy*, 7, 87–107.

10 For genocidal developments in such locales, see Adhikari M., ed. 2014. *Genocide on Settler Frontiers: When Hunter-Gatherers and Commercial Stock Farmers Clash*. Cape Town: UCT Press.

11 Weber M. 2015. 'Politics as vocation', in Waters T. & Waters D., eds.; *Weber's Rationalism and Modern Society: New Translations on Politics, Bureaucracy, and Social Stratification*. Houndmills: Palgrave Macmillan, 129–198.

12 This is a political dispensation that can be explored in its ongoing development. See Nutt S. 2018. 'Pluralized sovereignties: Autochthonous lawmaking on the settler colonial frontier in Palestine'. *Interventions: International Journal of Postcolonial Studies*, 21, no. 4.

that elsewhere, as Weber influentially argued, fundamentally defines the state. Out there, they claim special constitutive capabilities. Not only is the state not really there, the settlers are often themselves escaping the absolutist state. They undo its consolidation of sovereign capabilities by way of displacement. And when the state reaches the frontier, the settlers are often able to control it in its local reach. This is one of the results of the settler revolution: the settlers are hegemonic. Searching for the state in frontier genocides can be a moot undertaking. Conversely and paradoxically, as some of the essays gathered in this volume demonstrate, it is precisely because the state is distant and nimble, and because there is a political vacuum, that an even minimal state presence can become immediately and murderously significant.

As a massive literature has demonstrated, genocide at the centre is one response to social crisis. But the escape of settlers is a pre-emptive response to crisis: a displacement in the face of crisis therefore often results in genocides on remote frontiers. Enzo Traverso's work linked genocide and colonialism by pointing out that the colonies had been a long-lasting laboratory of genocidal practic1314es and that these practices were eventually reimported to Europe. He was developing an argument that Aimé Césaire and Hannah Arendt had already put forward.15 But it goes the other way round as well. Europe had been a laboratory of statecraft and centralisation, which had prompted the settler escape in the first place ('first place' seems an especially apt metaphor in this context) and the dispersal and genocides that followed. As Dirk Moses has concluded, genocide and modernity are intimately imbricated at the centre and at the periphery. We should take political geometry seriously, especially when displacement fundamentally defines all colonial formations. It is important that civilian-driven genocides in relatively remote locations should be understood in the context of a comparative analysis.

Colonialism as dissipated or accumulated violence

All unequal relationships are inherently violent: we are clear on this. Equal relationships can be violent too, of course, despite what Hegel presumed about an imagined 'legal state', but unequal ones are invariably violent. Colonialism unleashes violence as it is constituted in institutional forms.

---

13 See Traverso E. 2003. *The Origins of Nazi Violence*. New York: The New Press; and Moses, 'Genocide and modernity', 171.

14 See Césaire A. 1972 [1950]. *Discourse on Colonialism*. New York: Monthly Review, 36; Arendt A. 1994 [1955]. *The Origins of Totalitarianism*. New York: Harcourt, 155.

15 Moses, 'Genocide and modernity', 156–193.

That is why Marx, for example, who was developing an understanding of 'primitive accumulation' as stored-up violence for future use — as violence that had been contained and could appear as 'silent compulsion of economic relations', a powerful manufacturer of unequal relations — looked at in the colonies as well as in England.[16] In the case of chattel slavery, in a tropical plantation on some island somewhere producing colonial commodities to be traded in an expanding capitalist global network, violence is literally and periodically unleashed — there is leash in unleashing. If it is stored properly, if violence is unleashed and controlled at once, violence appears safely contained, but everyone knows that it is always and only superficially contained — slave rebellions and maroon republics populate the history of colonialism, as well as the nightmares of colonialists. When it is contained, one does not see violence precisely because it is effectively repressed. It is a paradox of colonial relationships: the absence of evidence is not evidence of absence, and references to 'peaceful settings' always invite a closer look.

So, just as capital is stored-up labour, colonialism can be understood as stored-up violence. Just as capital can be reproduced or is expended, colonialism as stored-up violence can be reproduced or superseded. Colonialism and settler colonialism can thus be conceptualised as distinct modes of domination because they rely on violence to, respectively, reproduce or supersede themselves: store it up or dissipate it. Primitive accumulation — violent appropriation and dispossession — in the case of colonialism is originary and results in an ongoing relationship. But in the case of settler colonialism as a mode of domination, premised on a logic of elimination, it is at once originary and final, hence continually repeated. Wolfe's famous conclusion that 'settler colonialism is a structure' in this context is another way of saying that settler colonialism perpetually appropriates in an originary way.[17] In the case of settler colonialism, violence enables the primitive accumulation of land, but violence is not stored up in relation to Indigenous labour, it is dissipated. When it comes to Indigenous labour, settler colonialism does not lead to primitive accumulation or proletarianisation; it is a process that might be described as primitive dissipation. Cedric Robinson's notion of 'racial capitalism' can be mobilised in order to understand the relationship between primitive accumulation and primitive dissipation: Robinson emphasised capitalism's

---

16 Marx K. 1967. *Capital*, vol. 1, c h 28. Available at: https://www.marxists.org/archive/marx/works/1867-c1/ch28.htm, accessed 27 May 2018.
17 Wolfe P. 1999. *Settler Colonialism and the Transformation of Anthropology: The Politics and Poetics of an Ethnographic Event*. London: Cassell, 163.

CHAPTER 11: Colonialism, Frontiers, Genocide

inability to universalise waged labour. Unfree labour was then racialised.[18] This is the key to relating capitalism's theft of time and settler colonialism's theft of space. Colonialism's theft of bodies constitutes a mix of two modes of domination: like capitalism, it exploits and extracts a surplus; and like settler colonialism, it results in permanent primitive accumulation. The wage relation is deferred. When and if the wage relation arrives, it is already neocolonial.

Settler colonialism is permanent primitive accumulation, not a type of primitive accumulation that is superseded by compulsion. The 'killing time' does not yield to the time of exploitation, and the moment of dispossession is never superseded. The theft of space does not yield to the theft of bodies and/or time. Bodies are indeed stolen, but typically for the purpose of dispossession, not accumulation, or for the purpose, as we will see below, of exploitation somewhere else.[19] It is interesting to note that recent debates about primitive accumulation as an ongoing phenomenon, a proposition that critiqued 'orthodox' Marxist narratives of primitive accumulation as a finite stage in capitalism's development, are paralleled by the emergence of settler colonial studies as an intellectual endeavour beside postcolonial perspectives: settler colonialism is as ongoing as the 'accumulation by dispossession' that characterises current capitalist dispensations.[20]

Violence that is originary and final is as good a definition of genocide as I can think of. At the end of settler colonialism, just as at the end of genocide, there is no relationship. It is in this sense that I argue that genocide is always settler colonial. Biopolitics in the metropole turns necropolitics in the colony — Foucault was inclined to neglect colonial settings, but Achille Mbembe does not.[21] But necropolitics turns thanatopolitics in settler colonial conditions. The difference between biopolitics and necropolitics is a crucial shift in focus from those the sovereign 'makes live' to those he 'lets die'; the difference between necropolitics and thanatopolitics is a shift in method; make live and let die are decoupled. In other words, biopolitics is famously about 'make live and let die'; necropolitics is about a colonial 'make die and let live'. In both instances life and death are simultaneous. Thanatopolitics is about

---

18 On the current relevance of Robinson's work, see for example, Kelley R.D.G. 2017. 'What did Cedric Robinson mean by racial capitalism?'. *Boston Review*, 12 January 2017. Available at: http://bostonreview.net/race/robin-d-g-kelley-what-did-cedric-robinson-mean-racial-capitalism, accessed 25 October 2018.

19 See Coulthard G.S. 2010. 'Place against empire: Understanding indigenous anti-colonialism', *Affinities*, 4, no. 2, 79–83.

20 See Harvey D. 2003. *The New Imperialism*. Oxford: Oxford University Press.

21 Foucault M. 1977. 'The birth of biopolitics', in *Ethics, Subjectivity and Truth*. New York: The New Press, 73–79; Mbembe A. 2003. 'Necropolitics'. *Public Culture*, 15, no. 1, 11–40.

'make die' in a project of replacement; and settler colonialism is a project of replacement. Death and life remain nonsynchronous. Biopolitics is conducive to necropolitics — the result of colonialism is an unequal relationship that reproduces itself through time. Thanatopolitics is conducive to biopolitics — the result of settler colonialism is a sociopolitical collective that reproduces itself through time. Foucault intuited that the 'inverse' of biopolitics is 'thanatopolitics', which is genocide. Necropolitics is its opposite.[22] Opposite and inverse, of course, are not the same.

This brings me to another paradox: it is precisely because third-wave colonialisms are based on a foundational violence that is originary and final that settler colonial frontiers can often be represented as 'peaceful' and 'serene' settings. It is not just wishful thinking; peace is one result of unleashing violence without the intention of reproducing a relationship. Violence on settler frontiers erases the conditions for its reproduction — and yet its ostensible absence is ultimate evidence of its foundational pervasiveness. The ubiquitous myth of the 'peaceful settler' is a myth premised on a patently false comparative observation and syllogism. It goes like this: since in first- and second-wave colonial settings violence reproduces the conditions for its possibility, its nonreproduction on settler colonial frontiers must mean that settler colonialism is nonviolent. It is in this sense that I have argued elsewhere that colonialism and settler colonialism as modes of domination constitute each other in dialectical tension.[23] In the imagination of the settler, the settler is the end of history because in settler colonial settings — and especially in the settler's headspace, which is space after all — there is no further dialectic, no further relationship. Settler colonial spaces, or third-wave settings, are locales where violence is unleashed but not stored up. First- and second-wave colonialisms are, on the contrary, characterised by systematic endeavours to store it up. There are periodic outbursts in these settings — patently violent moments. In these cases, violence must be periodically released precisely because it must be reproduced.

Civilian-driven genocides

When it comes to figuring out unequal relationships, we have a variety of intellectual instruments at our disposal. The master-slave parable and colonial relationships are clearly related, even if Hegel did not necessarily have the colonies in mind when he figured it out — and even if a Fanonian

---

22 See Moses, 'Genocide and modernity', 175.
23 Veracini L. 2014. 'Understanding colonialism and settler colonialism as distinct formations'. *Interventions: International Journal of Postcolonial Studies*, 16, no. 5, 615–633.

CHAPTER 11: Colonialism, Frontiers, Genocide

critique of Hegel's logic of recognition demands a decolonising moment of violent rupture that Hegel did not consider.[24] The parable begins with a struggle, a struggle to the death between two individuals. It is significant that this struggle happens *before* the state, that is, that this struggle happens on a frontier.[25] One wins, one loses — it is a foundational moment. Then it can go either way. Violence can be stored up and reproduced; the slave becomes slave and the master becomes master. Or the violence can be dissipated and expended. More paradoxes: the storing-up of violence that underpins its reproduction is premised on a foundational act of mercy, as the future slave is spared and becomes a 'bondsman'; while ostensibly 'peaceful' settings — the 'whole world', which 'was once America' according to the Lockean *dictum* — are one result of mad, senseless vengeance. For the record: Hegel did not think that the future master could be as callous as to actually kill in cold blood, and assumed that the potential master knew that a master needs the bondsman, if not for the purpose of exploitation, then at least for the purpose of recognition, emancipation and developing his self-consciousness. But the settler annihilates Indigenous alterities. Perhaps the settler knows that at the end of the parable, there is a reversal and the master moves from independent freedom to dependency; perhaps the settler feels that he is not the end of history after all and lashes out.

If the centre is at the margin, and if the margin is out of the sovereign's reach, and if the settler is unleashing violence without the intention of reproducing it, and if he sees himself as the end of history, chances are that one is facing a civilian-driven genocide. Bauman believes that genocides are most likely when the sovereign has consolidated, when it has developed powerful destructive capabilities. But it is at the other extreme of this spectrum of possibility that genocide is also most likely: where the state has not even entered the scene, and where bureaucratic apparatuses are unable or unwilling to exercise their equally powerful restraining potential. The modern state is powerful whether it commits to genocide or whether it endeavours to prevent it.[26] Or where there is 'no consensus', as Westermann notes, which means equally that there is no ability to enforce state-driven

---

24 See Buck-Morss S. 2000. 'Hegel and Haiti'. *Critical Inquiry*, 26, no. 4, 821–865; Sankar A. 2019. 'Radical dialectics in Benjamin and Fanon: On recognition and rupture'. *Parrhesia*, 30, 120–136. Sankar cites Fanon: '[F]or Hegel, there is reciprocity; here [in the context of a colonial relation] the master laughs at the consciousness of the slave. What he wants from the slave is not recognition but work.' See Sankar, 'Radical dialectics', 123.

25 Hegel G.W.F. 1977 [1807]. 'Philosophy of right', in *Phenomenology*. Oxford: Oxford University Press, 57.

26 For a critique of Bauman's contention, see Moses, 'Genocide and modernity', 175.

CIVILIAN-DRIVEN VIOLENCE AND THE GENOCIDE OF INDIGENOUS PEOPLES

genocidal policies *and* no ability to prevent civilian-driven genocide from happening. But inability can and should be read as unwillingness. It is a slippery slope.

The essays collected in this volume offer a privileged point for observing this slope. They collectively explore the shifting dynamics of colonial violence, the shifting relationship between violence that is inflicted for the purpose of its storage and future use, and violence that is inflicted and dissipated at once for the purpose of pre-empting the possibility of its repetition. This collection offers a veritable global exploration of settler-driven genocidal violence over the *longue durée* across four continents. Historically, seafaring colonising Europeans encountered Africa first and then the Americas. Australia was last. Partially upending this volume's structure in the next paragraphs, I will review the essays collected in this volume following the same heliotropic imperial course.

Mohamed Adhikari's analysis of the first modern instance of settler colonial conquest demonstrates that the dialectic between dissipating and concentrating violence is at the very heart of the colonial relation — one of its foundational codes. The last recorded Indigenous insurrection in the Canary Islands was eventually repressed in 1496. Freebooters and marauders from a variety of European polities targeted the islands first, then slavers and *conquistadors* operated in the archipelago. Last were the settlers. It is significant that the conquest was funded through 'private means', that it was civilian-driven. The state could not reach because it was distant and because it had not yet even consolidated at home. Adhikari demonstrates that it was a recognisably genocidal process: slavery and deportation were the fate of the Indigenous peoples. Only a few were allowed to remain.

The acquisition of slaves remained the focus of the conquering Europeans because the islands lacked large-scale native settlements, mineral riches or tradeable spices, all features that could have sustained other modes of colonial interaction, and because Canarian slaves were needed in nearby Atlantic archipelagos. These islands had been uninhabited at the time of European discovery, with Madeira especially suitable for sugar production. There was a succession of conquests; the islands were conquered one by one: isolation undermined Indigenous resistance. Lanzarote and Fuerteventura were conquered by Normans who had to rely on some local allies; the larger and more populated islands were conquered at a later stage. By that time Spain and Portugal had become the main actors, even if they acted by proxy, allowing private agents to act in their name. Deporting resisters across the water was especially devastating for Indigenous collectivities. All island-conquests crucially relied on Indigenous allies, Indigenous collectives and

276

CHAPTER 11: Colonialism, Frontiers, Genocide

individuals who had decided to support invading Europeans in order to reduce the risk of their deportation. And yet, irrespective of whether they had sued for peace or even collaborated with the invaders, or whether they had been explicitly promised they would not be enslaved, all Indigenous Canarians were treated as 'enslaveable' and deported. Sugar production elsewhere made enslavement and transportation profitable, certainly more profitable in the short run than localised exploitation. As the islands were depopulated, conquistadors sought and obtained European settlers to repopulate them. They also imported slaves from the African mainland to grow sugar, a practice that further contributed to the erasure of Indigenous Canarian societies. In this instance, violence was stored up in order to be used elsewhere.

If Adhikari focuses on the West's first settler colonial genocide, Susan Thomson's chapter deals with one of genocide's most recent instantiations. Her intuition is that a settler colonial framework of interpretation underpins ethnic relationships in Rwanda. Ethnic Tutsi were routinely represented as inherently foreign. This is 'an idea that has received relatively little attention on the causes of the 1994 Rwandan genocide', she notes. Relatedly, Tutsi were represented as 'arrogant and wily invaders who sought to dominate the majority Hutu', which means that Tutsi were represented as settlers: exogenous dominators who must be prevented at all costs from dominating again. The 'Hamitic hypothesis' proffered by the colonial authorities before independence further reinforced this representational regime. Colonialism 'extended the reach of the state' and reinforced this representational regime, but Thomson argues that this system of representation existed already. It coalesced before the state in two senses: chronologically and, leading to the genocide, in everyday practices operating in front of the state. It was the 'practice of civil defence' that 'provided poorer, rural Hutu with the necessary training to kill', Thomson concludes. In this instance, genocidal violence was 'state-sponsored', not state-led. Violence was not to be stored for later use.

Lance van Sittert and Thierry Rousset's essay offers numerous insights to explore the shifting relationship between settlers and distant authorities, and the settlers' contradictory need to acquire land and labour: to dissipate colonial violence to acquire the former, or to concentrate it for later use. The settler militia on the Cape frontier was, van Sittert and Rousset argue, 'the key instrument of settler primitive accumulation through the extirpation and enslavement of the San'. 'Instrument' of whom? The authors convincingly demonstrate that the militia was able to pursue the interests of its members, that the conquest of this frontier was indeed civilian-driven. The settlers

277

needed both the land and forced Indigenous labour. Killing Indigenous resisters would secure the former, but land that could not be exploited with Indigenous labour was relatively useless. Moreover, due to military considerations, the Indigenous resisters were *not* isolated as the Canarians were; Bastard and Khoisan individuals under settler control had to be armed, and the 'general commando' as a military institution to be instituted. Both developments had profound implications: the former fundamentally challenged the colonial relation, while the demands of extended military service often undermined the settler's ability to self-reproduce. Only wealthy settlers could abandon their economic units for extended periods of time, but they wouldn't. As the settlers' 'firearm monopoly broke down', creative solutions had to be sought. Chests with locks were ordered to lock away at night the weapons that Khoisan personnel were allowed to carry during daytime. It was a time-bound type of partial emancipation.

Violence had to be concentrated and dissipated simultaneously. It could not be stored up for use elsewhere, and the slave and Khoisan populations under settler control were not 'self-reproducing'. Van Sittert and Rousset calculate that approximately three Indigenous resisters were killed for every one that was enslaved. It was, they note, a 'killed-to-capture ratio that was socially, if not economically, efficient'. In any case, violence was not being stored up at a satisfactory rate, or, to put it another way, what a satisfactory rate would be depended on each settler's economic standing. Why have slaves when you don't have land? Van Sittert and Rousset note that the settler polity was divided, the '12 per cent' on the one hand, and the '88 per cent' on the other, had strategically different interests. When settler solidarity broke down, the frontier was 'rolled back a third of the way to Cape Town'. In the end, the militia generally served the interests of the settler 'common men' (the '88 per cent'). Genocide on the frontier resulted from this fissure because the '88 per cent' had no particular interest in storing up violence and found it easier to dissipate it. This development resulted in a localised instance of colonialism's general crisis. The slaves were dispersed, no social reproduction means no reproduction, and 'heavy labour demands' and 'poor subsistence' made the reproduction of slaves unviable; their numbers 'stagnated'. More creative solutions were needed, and settlers assumed parental responsibility over Indigenous children. They began considering San parents as 'unnatural parents'. This categorisation is crucial, as it identifies a collective that is primarily defined by the inability to reproduce, a failure that allegedly characterises all Indigenous peoples facing settler colonialism as a mode of domination. Offal for rations, deliberately distributed narcotics, ongoing outbursts of exceptional violence, such as

CHAPTER 11: Colonialism, Frontiers, Genocide

public floggings, iron branding, and hard labour: the destruction and the reproduction of colonised labour coexisted and codefined each other in an unstable fashion throughout the nineteenth century in the area.

Robert Gordon's analysis of German South West Africa begins with the German discovery, during the genocidal wars of 1904–1908, of the impossibility of simultaneously concentrating and dissipating colonial violence. The 'extermination policies' of 1904–1908 had run against settler demands for cheap labour. Then again, the colonial state was not really there; it was 'weak', 'improvisational' and 'ceremonial'. After the acute conflict phase ended, the conundrum remained: the consolidation of land acquisition required violence to be stored up, but a genocidal legacy made it quite difficult. The solution was not that creative: German South West African farmers were 'unofficially' devolved authority. The state was not there and knew it. But the farmers proved callous and short-sighted; dispersed and isolated, their community fearful and alienated, paranoiac responses were widespread. Further genocide was a response to genocide. The farmers, Gordon concludes, 'played a key role in facilitating Bushman genocide'.

And yet in the post-war period the settler farms became more numerous and the agricultural sector, taking advantage of generously subsidised incentives, recovered rapidly. Settler empowerment proceeded via the *Landesrat* level of government, and the *Landesrat* eventually acquired the ability to shape the modes of settler access to Indigenous labour. Accessing labour required accelerated primitive accumulation, and the Indigenous collectives were systematically deprived of their 'traditional livelihood'. Once separated from their subsistence, it was assumed, they would enter the colonial workforce, and the 1907 ordinances were meant to ensure that this would happen at a rapid pace. Pass laws tied labour to specific locations, but the settlers' right to engage in 'fatherly chastisement' of their Indigenous charges was a crucial lynchpin in this suite of measures — a provision that echoed the acquisition of paternal prerogatives that the settlers of the Cape frontier had arrogated to themselves nearly a century before and a country away. The farmers ended up seeing themselves as 'little kings', but labour shortages were acutely felt. It seems significant, as Gordon remarks, that in the mandatory era Bushmen would be 'tamed' rather than 'erased'. The poor Afrikaners sent as settlers to what would become Namibia by the mandatory authorities did not commit genocide; they prioritised storing up violence.

Argentina and Chile resolved their dispute over Tierra del Fuego diplomatically in 1881. The state was still absent; these powers had merely agreed not to subsequently enter what each understood as its rival's legitimate claim. Corporate entities operated on the ground without state supervision. For Indigenous peoples elsewhere in Chile and Argentina, the state's extended reach had had fateful consequences, but as Alberto Harambour notes, it was the island's integration into the world economy after the late 1870s that had 'devastating consequences' for them. Miners had operated murderously in the area, but had limited impact. The colonists linked to the expanding pastoral frontier were more systematic: they had horses and repeating rifles, and an uncontested advantage. Sheep farming and corporate control mixed genocidally. There was an interest in keeping the labour force limited. The state had relinquished control to 'Indian hunters' paid by the pastoral industry and 'Indian gatherers', the Salesian Catholic mission across a narrow strait. The former benefited from the latter and the latter from the former. The hunters killed 'men, children and elders' even though they often 'captured women as sexual slaves'; the gatherers welcomed survivors but witnessed infective epidemics decimating their flock.

One of Sidney L. Harring's essay's primary tasks is to recover violence from Canada's officially endorsed and cultivated collective amnesia. Residential schools and their genocidal implications recently entered the analytical frame and the general public's attention, but what about the sheer violence that preceded them and made the system a possibility? There *was* indeed violence, and there was no state control on many frontiers, the very opposite of widely held interpretations of Canada's development. Indeed, as Harring argues, it was *precisely* because there had been no control elsewhere in Canada, and not only elsewhere in North America, that a decision to establish state pre-emption had been taken in the first place — the first place being, on the contrary, a place of settler, not state pre-emption. In Newfoundland, a civilian-driven genocide had happened first. It was, after all, an island like the ones that are the subject of Adhikari's essay. Forced Indigenous displacement to an inhospitable interior and away from traditional resources was the mode of destruction, but it was settler violence that had made forced displacement a reality, even if the settlers had failed to occupy contested sites continously. Remoteness and a difficult geography had made the reach of the state tenuous or non-existent. Elsewhere in what would become Atlantic Canada, the aim was to remove Indigenous communities and their claims to lands targeted for agricultural settlement. Forced removal was the cheapest option. Hostile land invasions by settlers were the norm. The settlers would have an interest in hiding or not documenting their violent deeds; the authorities had an interest in not hearing about their violence.

Thus, on the basis of an assessment about failures further east, the Crown decided it had to obtain title to land before settlement could be authorised in what would become Ontario. Treaties were negotiated before settlers could enter the scene, but if treaties in themselves were not genocidal, their consequences often were, and Indigenous impoverishment, a notion Harring returns to several times, was also the norm. Even then, reserved Indian land was illegally and routinely occupied. Squatting without legal sanction was not that different from squatting against a legal sanction that could not be uttered let alone enforced, and the legal system denied Indian communities all avenues for redress. Reserves were rarely viable or sustainable, and Harring convincingly argues that the prospect of forced assimilation was predicated on their deliberately engineered collapse.

In the prairies further west, the state was present but it was in the context of a tradition fundamentally shaped by squatting settlers. As such, it was still a civilian-driven process. The reservations in the prairies were locales where Indians would allegedly become 'small farmers or wage labourers'. But if this outcome was hoped for, nothing was done to sustain the hope. On the contrary, the reserves effectively operated as prisons. A pass system constraining the mobility of indigenous Individuals made sure that their options would be limited; famine, mass starvation and disease followed. Not only was this predictable; it had been predicted. Disease was not the beginning of colonisation, a prodrome, as some scholarship on ecological imperialism has argued.[27] Disease was its end. And, indeed, it was its means, as Prime Minister John A. MacDonald endeavoured to keep reserve Indians just above starvation level, as he himself candidly noted. He suggested, as Harring remarks, to refuse 'food until the Indians are on the verge of starvation' in order to make their labour available and cheap. But his policy failed. Yet again, one could argue that deliberately engineered famine, a recognisably genocidal policy, was indeed a testament to his policy's success. Failure and accomplishment, after all, crucially depend on what one is aiming for.

One of the creative solutions that was developed in the case of Canada replicated what had happened elsewhere: a unilateral assumption of settler control over Indigenous children. Andrew Woolford's essay, which also deals with parallel developments in the US, takes up from where Harring concludes. The state now was present and overbearing, even if in the case of Canada's Indigenous education system it willingly and strategically abdicated to churches and their organisations. In this sense, genocide at

---

27 See Crosby, *Ecological Imperialism.*

boarding schools was still a civilian-driven process, and the government only provided 'general oversight'. Woolford focuses on the role of 'civilian workers' and the ways their agency interacted with 'collective action frames' in the context of settler colonialism as a mode of domination aimed at eliminating Indigenous alterities, but it is significant that sequestering Indigenous children was seen by many as a way of directing them towards menial employment.

Mobilising indigenous labour was distinct but in no way incompatible with other aims coalescing in the boarding school system, such as saving souls, saving indigenous children from 'corrupting' influences, and assimilating them to the settler body politic. Individuals related to the action frames differently, and dissonances should be taken into account — as Woolford does. But they were managing an invariably industrial-style education system; it was work training, an apparatus aiming to boost the availability of labour. The structural reference of this system was the workhouses for the poor, sites of disciplining, forced labour and corporal punishment. Scholars have rightly focused on the eliminatory intent that underwrote the operation of the Canadian boarding school archipelago. But releasing productive capacity was always a declared priority, even though, comparatively speaking and in the light of the essays collected in this volume, we can deduce that there was less settler need for Indigenous labour in twentieth-century Canada than there was on, say, the early-nineteenth-century Cape frontier. Still there was a ratio between enslaved and killed, a ratio underpinning a specifically settler colonial relationship between land and labour.[28]

And then, Australia: Lyndall Ryan's paper explores a circumstance in which there seemed to be no interest in obtaining Indigenous labour, no interest in setting a socially, if not an economically, efficient ratio. Ryan notes a 'determination to annihilate Aboriginal people on the frontier', a determination that characterised the expanding New South Wales frontier in the first half of the nineteenth century. A majority of the perpetrators were assigned convicts and employees of absentee landlords; they were perhaps not interested in maximising the economic viability of the pastoral runs. Besides, the raw-wool industry was export-driven and more interested in acquiring extensive tracts than in intensive exploitation; it did not require Indigenous labour. When an economic recession hit in the 1840s, genocidal violence on the frontier became even more widespread. There is rarely a

---

28 Wolfe P. 2001. 'Land, labor, and difference: Elementary structures of race'. *American Historical Review,* 106, no. 3, 866–905.

CHAPTER 11: Colonialism, Frontiers, Genocide

need for a potential industrial reserve army when the price of a particular industry's output has collapsed. Crucially, Ryan refers to the insight of one settler who noted that after a terrifying massacre the property that had been cleared of its indigenous owners had become 'fifty per cent more valuable'.

Massacres were everywhere on this frontier. They were perpetrated systematically. Much more than in the difficult terrain of the Cape frontiers, the newly acquired horseback mobility gave the invaders of New South Wales a big military advantage. British forces initially brought resisters under control by perpetrating massacres, but then in each region private violence executed by settlers and stockmen became the norm. The transition in this pattern of violence was imperceptible and made little difference on the ground — the two groups had developed a 'close relationship' and always collaborated. In this sense, as the role of the state and that of the settlers were often indistinguishable, this one was still a civilian-driven genocide. Crucially, Ryan demonstrates that massacres were designed to annihilate the Aboriginal presence or to induce fear and prompt surrender, not to extract labour.

Further north and slightly later, Queensland was an even more violent frontier. Raymond Evans and Robert Ørsted-Jensen assess the devastation and challenge a consistent pattern of historiographical denial. The Native Police, which was instrumental in carrying out the dirty work of eliminating Indigenous resistance, was mounted and was provisioned with new-generation rifles. Enhanced mobility and concentrated firepower resulted in an even more unbalanced confrontation. If Ryan endeavours to map the massacres, Evans and Ørsted-Jensen give up — for them, the map of the state is itself a map of Queensland frontier massacres. As happened further south, state-sponsored violence and 'private violence' were often indistinguishable. The colonial state had caught up, but it was entirely subservient to the settler community — violence was still settler-driven. Admittedly, some of the settlers were interested in treating Aborigines with 'justice and kindness'. They related differently to the collective action frames. But violence was everywhere, and Evans and Ørsted-Jensen implicate these settlers as well: an 'exterminatory cultural *Zeitgeist* enveloped them all', they conclude. Thus, the ratio between killed and enslaved in the case of Queensland is much higher than the one that ensued on the Cape frontier. Evans and Ørsted-Jensen focus on natural figures, the head count, not on rational ones. But that their work does not even refer to enslaved indigenous people is telling. Violence was dissipated with no consideration for its storage. It was a 'murderous frenzy'; 'mass killings were wanton, furtive and unprosecuted'. And yet, many Aboriginal individuals ended up as pastoral workers, able to move

283

CIVILIAN-DRIVEN VIOLENCE AND THE GENOCIDE OF INDIGENOUS PEOPLES

for mutually agreed seasonal 'walkabouts', working for rations, determined to remain in 'country'. Their extended families resided with them, and as a significant scholarship has explored, the Aboriginal contribution to the northern Australian pastoral industry was substantive.[29] Evans and Ørsted-Jensen focus on the body count to counter a denialist historiography, but the formulation of a ratio between killed and enslaved would demonstrate a relationship between violence that is dissipated and violence that is stored up even in this case. The pastoral industry eventually became a site for indigenous survival.

'Dispersal' was the euphemism officially adopted to refer to these homicidal forays, and in a sense it is an apt descriptor: violence on the Queensland frontier *was* indeed dispersed, dissipated. One result of an extremely violent frontier was that captive labour had to be imported to Queensland during the second half of the nineteenth century in order to sustain the developing sugar industry. These quasi-slaves were kidnapped from islands across the Coral Sea that were then the subject of private-led incursions that closely resembled the forays of European adventurers and freebooters in the fourteenth-century Canary Islands. Sugar again; and again, a coloniser-made depopulation prompting enslavement, deportation and the destruction of Indigenous societies elsewhere. By then, many waves had washed in and away in the colonial world. The addiction and the means to satisfy it had remained remarkably stable, as had the pattern of colonial destruction.

---

29 See for example May D. 1994. *Aboriginal Labour and the Cattle Industry: Queensland from White Settlement to the Present.* Melbourne: Cambridge University Press; McGrath A. 1987. *Born in the Cattle: Aborigines in Cattle Country.* Sydney: Allen & Unwin; Veracini L. 2001. 'Towards a further redescription of the Australian pastoral frontier'. *Journal of Australian Studies,* 26, no. 72, 29–39, 260–263.

BIBLIOGRAPHY

Abulafia D. 2008. *Discovery of Mankind: Atlantic Encounters in the Age of Columbus*. New Haven: Yale University Press.

Adams D.W. 2005. *Education for Extinction: American Indians and the Boarding School Experience, 1875–1928*. Lawrence: University Press of Kansas.

Adhikari M. 2010a. *The Anatomy of a South African Genocide: The Extermination of the Cape San Peoples*. Cape Town: UCT Press.

Adhikari M. 2010b. 'A total extinction confidently hoped for: The destruction of Cape San society under Dutch colonial rule, 1700–1795'. *Journal of Genocide Research*, 12, no. 1–2.

Adhikari M., ed. 2014. *Genocide on Settler Frontiers: When Hunter-gatherers and Commercial Stock Farmers Clash*. Cape Town: UCT Press.

Adhikari M. 2015. *Genocide on Settler Frontiers: When Hunter-gatherers and Commercial Stock Farmers Clash*. New York: Berghahn Books.

Adhikari M. 2017. 'Europe's first settler colonial incursion into Africa: The genocide of aboriginal Canary Islanders'. *African Historical Review*, 49, no. 1.

Agamben G. 2005. *State of Exception*. Chicago: University of Chicago Press.

Aitken R. 2007. *Exclusion and Inclusion: Gradations of Whiteness and Socio-economic Engineering in German Southwest Africa 1884–1914*. Oxford: Peter Lang.

Aliaga F. 2000. *La Misión Salesiana en Isla Dawson*. Santiago: Salesianos.

Alvarado M., Odone C., Maturana F. & Fiore D., eds. 2007. *Fueguinos: Fotografías Siglos XIX y XX. Imágenes e Imaginarios del Fin del Mundo*. Santiago: Pehuén.

Alvarez A. 2014. *Native America and the Question of Genocide*. Lanham: Rowman & Littlefield.

Anderson G.A. 2014. *Ethnic Cleansing and the Indian: The Crime that Should Haunt America*. Norman: University of Oklahoma Press.

Anon. 1909. *Our First Half-Century: A Review of Queensland Progress*. Brisbane: Anthony J. Cumming.

Anon. 1985. 'The evidence of murder'. *The Push from the Bush*, no. 20.

Ansel B. 1970. 'European adventurer in Tierra del Fuego: Julio Popper'. *Hispanic American Historical Review*, 50, no. 1.

Arendt H. 1969. *On Violence*. New York: Penguin Books.

Arendt A. 1994 [1955]. *The Origins of Totalitarianism*. New York: Harcourt.

Armstrong R. n.d. *The Kalkadoons: A Study of an Aboriginal Tribe on the Queensland Frontier*. Brisbane: William Brooks.

Athearn F.J. 1976. *An Isolated Empire: A History of Northwest Colorado*. Denver: Department of the Interior, Bureau of Land Management, Colorado Division.

Aveling M. & Ryan L. 1987. 'At the boundaries', in *Australians 1838*, eds. A. Atkinson & M. Aveling. Sydney: Fairfax, Syme & Weldon Associates.

Azurara G. 1971. *The Chronicle of the Discovery and Conquest of Guinea*, trans. C. Beazley & E. Prestage. New York: Franklin.

Baily G., Phillips C. & Voigt L. 2009. 'Spain and Spanish America in the early modern Atlantic world: Current trends in scholarship'. *Renaissance Quarterly*, 62.

Baines E. 2003. 'Body politics and the Rwandan crisis'. *Third World Quarterly*, 24, no 3.

Banner S. 2007. *Possessing the Pacific: Land, Settlers and Indigenous People from Australia to Alaska*. Cambridge: Harvard University Press.

Barr D. 2006. '"The land is ours and not yours": The Western Delawares and the Seven Years War in the Upper Ohio Valley, 1755–1758', in *The Boundaries Between Us: Natives and Newcomers Along the Frontiers of the Old Northwest Territory, 1750–1850*, ed. D. Barr. Kent, OH: Kent State University Press.

Barrow J. 1806. *Travels into the Interior of Southern Africa*. vol. 1. London: T. Cadell & W. Davies.

Barta T. 2000. 'Relations of genocide: Land and lives in the colonisation of Australia', in *genocide and the Modern Age: Etiology and Case Studies of Mass Death*, eds. I. Walliman & M. Dobkowski. Syracuse: Syracuse University Press.

Barta T. 2008. '"They appear actually to vanish from the face of the earth." Aborigines and the European Project in Australia Felix'. *Journal of Genocide Research*, 10, no. 4.

Barta T. 2015. '"A fierce and irresistible cavalry": Pastoralists, homesteaders and hunters on the American plains frontier', in *Genocide on Settler Frontiers: When Hunter-Gatherers and Commercial Stock Farmers Clash*, ed. M. Adhikari. New York: Berghahn Books.

Bascopé J. 2010. 'El oro y la vida salvaje en Tierra del Fuego, 1880–1914'. *Magallania*, 38, no. 2.

Bauman Z. 1989. *Modernity and the Holocaust*. Cambridge: Polity Press.

Bauman Z. 2000. 'The duty to remember: But what?', in *Enlightenment and Genocide, Contradictions of Modernity*, eds. J. Kay & B. Strath. Brussels: Presses Interuniversitaires Européennes & Peter Lang.

Bays E. 2009. *Indian Residential Schools: Another Picture*. Ottawa: Baico Publishing.

Belich J. 2009. *Replenishing the Earth: The Settler Revolution and the Rise of the Anglo-World, 1783–1939*. Oxford: Oxford University Press.

Bell F.M. 1947. 'Camboon reminiscences'. *Royal Historical Society of Queensland*, IV, no. 1.

Bellamy A. 2012a. 'Massacres and morality: Mass killing in an age of immunity'. *Human Rights Quarterly*, 34, no. 4.

Belshaw J. 1978. 'Population distribution and the pattern of seasonal movement in northern New South Wales', in *Records of Times Past: Ethnohistorical Essays on the Culture and Ecology of the New England Tribes*, ed. by I. McBryde. Canberra: Australian Institute of Aboriginal Studies.

Belza J.E. 1973. 'Capelo, el Ona Guerrillero'. *Karukinka*, 5 (July).

Belza J.E. 1975. *En la Isla del Fuego. Vol. II. Colonización*. Buenos Aires: IIHTF.

Benjamin T. 2009. *The Atlantic World: Europeans, Africans, Indians and Their Shared History, 1400–1900*. Cambridge: Cambridge University Press.

Bennett M.M. 1927. *Christison of Lammermoor*. London: Alston River.

Benzoni G. 1858. *A History of the New World*, trans. W. Smyth. London: Hakluyt Society.

Berger P. & Luckmann T. 1966. *The Social Construction of Reality*. New York: Vintage.

Bischoping K. & Fingerhut N. 1996. 'Border lines: Indigenous peoples in genocide studies'. *Canadian Review of Sociology and Anthropology*, 33, no. 4.

Blair P. 2008. *Lament for a First Nation: The Williams Treaties of Southern Ontario*. Vancouver: University of British Columbia Press.

Bley H. 1971. *South-West Africa under German Rule*. Evanston: Northwestern University Press.

Blomfield G. 1981. *Baal Belbora: The End of the Dreaming*. Sydney: Alternative Publishing Co-operative.

Bonn M. 1910. 'Siedlungsfragen und Eingeborenenpolitik II: Die Entstehung der Gutsherrschaft in Südafrika'. *Archiv für Sozialwissenschaft und Sozialpolitik*, 31.

Bonn M.J. 1910. 'Siedlungsfragen und Eingeborenenpolitik III: Die Entstehung der Gutsherrschaft in Südafrika'. *Archiv für Sozialwissenschaft und Sozialpolitik*, 31.

Bonn M.J. 1914. 'German colonial policy'. *United Empire*, 5 (2 February).

Bonn M.J. 1932. 'Imperialism', in *Encyclopaedia of the Social Sciences*, eds. E. Seligman & A. Johnson. New York: Macmillan.

Bonn M.J. 1938. *The Crumbling of Empire: The Disintegration of World Economy*. London: Allen & Unwin.

Bonn M.J. 1948. *Wandering Scholar*. New York: John Day.

Borch M. 2001. 'Rethinking the origins of *terra nullius*'. *Australian Historical Studies*, 32, no. 117.

Borgatello M. 1920. *Florecillas Silvestres*, trans. G. Roca. Turin: Scuola Tipográfica Salesiana.

Borrero J.M. 1989 [1928]. *La Patagonia Trágica*. Ushuaia: Zagier & Urruty.

Bortolini M., Thomas M.G., Chikhi L., Aguilar, J.A., Castro-De-Guerra D., Salzano F.M. & Ruiz-Linares A. 2004. 'Ribeiro's typology, genomes, and Spanish colonialism, as viewed from Gran Canaria and Colombia'. *Genetics and Molecular Biology*, 27, no. 1.

Bottoms T. 2013. *Conspiracy of Silence: Queensland's Frontier Killing Times*. Sydney: Allen & Unwin.

Bourdieu P. 1999. 'Rethinking the state: Genesis and structure of the bureaucratic field', in *State/Culture: State-formation after the Cultural Turn*, ed. G. Steinmetz. Ithaca: Cornell University Press.

Bourdieu P. 2001. *Masculine Domination*. Stanford: Stanford University Press.

Bourdieu P. & Wacquant L. 1992. *An Invitation to Reflective Sociology*. Chicago: University of Chicago Press.

Bourgois P. 2001. 'The power of violence in war and peace: Post-cold War lessons from El Salvador'. *Ethnography*, 2, no. 1.

Bradlow E. & Bradlow F., eds. 1979. *William Somerville's Narrative of His Journeys to the Eastern Cape Frontier and to Lattakoe, 1799–1802*. Cape Town: Van Riebeeck Society.

Braun M. 1985. *Memorias de una Vida Colmada*. Buenos Aires: Autoedición.

Bridges L. 1948. *Uttermost Part of the Earth*. London: Hodder & Stoughton.

Bridges T. 2001. *Los Indios del Confín del Mundo: Escritos para la South American Missionary Society*, trans. by A. Canclini. Ushuaia: Zagier & Urruty.

Briscoe G. 1993. 'Aboriginal Australian identity: The historiography of relations between indigenous ethnic groups and other Australians', *History Workshop Journal*, 36.

Brockmann C. 1912. *Briefe Eines Deutschen Mädchen aus Südwest*. Berlin: E.S. Mitler.

Broome R. 1982. *Aboriginal Australians: Black Response to White Domination*. Sydney: Allen & Unwin.

Broome R. 2003. 'Statistics of frontier conflict', in *Frontier Conflict: The Australian Experience*, eds. B. Attwood & S. Forster. Canberra: National Museum of Australia.

Broome R. 2010. *Aboriginal Australians: A History Since 1788*. Sydney: Allen & Unwin.

Browning C. 1998. *Ordinary Men: Reserve Police Battalion 101 and the Final Solution in Poland*. New York: Harper Perennial.

Brownlie R.J. 2003. *A Fatherly Eye: Indian Agents, Government Power, and Aboriginal Resistance in Ontario, 1918–1939*. Toronto: Oxford University Press.

Buckley H. 1992. *From Wooden Ploughs to Welfare: Why Indian Policy Failed in the Prairie Provinces*. Montreal: McGill-Queen's University Press.

Buck-Morss S. 2000. 'Hegel and Haiti'. *Critical Inquiry*, 26, no. 4.

Budgel R. 1992. 'The Beothuks and the Newfoundland mind'. *Newfoundland Studies*, 8.

Burchell W. 1824. *Travels in the Interior of Southern Africa*, vol. 2. London: Longman.

Burnet J.E. 2012a. *Genocide Lives in Us: Women, Memory, and Silence in Rwanda*. Madison: University of Wisconsin Press.

Burnet J.E. 2012b. 'Sexual violence, female agencies, and sexual consent: Complexities of sexual violence in the 1994 Rwandan genocide'. *African Studies Review*, 55, no 2.

Burnet J.E. 2019. 'Rwanda: Women's political representation and its consequences', in *The Palgrave Handbook of Women's Political Rights*, eds. S. Franceschet, M.L. Krook & N. Tan. London: Palgrave Macmillan.

Byrne J.C. 1848. *Twelve Years Wandering in the British Colonies 1*. London: Richard Bentley.

Caldwell J.C. 1987. 'Population', in *Australian Historical Statistics*, ed. W. Vamplew. Sydney: Fairfax, Syme & Weldon Associates.

Campbell B. 2009. 'Genocide as social control'. *Sociological Theory*, 27, no. 2.

Campbell J. 1815. *Travels in South Africa Undertaken at the Request of the London Missionary Society*. vol. 1. London: Black & Parry.

Campos C. 2013. 'The Atlantic islands and the development of southern Castile at the turn of the fifteenth century', in *Spain, Portugal and the Atlantic Frontier of Medieval Europe*, ed. by J. Lopez-Portillo. Farnham: Ashgate Variorum.

Carew J. 1992. 'The end of Moorish enlightenment and the beginning of the Columbian era'. *Race and Class*, 33, no. 3.

Carney R. 1995. 'Aboriginal residential schools before Confederation: The early experience'. *CCHA Historical Studies*, 61.

Carr A. 1870. *Where not to Immigrate: Queensland as It Is*. London: T. Cooper.

Carrington G. 1871. *Colonial Adventures and Experiences*. London: Bell & Daldy.

Carter S. 1990. *Lost Harvests: Prairie Indian Reserve Farmers and Government Policy*. Montreal: McGill-Queen's University Press.

Casali R. 2008. 'Contacto interétnico en el Norte de Tierra del Fuego: Primera aproximación a las estrategias de resistencia Selk'nam'. *Magallania*, 36, no. 2.

Casali R. 2013. *Conquistando el Fin del Mundo: La Misión la Candelaria y la Salud de la Población Selk'nam (Tierra del Fuego 1895–1931)*. Rosario: Prohistoria.

Casali R., Fugassa M. & Guichón R. 2006. 'Aproximación epidemiológica al proceso de contacto interétnico en el norte de Tierra del Fuego'. *Magallania*, 34, no. 1.

Cavanagh E. 2014. '"We exterminated them, and Dr. Philip gave the country": The Griqua people and the elimination of San from South Africa's Transorangia region', in Adhikari M., ed. 2015. *Genocide on Settler Frontiers: When Hunter-gatherers and Commercial Stock Farmers Clash*. New York: Berghahn Books.

Césaire A. 1972 [1950]. *Discourse on Colonialism*. New York: Monthly Review.

Challis S. 2012. 'Creolisation on the nineteenth-century frontiers of Southern Africa: A case study of the AmaTola Bushmen in the Maloti-Drakensberg'. *Journal of Southern African Studies*, 38, no. 2.

Chapman A. 2002. *Fin de un mundo: Los Selk'nam de la Tierra del Fuego*. Santiago: Taller Experimental Cuerpo Pintados.

Chapman A. 2012. *Yaganes del Cabo de Hornos: Encuentros con los Europeos Antes y Después de Darwin*. Santiago: Pehuén-Liberalia.

Child B.J. 1996. 'Runaway boys, resistant girls: Rebellion at Flandreau and Haskell, 1900–1940'. *Journal of American Indian Education*, 35, no. 3.

Childs H. 1997 [1936]. *El Jimmy: Bandido de la Patagonia*, trans. E. Pisano. Punta Arenas: Ediciones de la Universidad de Magallanes.

Chrisjohn R. & Young S. 1997. *The Circle Game: Shadows and Substance in the Indian Residential School Experience*. Penticton, BC: Theytus Books.

Churchill W. 1997. *A Little Matter of Genocide: Holocaust and Denial in the Americas, 1492 to the Present*. San Francisco: City Lights Books.

Cilliers J. & Green E. 2018. 'The land-labour hypothesis in a settler economy: Wealth, labour and household composition on the South African frontier'. *International Review of Social History*, 63, no. 2.

Clark I.D. 1995. *Scars in the Landscape: A Register of Massacre Sites in Western Victoria, 1803–1859*. Canberra: Australian Institute of Aboriginal and Torres Strait Islander Studies.

Coady C. 2007. 'Collateral immunity in war and terrorism', in *Civilian Immunity in War*, ed. by I. Primoratz. Oxford: Oxford University Press.

Coffey R. 2010. 'Frontier Violence at Gin Gin'. BA (Hons) thesis, University of Queensland.

Cohen Y. 2012. *The Spanish: Shadows of Embarrassment*. Brighton: Sussex Academic Press.

Collins D. 1975. *An Account of the English Colony in New South Wales*. vol 1; ed. B. Fletcher. Sydney: A.H & A.W. Reed, in association with the Royal Australian Historical Society.

Collins P. 2002. *Goodbye Bussamarai: The Mandandanji Land War, Southern Queensland 1842–1852. St Lucia*, Brisbane: University of Queensland Press.

Collins R. 2004. *Interaction Ritual Chains*. Princeton: Princeton University Press.

'Colonial frontier massacres in central and eastern Australia 1788–1930'. Digital map. The Centre for 21st Century Humanities, University of Newcastle. Available at https://c21ch.newcastle.edu.au/colonialmassacres/map.php; accessed 26 October 2019.

Conners L. 2017. 'Uncovering the shameful: Sexual violence on an Australia colonial frontier', in *Legacies of Violence: Rendering the Unspeakable Past in Modern Australia*, ed. R. Mason. New York: Berghahn Books.

Connor J. 2002. *The Australian Frontier Wars, 1788–1838*. Sydney: UNSW Press.

Cook A. 1900. 'The Aborigines of the Canary Islands'. *American Anthropologist*, New Series, 2, no. 3.

Cook J. 1955. *The Journals of Captain James Cook in his Voyages of Discovery, Vol. 1: The Voyage of the Endeavour 1768–1771*, ed. J.C. Beaglehole. Cambridge: Cambridge University Press.

Cooper F. 2005. *Colonialism in Question: Theory, Knowledge, History*. Berkeley: University of California Press.

Cornell F.C. 1986 [1920]. *The Glamour of Prospecting*. Cape Town: David Philip.

Coulthard G.S. 2010. 'Place against empire: Understanding indigenous anti-colonialism'. *Affinities*, 4, no. 2.

Coyle M. 2005. *Report: Addressing Aboriginal Land and Treaty Rights in Ontario: An Analysis of Past Policies and Options for the Future*. Attorney General of Ontario. Available at https://www.attorneygeneral.jus.gov.on.ca/inquiries/ipperwash/policy_part/research/pdf/Coyle.pdf, accessed 29 October 2019.

Crépeau P. & Bizimana S. 1979. *Proverbes du Rwanda*. Tervuren: Musée royale de l'Afrique centrale.

Crosby A. 2007. *Ecological Imperialism: The Biological Expansion of Europe, 900–1900*. 2nd ed. New York: Cambridge University Press.

Crosby A. 2013. 'An ecohistory of the Canary Islands: A precursor of European colonisation in the New World and Australasia', in *Spain, Portugal and the Atlantic Frontier of Medieval Europe*, ed. by J. Lopez-Portillo. Farnham: Ashgate Variorum.

Curr E. 1886. *The Australian Race: Its Origins, Language, Customs*. Melbourne: John Ferres, 209.

Curthoys A. 2014. 'Indigenous dispossession and pastoral employment in Western Australia during the nineteenth century: Implications for understanding colonial forms of genocide', in *Genocide on Settler Frontiers: When Hunter-gatherers and Commercial Stock Farmers Clash*, ed. M. Adhikari. Cape Town: UCT Press.

Darwin C. 1839. *The Voyage of the Beagle*. London: Henry Colburn.

Daschuk J.W. 2013. *Clearing the Plains: Disease, Politics of Starvation, and the Loss of Aboriginal Life*. Regina: University of Regina Press.

Day D. 1997. *Claiming a Continent: A New History of Australia*. Sydney: Angus & Robertson.

De Bethencourt J. 1970. *The Canarian, or Book of the Conquest and Conversion of the Canarians in the Year 1402*, trans. R. Major. New York: Burt Franklin (first published London: Hakluyt Society 1872).

De Espinosa A. 1907 [1594]. *The Guanches of Tenerife: The Holy Image of Our Lady of Candelaria and the Spanish Conquest and Settlement*, trans. & ed. C. Markham. London: Hakluyt Society.

Dearing S. 2009. 'Harper in Pittsburgh: Canada has no history of colonialism'. *Digital Journal*, 3 October 2009. Available at digitaljournal.com/article/280003, accessed on 29 October 2019.

Des Forges A. 1995. 'The ideology of genocide'. *Issue: A Journal of Opinion*, 23, no. 2.

Des Forges A. 1999. *Leave None to Tell the Story: Genocide in Rwanda*. New York: Human Rights Watch.

Des Forges A. 2011. *'Defeat is the only bad news': Rwanda under Musinga, 1896–1931*, ed. D. Newbury. Madison: University of Wisconsin Press.

De Lame D. 2005. *A Hill Among a Thousand: Transformations and Ruptures in Rural Rwanda*, trans. H. Arnold. Madison: University of Wisconsin Press.

Desrosiers M.-E. 2014. 'Rethinking political rhetoric and authority during Rwanda's First and Second Republics'. *Africa*, 84, no. 2.

Diffie B. & Winius G. 1977. *Foundations of the Portuguese Empire, 1415–1580*. Minneapolis: University of Minnesota Press.

Disney A. 2009. *A History of Portugal and the Portuguese Empire, Vol. II*. Cambridge: Cambridge University Press.

Docker J. 2008. 'Are settler colonies inherently genocidal? Rereading Lemkin', in *Empire, Colony, Genocide: Conquest, Occupation and Subaltern Resistance in World History*, ed. by A.D. Moses. New York: Berghahn Books.

Downes A. 2008. *Targeting Civilians in War*. Ithaca: Cornell University Press.

Drinnon R. 1997. *Facing West: The Metaphysics of Indian-hating and Empire Building*. Norman: University of Oklahoma Press.

Du Pisani A. 1985. *SWA/Namibia: The Politics of Continuity and Change*. Johannesburg: Jonathan Ball.

Dwyer P. & Nettelbeck A. 2018. '"Savage wars of peace": Violence, colonialism and empire in the modern world', in *Violence, Colonialism and Empire*, eds. P Dwyer & A Nettelbeck. Basingstoke: Palgrave MacMillan.

Dye A. & La Croix S. 2018. 'Institutions for the taking: property rights and the settlement of the Cape Colony, 1652–1750'. *Economic History Review*, 8 November 2018.

Elbourne E. 2003. 'The sin of the settler: The 1835–36 Select Committee on Aborigines and debates over virtue and conquest in the early nineteenth-century British white settler empire'. *Journal of Colonialism and Colonial History*, 25, no. 3.

Elder B. 1988. *Blood on the Wattle: Massacres and Maltreatment of Australian Aborigines since 1788*. Sydney: Child & Associates.

Elkins E. & Pedersen C., eds. 2005. *Settler Colonialism in the Twentieth Century: Projects, Practices, Legacies*. Abingdon: Routledge.

Elliott J.H. 1963. *Imperial Spain, 1469–1716*. London: Arnold.

Eltringham N. 2006. '"Invaders who have stolen the country": The Hamitic hypothesis, race and the Rwandan genocide'. *Social Identities*, 12, no. 4.

Enns R.A. 2009. '"But what is the object of educating these children, if it costs their lives to educate them?" Federal Indian education policy in Western Canada in the late 1800s.' *Journal of Canadian Studies*, 43, no. 3.

Evans J. 2009. 'Where lawlessness is law: The settler-colonial frontier as a legal space of violence'. *Australian Feminist Law Journal*, 30, no. 1.

Evans R. 1995. 'Blood dries quickly: Conflict study and Australian historiography'. In *Historical Disciplines in Australasia: Themes, Problems and Debates*, ed. A. Moses. Special issue of *Australian Journal of Politics and History*, 41.

Evans R. 1999. *Fighting Words: Writing about Race*. St Lucia: University of Queensland Press.

Evans R. 2003. 'Across the Queensland frontier', in *Frontier Conflict: The Australian Experience*, eds. B. Attwood & S.G. Foster. Canberra: National Museum of Australia.

Evans R. 2004. '"Plenty shoot 'em": The destruction of Aboriginal societies along the Queensland frontier', in *Genocide and Settler Society: Frontier Violence and Stolen Indigenous Children in Australian History*, ed. A. Moses. New York: Berghahn Books.

Evans R. 2007. *History of Queensland*. Cambridge: Cambridge University Press.

Evans R. 2008a. 'Done and dusted'. *Griffith Review*, 21.

Evans R. 2008b. '"On the utmost verge": Race and ethnic relations at Moreton Bay, 1799–1842', *Queensland Review*, 15, no. 1.

Evans R. 2009. 'Queensland 1859: Reflections on the act of becoming'. *Queensland Review*, 16, no. 1.

Evans R. 2010. 'The country has another past: Queensland and the history wars', in *Passionate Histories: Myth, Memory and Indigenous Australia*, eds. F. Peters-Little, A. Curthoys & J. Docker. Canberra: ANU Press.

Evans R. 2013. 'Foreword', in Bottoms T. 2013. *Conspiracy of Silence: Queensland's Frontier Killing Times*. Sydney: Allen & Unwin.

Evans R., Saunders K. & Cronin K. 1988. *Race Relations in Colonial Queensland: A History of Exclusion, Exploitation and Extermination*. St Lucia: University of Queensland Press.

Fanon F. 1963. *The Wretched of the Earth*. New York: Grove Press.

Farmer P. 1997. 'On suffering and structural violence: A view from below', in *Social Suffering*, eds. A. Kleinman, V. Das & M. Lock. Berkeley: University of California Press.

Farrujia de la Rosa A. 2005. *Imperialist Archaeology in the Canary Islands: French and German Studies on Prehistoric Colonization at the End of the Nineteenth Century*. Oxford: John & Erica Hedges.

Farrujia de la Rosa A. 2014. *An Archaeology of the Margins: Colonialism, Amazighity and Heritage Management in the Canary Islands*. New York: Springer.

Fear-Segal J. 2007. *White Man's Club: Schools, Race, and the Struggle of Indian Acculturation*. Lincoln: University of Nebraska Press.

Fein H. 1990. *Genocide: A Sociological Perspective*. London & Newbury Park: Sage Publications.

Fenn E. 2001. *Pox Americana: The Great Smallpox Epidemic of 1775–82*. New York: Hill & Wang.

Fernández-Armesto F. 1982. *The Canary Islands after the Conquest: The Making of a Colonial Society in the Early Sixteenth Century*. Oxford: Oxford University Press.

Fernández-Armesto F. 1987. *Before Columbus: Exploration and Colonization from the Mediterranean to the Atlantic, 1229–1492*. London: Macmillan.

Fernández-Armesto F. 2006. *Pathfinders: A Global History of Exploration*. Oxford: Oxford University Press.

Fernández-Armesto F. 2009. *1492: The Year the World Began*. New York: HarperCollins.

Finger C. 1968 [1936]. *Valiant Vagabonds*. New York: Books for Libraries Press.

Finnane M. & Richards J. 2010. 'Aboriginal violence and state response: Histories, policies, legacies in Queensland 1860–1940'. *ANZ Journal of Criminology*, 43, no. 2.

Finzsch N. 2008. '"The Aborigines … were never annihilated, and still they are becoming extinct": Settler imperialism and genocide in nineteenth-century America and Australia', in *Empire, Colony, Genocide: Conquest, Occupation and Subaltern Resistance in World History*, eds. A.D. Moses. New York: Berghahn Books.

Fisher R. 1977. *Contact and Conflict: Indian–European Relations in British Colombia, 1774–1890*. Vancouver: University of British Columbia Press.

Fisk A. & Rai T. 2015. *Virtuous Violence: Hurting and Killing to Create, Sustain, End, and Honor Social Relationships*. Cambridge: Cambridge University Press.

Fitzmaurice A. 2007. 'The genealogy of *terra nullius*'. *Australian Historical Studies*, 38, no. 129.

FitzRoy R. 1839. *Narrative of the Surveying Voyages of His Majesty's Ships Adventure and Beagle between the Years 1826 and 1836*. London: Henry Colburn.

Flores C., Maca-Meyer N., Pérez J.A., González A.M., Larruga J.M. & Cabrera V.M. 2003. 'A predominant European ancestry of paternal lineages from Canary Islands'. *Annals of Human Genetics*, 67.

Fontaine T. 2012. *Broken Circle: The Dark Legacy of Indian Residential Schools, a Memoir*. Victoria: Heritage House.

Forster W. 1877. 'The brothers', quoted in Evans R. 2007. *A History of Queensland*. Melbourne: University of Cambridge Press.

Bibliography

Foster S. 2010. *A Private Empire*. Sydney: Pier 9 Books.

Foucault M. 1977. 'The birth of biopolitics', in *Ethics, Subjectivity and Truth*. New York: The New Press.

Fourie J. & Green E. 2018a. 'Building the Cape of Good Hope Panel'. *History of the Family*, 23, no. 3.

Fourie J. & Green E. 2018b. 'Wage labour and slavery on the Cape frontier: The impact of the abolition of slave imports on labour relations in the Graaff-Reinet district', in *Colonialism, Institutional Change and Shifts in Global Labour Relations*, eds. K. Hofmeester & P. de Zwart. Amsterdam: Amsterdam University Press.

Fradera J. 2004. 'Spanish colonial historiography: Everyone in their place'. *Social History*, 29, no. 3.

Frederickson G. 2002. *Racism: A Short History*. Princeton: Princeton University Press.

Freeden M. 2003. *Ideology: A Very Short Introduction*. Oxford: Oxford University Press.

Fregel R., Gomes V., Gusmão L., González A.M., Cabrera, V.M., Amorim A. & Larruga J.M. 2009. 'Demographic history of Canary Islands male gene-pool: Replacement of native lineages by European'. *BMC Evolutionary Biology*, 9.

French M. 1989. *Conflict on the Condamine: Aborigines and the European Invasion*. Toowoomba: Darling Downs Institute Press.

Fujii L.A. 2004. 'Transforming the moral landscape: The diffusion of a genocidal norm in Rwanda'. *Journal of Genocide Research*, 6, no. 1.

Fujii L.A. 2009. *Killing Neighbors: Webs of Violence in Rwanda*. Ithaca: Cornell University Press.

Galton F. 1855. *The Art of Travel*. London: John Murray.

Galtung J. 1969. 'Violence, peace and peace research'. *Journal of Peace Research*, 6, no. 3.

Gammage B. 2011. *The Biggest Estate on Earth: How Aborigines Made Australia*. Sydney: Allen & Unwin.

Gann L. & Duignan P. 1987. *Rulers of German Africa*. Stanford: Stanford University Press.

Gapps S. 2018. *The Sydney Wars: Conflict in the Early Colony, 1788–1817*. Sydney: NewSouth Books.

García-Moro C. 1992. 'Reconstrucción del proceso de extinción de los Selknam a través de los libros misionales'. *Anales del Instituto de la Patagonia*, 21.

Gardiner A. 1896. *Records of the South American Missionary Society, or Fifty Years Work of the Church of England in South America (British Guiana Excepted)*. 4th ed. London: South American Missionary Society.

Gardner P.D. 2000. *Gippsland Massacres*. Ensay: Ngarak Press.

Gavigan S. 2012. *Hunger, Horses, and Government Men: Criminal Law on the Aboriginal Plains, 1870–1905*. Vancouver: University of British Columbia Press.

Gil J. & Martin F. 1993. *History of the Canary Islands*. Santa Cruz: Centro de la Cultura Popular Canaria.

Glas G. 2006. *The History of the Discovery and Conquest of the Canary Islands*. London: Adamantine Media Corporation (first published London: R. & J. Dodsley, 1764. Translation of Abreu de Galindo J. 1632. *Historia de las siete Islas de Canarias*).

Goffman E. 1974. *Frame Analysis: An Essay on the Organization of Experience*. Cambridge, MA: Harvard University Press.

Goodman J. 1998. *Chivalry and Exploration, 1298–1630*. Woodbridge: Boydell Press.

Gordon R. 2013. 'Moritz Bonn, Southern Africa and the critique of colonialism'. *African Historical* Review, 45, no. 2.

Gordon R. & Meggitt M. 1985. *Law and Order in the New Guinea Highlands.* Hanover, NH: University Press of New England.

Gordon R.J. 1992. *The Bushman Myth and the Making of a Namibian Underclass.* Boulder: Westview.

Gordon R.J. 1998. 'Vagrancy, law and "shadow knowledge": Internal pacification 1915–1939', in *Namibia Under South African Rule: Mobility and Containment*, eds. P. Hayes, J. Silvester, M. Wallace & W. Hartmann. Windhoek: Out of Africa.

Gordon R.J. 2009. '"Hiding in full view": The forgotten Bushman genocides in Namibia'. *Genocide Studies & Prevention*, 4.

Gordon R.J. 2017. '"Taming" Bushman farm labour: A villeinous era in neo-feudal Namibia?' *Anthropology Southern Africa*, 40, no. 4.

Gough B. 1984. *Gunboat Frontier: British Maritime Authority and Northwest Coast Indians, 1846–1890.* Vancouver: University of British Columbia Press.

Gourevitch P. 1998. *We Wish to Inform You that Tomorrow We Will Be Killed with Our Families: Stories from Rwanda.* New York: Farrar Straus & Giroux.

Gram J. 2012. 'Education on the Edge of Empire: Pueblos and the Federal Boarding Schools, 1880–1930'. PhD dissertation, Southern Methodist University.

Grandy L. 2017. 'First nations and local courts of New Brunswick: Negotiated relationships, Atlantic Loyalist connections'. The Loyalist Collection, University of New Brunswick. Available at https://loyalist.lib.unb.ca/atlantic-loyalist-connections/first-natins-and-local-courts-new-brunswick, accessed 29 October 2019.

Guelke L. & Shell R. 1992. 'Landscape of conquest: Frontier water alienation and Khoikhoi strategies of survival 1652–1780'. *Journal of Southern African Studies*, 18, no. 4.

Guerrero M. 1897. *Memoria que el Delegado del Supremo Gobierno en el Territorio de Magallanes don Mariano Guerrero Bascuñan presenta al señor Ministro de Colonización.* Santiago: Imprenta i Librería Ercilla.

Guichaoua A. 2015. *From War to Genocide: Criminal Politics in Rwanda, 1990–1994*, trans. D.E. Webster. Madison: University of Wisconsin Press.

Gunn D. 1937. *Links with the Past.* Brisbane: John Mills.

Hagedorn H. 1921. *Roosevelt in the Bad Lands.* Boston: Houghton Mifflin.

Haig-Brown C. & Nock D.A., eds. 2006. *With Good Intentions: Euro-Canadian & Aboriginal Relations in Colonial Canada.* Vancouver: University of British Columbia Press.

Halenke H. 1985. 'Farmvereine und Genossenschaften', in *Vom Schutzgebiet bis Namibia, 1884–1984*, eds. H. Becker & J. Hecker. Windhoek: Interessengemeinschaft Deutschsprachiger Südwester.

Hall S. 1986. 'Pastoral adaptations and forager reactions in the Eastern Cape'. *South African Archaeological Society, Goodwin Series*, 5.

Hamilton M. 1987. 'The elements of the concept of ideology'. *Political Studies*, 35, no. 1.

Hannaford I. 1996. *Race: The History of an Idea in the West.* Baltimore: Johns Hopkins University Press.

Harambour A. 2012. 'Borderland Sovereignties: Postcolonial Colonialism and State Making in Patagonia, Argentina and Chile, 1840s–1922'. PhD dissertation, Department of History, Stony Brook University, New York.

Harambour A. 2015. 'El ovejero y el bandido: Trayectorias, cruces y genocidio en dos relatos de viaje británicos en Tierra del Fuego (década de 1890)'. *Anales de Literatura Chilena*, 16, no. 24.

Harambour A. 2016. *Un Viaje a las Colonias: Memorias de un Ovejero Escocés en Malvinas, Patagonia y Tierra del Fuego (1878–1898)*, trans. M. Azara & A. Harambour. Santiago: DIBAM-Centro de Investigaciones Diego Barros Arana.

Harambour A. 2017. 'Soberanía y corrupción: La construcción del estado y la propiedad en Patagonia austral (Argentina y Chile, 1840s–1920s)'. *Historia*, 50, no. 2.

Harambour A. 2018. 'Los prohombres y los extintos: Patrimonio, identidad e historiografía regional en Magallanes'. *Cuadernos de Historia*, 48.

Harambour A. & Barrena J. 2019. 'Barbarie o justicia en la Patagonia occidental: Las violencias coloniales en el ocaso del pueblo kawésqar, finales del siglo XIX e inicios del siglo XX'. *Historia Crítica*, 71.

Harari Y. 2014. *A Brief History of Humankind*. London: Harvill Secker.

Harring S.L. 1998. *White Man's Law: Native People in Nineteenth Century Canadian Jurisprudence*. Toronto: University of Toronto Press.

Harring S.L. 2015. 'Dispossession, ecocide, genocide: Cattle ranching and agriculture in the destruction of hunting cultures on the Canadian Prairie', in *Genocide on Settler Frontiers: When Hunter-gatherers and Commercial Stock Farmers Clash*, ed. M. Adhikari. Cape Town: UCT Press.

Harris C. 1997/1998. 'Social power and cultural change in pre-colonial British Columbia'. *BC Studies*, no. 115/116.

Harris C. 2002. *Making Native Space: Colonialism, Resistance, and Reserves in British Columbia*. Vancouver: University of British Columbia Press.

Harris C. 2004. 'How did colonialism dispossess? Comments from the edge of empire'. *Annals of the Association of American Geographers*, 94, no. 1.

Harris C. 2008. *The Reluctant Land: Society, Space, and Environment in Canada before Confederation*. Vancouver: University of British Columbia Press.

Harris J. 2003. 'Hiding the bodies: The myth of humane colonization of Aboriginal Australia'. *Aboriginal History*, 27.

Harrison B. 1978. 'The Myall Creek massacre', in *Records of Times Past: Ethnohistorical Essays on the Culture and Ecology of the New England Tribes*, ed. I. McBryde. Canberra: Australian Institute of Aboriginal Studies.

Hart T. 1989. 'Haaskraal and Volstruisfontein: Late Stone Age Events at Two Rock Shelters in the Zeekoe Valley, Great Karoo, South Africa'. MA dissertation, University of Cape Town.

Harvey D. 2003. *The New Imperialism*. Oxford: Oxford University Press.

Hasian M. 2019. *Debates on Colonial Genocide in the 21st Century*. Houndmills: Palgrave.

Haussler M. 2013. '"Kultur der Grausamkeit" und die Dynamik "eradierender Praktiken": Ein Beitrag zur Erforschung extremer Gewalt'. *Sociologus*, 63.

Hegel G.W.F. 1977 [1807]. 'Philosophy of right', in *Phenomenology*. Oxford: Oxford University Press.

Heller-Roazen D. 2009. *The Enemy of All: Piracy and the Law of Nations*. New York: Zone Books.

Herrera S. 1978. *The Canary Islands through History*. Madrid: Editorial Drosbe.

Hixson W. 2013. *American Settler Colonialism: A History*. New York: Palgrave Macmillan.

Hoernlé A.W. 1987. *Trails in the Thirstland: The Anthropological Field Diaries of Winifred Hoernlé*, eds. P. Carstens, G. Klinghardt & M. West. Cape Town: University of Cape Town.

Hoxie F. 1983. *The Final Promise: The Campaign to Assimilate the Indian, 1880–1920*. Lincoln: University of Nebraska Press.

Hudson V.M, Ballif-Spanvill B., Caprioli M. & Emmet C.F. 2014. *Sex and World Peace*. New York: Columbia University Press.

Hull I. 2003. 'Military culture and the production of "Final Solutions" in the colonies: The example of Wilhelmian Germany', in *The Specter of Genocide*, eds. R. Gellately & B. Kiernan. New York: Cambridge University Press.

Huseman J. & Short D. 2012. *Extreme Energy as Genocidal Method: Tar Sands and the Indigenous Peoples of Northern Alberta*. Extreme Energy Initiative Research Paper. Available at http://extrmeenergy.org/files/2013/07/EEI-Tar-Sands-RP.pdf, accessed 29 October 2019.

Hutchings K. 2016. 'Cultural genocide and the first nations of Upper Canada: Some romantic-era roots of Canada's residential school system'. *European Romantic Review*, 27, no. 3.

Hyer S. 1990. *One House, One Voice, One Heart: Native American Education at the Santa Fe Indian School*. Santa Fe: Museum of New Mexico Press.

Inda E. 2008. *The Extermination of the Onas*. Buenos Aires: Cofomar.

Jacobs M.D. 1999. *Engendered Encounters: Feminism and Pueblo Cultures, 1879–1934*. Lincoln: University of Nebraska Press.

Jacobs M.D. 2009. *White Mother to a Dark Race: Settler Colonialism, Maternalism, and the Removal of Indigenous Children in the American West and Australia, 1880–1940*. Lincoln: University of Nebraska Press.

Jahoda G. 1999. *Images of Savages: Ancient Roots of Modern Prejudice in Western Culture*. New York: Routledge.

Jefremovas V. 1991. 'Loose women, virtuous wives, and timid virgins: Gender and the control of resources in Rwanda'. *Canadian Journal of African Studies*, 25, no. 3.

Jefremovas V. 1995. 'Acts of human kindness: Hutu, Tutsi and genocide'. *Issue: A Journal of Opinion*, 23, no. 2.

Johnson A. & Lawson A. 2005. 'Settler colonies', in *A Companion to Postcolonial Studies*, eds. S. Ray & H. Schwarz. Malden: Blackwell.

Jones A. 2009. '"When the rabbit's got the gun": Subaltern genocide and the genocidal continuum', in *Genocides by the Oppressed: Subaltern Genocide in Theory and Practice*, eds. N.A. Robins & A. Jones. Bloomington: Indiana University Press.

Jones A. 2011. *Genocide: A Comprehensive Introduction*. Abingdon: Routledge.

Kalekin-Fishman D. 2013. 'Sociology of everyday life'. *Current Sociological Review*, 61, nos. 5–6.

Kalyvas S. 2006. *The Logic of Violence in Civil War*. New York: Cambridge University Press.

Kamen H. 1983. *Spain, 1469–1714*. London: Longman.

Karskens G. 2009. *The Colony*. Sydney: Allen & Unwin.

Karskens G. 2013. 'The early colonial presence', in *The Cambridge History of Australia*, vol. 1, eds. A. Bashford & S. Macintyre. Melbourne: Cambridge University Press.

Keen M. 1986. 'Gadifer de La Salle: A late medieval knight errant', in *The Ideals and Practices of Medieval Knighthood: Papers from the First and Second Strawberry Hill Conferences*, eds. C. Harper-Bill & R. Harvey. Dover: Boydell Press.

Keller R.H. 1983. *American Protestantism and the United States Indian Policy, 1869–82*. Lincoln: University of Nebraska Press.

Kesselring R. 2017. *Bodies of Truth: Law, Memory, and Emancipation in Post-apartheid South Africa*. Stanford: Stanford University Press.

Kicza J. 1992. 'Patterns in early Spanish overseas expansion'. *William and Mary Quarterly*, 49, no. 2.

Kiernan B. 2007. *Blood and Soil: A World History of Genocide and Extermination from Sparta to Darfur*. New Haven: Yale University Press.

Kimonyo J-P. 2014. *Rwanda's Popular Genocide: A Perfect Storm*. Boulder, CO: Lynne Rienner.

King R. 2017. 'Cattle, raiding and disorder in southern African history'. *Africa*, 87, no. 3.

King R. & Challis S. 2017. 'The interior world of the nineteenth-century Maloti-Drakensberg Moutains'. *Journal of African History*, 58, no. 2.

Kingston B. 2007. *A History of New South Wales*. Melbourne: Cambridge University Press.

Kohen J. & Lampert R. 1987. 'Hunters and fishers in the Sydney region'. in *Australians to 1788*, eds. D.J. Mulvaney & J.P White. Sydney: Fairfax, Syme & Weldon Associates.

Köhler O. 1957. 'Dokumente zur Enstehung des Buschmannproblems in Südwestafrika', in *Afrikanischer Heimatkalender*.

Kulchyski P. 2005. *Like the Sound of a Drum: Aboriginal Cultural Politics in Denendeh and Nunavut*. Winnipeg: University of Manitoba Press.

Laderman S. 2002. '"It is cheaper and better to teach a young Indian than to fight an old one": Thaddeus Pound and the logic of assimilation'. *American Indian Culture and Research Journal*, 26, no. 3.

Laforteza E. 2018. 'Teaching nationhood: An Asian Australian story'. Kardla (Fire)/News/Symposia, 27 April. Australian Critical Race and Whiteness Studies Association. Available at https://acrawsa.org.au/2018/04/27/teaching-nationhood-an-asian-australian-storyteaching-nationhood-an-asian-australian-story/, accessed 30 October 2019.

Landry M. 2010. 'Pokemouche Mi'kmaq and the Colonial Regimes'. MA dissertation, St Mary's University, Halifax.

Lantian A, Muller D., Nurra C. & Douglas K.M. 2017 '"I know things they don't know!": The role of need for uniqueness in conspiracy theories'. *Social Psychology*, 48.

Latour B. 1987. *Science in Action: How to Follow Scientists and Engineers through Society*. Cambridge, MA: Harvard University Press.

Lawrence B. 2003. 'Gender, race, and the regulation of native identity in Canada and the United States: An overview'. *Hypatia*, 18, no. 2.

Legassick M. & Wolpe H. 1976. 'The bantustans and capital accumulation in South Africa'. *Review of African Political Economy*, 7.

Lemkin R. 1944. *Axis Rule in Occupied Europe: Laws of Occupation, Analysis of Government, Proposals for Redress*. New York: Columbia University Press.

Leser H. 1982. *Namibia*. Stuttgart: Ernst Klett.

Levi P. 2017 [1958]. *Si Esto es un Hombre*, trans. P. Gómez. Buenos Aires: Ariel.

Lewy G. 2007. 'Can there be genocide without the intent to commit genocide?'. *Journal of Genocide Research*, 9, no. 4.

Lindner E.G. 2004. 'Genocide, humiliation, and inferiority: An interdisciplinary perspective', in *Genocides by the Oppressed: Subaltern Genocide in Theory and Practice*, eds. N.A. Robins & A. Jones. Bloomington: Indiana University Press.

Lindsay B. 2012. *Murder State: California's Native American Genocide, 1846–1873*. Lincoln: University of Nebraska Press.

Lista R. 1887. *Viaje al País de los Onas: Tierra del Fuego*. Buenos Aires: Establecimiento Tipográfico de Alberto Núñez.

Livermore H. 1968. *A History of Spain*. New York: Minerva.

Lockner L. 1942. *What About Germany?* New York: Dodd, Mead.

Longman T. 2004. 'Placing genocide in context: Research priorities for the Rwandan genocide'. *Journal of Genocide Research*, 6, no. 11.

Loo T. 1994. *Making Law, Order, and Authority in British Columbia, 1821–1871*. Toronto: University of Toronto Press.

Loos N. 1982. *Invasion and Resistance: Aboriginal-European Relations on the North Queensland Frontier 1861–1897*. Canberra: Australian National University Press.

Loos N. & Reynolds H. 1976. 'Aboriginal resistance in Queensland'. *Australian Journal of Politics and History*, 22, no. 2.

Lopez-Portillo J., ed. 2013. *Spain, Portugal and the Atlantic Frontier of Medieval Europe*. Farnham: Ashgate Variorum.

Lord W.B. & Baines T. 1871 *Shifts and Expedients of Camp Life, Travel and Exploration*. London: Horace Cox.

Lourandos H. 1997. *Continent of Hunter-gatherers: New Perspectives on Australian Prehistory*. Cambridge: Cambridge University Press.

Lux M. 2001. *Medicine that Walks: Disease, Medicine and Canadian Native People, 1880–1940*. Toronto: University of Toronto Press.

Lydon J. 1996. '"No moral doubt": Aboriginal evidence and the Kangaroo Creek poisoning, 1847–1849'. *Aboriginal History*, 20.

Lydon J. & Ryan L., eds. 2018. *Remembering The Myall Creek Massacre*. Sydney: NewSouth Books.

Maca-Meyer N., Arnay M., Rando J.C., Flores C., González A.M., Cabrera V.M. & Larruga J.M. 2004. 'Ancient mtDNA analysis and the origin of the Guanches'. *European Journal of Human Genetics*, 12.

Maca-Meyer N., Villar J., Pérez-Méndez L., Cabrera de Léon A. and Flores C. 2004. 'A tale of aborigines, conquerors and slaves: Alu insertion polymorphisms and the peopling of Canary Islands'. *Annals of Human Genetics*, 68.

MacDonald L. 1981. *Rockhampton: A History of City and District*. St Lucia: University of Queensland Press.

MacDonald D.B. & Hudson G. 2012. 'The genocide question and Indian residential schools in Canada'. *Canadian Journal of Political Science*, 45, no. 2.

Mac Ginty R. 2014. 'Everyday peace: Bottom-up and local agency in conflict-affected societies'. *Security Dialogue*, 43, no. 3.

Macleod R.C. 1976. *The North-West Mounted Police and Law Enforcement, 1873–1905*. Toronto: University of Toronto Press.

Madley B. 2016. *An American Genocide: The United States and the California Indian Catastrophe, 1846–1873*. New Haven: Yale University Press.

Major R. 1967. *The Life of Prince Henry of Portugal, Surnamed the Navigator, and its Results; from Authentic Contemporary Documents*. London: Cass (first published 1868 London: Major R. 1970. A. Ascher & Co.).

Malherbe V.C. 1978. 'Diversification and Mobility of Khoikhoi Labour in the Eastern Districts of the Cape Colony Immediately prior to the Labour Law of 1 November 1809'. MA dissertation, University of Cape Town.

Malherbe V.C. 1980. 'David Stuurman: Last chief of the Hottentots'. *African Studies*, 39, no. 1.

Malherbe V.C. 1982. 'Hermanus and his sons: Khoi bandits and conspirators in the post-rebellion period, 1803–1818'. *African Studies*, 41, no. 2.

Malherbe V.C. 1997. 'The Cape Khoisan in the Eastern Districts of the Colony before and after Ordinance 50 of 1828'. PhD dissertation, University of Cape Town.

Mamdani M. 2002. *When Victims Become Killers: Colonialism, Nativism and the Genocide in Rwanda*. Princeton: Princeton University Press.

Mann B.A. 2013. 'Fractal massacres in the Old Northwest: The example of the Miamis'. *Journal of Genocide Research*, 15, no. 2.

Manne R. 2004. *Whitewash*. Melbourne: Black Inc.

Maquet J.J. 1961. *The Premise of Inequality in Ruanda: A Study of Political Relations in a Central African Kingdom*. London: Oxford University Press.

Marais J.S. 1944. *Maynier and the First Boer Republic*. Cape Town: Maskew Miller.

Marchante J.L. 2014. *Menéndez, Rey de la Patagonia*. Santiago: Catalonia.

Marquez X. 2013. 'Engines of sacrality: A footnote on Randall Collins' *Interaction Ritual Chains*'. Blog post, Abandoned Footnotes, 14 April. Available at *http://abandonedfootnotes.blogspot.co.uk/2013/04/engines-of-sacrality-footnote-on.html*, accessed 31 October 2019.

Marshall I. 2001. *The Beothuk*. St John's: Newfoundland Historical Society.

Martinic M. 1973. 'Panorama de la colonización en Tierra del Fuego entre 1881 y 1900'. *Anales del Instituto de la Patagonia*, IV, no. 1.

Martinic M. 1981. *La Tierra de los Fuegos*. Porvenir: Municipalidad de Porvenir.

Martinic M. 1996. 'Diario de vida de William Blain. Ovejero on Tierra de Fuego (1891–1898) *Magallania*, 27, no. 1.

Martinic M. 2003. 'La minería aurífera en la región austral americana (1869–1950)'. *Historia*, 36.

Martinic M. 2011. 'Centenario del cierre de la misión de Dawson: Reflexiones sobre un esfuerzo admirable e infructuoso'. *Magallania*, 39, no. 2.

Martinic M. 2015. Review of *Menéndez, rey de la Patagonia*. *Magallania*, 43, no. 1.

Mason J. & A. 1976. *The Canary Islands*. London: Batsford.

May D. 1994. *Aboriginal Labour and the Cattle Industry: Queensland from White Settlement to the Present*. Melbourne: Cambridge University Press.

Maynard J.L. 2014. 'Rethinking the role of ideology in mass atrocities'. *Terrorism and Political Violence*, 26, no. 5.

Mbembe A. 1992. 'The banality of power and the aesthetics of vulgarity in the postcolony'. *Public Culture*, 4, no. 2.

Mbembe A. 2003. 'Necropolitics'. *Public Culture*, 15, no. 1.

McDonald J. 2015. 'Subjects of the Crown: Khoesan Identity and Assimilation in the Cape Colony, c. 1795–1858'. PhD dissertation, University of London.

McDonald J. 2016. '"We do not know who painted our pictures": Child transfers and cultural genocide in the destruction of Cape San societies along the Cape Colony's north-eastern frontier, c. 1770–1830'. *Journal of Genocide Research*, 18, no. 4.

McGranaghan M. 2015. 'Hunters-with-sheep: The /Xam Bushmen of South Africa between pastoralism and foraging'. *Africa*, 85, no. 3.

McGrath A. 1987. *Born in the Cattle: Aborigines in Cattle Country*. Sydney: Allen & Unwin.

McKenna M. 2018. moment of truth: History and Australia's future. *Quarterly Essay*, 69.

McNamara P. 2011. '"Nuclear genocide" at Serpent River First Nation, Elliot Lake, Ontario'. *Beyond Nuclear*, 26 November. Available at http://www.beyondnuclear. org/uranium-mining/2011/11/26/nuclear-genocide-at-serpent-river, accessed 29 October 2019.

Memmi A. 1968. *The Colonizer and the Colonized*. Boston: Beacon Press.

Mercer J. 1979. 'The Canary Islanders in Western Mediterranean politics'. *African Affairs*, 78, no. 3.

Mercer J. 1980. *The Canary Islanders: Their Prehistory, Conquest and Survival*. London: Rex Collings.

Merediz E. 2001. 'Travelling icons: The Virgin of Candelaria's transatlantic journeys'. *Arizona Journal of Hispanic Cultural Studies*, 5.

Merediz E. 2004. *Refracted Images: The Canary Islands through a New World Lens*. Tempe: Arizona Center for Medieval and Renaissance Studies.

Meston A. 1889. 'Report on the government scientific expedition to the Bellenden-Kerr Range (Wooroonooran), North Queensland'. *Queensland Legislative Council Votes and Proceedings* II, 1213.

Meyn S.L. 2001. *More than Curiosities: A Grassroots History of the Indian Arts and Crafts Board and its Precursors, 1920–1942*. Lanham: Lexington Books.

Miller J.R., ed. 1991. *Sweet Promises: A Reader on Indian–White Relations in Canada*. Toronto: University of Toronto Press.

Miller J.R. 1996. *Shingwauk's Vision: A History of Native Residential Schools*. Toronto: University of Toronto Press.

Miller J.R. 2017. *Residential Schools and Reconciliation: Canada Confronts its History*. Toronto: University of Toronto Press.

Miller P. & Rose N. 1990. 'Governing economic life'. *Economy and Society*, 19, no. 1.

Miller R.J. 2010. 'The doctrine of discovery', in *Discovering Indigenous Lands: The Doctrine of Discovery in the English Colonies*, eds. R.J. Miller, J. Ruru, L. Behrendt & T. Lindberg. Oxford: Oxford University Press.

Milliss R.1992. *Waterloo Creek: The Australia Day Massacre of 1838. George Gipps and the British Conquest of New South Wales*. Melbourne: McPhee Gribble.

Milloy J. 1999. *A National Crime: The Canadian Government and the Residential School System*. Winnipeg: University of Manitoba Press.

Molony J. 1973. *An Architect of Freedom: John Hubert Plunkett in New South Wales 1832–1869*. Canberra: Australian National University Press.

Moodie D. 1838/1839. *The Record or Official Papers Relative to the Condition and Treatment of the Native Tribes of South Africa*. Cape Town: A.S. Robertson (for published parts) and Cape Town Archives Repository (KAB), VC 871-897 (for drafts of unpublished parts II and IV).

Moreno M. 2017. 'Estado, soberanía y resistencia indígena: La colonización ovina de Tierra del Fuego y la resistencia Selk'nam, 1881–1911', in *Seminario Simon Collier*. Santiago: Instituto de Historia P. Universidad Católica de Chile.

Moses A.D. 2004. 'Genocide and settler society in Australian history', in *Genocide and Settler Society: Frontier Violence and Stolen Indigenous Children in Australian History*, ed. A.D. Moses. New York: Berghahn Books.

Moses A.D., ed. 2005. *Genocide and Settler Society: Frontier Violence and Stolen Indigenous Children in Australian History*. New York: Berghahn Books.

Moses A.D., ed. 2008a. *Empire, Colony, Genocide: Conquest, Occupation and Subaltern Resistance in World History*. New York: Berghahn Books.

Moses A.D. 2008b. 'Genocide and modernity', in *The Historiography of Genocide*, ed. D. Stone. Houndmills: Palgrave Macmillan.

Moses A.D. & Stone D., eds. 2008. *Colonialism and Genocide*. Abingdon: Routledge.

Muschalek M. 2014. 'Everyday Violence and the Production of Colonial Order: The Police in German Southwest Africa 1905–1915'. PhD dissertation, Cornell University.

Muschalek M. 2019. *Violence as Usual: Everyday Police Work and the Colonial State in German Southwest Africa*. Ithaca: Cornell University Press.

Naude S.D. & Venter P.J. 1949. *Kaapse Plakkaatboek*. Part 4. Cape Town: *Cape Times*.

Nettelbeck A. & Ryan L. 2018. 'Salutary lessons: Native police and the "civilising" role of legalised violence in colonial Australia'. *Journal of Imperial and Commonwealth History*, 46, no. 1.

Neville D. 1996. 'European Impacts on the Seacow River Valley and its Hunter-gatherer Inhabitants, AD 1770–1900'. MA dissertation, University of Cape Town.

Newbury C. 1988. *The Cohesion of Oppression: Rwanda, 1860–1960*. New York: Columbia University Press.

Newbury C. 1998. 'Ethnicity and the politics of history in Rwanda'. *Africa Today*, 45, no. 1.

Newbury D. 2012. 'Canonical conventions in Rwanda: Four myths of recent historiography in Central Africa'. *History in Africa*, 39, no. 1.

Newbury D. & Newbury C. 2000. 'Bringing the peasants back in: Agrarian themes in the construction and corrosion of statist historiography in Rwanda'. *American Historical Review*, 105, no. 3.

Newton-King S. 1999. *Masters and Servants on the Cape Eastern Frontier*. Cambridge: Cambridge University Press.

Newton-King S. & Malherbe V.C. 1981. *The Khoikhoi Rebellion in the Eastern Cape, 1799–1803*. Communication no. 5. Cape Town: Centre for African Studies, University of Cape Town.

Nicholas A. 2011. 'Settler imperialism and the dispossession of the Maliseet, 1758–1765', in *Shaping an Agenda for Atlantic Canada*, eds. J. Reid & D. Savoie. Halifax: Fernwood Publishers.

Nichols A. 2015. 'The role of colonial artists in the dispossession and displacement of the Maliseet, 1790–1850s'. *Journal of Canadian Studies/Revue d'études canadiennes*, 49, no. 2.

Nichols R.L. 1998. *Indians in the United States and Canada: A Comparative History*. Lincoln: University of Nebraska Press.

Niezen R. 2013. *Truth & Indignation: Canada's Truth and Reconciliation on Indian Residential Schools*. Toronto: University of Toronto Press.

Nutt S. 2018. 'Pluralized sovereignties: Autochthonous lawmaking on the settler colonial frontier in Palestine'. *Interventions: International Journal of Postcolonial Studies*, 21, no. 4.

O'Callaghan J. 1975. *A History of Medieval Spain*. Ithaca: Cornell University Press.

O'Callaghan J. 2013. 'Castile, Portugal and the Canary Islands: Claims and counterclaims, 1344–1479', in *Spain, Portugal and the Atlantic Frontier of Medieval Europe*, ed. J. Lopez-Portillo. Farnham: Ashgate Variorum.

O'Flanagan P. 2017. 'Mediterranean and Atlantic settler colonialism from the late fourteenth to the early seventeenth centuries', in *The Routledge Handbook of the History of Settler Colonialism*, eds. E. Cavanagh & L. Veracini. Abingdon: Routledge.

Oliver P. & Johnston H. 2000. 'What a good idea! Ideologies and frames in social movement research'. *Mobilization: An International Quarterly*, 5, no. 1.

Ørsted-Jensen R. 2011. *Frontier History Revisited: Colonial Queensland and the 'History War'*. Brisbane: Lux Mundi Publishing.

Otis E.S. 1878. *The Indian Question*. New York: Sheldon & Company.

'Ovejero en Tierra del Fuego (1891–1898)'. *Magallania*, 27, no. 1.

Palmater P. 2014. 'Genocide, Indian policy, and legislated elimination of Indians in Canada'. *Aboriginal Policy Studies*, 3, no. 3.

Palmater P. 2016. 'The ongoing legacies of Canadian genocide'. *Canadian Dimension*, 50, no. 1.

Palmer A. 2002. *Colonial Genocide*. Adelaide: Crawford House Publishing.

Pascoe B. 2013. *Dark Emu, Black Seeds: Agriculture or Accident?* Broome: Magabala Books.

Pastore R. 1987. 'Fishermen, furriers, and Beothuks: The economy of extinction'. *Man in the Northeast*, 33.

Pastore R. 1993. 'Archaeology, history and the Beothuks'. *Newfoundland Studies*, 9, no. 2.

Pastore R. & Story G. 1987. 'Demasduwit', in *Dictionary of Canadian Biography*. Toronto: University of Toronto/University of Laval Press.

Patterson S. 1993. 'Indian–White relations in Nova Scotia, 1749–61: A study in political interaction'. *Acadiensis*, 23, no. 1.

Paul D. 2006. *We Are not Savages*. 3rd ed. Winnipeg: Fernwood Publishing.

Paul D. 2011. 'The hidden history of the Americas: The destruction and depopulation of the Indigenous civilizations of the Americas by European invaders'. *Settler Colonial Studies*, 1, no. 2.

Peters M. 2016. 'A Respectable Solution to the Indian Problem: Canadian Genocidal Intent, Non-Physical Conceptions of Destruction and the Nova Scotia Mi'kmaq, 1867–1969'. BA Honours thesis, Acadia University.

Penn N. 2005. *The Forgotten Frontier: Colonist and Khoisan on the Cape's Northern Frontier in the 18th Century*. Cape Town: Double Storey.

Penn N. 2013. 'The British and the Bushmen: The massacre of the Cape San, 1795 to 1828'. *Journal of Genocide Research*, 15, no. 2.

Penn N. 2014. 'The destruction of hunter-gatherer societies on the pastoralist frontier: The Cape and Australia compared', in *Genocide on Settler Frontiers: When Hunter-gatherers and Commercial Stock Farmers Clash*, ed, M. Adhikari. Cape Town: UCT Press.

Penrose R. 1908. 'The gold regions of the Strait of Magellan and Tierra Del Fuego'. *Journal of Geology*, 16, no. 8.

Pérez M. 2011. 'The role of interpreters in the conquest and acculturation of the Canary archipelago'. *Interpreting*, 13, no. 2.

Philip J. 1828. *Researches in South Africa Illustrating: the Civil, Moral and Religious Condition of the Native Tribes.* 2 vols. London: James Duncan.

Plug I. & Sampson C.G. 1996. 'European and Bushmen impacts on Karoo fauna in the nineteenth century: An archaeological perspective'. *South African Archaeological Bulletin*, 51, no. 163.

Pool G. 1979. *Die Herero-Opstand, 1904–1907.* Cape Town: HAUM.

Popper J. 1887. *Exploration of Tierra del Fuego: A Lecture Delivered at the Argentine Geographical Institute on the 5th of March, 1887.* Buenos Aires: L. Jacobsen & Co.

Popper J. 2003. *Atlanta: Proyecto para la Fundación de un Pueblo Marítimo en Tierra del Fuego, y Otros Escritos.* Buenos Aires: Eudeba.

Poulantzas N. 1991 [1978]. *Estado, Poder y Socialismo.* Mexico City: Siglo XXI.

Powell C. 2011. *Barbaric Civilization: A Critical Sociology of Genocide.* Montreal: McGill-Queen's University Press.

Pratt R.H. 1973 [1892]. 'The advantages of mingling Indians with whites', in *Americanizing the American Indians: Writings by the 'Friends of the Indian' 1880–1900*, ed. F.P. Prucha. Cambridge, MA: Harvard University Press.

Price R. 2018. 'The psychology of colonial violence', in *Violence, Colonialism and Empire in the Modern World*, eds. P. Dwyer & A. Nettelbeck. Basingstoke: Palgrave Macmillan.

Prieto A. 2011. *Arquería de Tierra del Fuego.* Santiago: Cuarto Propio.

Prucha F.P. 1984. *The Great Father: The United States Government and the American Indians, Vols. I & II.* Lincoln: University of Nebraska Press.

Purdeková A. 2015. *Making Ubumwe: Power, State and Camps in Rwanda's Unity-Building Project.* New York: Berghahn Books.

Radcliffe-Brown A.R. 1940. 'Preface', in *African Political Systems*, eds. M. Fortes & E.E. Evans-Pritchard. London: Oxford University Press.

Radkau J. 2011. *Max Weber: A Biography.* New York: Polity.

Raibmon P. 1996. '"A new understanding of things Indian": George Raley's negotiation of the residential school experience'. *BC Studies*, 110, Summer.

Ramsey J. 1973. *Spain: The Rise of the First World Power.* Birmingham: University of Alabama Press.

Rathenau W. 1985. *Walther Rathenau: Industrialist, Banker, Intellectual and Politician: Notes and Diaries 1907–1922*, ed. H. Pogge von Strandmann. Oxford: Oxford University Press.

Ray A. 1974. *Indians in the Fur Trade: Their Role as Trappers, Hunters, and Middlemen in the Lands Southwest of Hudson Bay, 1660–1870.* Toronto: University of Toronto Press.

Reece R.H.W. 1974. *Aborigines and Colonists: Aborigines and Colonial Society in New South Wales in the 1830s and 1840s.* Sydney: Sydney University Press.

Reid G. 1982. *A Nest of Hornets: The Massacre of the Fraser Family at Hornet Bank Station, Central Queensland 1857, and Related Events.* Melbourne: Oxford University Press.

Reid J. 2009. 'Empire, the maritime colonies, and the supplanting of Mi'kma'ki/Wulstukwik, 1780–1820'. *Acadiensis*, 38, no. 2.

Reiner O. 1924. *Achtzehn Jahre Farmer in Afrika.* Leipzig: Paul List.

Restall M. 2003. *Seven Myths of the Spanish Conquest.* Oxford: Oxford University Press.

Reyhner J. & Eder J. 2004. *American Indian Education: A History*. Norman: University of Oklahoma Press.

Reynolds H. 1972. 'Violence, the Aboriginals and the Australian historian'. *Meanjin*, 31, no. 4.

Reynolds H. 1981. *The Other Side of the Frontier*. Townsville: James Cook University Press.

Reynolds H. 1987. *Frontier: Aborigines, Settlers and Land*. Sydney: Allen & Unwin.

Reynolds H. 2013. *Forgotten War*. Sydney: University of New South Wales Press.

Reyntjens F. 2018. 'Understanding Rwandan politics through the *longue durée*: From the precolonial to the post-genocide era'. *Journal of Eastern African Studies*, 12, no. 3.

Richards J. 2005. 'A Question of Necessity: The Native Police in Queensland'. PhD dissertation, Griffith University.

Richards J. 2008a. 'The Native Police of Queensland'. *History Compass*, 6, no. 4.

Richards J. 2008b. *The Secret War: A True History of Queensland's Native Police*. St Lucia, Brisbane: University of Queensland Press.

Roberts T. 2005. *Frontier Justice: A History of the Gulf Country to 1900*. St Lucia: University of Queensland Press.

Rodger N. 2011. 'Atlantic seafaring', in *The Oxford Handbook of the Atlantic World, 1450–1850*, eds. N. Canny & P. Morgan. Oxford: Oxford University Press.

Rohrbach P. 1915. *German World Politics*. New York: Macmillan.

Roosevelt T. 1889. *The Winning of the West: From the Alleghenies to the Mississippi, 1769–1776*. New York: G.P. Putnam's Sons.

Roux P.E. 1925. 'Die Vedigingstelsel aan die Kaap onder die Hollandse-Oosindiese Kompanje, 1652–1795'. MA dissertation, University of Stellenbosch.

Rowe E. 1977. *Extinction: The Beothuks of Newfoundland*. Toronto: McGraw-Hill Ryerson.

Ruiz T. 2001. *Spanish Society, 1400–1600*. Harlow: Pearson Education.

Russell P. 2000. *Prince Henry the Navigator: A Life*. New Haven: Yale University Press.

Ryan L. 2003. 'Waterloo Creek, northern New South Wales, 1838', in *Frontier Conflict: The Australian Experience*, eds. B. Attwood & S.G. Foster. Canberra: National Museum of Australia.

Ryan L. 2010. 'Settler massacres in the Port Phillip District, 1836–1851'. *Journal of Australian Studies*, 23, no. 3.

Ryan L. 2012. *Tasmanian Aborigines: A History since 1803*. Sydney: Allen & Unwin.

Ryan L. 2013. 'Untangling Aboriginal resistance and the settler punitive expedition: The Hawkesbury frontier in New South Wales, 1794–1810'. *Journal of Genocide Research*, 15, no. 2.

Ryan L. 2014. '"No right to the land": The role of the wool industry in the destruction of Aboriginal societies in Tasmania (1817–1832) and Victoria (1835–1851) compared', in *Genocide on Settler Frontiers: When Hunter-gatherers and Commercial Stock Farmers Clash*, ed. M. Adhikari. Cape Town: UCT Press.

Ryan L. 2016. 'Frontier massacres in the Australian colonies'. Interview, University of Newcastle.

Ryan L. 2018. '"A very bad business": Henry Dangar and the Myall Creek massacre 1838', in *Remembering the Myall Creek Massacre*, eds. J. Lydon & L. Ryan. Sydney: NewSouth Books.

Bibliography

Sampson C.G. 1993. 'Zeer grote liefhebbers van tobak: Nicotine and cannabis dependency of the Seacow River Bushmen'. *Digging Stick*, 10, no. 1.

Sampson C.G. 1995. 'Acquisition of European livestock by the Seacow River Bushmen between AD 1770–1890'. *South African Field Archaeology*, 4, no. 1.

Sampson C.G., Sampson B.E. & Neville D. 1994. 'An early Dutch settlement pattern on the north east frontier of the Cape Colony'. *South African Archaeological Bulletin*, 3, no. 2.

Sanders E. 1969. 'The Hamitic hypothesis: Its origin and functions in time perspective'. *Journal of African History*, 10, no. 4.

Sankar A. 2019. 'Radical dialectics in Benjamin and Fanon: On recognition and rupture'. *Parrhesia*, 30.

Satzewich V. & Mahood L. 1995. 'Indian agents and the residential school system in Canada, 1946–1970.' *Historical Studies in Education*, 7, no. 1.

Saunders F. 1912. *The Indians of the Terraced Houses*. New York: G.P. Putnam's Sons.

Scheper-Hughes N. 1993. *Death Without Weeping: The Violence of Everyday Life in Brazil*. Berkeley: University of California Press.

Schmalz P.S. 1991. *The Ojibwa of Southern Ontario*. Toronto: University of Toronto Press.

Schoeman K. 1993. 'Die Londense Sendinggenootskap en die San: Die Stasies Toornberg en Hephzibah, 1814–1818'. *South African Historical Journal*, 28, no. 1.

Schwartz T. 1973. 'Cult and context: The paranoid ethos in Melanesia'. *Ethos*, 1, no. 2.

Schwidetzky I. 1976. 'The pre-Hispanic population of the Canary Islands', in *Biogeography and Ecology in the Canary Islands*, ed. G. Kunkel. The Hague: Dr W. Junk Publishers.

Schwirck H. 1998. 'Violence, Race and the Law in German South West Africa 1884–1914'. PhD dissertation, Cornell University.

Schwirck H. 2002. 'Law's violence and the boundary between corporal punishment and physical abuse in German South West Africa'. *Akron Law Review*, 36.

Scott G.S. 1865. *The Aborigines in Australia: In their Original Conditions and their Relations with the White Men*. Melbourne: Wilson & McKinnon.

Scott J. 1990. *Domination and the Arts of Resistance: Hidden Transcripts*. New Haven: Yale University Press.

Semelin J. 2007. *Purify and Destroy: The Political Uses of Massacre and Genocide*, trans. C. Schoch. London: Hurst.

Sennett R. 2006. *The Culture of the New Capitalism*. New Haven: Yale University Press.

Señoret M. 1895. *Memoria del Gobernador de Magallanes: La Tierra del Fuego i sus Naturales*. Santiago: Imprenta Nacional.

Serrano R. 1929. 'Diario de la escursión a la isla grande de la Tierra del Fuego durante los meses de enero i febrero de 1879 por el Teniente 2 de la Armada de Chile Ramón Serrano Montaner', in *Exploraciones y Estudios Hidrográficos: Contribución de la Armada de Chile a la Exposición de Sevilla*. Santiago: Imprenta de la Armada.

Shaw M. 2015. *What is Genocide?* Cambridge: Polity Press.

Short D. 2010. 'Australia: A continuing genocide?'. *Journal of Genocide Research*, 12, nos. 1–2.

Short D. 2016. *Redefining Genocide: Settler Colonialism, Social Death and Ecocide*. London: Zed Books.

Shrubb R. 2014. '"Canada Has No History of Colonialism." Historical Amnesia: The Erasure of Indigenous Peoples from Canadian History'. MA dissertation, University of Victoria.

Skaggs D. & Nelson L. 2010. *The Sixty Years War for the Great Lakes, 1754–1814*. East Lansing: Michigan State University Press.

Skinner L.E. 1975. *Police of the Pastoral Frontier: Native Police 1849–59*. St Lucia, Brisbane: University of Queensland Press.

Slim H. 2007. *Killing Civilians: Method, Madness and Morality in War*. London: Hurst.

Slim H. 2016. 'Civilians, distinction and the compassionate view of war', in *Protection of Civilians*, eds. H. Willmot, R. Mamiya, S. Sheeran & M. Weller. Oxford: Oxford University Press.

Smith K.W. 1976. *From Frontier to Midlands: A History of the Graaff-Reinet District, 1786–1910*. Grahamstown: Institute of Social and Economic Research.

Smith S. 2010. 'The mid-Atlantic islands: A theatre of early modern ecocide?'. *International Review of Social History*, 55, supplement 18.

Snow D.A. & Benford R.D. 1988. 'Ideology, frame resonance and participant mobilization'. *International Social Movement Research*, 1.

Snow D.A. & Benford R.D. 1992. 'Master frames and cycles of protest', in *Frontiers in Social Movement Theory*, eds. A.D. Morris & C. McClurg Mueller. New Haven: Yale University Press.

Sommers M. 2011. *Stuck: Rwandan Youth and the Struggle for Adulthood*. Athens: University of Georgia Press.

Sparrman A. 1977. *A Voyage to the Cape of Good Hope: Towards the Antarctic Polar Circle, and Round the World but Chiefly into the Country of the Hottentots and Caffres, from the Year 1772 to 1776*. vol. 2. Cape Town: Van Riebeeck Society.

Spears J.R. 1895. *The Gold Diggings of Cape Horn: A Study of Life in Tierra del Fuego and Patagonia*. New York: G.P. Putnam's Sons.

Stanley T. 2015. 'John A. Macdonald's Aryan Canada: Aboriginal genocide and Chinese exclusion'. *Active History*, 7 January. Available at http://activehistory.ca/2015/01/john-a-macdonalds-aryan-canada-aboriginal-genocide-and-chinese-exclusion/, accessed 29 October 2019.

Stannard D.E. 1992. *American Holocaust: The Conquest of the New World*. Oxford: Oxford University Press.

Stevens-Arroyo A. 1993. 'The inter-Atlantic paradigm: The failure of Spanish medieval colonization of the Canary and Caribbean islands'. *Comparative Studies in Society and History*, 35, no. 3.

Stoecker H., ed. 1986. *German Imperialism in Africa*. London: Hurst.

Stone P. 2014. *The Canary Islands: A Cultural History*. Oxford: Signal Books.

Storey W.K. 2008. *Guns, Race and Power in Colonial South Africa*. Cambridge: Cambridge University Press.

Straus S. 2006. *The Order of Genocide: Race, Power and War in Rwanda*. Ithaca: Cornell University Press.

Straus S. 2015. *Making and Unmaking Nations: War, Leadership, and Genocide in Modern Africa*. Ithaca: Cornell University Press.

Surtees R. 1969. 'The development of an Indian reserve policy in Canada'. *Ontario History*, 61, no. 2.

Surtees R. 1984. *Report: Indian Land Surrenders in Ontario, 1763–1867*. Canadian Department of Indian and Northern Affairs Treaty Research Centre.

Bibliography

Szalay M. 1995. *The San and the Colonisation of the Cape, 1770–1879: Conflict, Incorporation, Acculturation*. Köln: Rüdiger Köppe.

Szasz M.C. 1988. *Indian Education in the American Colonies, 1607–1783*. Albuquerque: University of New Mexico Press.

Szasz M.C. 1999. *Education and the American Indian: The Road to Self-determination since 1928*. Albuquerque: University of New Mexico Press.

Tang E. 2003. 'Agriculture: The relationship between aboriginal farmers and non-aboriginal farmers'. Research paper, Western Development Museum/Saskatchewan Indian Cultural Centre Partnership Project, 24 April.

Taussig, M. 1992. *The Nervous System*. New York: Routledge.

Taylor A. 2006. *The Divided Ground: Indians, Settlers, and the Northern Borderland of the American Revolution*. New York: Random House.

Taylor A. 2010. *American Citizens, British Subjects, Irish Rebels, and Indian Allies*. New York: Alfred Knopf.

Taylor C. 2004. 'Visions of the "oppressor" in Rwanda's pre-genocidal media', in *Genocides by the Oppressed: Subaltern Genocide in Theory and Practice*, eds. N.A. Robins & A. Jones. Bloomington: Indiana University Press.

Tedeschi M. 2016. *Murder at Myall Creek: The Trial that Defined a Nation*. Sydney: Simon & Schuster.

Tennant P. 1990. *Aboriginal People and Politics: The Indian Land Question in British Columbia, 1849–1989*. Vancouver: University of British Columbia Press.

Theal G.M., comp. 1897–1905. *Records of the Cape Colony*. 36 vols. London: Clowes Printers for the Government of the Cape Colony.

Thompson G. 1967. *Travels and Adventures in Southern Africa*. vol. 1. Cape Town: Van Riebeeck Society.

Thompson G. 1968. *Travels and Adventures in Southern Africa*. vol. 2. Cape Town: Van Riebeeck Society.

Thomson S. 2010. 'Getting close to Rwandans since the genocide: Studying everyday life in highly politicized research settings'. *African Studies Review*, 53, no. 3.

Thomson S. 2013a. 'Academic integrity and ethical responsibilities in post-genocide Rwanda: Working with research ethics boards to prepare for fieldwork with "human subjects"', in *Emotional and Ethical Challenges for Field Research in Africa: The Story Behind the Findings*, eds. S. Thomson, A. Ansoms & J. Murison. London: Palgrave Macmillan.

Thomson S. 2013b. *Whispering Truth to Power: Resistance to Reconciliation in Post-genocide Rwanda*. Madison: University of Wisconsin Press.

Thomson S. 2016. 'Genocide in Rwanda', in *Oxford Bibliographies in African Studies*, ed. T. Spear. New York: Oxford University Press.

Thomson S. 2017. 'The long shadow of genocide in Rwanda'. *Current History*, 116, no. 790.

Thomson S. 2018a. *Rwanda: From Genocide to Precarious Peace*. New Haven: Yale University Press.

Thomson S. 2018b. 'Engaged silences as political agency in postgenocide Rwanda: Jeanne's story', in *Rethinking Silence, Voice and Agency in Contested Gendered Terrains*, eds. S. Parashar & J. Parpart. London: Routledge.

Thorne E. 1901. 'A "white Australia": The other side'. *United Australia*, 2, no. 4.

Thornton J. 1998. *Africa and Africans in the Making of the Atlantic World, 1400–1800.* Cambridge: Cambridge University Press.

Thornton J. 2012. *A Cultural History of the Atlantic World, 1250–1820.* Cambridge: Cambridge University Press.

Thornton R. 1987. *American Indian Holocaust and Survival: A Population History since 1492.* Norman: University of Oklahoma Press.

Tilly C. 2003. *The Politics of Collective Violence.* Cambridge: Cambridge University Press.

Titley E.B. 1986. *A Narrow Vision: Duncan Campbell Scott and the Administration of Indian Affairs in Canada.* Vancouver: UBC Press.

Tobias J. 1991. 'Protection, civilization, assimilation: An outline history of Canada's Indian policy', in *Sweet Promises: A Reader on Indian-White Relations in Canada*, ed. J.R. Miller. Toronto: University of Toronto Press.

Todorov T. 1984. *The Conquest of America: The Question of the Other.* New York: Harper & Row.

Tough F. 1996. *As their Natural Resources Fail: Native Peoples and the Economic History of Northern Manitoba, 1870–1930.* Vancouver: UBC Press.

Trafzer C.E., Keller J.A. & Sisquoc L., eds. 2006. *Boarding School Blues: Revisiting American Indian Educational Experiences.* Lincoln: University of Nebraska Press.

Traverso E. 2003. *The Origins of Nazi Violence.* New York: The New Press.

Trevithick S. 1998. 'Native residential schooling in Canada'. *Canadian Journal of Native Studies*, 18, no. 1.

Trigger B.R. 1985. *Natives and Newcomers: Canada's 'Historic Age' Reconsidered.* Kingston: McGill-Queen's University Press.

Truth and Reconciliation Commission of Canada. 2015b. *The Final Report of the Truth and Reconciliation Commission of Canada. Vol. 6: Reconciliation: Canada's Residential Schools.* Montreal: McGill-Queen's University Press.

Twagiramungu N. 2010. 'The anatomy of leadership: A view-from-within of post-genocide Rwanda'. Unpublished paper presented at the 53rd Annual Conference of the African Studies Association.

Ülgen Ö. 2002. 'Developing the doctrine of aboriginal title in South Africa: Source and content'. *Journal of African Law*, 46, no. 2.

Upton L. 1974. 'Indian affairs in colonial New Brunswick'. *Acadiensis*, 3, no. 2.

Upton L. 1977. 'The extermination of the Beothuks of Newfoundland'. *Canadian Historical Review*, 58, no. 2.

Upton L. 1979. *Micmacs and Colonists: Indian-White Relations in the Maritime Provinces, 1713–1867.* Vancouver: University of British Columbia Press.

Upton L. 1991. 'Extermination of the Beothuks', in *Sweet Promises: A Reader on Indian-White Relations in Canada*, ed. J.R. Miller. Toronto: University of Toronto Press.

Uvin P. 1998. *Aiding Violence: The Development Enterprise in Rwanda.* West Hartford, CT: Kumarian Press.

Valentino B.A. 2004. *Final Solutions: Mass Killing and Genocide in the Twentieth Century.* Ithaca: Cornell University Press.

Vallejo E. 1994. 'The conquests of the Canary Islands', in *Implicit Understandings: Observing, Reporting and Reflecting on the Encounters between Europeans and Other Peoples in the Early Modern Era*, ed. S. Schwartz. Cambridge: Cambridge University Press.

Bibliography

Van der Merwe P.J. 1937. *Die Noordwaartse Beweging van die Boere voor die Groot Trek, 1770–1842*. The Hague: W.P. van Stockum & Zoon.

Vansina J. 2004. *Antecedents to Modern Rwanda: The Nyiginya Kingdom*. Madison: University of Wisconsin Press.

Vansina J. 2010. *Being Colonized: The Kuba Experience in Rural Congo, 1880–1960*. Madison: University of Wisconsin Press.

Veracini L. 2001. 'Towards a further redescription of the Australian pastoral frontier'. *Journal of Australian Studies*, 26, no. 72.

Veracini L. 2010. *Settler Colonialism: A Theoretical Overview*. London: Palgrave Macmillan.

Veracini L. 2015. *The Settler Colonial Present*. Basingstoke: Palgrave Macmillan.

Veracini L. 2014. 'Understanding colonialism and settler colonialism as distinct formations'. *Interventions: International Journal of Postcolonial Studies*, 16, no. 5.

Verlinden C. 1970. *The Beginnings of Modern Colonization*. Ithaca: Cornell University Press.

Verlinden C. 2013.'Feudal and demesnial forms of Portuguese colonisation in the Atlantic zone in the fourteenth and fifteenth centuries, especially under Prince Henry the Navigator', in *Spain, Portugal and the Atlantic Frontier of Medieval Europe*, ed. J. Lopez-Portillo. Farnham: Ashgate Variorum.

Vicens Vives J. 1969. *An Economic History of Spain*. Princeton: Princeton University Press.

Vieira A. 2004. 'The sugar economy of Madeira and the Canaries, 1450–1650', in *Tropical Babylons: Sugar and the Making of the Atlantic World, 1450–1680*, ed. S. Schwartz. Chapel Hill: University of North Carolina Press.

Von Weber O. 1982. *Geschichte des Schutzgebietes Deutsch-Südwest-Afrika*. Windhoek: SWA Wissenschaftlichen Gesellschaft.

Wagner M.D. 1998. 'All the *bourgmestre*'s men: Making sense of genocide in Rwanda'. *Africa Today*, 25, no. 1.

Waiser B. & Stonechild B. 1997. *Loyal Till Death: Indians and the North West Rebellion*. Calgary: Fifth House.

Walker F.A. 1874. *The Indian Question*. Boston: James R. Osgood & Company.

Wallis L., Cole N., Barker B., Bruce H., Lowe K., Davidson I. & Hatte E. 2016. *Rewriting the History of the Native Mounted Police in Queensland*. Nulungu Publication Series, Nulungu Insights No. 1. Broome: Nulungu Research Institute, University of Notre Dame, Australia.

Walther D. 2002. *Creating Germans Abroad*. Athens: Ohio University Press.

Walzer M. 2006. *Just and Unjust Wars: A Moral Argument with Historical Illustrations*. New York: Basic Books.

Wattam J. 2016. 'Dr Peter Henderson Bryce: A story of courage'. First Nations Child and Family Caring Society of Canada, July. Available at https://fncaringsociety.com/sites/default/files/dr._peter_henderson_bryce_information_sheet.pdf, accessed 29 October 2019.

Weaver J. 2003. *The Great Land Rush and the Making of the Modern World, 1650–1900*. Montreal: McGill-Queen's University Press.

Wegner T. 2009. *We Have a Religion: The 1920s Pueblo Indian Dance Controversy and American Religious Freedom*. Chapel Hill: University of North Carolina Press.

Westermann E. 2016. 'Stone-cold killers or drunk with murder?: Alcohol and atrocity during the Holocaust'. *Holocaust and Genocide Studies*, 30, no. 1.

Westermann E.B. 2016. *Hitler's Ostkrieg and the Indian Wars: Comparing Genocide and Conquest*. Norman: University of Oklahoma Press.

White J.P. & Mulvaney D.J. 1987. 'How many?', in *Australians to 1788*, eds. D.J. Mulvaney & J.P. White. Sydney: Fairfax, Syme & Weldon Associates.

White R. 1991. *The Middle Ground: Indians, Empires, and Republics in the Great Lakes Region, 1650–1815*. Cambridge: Cambridge University Press.

Whitt L. & Clarke A. 2019. *North American Genocides: Indigenous Nations, Settler Colonialism, and International Law*. Cambridge: Cambridge University Press.

Wildenthal L. 2001. *German Women for Empire, 1884–1945*. Durham: Duke University Press.

Williams T. & Pfeiffer D. 2017. 'Unpacking the mind of evil: A sociological perspective on the role of intent and motivations in genocide'. *Genocide Studies and Prevention*, 11, no. 2.

Windschuttle K. 2004. *The Fabrication of Aboriginal History, Vol. 1, Van Diemen's Land, 1803–1847*. Sydney: Macleay Press.

Withycombe P. 2018. 'The twelfth man: John Henry Fleming and the Myall Creek massacre', in eds. J. Lydon & L. Ryan. *Remembering the Myall Creek Massacre*, Sydney: NewSouth Books.

Wolf E. 1982. *Europe and the People Without History*. Berkeley: University of California Press.

Wolfe P. 1999. *Settler Colonialism and the Transformation of Anthropology: The Politics and Poetics of an Ethnographic Event*. London: Cassell.

Wolfe P. 2001. 'Land, labor, and difference: Elementary structures of race'. *American Historical Review*, 106, no. 3.

Wolfe P. 2006. 'Settler colonialism and the elimination of the native'. *Journal of Genocide Research*, 8, no. 4.

Wolfe P. 2008. 'Structure and event: Settler colonialism, time and the question of genocide', in *Empire, Colony, Genocide: Conquest, Occupation and Subaltern Resistance in World History*, ed. A.D. Moses. New York: Berghahn Books.

Wolfe P. 2016. *Traces of History: Elementary Structures of Race*. London: Verso.

Woolford A. 2009. 'Ontological destruction: Genocide and Canadian Aboriginal peoples in Canada'. *Genocide Studies and Prevention*, 4, no. 1.

Woolford A. 2015. *This Benevolent Experiment: Indigenous Boarding Schools, Genocide and Redress in North America*. Lincoln & Winnipeg: University of Nebraska Press & University of Manitoba Press.

Woolford A. & Benvenuto J. 2015. 'Canada and colonial genocide'. *Journal of Genocide Research*, 17, no. 4.

Woolford A., Benvenuto J. & Hinton A., eds. 2014. *Colonial Genocide in Indigenous North America*. Durham: Duke University Press.

Woollacott A. 2015. *Settler Society in the Australian Colonies*. Oxford: Oxford University Press.

Young C. 1994. *The African Colonial State in Colonial Perspective*. New Haven: Yale University Press.

Young I. 2004. 'Five faces of oppression', in *Oppression, Privilege, & Resistance: Theoretical Perspectives of Racism, Sexism and Heterosexism*, eds. L. Heldke & P. O'Connor. Boston: McGraw-Hill.

Young R. 1905. *From Cape Horn to Panama: A Narrative of Missionary Enterprise among the Neglected Races of South America, by the South American Missionary Society*. London: South American Missionary Society.

Bibliography

Zollmann J. 2010. *Koloniale Herrschaft und ihre Grenzen: Die Kolonialpolizei in Deutsch Südwest-Afrika*. Göttingen: Vandenhoeck & Ruprecht.

Zollmann J. 2011. 'Communicating colonial order: The police in German South-West Africa'. *Crime, History & Societies*, 15, no. 1.

Index

A

Aboriginal troopers (Queensland) 21, 142, 149, 155

Acaymo 53–54

Afche 40–41

Afrikaner farmers 70, 240, 279

Agricultural Bank 224

Agricultural Council 224

agro-pastoralists 35

Aht (Nuu-chah-nulth) 79

Alacalufes 169

Alberta tar sands 83

Albuquerque Indian School (AIS) in New Mexico 189, 205–208, 211, 213, 216

alcohol consumption 233–234, 238, 239

Allman, Francis 132, 138

Anaga 51, 52, 53

Anderson, George 115–116

Argentina
claims relating to Tierra del Fuego 170, 179–180
expedition to Tierra del Fuego 169
use of police force against Selk'nam people 183

arms and ammunition
Native Police (Queensland) 149
San communities 93, 278

arts 208–209, 216

assimilative schooling / education 188, 191, 196, 199, 200, 202, 206, 212

Atkins, John 196–197

Australian Aborigines
1828–1838 massacres 127–130
1839–1848 massacres 130–133
1849–1859 massacres 133–136
aboriginal troopers 21, 142, 149, 155
Bediagal clan 125
bushwhacks 129–130, 137–138
Carbucky Station massacre, 1849 135
colonial government's role 136–137
conflict between clans 123
contribution to pastoral industry 283–284
description 122–124
Dharawal people 126
dispossession 21
Dreaming 122

Gamilaraay people 128–130, 138

Gumbaynggir people 132–133

hearth groups 122

Hornet Bank massacre, 1858 118, 134, 155–156

Imbil Station 152

inquests into deaths 133

'invader casualties' 156

Jiman people massacre 138

land management practices 122–123

Mandandanji people massacre 135, 138

Manumbar Station, 10 February 1861 151–152

martial law 126, 127, 128

massacres of colonists by 134

military-led massacres 119, 126–127, 136

mortality rate 136, 161–162

Myall Creek massacre, 1838 20–21, 114–120, 137–138

native police force massacres 133–136

number of collisions between Native police and 150–151

poisoning 120, 132–133, 137, 157, 160

population size 123–124, 142

private vigilante casualties 156–161

prolonged drought 133

protected by Crown Lands Commissioner 131, 138

Raglan Creek, November 1860 152–154

serving in native police force 133–134

singing the country 122

state-led and private assault casualties 154–161

stockmen-led massacres 114, 115, 117–118, 127, 128–129, 130, 131–132, 134, 137, 151, 283

understatement of frontier casualties 22

violent mortality 144–154

visiting rights to neighbouring clans and nations 123

Waiwan massacres 132

Wiradjuri people 126

Wirrayaraay people 115–116, 128, 138

Wonnarua people 126, 128
Worimi people 126, 128
Yabba stations 152
Australian squatters 157, 159, 162
Azores 31, 38, 44

B

Bagosora, Théoneste (Colonel) 264
bandos de guerra 50–51
bandos de pazes 50
baptism 41, 42, 46, 47, 49, 50, 55
Barba, Pedro 43
Bastard (Griqua) militias 110
Batavian regime (1803–1806) 105
Bediagal clan 125
Belgian control of Rwanda (1916–1962) 246, 249
Beothuk of Newfoundland
  competition for land and resources 64
  demographic shift 64
  extermination of 17, 63–66
  genocide against 66
  Mi'kmaq used against 65
  protection by colonial government 66
  traditional economy 64
  violence against 64–65
Berber societies of northwest Africa 34–35
besiegement 220
Bethencourt, Jean de 39–42, 44
Bethencourt, Maciot de 42, 43, 49, 58
Big Bear 76
biopolitics 273–274
Black Association 117
Blain, William 178–179
Blake, Samuel H. 201
boarding schools *see* indigenous boarding schools (1879–1975)
Bonn, Moritz 236–237
Borgatello, Maggiorino 176
Boundary Treaty of 1881 (Tierra del Fuego) 22
bounty hunters 8
Braddock, Edward (Major General) 1–2
Braun, Moritz 165, 166, 170, 174, 175, 177, 181, 182
Bridges, Lucas 172, 184–185
Briggs, Fanny 152–153
British Columbia

fur trade 80
gold rush 80–81
settler-driven settlement 79–81
British Empire, policy on rights of indigenous peoples 114–115
Bryan, Richard W.D. 206, 215
Burke, Edmund 12
Bushmen
  Afrikaner farmers 239, 279
  assisting police 227
  behaviour of German farmers towards 26–27
  deviant behaviour 219
  fatherly chastisement 225, 228–231, 279
  flogging 227, 231, 238, 279
  forceful separation of families 228
  genocide against 26–27
  legislation facilitating genocide of 225
  on mission stations 232
  pass law 225, 229, 233, 279
  punished as 'vagrants' 225
  reserves for 231–232
  South African *see* San communities
  tamed 219, 279
  trade in 232
bushwhacks (Australia) 129–130, 137–138

C

Californian Indian societies
  destruction of 23
  paid militia units 23–24
  voluntary militia units 23–24
Cameron, Alexander 180–182, 185
Canada
  assumption of settler control over indigenous children 281
  British Columbia 78–81
  child confiscation 84
  civilian-driven violence 17–18
  collective amnesia 280
  colonies 63
  displacement 280
  education 189
  effect of Britain's loss of American colonies 70–71
  extermination of Beothuk of Newfoundland 63–66

Index

forced assimilation 84–85
forced removal 280
French settlers 81–82
fur trade 73, 80–82, 188
genocidal impact of residential
    schooling 18
Indian agents 203–204
Indian policy 69–71, 73, 75, 78, 81
indigenous boarding schools (1879–
    1975) see indigenous boarding
    schools (1879–1975)
indigenous peoples of Ontario 69–78
Manitoba see Manitoba
mining 83
myth of peaceful frontier 61–62
reserves 85, 281
residential school system 18, 25, 61,
    69, 84, 280
role of missionaries in school system
    200–202
seasonal white settler settlements 64
settler violence against indigenous
    peoples of Nova Scotia and New
    Brunswick 66–69
settlers and Indian land in Quebec and
    North 81–83
squatters 67–68, 70, 71, 72, 73, 74, 281
strictly administered colony 70
treaty system 70–72, 82, 281
Truth and Reconciliation Commission
    84, 198, 213
Western Canada see Canadian prairies
white racism 62
Canadian exceptionalism 18
Canadian prairies
American Indian policy 78
disease and death in reserves 76–77,
    281
forced assimilation 75
interaction with American settlers
    74–75, 78
North-West Mounted Police (NWMP)
    74–75, 77
North-West Rebellion of 1885 75–76
policed frontier 74
racial segregation 77
removal of Indians and settlement on
    74–78
reserves 75, 77–78, 281

residential school system 77–78
starvation 77, 281
Canarian slaves 36–38, 276
Canary Islands
Castilian control 39–42, 43, 60
civilian-driven genocide 276
civilian-driven nature of expansion
    59–60
collaborators in Spanish campaign 46
colonial economy 45, 57, 60
commodities obtained from 37
conquest of Lanzarote, Fuerteventura
    and Hierro 39–42
conquest of Tenerife 51–56
conquistadors 17, 31, 44, 45, 56, 60,
    276, 277
deportation of captives / survivors 17,
    31, 40, 56, 276–277
diseases 54
enslavement 17, 31, 40, 56
feudal overlordship by European
    aristocrats 37–38
genocide 56–59
geographic description 32–34
importation of slaves 57
indigenous economy 34, 35, 38
indigenous peoples see Indigenous
    Canarian peoples
initial conquest 17
Norman enterprises 39–42
occupation of Gomera 48–49
plundering expeditions prior to 1402
    35
Portuguese intervention 42–44
position by 1492 31
pre-contact population 35
principals 206–212
private claims to 17, 43, 44–45, 48–49
raiding 36–39
reasons for reconnaissance and
    colonisation 31–32
reconnaissance 31–32, 36–39
royal islands 45
seigneurial control 45, 60
slave raiding 36–39, 42, 48, 49, 56, 276
social destruction 56–57
Spanish campaign 44–48
Spanish intervention 52–56
state agents acting in private capacity 8

315

subjugation of Gran Canaria 44–48
sugar production 17, 38–39, 44, 45, 49, 51, 55, 56, 276, 277, 278
vanquishing of La Palma 49–51
Cape Colony
abolition of import slave trade, 1807 106
clandestine militia activity 19
commandos 19–20, 278
enslavement and extermination of San 86–113, 177–178
field cornets 105, 107
state-sanctioned militia 19–20
violence by farmers against San communities 18
captives, taking of 13, 46, 89, 91, 94, 99, 102–103, 108
Carbucky Station massacre in 1849 135
Carnino, Luis 177
Carrington, George 2
Cart, Samuel 206–208, 215
Castilian control, Canary Islands 39–42, 43, 60
Castilian empire, struggle between Portugal and for Gomera 48–49
Castillo, Gonzalo del 58
Castro, Fernando de 44
Catholic schools 200, 202, 211, 216
cattle-sharing 247–248, 250
Charles Eyles 126
chastisement, fatherly 225, 228–231, 279
child confiscation 13, 15, 17, 31, 57, 84, 140, 282
child slavery
San communities 109–111, 278
Tswana and Korana 'orphans' 110–111
children, violence against in Canada 84–85
Chile
claims relating to Tierra del Fuego 170, 174, 179–180
expedition to Tierra del Fuego 169
Christianity, conversion to 50, 52, 55
Christison, Robert 158
civilians
combatant distinguished from 6–7
expansion to Canary Islands mainly driven 59–60

genocide by 5–9, 10–11, 24–25, 29, 274–284
meaning of 5–7
mindsets of perpetrators 24–25, 29
partnerships with military and non-military state actors 11
code of silence, Australian massacres 21, 116, 119, 121, 130, 138
collective action frames
definition of 25
Indian agents 205
indigenous boarding schools (1879–1975) 26, 191–195, 196, 199, 201–202, 206, 208, 210, 212, 214, 215–217, 282
intent 193
missionaries 201, 202
principals 209
residential school system 25–26
teachers 214, 216
collective punishment 10, 21
Collier, John 197, 212, 214
colonialism
arboreal 270
dissipated or accumulated violence 271–274
indigenous containment 269
phases of 268–269
relationship to violence 28
stored-up violence 272
third-wave 269, 274
what is 268–271
colonisation, explosive 9
combatants, civilians distinguished from 6–7
commandos (Cape Colony)
general versus traditional 94, 278
horses 93–94
Khoisan 8, 90
system 19–20, 90–91
war captives 91, 94, 96, 99
'common men,' settler militia (Cape Colony) 93, 95, 98–99, 101, 102, 103, 104, 278
communicable diseases 23, 57
communis hostis omnium (the common enemy of all) 219
Como, Ben 52–53, 54, 55

Index

conquistadors 17, 31, 44, 45, 56, 60, 276, 277
Cornwallis (Lord) 66–67
corporal punishment 15, 209, 230, 282
Coutts, Thomas 132–133
Crandall, Clinton J. 208
Cressbrook Station (Queensland) 157
Crown Lands Commissioner, Australia 131, 138
Cruz Ramírez, Daniel (Lieutenant Colonel) 176
cult of Candelaria 52–53
cultural genocide 71, 84, 189
cultural suppression 13, 15, 31, 57
Curr, Edward 162

D

Darwin, Charles 167, 168
Davin, Nicholas Flood 196
Dawson Island 165, 174, 175, 176, 178, 181, 182, 184
Day, David 146, 162
De la Cerda, Luis 38
De Lugo, Alonso 50, 52–56
De Vera, Pedro 46–50
DeHuff, John 208–209, 211, 216
dehumanisation 14
Delawares 2
Demasduwit 65
deportation of captives / survivors
Canary Islands 17, 31, 40, 56, 276–277
to Madeira 56
mass 17, 31, 56
Deutsch-Südwestafrikanischer Farmerbund 224
Dharawal people 126
diseases
among the Guanches 54
communicable 23, 57
indigenous boarding schools 198, 201
Indigenous Canarian peoples 58–59
Selk'nam people 177, 178, 180
dispersals, Queensland 143, 150–152, 154, 155, 166, 284
displacement
Canada 280
consequences of 13
dispossession
consequences of 13

homicidal phase 15
post-frontier phase 15
dogs 179, 187
dragon's blood 37
Drake, Francis 168
Dunn, Dorothy 212, 214, 216, 217
Durbin, John 135, 138
Durieu system 216
Dutch East India Company (VOC) 18, 19, 90

E

Eaton, Daniel 116
economy
Beothuk of Newfoundland 64
colonial Canary Islands 45, 57, 60
German South West Africa 26
global industrial 16
indigenous Canarian 34, 35, 38
indigenous peoples of Nova Scotia 66
education
assimilative 188, 196, 202, 206, 212
Canada 189
industrial-style 196
schools see schools
United States 188–189
Eliot, John 199
elitism 258
empire-building in Mediterranean 32
encomienda system 269
enslavement *see also* slave labour
Canary Islands 17, 31, 40, 56
San communities 20, 90–100, 108
ethnic cleansing 10, 16, 18, 30, 138, 159, 183
European maritime expansion 3
explosive colonisation 9
exterminatory cultural *Zeitgeist* 158, 283
Eyles, Charles 130

F

Fagnano, Giuseppe 168, 174, 175–177, 186
Falkland Islands 166, 170, 178
Falkland Islands Company 170, 178
famine 75, 263
Faris, Chester 208, 209
Farmerbund (Farmers' Union) 224
fatherly chastisement 225, 228–231, 279

317

CIVILIAN-DRIVEN VIOLENCE AND THE GENOCIDE OF INDIGENOUS PEOPLES

Ferdinand and Isabella 44–45, 46, 49
field cornets, Cape Colony 105, 107
Finger, Charles 178–179, 180
First Nation peoples 141
Fitzroy, Charles (Governor) 133–134
Fleming, John Henry 115–118, 130
flogging 227, 231, 238, 279
forced assimilation 15, 18, 69, 73, 75, 85,
    184, 190, 196, 205, 206, 217, 281
forced labour 7, 13, 15, 20, 38, 57, 162,
    278, 282
forced removal in Canada 69, 72–73, 280
Fort Alexander Indian Residential School
    (FAIRS) in Manitoba 189, 211, 213,
    216
Fraser family massacre 155
freebooters 17, 31, 37, 276, 284
free-trade colonialism 269
French and Indian War (1754–1763) 1–2
Fry, Oliver 133
Fuegian natives 168–169
Fuerteventura
    conquest of 41–44
    French attacks on 42
    repopulation by Normandian settlers
        42
fur trade 73, 80–82, 188

G

Gamilaraay people 128–130, 138
genocidal violence
    civilians as perpetrators of 5–9
    indigenous peoples as agents 8
genocide
    Beothuk of Newfoundland 66
    Bushmen 225
    Canada 83–85
    Canary Islands 56–59
    civil-driven 274–284
    cottage-industry 264
    cultural 71, 84, 189
    definition of 166, 219
    dolus specialis 193
    intent 193
    intentional 262, 266
    normalising genocidal violence 244
    perpetrators 194–195
    privatisation of see Selk'nam people;
        Tierra del Fuego

Rwanda see Rwandan genocide
settler see settler genocide
settler colonialism 267, 270
German Colonial League 224
German control of Rwanda (1897–1916)
    246, 250
German farmers (German South West
    Africa)
    alcohol consumption 233, 238, 239
    behaviour toward San 26–27
    as 'dependent masters' 235, 237
    difficulties experienced 234–235
    emigration and immigration records
        234
    empowerment of 222–231, 279
    erasive practices of 218–240
    government support for 224
    as little kings 230–235, 279
    nationalism among settlers 237–238
    post-war increase in number of
        220–221
    settler networks 238
    Spiessburgertum 238
    swearing 238
    war compensation 222, 223
German South West Africa
    African assistants in police 227
    Agricultural Bank 224
    Agricultural Council 224
    assessment of 233
    besiegement 220
    Bismark's new form of bureaucratic
        organisation 226
    Bushmen see Bushmen
    discovery of diamonds 223, 225, 233
    extermination policies 279
    Farmerbund (Farmers' Union) 224,
        230
    Gemütlichkeit (geniality) towards
        insiders 239
    Gouvernmentsrat 222
    Landesrat 222–223, 225, 228, 231, 279
    law enabled colonial abuse 226
    military utilised in anti-banditry and
        stock-theft patrols 228
    mobile police stations 232
    Native Commissioner 225
    native labour 225
    necessity of decolonisation 236

neo-feudalism 219–220, 236–237, 240
non-commissioned officers in police
227
pass laws 225, 229, 233, 279
Platzgeist fantasyland 236–238
police 226–228, 235
settler politicisation 222
social hierachy 233
Verordnungstaat 226
villeinage 220
weak, improvisational and ceremonial
colonial state 218–219, 279
gold rush 23, 80–81,170–172, 180
Gomera
occupation of 48–49
struggle between Castile and Portugal
for supremacy 48–49
Graaff-Reinet district, 1776–1825 (Cape
Colony)
administrative district and
drostdy,1786 96
borders 87–88
child slavery 109–111
class differentiation 93–94
communication 105–106
enslavement and extermination of San
86–113
establishment of 87–88
increasing land prices 98–99
San communities between 1799–1824
100–101
stagnation of slave population 106
violence against indigenous slaves
105–106
Gracemere Station (Queensland) 157
Gran Canaria
1404 attacks 41
1405 attacks 42
1470s incursions 42
1490 incursion 51
pre-contact settlements 35
slavers 38
subjugation of 44–48, 50
great land rush 10
group destruction
by civilian actors 26
indigenous boarding schools (1879–
1975) 189, 190, 194, 195
Guanche, Anton 52

Guanches 51–55
Guimar 51–53
Gumbaynggir people 132–133
Guzman of Niebla 43
Gwydir River massacres 115–116,
129–130

H

Habyarimana, Juvénal (1973–1994) 8,
245, 263
Hamitic hypothesis 27, 247, 277
Haush 167
Hektliohih 184
Hendry, William A. 209
Henry III of Castile 41, 43
Herrera, Diego de 44, 45, 48, 51
Hierro, conquest of 42
Hintrager, Oskar 224
historiography of frontier massacres
118–122, 284
Hobbs, William 114–115, 116–117
Hornet Bank massacre in 1858 118–119,
134, 155–156
horses 127, 137
Hottentots see Khoisan
Hutu (Rwanda)
civic duty to commit genocide 260
framing of 247–248, 254–255
inequalities between Tutsi and 249
nationalists 27–28
number of civilians participating in
genocide 264
practice of civil defence 277
as rightful inhabitants 262, 263, 265
Hybeb, Jacob 227
Hyslop, Sam 180

I

Iberian colonialism 31–32
Imbil Station 152
Imperial Mounted Police (German South
West Africa) 226–228
imperialism 238, 252, 269
Indian agents
indigenous boarding schools (1879–
1975) 203–205, 215
responsibilities of 203–204
Indian policy
Canada 69–71, 73, 75, 78, 81

CIVILIAN-DRIVEN VIOLENCE AND THE GENOCIDE OF INDIGENOUS PEOPLES

United States 78, 81
Indian Residential School Settlement
  Agreement of 2007 198
Indians (Canadian)
  fur trade 81
  pass law 77, 279
  settlers and Indian land in Quebec and
    North 81–83
indigenous arts 208–209, 216
indigenous boarding schools (1879–
  1975) *see also* residential school
  system
  Albuquerque Indian School (AIS) in
    New Mexico 189, 205–208, 211,
    213, 216
  Canada 195–198, 281–282
  civilian-driven 281–282
  collective action frames 26, 196, 199,
    201–202, 206, 208, 210, 212, 214,
    215–217, 281
  compensation programme 198
  diseases 198, 201
  federal boarding schools 197
  forced assimilation 190, 196, 206
  Fort Alexander Indian Residential
    School (FAIRS) in Manitoba 189,
    211, 213, 216
  group destruction 189, 190, 194, 195
  health inspections 215–216
  humanitarian motivations 190
  Indian agents 203–205, 215
  indigenous arts 208–209, 216
  indigenous dancing 211, 216
  industrial-style 196, 197, 282
  to 'Kill the Indian in him, and save the
    man' 196
  less dynamic system in Canada 197
  military discipline 197, 215–216
  missionaries 199–202, 215
  mission-based contract schools 197
  monastic discipline 197, 216
  origins of 195
  Portage la Prairie Indian Residential
    School (PLPIRS) in Manitoba 189,
    204, 210, 211, 213, 216
  power struggling between staff and
    parents 207
  preservation of culture 197
  principals 206–212

Pueblo Indians 202, 206, 208–209
purpose of 282
Santa Fe Indian School (SFIS) in New
    Mexico 189, 202, 206, 207–209,
    211, 212, 214, 216
securing students 206–207
smaller, reserve-based 197
spiritual reflection 216
student home visits 207–208
suffering 198
superintendents 206–212
survivor-led class action lawsuits 198
teachers 212–214
Truth and Reconciliation Commission
    198
United States 195–198
violence in 214
Indigenous Canarian peoples
  agro-pastoralists 35
  captives and chattels enlisted in
    Spanish slaving or conquering
    sorties 7–8
  cutting levadas 39
  derived from Berber societies of
    northwest Africa 35–36, 59
  diseases 58–59
  enslavement 17, 31, 40, 56
  fighting forces 36, 44
  hierarchical social structures 35–36
  island warriors 36
  land grants 58–59
  marriages between Canarian women
    and settler men 58
  migrants from Africa 34–35
  political organisation 36
  recruited as fighters 57
  settlements 35–36
  sexual exploitation 58
  skills as drovers 39
  societies 35
  survival 57
  viewed as culturally and spiritually
    inferior 59
indigenous conscripts and collaborators
    7–8
indigenous dancing 208–209, 211,
    216
indigenous labour 15, 20, 57, 174, 272,
    278–279, 282

320

Index

indigenous peoples
  access to global markets 13
  Australia see Australian Aborigines
  Bushmen see Bushmen
  Canada see Beothuk of
    Newfoundland; Indians
    (Canadian); New Brunswick; Nova
    Scotia; Ontario
  Canary Islands see Indigenous
    Canarian peoples
  cheap labour 4
  consequences of expulsion from and
    dispossession 13
  destruction of societies 4
  displacement 4, 10, 13
  'elimination of the native' 10, 15, 269
  exterminatory violence against 4
  as perpetrators of genocidal violence
    8
  prior ownership of land not
    recognised 3
  racism against 2
  San communities see San communities
  Selk'nam people see Selk'nam people
  violence against 2
intermarriage 58, 258

J

Jesuits 199–200
Jicarilla Apache 207
Jiman people 138
Julia, Barnaby 68
just war 14

K

Kagame, Paul 264
Kangaroo Creek poisoning, 1847 132–
  133
Kawésqar 168, 176, 186
Kayibanda, Grégoire (1962–1973) 245,
  263
Keir, Andrew 131–132
Khoisan
  authority and status gained from
    militia service 91–92
  Batavian regime (1803–1806) 105
  commandos (Cape Colony) 90–91, 95
  employees in Graaff Reinet, 1805
    92–93

enslavement of San as slaves 88
'faithfulness' 92–93
labour contracting 102, 107, 109,
  110–111
labour statistics, 1805–1825 103
mission stations 101, 103
not self-reproducing 89, 278
offer of own land and protection from
  settlers 101
original sources of labour 107
pass-law 107, 279
'place of abode' 107
population statistics, 1805–1825 104
replenishment of slave labour 112
reproductive capacity 112
right to bear arms 91–93, 278
spies 90, 95, 100
Kilmeister, Charles 115–116
Kiumanga 115

L

La Candelaria mission 177, 178, 184
La Palma
  slave raids 49
  vanquishing of 49–51
La Salle, Gadifer de 39–41
labour
  forced 7, 13, 15, 20, 38, 57, 162, 278,
    282
  imported 269
  subjugated 269
laissez-faire capitalism 22
land grants to Indigenous Canarian
  peoples 58–59
land theft
  Nova Scotia and New Brunswick
    68–69
  Tierra del Fuego 173
Landesrat (German South West Africa)
  222–223, 225, 228, 231, 279
Lanzarote
  conquest of 39–42
  Portuguese occupation 44
  slave raids 38, 56
Lee, William 131–132
Leutwein, Theodor (Governor) 221
limited warfare 14
limpieza de sangre (purity of blood)
  59

321

CIVILIAN-DRIVEN VIOLENCE AND THE GENOCIDE OF INDIGENOUS PEOPLES

Lindequist, Friedrich von 221, 222, 224, 225
Lista, Ramón 169, 170, 174
Low, Jacob 156–157
Lowe, Lieutenant Nathanial 153
Lucio Cortés, Ramón 183

M

Macdonald, John A. 77
Macpherson, Allan 135, 138
Madeira
    deportation of captives to 56
    slave labour 17, 38–39
    sugar production 38–39, 44, 276
Magellan, Ferdinand 167, 168
Maldonado, Francisco 51
Maliseet 69
malnutrition 41, 54, 57, 77
Malocello, Lancelotto 36, 43
Mandandanji people massacre 135, 138
Mandanjanji land war 119
Manitoba, indigenous boarding schools (1879–1975) 22, 188–217
Manumbar Station, 10 February 1861 151–152
Maranoa pastoral district 119, 131, 135, 138
marriages between settlers and indigenous peoples 58, 258
martial law, Australian Aborigines 126, 127, 128
mass deportation 15, 17, 31, 56
massacre map project (Australia) 120, 121, 126–127, 131, 136–138, 283
massacres
    assessment of violent mortality (Queensland) 144–154
    Australian frontiers 127–136
    at campsites 121
    carried out in secret 120–121
    code of silence (Australia) 21, 116, 119, 121, 130, 138
    daylight 128–129, 130, 137
    definition of 121
    expression of weakness 120
    historiography of frontier 118–122
    map project (Australia) 121, 126–127, 131, 136–138, 283
    military-led 119, 126–127, 136

New South Wales 20–21, 118–119, 125–127, 282–283
McClelland, Peter 165, 166, 175, 176, 185
McConnell, David 157
McLennan, Alexander 183
McNeill, John A. 203
McRae, John 180–181
mercantilism 269
mercenaries 19, 22–23, 45
Métis 76, 200
Métis day school 200
metropole-driven settler colonialism 269
Mi'kmaq
    proclamation of bounty for every scalp 67
    survival of 69
    violence against Beothuk 65
    violence against in Nova Scotia 66–67
    War of 1749 67
military-led massacres against Australian Aborigines 119, 126–127, 136
militia slaving, San communities 93, 95, 96, 98, 108
mining
    Canada 83
    Tierra del Fuego 180
    uranian 83
mission stations
    Bushmen 232
    Khoisan 101, 103
    Selk'nam people 23, 178, 182, 185
    Tierra del Fuego 23
missionaries, indigenous boarding schools (1879–1975) 199–202, 215
morality 29
Morisset, Major James 126, 132
Morisset, Rudolph 152, 153
Morriset, Edwin 153
Mortimer, John 151–152
Mount Playfair (Queensland) 157
Müller, Hauptmann 232
Musinga, Yuhi 250–251
Myall Creek massacre, 1838
    aboriginal people (New South Wales Frontier, 1788–1859) 20–21, 114–120, 137–138
    assassins 118
    divided the colony 117
    'guilty' verdict 117

322

Index

historiography of 118–122

perpetrators brought to justice 114–115

N

Nahrung, Konrad 153

Namibia

exterminatory wars (1904-1908) 14, 26

San see Bushmen

narcotic addiction 13, 111, 278

Native Americans, violence against in California 23

native police force (Australia)

ammunition of 149

Australian Aborigines serving in 133–134

barracks of 147–150

campsites of 21, 149

destruction of 147–149

massacres by 21–22, 133–136

New South Wales 119, 133–135, 138, 142, 160

number of collisions between Australian Aborigines and 150–151

patrols by 148–150

Queensland 8, 21–22, 142, 147–150, 155, 157, 159, 160–161

records of 147–149, 151

natural environment, destruction of 13, 23

necropolitics 273–274

New Brunswick

forced removal 69

land theft 68–69

settler violence against indigenous peoples of 67–69

New Mexico (United States), indigenous boarding schools (1879–1975) 22, 188–217

New South Wales (Australia)

1788–1827 massacres 125–127

1828–1838 massacres 127–130

Aboriginal peoples of see Australian Aborigines

Bediagal clan massacres 125

code of silence concerning massacres 21, 116, 119, 121, 130, 138

covert civilian-driven assaults together with state-sponsored violence 19

development of 127

Dharawal people massacres 126

food production 124–125

Gamilaraay people massacres 128–130

genocidal massacres, 1788–1859 114–138, 282–283

geographical boundaries 124

Gwydir River massacres 115–116, 129–130

historiography of frontier massacres 118–122

Hornet Bank massacre 118–119

Mandanjanji land war 119

massacre map project 120, 121, 126–127, 131, 136–138

Myall Creek massacre, 1838 see Myall Creek massacre, 1838

native police force 119, 133–135, 138, 142, 160

penal outpost of British Empire. 124

policy and practice of frontier massacre 125

Port Phillip district massacres between 1835 and 1859 120–121

role of horses 127, 137

squatters 130

studies of frontier massacres in 118–119

Wirrayaraay people massacres 115–116, 128, 138

Newfoundland

Beothuk of 63–66

geography of 65

Nogueira, José 166

no-man's land 3, 167, 170

non-commissioned officers in GSWA police 227

non-lethal means of social destruction 13

Nonobawsut 65

Norman enterprises, conquest of Lanzarote, Fuerteventura and Hierro 39–42

North-West Mounted Police (NWMP) 74–75, 77

North-West Rebellion of 1885 75–76

CIVILIAN-DRIVEN VIOLENCE AND THE GENOCIDE OF INDIGENOUS PEOPLES

Nova Scotia
  economy 66
  forced removal 69
  Halifax settlement 66–67
  killings by British soldiers 67
  land theft 68–69
  settler violence against indigenous
    peoples of 66–69
  violence against Mi'kmaq 66–67
Nunn, James (Major) 129, 137
Nyiginya kingdom 249, 250

O

Ona *see* Selk'nam people
Ontario
  forced assimilation 73
  forced removals 72–73
  Indians drove to by American violence
    71
  open border between United States
    and Canada 71
  paternalistic system 73
  residential school system 73
  Robinson-Huron Treaties of 1850
    82
  settler demand for land 72
  settler displacement of indigenous
    peoples 69–78
  Treaty 3 (1873) 82
  treaty system 70–72, 82, 281
  uranium mining 83
orchil 37, 45, 48

P

paid militia units in California 23–24
Pan-German League 224
pass law
  Bushmen (German South West
    Africa) 225, 229, 233, 279
  Khoisan (Cape Colony) 107, 279
  reserve Indians (Canada) 77, 279
Patagonian Missionary Society 168
Patagonian Sheep Farming Company
  166
Peraza, Fernan 48, 51
Peraza, Inez 44
Peraza family 43, 44–45, 48–49, 51
Perry, Rueben 207–208, 211, 215
Philip, John 86, 111

Philip Bay Sheep Farming Company 166,
  182
Pikedale Station (Queensland) 157
Plunkett, John Hubert 115, 118
poisoning
  Australian Aborigines 120, 132–133,
    137, 157, 160
  Rwanda 249
  Selk'nam people of Tierra del Fuego
    177
police
  Argentinean police force in Tierra del
    Fuego 183
  German South West Africa 226–228,
    232, 235
  native police force (Australia) 119,
    129–130, 133–135, 138, 142, 147–
    148, 160
policed frontier, Canadian prairies 74–78
political culture, Rwanda 250, 260
Popper, Julius 170–171, 173
Port Phillip district massacres, 1835–
  1859 120–121
Portage la Prairie Indian Residential
  School (PLPIRS) in Manitoba 189,
  204, 210, 211, 213, 216
Portugal
  Canary Islands 42–44
  struggle between Castile and for
    Gomera 48
Pound, Thaddeus 195
Pratt, Richard (Lieutenant) 195, 196, 205,
  215
Prince Henry the Navigator of Portugal
  43
principals of indigenous boarding schools
  (1879–1975) 206–212
private vigilante actions (Queensland)
  156–159
proverbs, riddles and poetry 259–260
psychological distress 54, 57
psychological trauma 13
Pueblo Indians 202, 206, 208–209

Q

Quebec, settlers and Indian land in
  81–83
Queensland (Australia)
  Aboriginal dispossession 21

324

assessment of loss of life 21–22, 144–154, 283
combined state-led and private assault casualties 154–161, 283
cover-up of violence 140
dispersals 143, 150–152, 154, 155, 166, 284
ethnic cleansing 159
exterminatory cultural Zeitgeist 158, 283
gold-mining frontiers 141
importation of slaves 184
Manumbar Station, 10 February 1861 151–152
Native Police force 8, 21–22, 142, 147–150, 155, 157, 159, 160–161
paramilitary force 19
population prior to 1788 142
secondary punishment centre 142
self-government 142
size of 141
sugar production 278

R

racial capitalism 272
racism
    Canada 62
    Rwandan genocide 246, 247, 248, 251, 254–255, 258
racist ideology 59
Radburne, James 171, 178–180
Raglan Creek, November 1860 152–154
Raley, George 206
Read, James 106
Récollets 200
reconnaissance, Canary Islands 36–39
Reconquista 32
Rejon, Juan 45–46, 50
religious instruction 211
reserves
    Bushmen (German South West Africa) 231–232
    Canada 75, 77–78, 85, 281
residential school system *see also* indigenous boarding schools (1879–1975)
    Canada 18, 25, 61, 69, 73, 77–78, 84, 200, 280
    collective action frames 25–26

genocidal impact 18
    United States 25
revenge, Rwandan genocide 250, 252, 256
ritual suicide 47
Robinson-Huron Treaties of 1850 82
Russell, George 115–116
Rwanda
    Belgian control (1916–1962) 246, 249
    cattle-sharing 247–248, 250
    German control (1897–1916) 246, 250
    Hutu government 8
    Nyiginya kingdom 249, 250
    political culture 250, 260
    proverbs, riddles and poetry 259–260
Rwandan genocide
    civil defence 261, 277
    climate of fear and insecurity 251, 261–262, 264
    culture of impunity 259
    elite power struggles 256
    elitism 258
    everyday violence 28, 240–250, 251–260, 265
    extensive civilian participation 28
    genocidal norm 244
    Hamitic hypothesis 27, 247, 277
    humiliation 257, 259
    Hutu see Hutu (Rwanda)
    Hutu-Tutsi inequality 249
    ideology of genocide 260–265
    intimacy of tyranny 253
    myths of history 245
    political exclusion 257
    popular participation 28
    practice murders 261
    practice of civil defence 261, 277
    public displays of power and dominance 256
    racism 246, 247, 248, 251, 254–255, 258
    representational regime 277
    respect for authority and hierarchy 256–257
    revenge 250, 252, 256
    role of myths 245, 248, 256, 262, 263, 265
    role of state institutions 243
    ruler-ruled dominion 255

self-defence 241, 261, 262
settler genocide 246–251
state-driven 28, 277
subaltern genocide 27–28
Tutsi see Tutsi (Rwanda)
Rwandan Patriotic Front (RPF) 242, 243,
    262–264

S

Salesian missions 165, 174, 175, 176, 177,
    178, 181, 182, 183, 184, 186, 280
San communities
    availability of firearms 93, 278
    British administration 105
    child slavery 109, 278
    civil-driven genocide 277–278
    commandos used 19–20
    decline of militia's capture ratio 96–97
    defensive response to militia slaving
        98
    effect of British mobilisation of settler
        militia 108–109
    enslavement 20, 88, 90–100, 277–278
    extermination in Graaff-Reinet
        District of Cape Colony 86–113
    gift economy 108
    gifting to 102, 108, 111
    in Graaff-Reinet district, 1799–1824
        100–111
    killed-to-capture ratio 96, 109, 278
    labour contracting 105
    Namibia see Bushmen
    narcotic addiction 102, 111, 278
    officer corps of militia 20
    official policy of British rulers 100–
        101
    parental responsibility over indigenous
        children 278
    population in 1832 112–113
    reoccupation of territories after British
        demobilisation of settler militia 108
    reproductive capacity 104
    settler pastoralists and 89–90
    settler reconciliation and restraint
        101–103, 107–108
    slave labour 20
    state-sanctioned militia 19–20
    statistics on capturing and killing of
        97

surge in raiding 97, 98
violence by farmers against 18
Santa Fe Indian School (SFIS) in New
    Mexico 189, 202, 206, 207–209, 211,
    212, 214, 216
schools
    assimilative schooling / education see
        assimilative schooling / education
    indigenous boarding schools see
        indigenous boarding schools
        (1879–1975)
scorched-earth tactics 17, 31, 46, 57
self-defence, Rwandan genocide 241,
    261, 262
self-government 12, 135, 142
Selk'nam people
    Argentinean police force 183
    civilisation of 174–175, 177, 181, 182,
        185
    death rate at mission stations 177
    deportation of 177, 178, 182, 184
    diseases 177, 178, 180
    encounters during early expeditions
        169–170
    extermination of 22–23, 165–187
    extermination of Aboriginal dogs 179,
        187
    extra-legal status 181–182
    forced assimilation of survivors
        184
    genocidal colonialism materialised by
        sheep farming 173–177
    gold rush and 170–172
    intra-ethnic violence 183
    killing and capturing of 177–184, 280
    land grant decree (Chile) 174–175
    legal transfer of Selk'nam land to
        foreign companies 174
    marginal incorporation into colonial
        economy 183
    miners' violence against 170–172
    mission stations 23, 176–177, 178,
        182, 185, 280
    poisoning 177
    population statistics 184, 185
    resistance 175
    Salesian missions 165, 174, 175, 176,
        177, 178, 181, 182, 183, 184, 186,
        280

sexual exploitation of women 171–172

trial about humiliations against 181–182

violence against by contract workers 178

warrior-like hunter-gatherers 169

Semidan, Tenesor 46–48, 50, 52

Serrano Montaner, Ramón 169, 170, 174

settler colonial projects
land 2
reproduction of home societies 2–3

settler colonialism
civilian-driven violence 3–4
description 246
genocide 267, 270
primitive accumulation 273
relationship to violence 28–29
rhizomatic 270

settler genocide
description 246
Rwanda 246–251

settler militia (Cape Colony)
British mobilisation of in 1811 108
campaigns against Zuurveld Xhosa 108–109
child slavery 109–110
commando system 90–91, 278
'common men' 93, 95, 98–99, 101, 102, 103, 104, 278
demobilisation 89, 100, 103, 106, 108
enslavement and extermination of San in Cape Colony 86–113
horses 93–94
impact of new administrative district and drostdy, 1786 96
institutionalisation by Dutch East India Company government in 1774 90
Khoisan spies 90, 95, 100
non-compliance and resignations 98
overkill 95–96
rebellion of Zuurveld militia, 1815 108
reorganised and subsidised 94
settler-dependent 'Bastard' and Khoisan adult male servants subject to commando requisition 90
slaving 95, 104

settler regimes 3

settler revolution 9, 16, 22, 268, 271

settlers
demands for political autonomy 11
government control 12
homelands and consequences of expulsion from 13
insurgence and mass violence 9
land expropriation 12
metropolitan interests and 11
self-government 12, 135, 142
spirit of insubordination and independence 12

sexual exploitation 15, 58, 162, 172

sexual violence 13, 55, 175, 260

Shawandithit 65

sheep farming operations, Tierra del Fuego 19, 22–23, 166, 169–179, 181, 182, 183, 185–187, 280

ship design and navigation advances 31

slave labour see also enslavement
importation of slaves 184
Madeira 17, 38–39

slave populations (Cape Colony), reproductive capacity 89, 106

slave raiding, Canary Islands 38–39, 42, 48, 49, 56, 276

slave trade, abolition of import, 1807 (Cape Colony) 106

smallpox epidemics 12, 76, 141, 207

Social Darwinist thought 14

social erasure 4, 56

Sociedad Explotadora de Tierra del Fuego (Company for the Exploitation of Tierra del Fuego) 165–166, 174, 175, 176, 177, 178, 180, 181–183

Sociedad Ganadera Gente Grande 166, 182

Spanish crown, Canary Islands 44–48, 52–56

Sproat, Gilbert Malcolm 79

squatters
Australia 130, 157, 159, 162
Canada 67–68, 70, 71, 72, 73, 74, 281

St Catherine's School (New Mexico) 202

starvation 41, 57, 66, 75, 77, 82, 162, 188, 196, 281

state-sanctioned militia 19–20

stockmen (Australia) 114, 115, 117–118,

327

CIVILIAN-DRIVEN VIOLENCE AND THE GENOCIDE OF INDIGENOUS PEOPLES

127, 128–129, 130, 131–132, 134, 137, 151, 283
Strait of Magellan 166, 168–169, 170, 174, 178
sugar production
  Canary Islands 17, 38–39, 44, 45, 49, 51, 55, 56, 57, 276, 277, 278
  Madeira 38–39, 44, 276
  Queensland 278
superintendents of indigenous boarding schools 206–212
survivor-led class action lawsuits 198
swearing by farmers (German South West Africa) 238

T

Tanausu 50
tar sands 83
teachers 212 Canarian slaves 214
Teguise 58
Temple, John (Sergeant) 129, 137
temporary armed units 7
Tenerife
  conquest of 51–56
  Guanches 51–55
  pre-conquest population 51
  religious cult 51–52
terra nullius 3
Thanatopolitics 273–274
Tierra del Fuego
  Boundary Treaty of 1881 22
  Chilean land 174
  commercial companies 22
  communism and anarchism 180
  competing territorial claims by Chile and Argentinia 170, 173, 179–180
  extermination of Selk'nam people 22–23, 165–187, 279
  Fuegian natives 168
  geographical description 166–167
  gold rush 23, 170–172, 180
  Laissez-faire policy 22, 185, 187
  land grabs 173
  land grant decree (Chile) 174–175
  mercenaries 19, 22–23
  mission stations 23
  no-man's land 167
  penal colony in Beagle Channel 173

place of in context of late-19th-century Argentinian and Chilean geopolitical expansion 167
predatory colonialism 170–172
sheep farming operations 19, 22–23, 166, 169–179, 180, 181, 182, 183, 185–187, 280
Transorangia, child slavery 110–111
Treaty 3 (1873) 82
Treaty of Alcaçovas 44
treaty system
  Canada 70–72, 82, 281
  unequal in conception and execution 71
Truth and Reconciliation Commission, Canada 84, 198, 213
Tswana and Korana 'orphans,' child slavery 112
tuberculosis 23, 66, 76, 177, 198, 204
Tutsi (Rwanda)
  as foreigners 243, 244, 245, 254, 262, 264
  framing of 245, 247–248, 254
  inequalities between Hutu and 249
  minority status 245, 247, 255
  represented as settlers 244, 246–247, 277
  sense of superiority 248, 250, 258, 263
  'white Africans' 247
Twa (Rwanda) 248, 258, 263

U

ubuhake 247–248, 250
United States
  education 188–189
  Indian policy 78, 81
  indigenous boarding schools (1879–1975) see indigenous boarding schools (1879–1975)
  New Mexico see New Mexico
  residential school system 25
  role of missionaries in school system 200–202
  superintendents 206–212
uranium mining 83
US Bureau of Indian Affairs (BIA) 196, 197, 209, 211, 214
Ute 205

328

Index

V

Vancouver Island 79
venture capital 60
vernichtungspolitik (extermination politics) 218
villeinage 220
violence
    against children in Canada 84–85
    colonialism as dissipated or accumulated 271–274
    established by fur trade 80–82
    everyday forms of in Rwanda 251–260, 265
    exterminatory against indigenous peoples 4
    genocidal 5–9
    increased between indigenous groups 13
    against indigenous peoples of Nova Scotia and New Brunswick 66–69
    intergroup 28, 183
    primitive accumulation 272
    righteous 29
    sexual 13, 55, 175, 260
    spectrum of 12–13
    stored-up 272, 275
    structural forms of 254
voluntary militia units in California 23–24
Von Trotha, Lothar 14, 26, 222, 240

W

Waite, Joseph 203
Waiwan Aboriginal people 132
Wales, Ernst 179–182
war captives of commandos (Cape Colony) 91, 94, 96, 99
Wesleyan missionaries 200–201
Western global dominance 3, 5, 16, 17
Windschuttle, Keith 146
Wiradjuri people 126
Wirrayaraay people 115–116, 128, 138
Wonnarua people 126, 128
Wood, Norman 183
Worimi people 126, 128

X

Xhosas 108–109

Y

Yabba stations 152
Yaganes 168
Yintayintin 115–116

Z

Zeitgeist 158, 283
Zuurveld militias 99
Zuurveld Xhosa wars 108–109

Printed in the United States
by Baker & Taylor Publisher Services